ONE DAY IN THE LIFE OF
TELEVISION

ONE DAY IN THE LIFE OF
TELEVISION

Edited by Sean Day-Lewis

GRAFTON BOOKS
A Division of the Collins Publishing Group

LONDON GLASGOW
TORONTO SYDNEY AUCKLAND

Grafton Books
A Division of the Collins Publishing Group
8 Grafton Street, London W1X 3LA

Published by Grafton Books 1989

British Library Cataloguing in Publication Data

One day in the life of television
    1. Great Britain. Television programmes.
    Attitudes to audiences
    I. Day-Lewis, Sean
    302.2'345

ISBN 0-246-13424-0
ISBN 0-246-13497-6 (Pbk)

Typeset by Ace Filmsetting Ltd, Frome, Somerset
Printed in Great Britain by
Butler and Tanner Ltd, Frome, Somerset

CONTENTS

ACKNOWLEDGEMENTS

The *One Day in the Life of Television* project, of which this book is a by-product, was achieved through the sustained enthusiasm, persistence and flair of Richard Paterson and Janet Willis. They, and their colleagues of the British Film Institute's Television Unit, did wonders with the minimal resources put at their disposal. They are the first to acknowledge that it would have been impossible to open so many television industry doors without the project's five supportive Patrons: Paul Bonner, Paul Fox, Michael Grade, Jonathan Powell and Alan Yentob. Much gratitude to them all.

A number of television celebrities gave valuable assistance in generating nationwide publicity. They included Carol Barnes, Stephen Fry, Martyn Lewis, Alan Plater, Jean Rogers, Phillip Schofield, Peter Sissons and Moira Stuart. The distinctive diary leaflet, filled out by most One Day participants, was the work of Andrew Batley and Elaine Black and Collins Diary Division.

Although in the last stages of terminal cancer, the late Professor Hilde Himmelweit gave tireless thought and advice over the organization and use of research material. To the end her mental energy outstripped that of all who worked with her.

As book compiler I could not possibly have met the tight deadline, set for delivery of this manuscript, without the diligent attention to detail of the additional readers who helped the Television Unit make a first trawl through the 18,000 One Day diaries written and submitted to us. They were Samantha Cook, Lilie Ferrari, Susan Fleming, Jeanne Johnson, Betty Palmer, Liz Reddish and Terry Staples. Most of all, I am indebted to Janet Willis, who organized and advised at all stages of the editorial process; and to picture researcher Melanie Nieuwenhuys, who found the right photographs from the 5,000-plus taken during One Day.

Special thanks are due to those who helped with funds: the John and Mary R. Markle Foundation, the British Council, Channel Four Television, Independent Television Association and Yorkshire Television.

Our gratitude for the considerable help in kind from the television industry. In particular we would like to thank all departments and regions of BBC Television; Anglia Television; Border Television; Central Independent Television; Channel Television; Grampian Television; Granada Television; HTV; ITN; LWT; Scottish Television; Thames Television; Television South-West; Television South; Tyne-Tees Television; Ulster Television; Yorkshire Television; TV-am; Channel Four Television; Sianel 4 Cymru (S4C) and RTE (Radio-Telefis Eireann).

The present and former Directors of the British Film Institute, Wilf

Stevenson and Anthony Smith, were especially supportive of the project, and we were enormously helped by the assistance we received from the BFI Postroom and Despatch section.

Thanks also to Arts Channel; BARB (Broadcasters' Audience Research Board); British Airways; Cable Authority; Cablevision Bedfordshire; Ceefax; CNN (Cable News Network); CPL (Colour Processing Laboratories); Children's Channel; Clyde Cablevision; Coventry Cable; Croydon Cable; *Daily Express*; Independent Broadcasting Authority; IPPA and the independent production sector; Indra Dhnush/Cabletel; Intelfax; Landscape Channel; many public libraries; Mass-Observation Archive, University of Sussex (Professor David Pocock and Dorothy Sheridan); MTV Europe; NASTA (National Association of Student Television); National Museum of Photography, Film and Television, Bradford (Margaret Benton and Colin Ford); Oracle; Philips Consumer Electronics; Premiere; Scotch Film (3M Photo Colour Systems); SIS (Satellite Information Services); Sky Television; W. H. Smith Television; Super Channel; Swindon Cable; Visnews; Westminster Cable/Arabic Channel; Worldnet; WTN (World Television News) and all those other organizations and individuals without whom the project would not have been so comprehensive.

FOREWORD

By Sir Richard Attenborough
**CHAIRMAN OF THE
BRITISH FILM INSTITUTE**

Television has a unique role in the social and cultural life of
contemporary Britain. It is the forum where the nation speaks to itself;
where the different cultures and groups that make up our society can see
themselves represented; and from which most people obtain the
information they need as citizens.

One Day in the Life of Television demonstrates the complexity of the
relationship between the public and the programmes on offer as viewers
respond to them in their own homes. It also illustrates the determination
and commitment of those employed at every level of the television
industry as they go about their daily work.

As the name implies, the entire project was mounted and completed in a
single day, 1 November 1988, just before fundamental alterations in the
organization and availability of the leisure activity we value the most
began to take effect. It is part of the BFI's role both to chronicle that
change and to do its utmost to foster standards of excellence in the face of
impending legislation which may well pit market forces against true
choice and quality programming. Whatever the outcome, it is true to say
that television in Britain will never be the same again. The 18,000 diaries
written on that day, therefore, together with the 500 hours of
programming and 5,000 photographs also preserved in our archive,
constitute a vital historical benchmark against which we may measure the
future of this essentially twentieth-century medium.

The social purposes of broadcasting are best understood through the
audience's use of what is available. This selection of just some of the
many diaries written on 1 November gives a rare insight into this
phenomenon. It is immensely to the credit of all the organizations
involved in supporting the BFI in this endeavour that the viewing public
was granted such an opportunity and seized it with such ready
commitment.

INTRODUCTION

This is a book of 18,000 writers, the volunteers who accepted the nationwide invitation to keep a diary of their television day on Tuesday 1 November 1988. Not all are directly quoted between these covers, which can only contain a fraction of the fifteen million words contributed, but the book is a distillation of everything that was written. No strand of observation or opinion has been knowingly excluded. The diaries anthologized here, nearly 800 in all, are representative of the whole.

The *One Day in the Life of Television* project was conceived, developed and organized from the British Film Institute, based in London. The television industry itself is unavoidably centred in London. These facts of life did not prove inhibiting. Viewers throughout the British Isles became television critics for the day and their enthusiasm bubbled from Derry to Norwich, from the Scillies to the Shetlands, from St Peter Port, Guernsey, to Ramsey, Isle of Man.

All classes, conditions and ages of people took up their pens or set to work on typewriter or wordprocessor. A concerned ninety-two-year-old wondered if 'the younger generations' could appreciate the Victorian nuances of *The Importance of Being Earnest*. A wise five-year-old remarked, in the context of ITV's *Count Duckula*, that 'I like cartoons because if they are scary I know they are not real'. No diarist actually suggested that television is a medium which can raise the dead, but there were reports of the unborn dancing in the womb to the signature tune of *Neighbours*.

In addition to other viewers, around 2,500 people within the broadcasting community responded to invitations to write of their working lives. Many were meticulous in keeping a record; one BBC administrator even recorded the two precise times, during her working hours, when she 'went to the loo to spend a penny'. Enough were candid about their working methods and conditions, their aspirations and worries, to provide the most telling inside picture of the television industry that I have seen in twenty years as an observer.

When the BFI's Geoffrey Nowell-Smith first had a One Day idea he had in mind the fiftieth anniversary of Mass-Observation, that very 1930s concept of a nation looking at itself and, if possible, finding the inner strength to stand firm against Fascism. It would be good to think that we have in some sense been true to the Mass-Observation spirit. In telling about their use of television our diarists inevitably open a wider view of national diversities and similarities. Whether the project has helped strengthen resolve, to defend what is best about British public service broadcasting, remains to be seen.

As the One Day idea developed it became obvious that it was not a moment too soon. Whether channel multiplication makes for better or worse television, it is bound to diffuse the audience. The function of television as a shared experience, a topic of conversation akin to the weather, can only diminish. The figures suggest that on 1 November 1988, a majority of the entire population saw something on BBC1 or ITV or both. It may be that the new services are slow to catch on, but the next age of broadcasting can only be delayed, it cannot be cancelled. That is why the 1988 snapshot will have its value enhanced with every passing year.

Why 1 November and why not a whole week to ensure a comprehensive mix of programmes? These were questions often asked. In fact the broadcasting organizations, filming themselves at work for the Yorkshire Television documentary of the day, still less the BFI Television Unit, simply did not have the resources to sustain a week-long survey. In any event a week would have been much less well focused.

There was no very scientific reason for selecting 1 November. At the time it was chosen it was sufficiently far away for the project to be properly organized. As it was the first Tuesday of the month *First Tuesday* could be relied upon to ensure that the ITV schedule included at least one weighty programme.

Channel controllers were asked to make 1 November a typical day, not a special one. It has to be admitted that there was some tinkering at the

A young viewer greets posterity

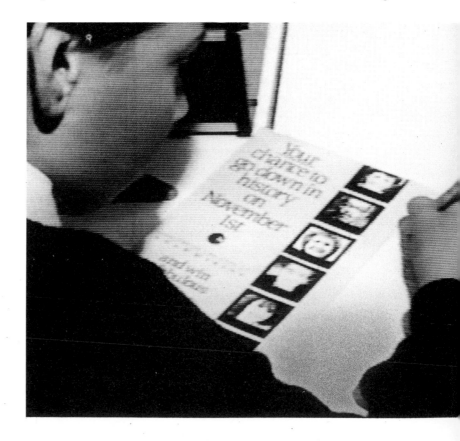

edges by BBC1. A forgettable afternoon film was replaced by *The Importance of Being Earnest*; in the late evening there was a third showing of *Meerkats United*, the most popular *Wildlife on One* for some time; and a repeat for the 'award-winning' Open University report on computer graphics, *The Search for Realism*. Otherwise all was as normal.

It might even be said that Channel 4 kept too closely to the rules for its own good. It did, and still does, maintain a reputation as the place to look for innovative British programming. On 1 November it had parts of two documentary series that might be expected to reinforce this reputation, *The Divided Kingdom* and *The Other Europe*. But a glance at the complete 9.30 a.m. to midnight schedule, leaving out Schools and Open College programmes, shows that the 330 minutes of British material was exactly balanced by 330 minutes from the USA. The American tinge was not limited to the infant satellite channels.

It has been said that there is no such person as a music lover. Only a deaf person, thinking about it in the abstract, could love all music. The rest of us love the particular idioms which suit us. It is the same with television. People have complained that 1 November was a weak television day on the four terrestrial channels. What they mean is that there was nothing to excite their taste buds at a time when they could watch.

It is true that the day lacked new up-market drama, a significant single documentary or sophisticated comedy. The only football relay was of the American kind. Against this it was a strong and diverse television day in the areas of popular drama, documentary series, sitcom, quiz and game shows, audience shows, children's programmes, news and current affairs. From the highest cultural peaks there was some music by Bach.

To some extent all surveys run into the problem that once people know they are being surveyed they will change their behaviour, however imperceptibly, to meet or challenge the presumed expectations of the surveyors. On 1 November there was a lot on television about television in general, and the One Day project in particular. And many viewers watched more than they usually do in order to write a more comprehensive diary. It is also true that outside the schools, where around 7000 students participated, and Mass-Observation, the survey sample was largely self-selecting. None of this should be thought to nullify the project. The vast majority of those who contributed are seen to care about television, its present and its future; and each participant may, on past survey experience, be presumed to represent many more who did not write.

There are, as television people might say, regional variations. It is a tribute to the determination of some in the Republic of Ireland, who are able to receive British television as well as that of Radio Telefis Eireann, that they found a way of participating with so little help from us. Such contributions were very welcome. Most of the Irish diaries were returned from the North, where the celebrations of All Saints' Day also made a difference to viewing patterns.

In Scotland many schools were closed by the teachers' 'day of action' protesting about the 'Anglicization' of Scottish education. In Wales there were renewed complaints from English speakers who are obliged to receive S4C rather than Channel 4. From the North of England there was an impression that people watched more television in order to take part.

Against this is much uniformity. The majority of the participants are middle class, either lower-middle or middle-middle. Far more women than men took part. A large proportion of women diarists are housebound and generally have a more complicated relationship with television than men. The feminist revolution remains as distant as ever. Female viewing is fitted into the gaps between household chores, or is seen as if through the eyes of their pre-school children, and they have a large capacity for guilt about their own 'telly addiction'. In contrast their husbands come home from work, take to the armchair, decide what is to be watched and often compound the female tendency towards effacement.

Many of the most delightful and bubbly diaries come from girls in their early and middle teens. They appear unselfconscious and confident in their tastes, and write as if talking to their friends. Other teenagers, of both sexes, write either in the censorious tones of parents or with their own blanket rebelliousness. For the latter group all television, beyond what they have discovered for themselves, is 'pathetic', 'patronizing', 'mindless' and, most of all, 'boring'.

After this it is not so surprising to find that teachers and lecturers, active or retired, form very much the largest group of professional contributors.

Many of the most moving and thoughtful diaries are written by people who are housebound by reason of age and infirmity, disablement or sickness. As a group they are fervently grateful for the 'godsend' of their 'window to the world', and almost as grateful for the opportunity to write about it. Some of the contributions from the lonely sound touchingly as if they must be scripts for Alan Bennett's next group of monologues.

There are many references to the use of television as 'moving wallpaper' and the like. In such households, where the set is left on as 'background', there is a constant challenge to programme-makers to grab and then sustain attention. On the other hand these non-viewers are outnumbered by others who report giving this or that programme 'my full attention'. Those pessimistic about the television future can take some comfort from the evidence of audience discrimination. At whatever level, popular or esoteric, the British viewer does have a firm idea of what constitutes acceptable, and trashy, television.

Our diarists also confirm that television is now less of a shared experience within families. Some mothers tell about what they will or will not allow their young children to watch. There are some sibling disputes over what is watched, and how quietly. But many households have several sets and many teenagers are able to watch alone in their own bedrooms. The consequent removal of embarrassment, felt when different generations watch together, may account for the comparative, and heartening, shortage of One Day complaints about 'sex 'n' violence' and 'bad language'.

Finally, a few words about my editorial method. The first rule has been to treat every contributor with respect, however violently I may disagree with the view being expressed. (I have endeavoured to save my opinions for the end of the book.) For space reasons only a handful of diaries could be used in full, but there has been no cutting to score points off the writer. The aim has been to show every writer in the best possible light. Where she or he is cut off in mid-flight I have indicated the fact with a . . .

I have corrected spelling and, within my own limitations, factual inaccuracy. I have only corrected grammar and punctuation where more clarity is essential. I have tried to be tolerant of cliché, except where words have literally lost all meaning. But I do have to plead guilty to chopping down several rain-forests of !s, sometimes axing two or three !!!s at a time. The nation appears almost as addicted to the ! as it is to *Neighbours*. Let humour and irony stand for themselves, and let the reader decide what is or is not funny. Even good jokes are likely to collapse when hammered on the head by a final !

Some obvious gaps will remain but every effort has been made to include at least something from all our major cities, from every county and from the smaller islands. Special attention has been given to people who watch in unusual conditions, such as hospital patients, lighthousekeepers, prisoners or whatever.

Beyond these considerations of geography and social circumstance the main imperative has been the search for variety. One Day happened to coincide with the height of the British craze for the Australian soap *Neighbours*, brilliantly scheduled by BBC1 to sustain its ratings success. Thousands of diarists enthused about this serial, and almost as many attempted and failed to give a rational explanation of its attraction. Perhaps the most sensible contributors are those who simply concluded: 'I am addicted, don't ask me why.'

Other refrains also echoed through a large proportion of diaries. There was the repeated view of the BBC1 soap *EastEnders* as 'gloomy 'n' depressing'; of the 'classic' 1970s sitcoms *Fawlty Towers* and *Rising Damp* as demonstrating the subsequent decline of the genre; of *Meerkats United* as showing televised natural history at its best.

All these very popular views are represented in this book, but not to the extent that they become tedious in their repetition. Thanks to the much appreciated BARB (Broadcasters' Audience Research Board) research, I have also given some space to 1 November head-counts. Otherwise statistics are ignored. It seemed more important to record the rich and enlightening range of opinion on particular programmes and the use of television in particular.

SEAN DAY-LEWIS
MARCH 1989

PROGRAMME LISTINGS FOR

BBC 1

7.00 BREAKFAST TIME with Jeremy Paxman and Kirsty Wark.

9.00 OPEN AIR, following the NEWS read by Lisa Davidson. Phil Redmond is the guide on the *Brookside* set, and Mike Shaft deals with viewers' calls.

9.20 KILROY! discusses 'marital rape' with female victims, male repentants and a studio audience.

10.00 GOING FOR GOLD with Henry Kelly, follows the NEWS read by Lisa Davidson. Repeat of yesterday's edition.

10.25 CHILDREN'S BBC presented by Andy Crane, begins with PLAYBUS and continues with JIMBO AND THE JET SET.

10.55 FIVE TO ELEVEN in which Patricia Routledge reads salutary animal poems by Elizabeth Jennings.

11.00 OPEN AIR follows the NEWS read by Lisa Davidson. Cheryl Baker is studio guest and Channel 4's Michael Grade talks about One Day in the Life of Television.

12.00 DAYTIME LIVE with Sue Cook, Alan Titchmarsh and Floella Benjamin follows the NEWS read by Lisa Davidson. Su Pollard and Eddie Shah are among the studio guests.

1.00 ONE O'CLOCK NEWS with Philip Hayton.

1.30 NEIGHBOURS . . . First visit of the day to suburban Melbourne, where Mrs Mangel cooks a steak for vegetarian Harold.

1.50 GOING FOR GOLD with Henry Kelly. More Euro-competitors struggle over simple general knowledge questions.

2.15 THE IMPORTANCE OF BEING EARNEST starring Michael Redgrave, Michael Denison, Edith Evans, Dorothy Tutin and Joan Greenwood. Another showing for Anthony Asquith's reverent 1952 cinema version of Oscar Wilde's play.

3.45 BEHIND THE SCREEN with Rob Curling. A repeat of yesterday's edition looking behind BBC scenes.

3.50 CHILDREN'S BBC with Andy Crane. In WHAT'S YOUR STORY? a company led by Sylvester McCoy acts a live serial with telephoned storyline ideas from the audience. Also today are PC PINKERTON, FIREMAN SAM, RATMAN, KNOWHOW, NEWSROUND and a GRANGE HILL repeat.

5.35 NEIGHBOURS again. A repeat of the lunch-time episode.

6.00 SIX O'CLOCK NEWS with Nicholas Witchell and Laurie Mayer.

6.30 REGIONAL NEWS MAGAZINES and the national weather picture from Ian McCaskill.

7.00 TELLY ADDICTS with Noel Edmonds. The Blakemore family from Bolton struggle to remember more of television past and present than the Moore family of Sutton.

7.30 EASTENDERS in trouble. In Albert Square perennial victim Kathy has been burgled, and in prison Den is suspected of grassing.

8.00 FAWLTY TOWERS by John Cleese and Connie Booth. Another repeat for the one about Basil's fear of sex.

8.30 A QUESTION OF SPORT with David Coleman asking the questions. Competing teams led by Ian Botham and Bill Beaumont manage some of the answers.

9.00 NINE O'CLOCK NEWS with Michael Buerk.

9.30 SOUTH OF THE BORDER by Susan Wilkins. Second of the South London-set crime series in which Buki Armstrong and Rosie Rowell are the inexperienced private eyes.

10.25 WILDLIFE ON ONE: MEERKATS UNITED. Another repeat for this favourite view of teamwork in the Kalahari. David Attenborough narrates.

10.55 NETWORK with Anna Ford. A studio discussion about televised football in particular and televised sport in general.

11.45 THE SEARCH FOR REALISM with Anna Ford. An Open University film showing the possibilities of computer graphics.

BBC 2

9.30 DAYTIME ON TWO for schools, and pre-school children.

2.15 SEE HEAR! with Clive Mason and Maureen Denmark. A repeat of the Sunday magazine for the deaf and hard-of-hearing.

2.40 CHAMPIONSHIP BOWLS at Preston. A round two match in the CIS Insurance United Kingdom Indoor Bowls Championship.

3.00 SUITE DREAMS follows the NEWS read by Lisa Davidson. An Open University film about design.

3.30 CHAMPIONSHIP BOWLS and more of the same.

4.25 THE COLLEGE, Britain's first City Technology College at Solihull in the West Midlands. A progress report made for the Midland region.

4.55 NORTHERN LIGHTS, this one being landscape painter David Blackburn. A repeat from BBC Leeds.

5.00 ADVICE SHOP with Hugh Scully and Helen Madden. Advice for people in need of welfare and public services.

5.30 FIRST TIME GARDEN with Geoff Hamilton, Gay Search and Roy Lancaster. Advice on making a garden out of a quagmire, first shown the previous Friday.

6.00 THE TUESDAY WESTERN: GUNS OF DIABLO starring Charles Bronson, Susan Oliver and Kurt Russell. A 1963 cinema film carved from the television series revolving round Jaimie McPheeters.

7.20 PERSONAL NOTES both musical and verbal. A conversation between conductor André Previn and cellist Yo-Yo Ma punctuated by Bach and Elgar.

8.00 FLOYD ON BRITAIN AND IRELAND, he being culinary joker Keith Floyd. He completes his series with mouth-watering fish dishes on the Orkneys.

8.30 BRASS TACKS looks at the way game poaching has lost its rustic charm to become an unappetizing big business.

9.00 COLIN'S SANDWICH by Paul Smith and Terry Kyan. Third of the Hancock-tinged sitcom series in which Mel Smith is a floundering British Rail clerk with writing ambitions.

9.30 THE MIND MACHINE and its provision of sight. Seventh of the series in which Colin Blakemore is the guide to the human brain.

10.20 BUILDING SIGHTS, this one the Isle of Dogs Pumping Station, enthused over by architect Piers Gough. First of a series on 20th-century British architecture.

10.30 NEWSNIGHT with Donald MacCormick in the studio and Peter Snow in Israel.

11.20 CHAMPIONSHIP BOWLS with David Icke. The last visit of the day to the Guild Hall at Preston.

TUESDAY 1 NOVEMBER 1988

ITV

5.00 ITN MORNING NEWS with Brenda Rowe.

6.00 THE MORNING PROGRAMME with Richard Keys and newscaster Gordon Honeycombe.

7.00 GOOD MORNING BRITAIN with Anne Diamond and Mike Morris.

9.00 AFTER NINE with Jayne Irving.

9.25 LUCKY LADDERS with presenter Lenny Bennett. Two couples compete for distant prizes.

10.00 THE TIME . . . THE PLACE . . . with Mike Scott. Today this audience show is in Central's Nottingham studios and the topic is financial credit, and debt.

10.40 THIS MORNING with Judy Finnigan and Richard Madeley in Liverpool's docklands. Barbara Cartland is graciously pleased to receive respectful Richard at her pink beehive in the home counties.

12.10 RAINBOW includes 'some very funny noises' for the little ones, made by Geoffrey Hayes.

12.30 REGIONAL VARIATIONS.

1.00 ITN NEWS AT ONE with Julia Somerville.

1.20 REGIONAL VARIATIONS.

3.00 GIVE US A CLUE with Michael Parkinson. All but one ITV region show this contest in celebrity charades, with Lionel Blair and Liz Goddard the team captains.

3.25 REGIONAL VARIATIONS.

4.00 CHILDREN'S ITV presented by Mark Granger. On show today are TICKLE ON THE TUM, THE ADVENTURES OF TINTIN, THE SOOTY SHOW, and COUNT DUCKULA.

5.15 BLOCKBUSTERS with Bob Holness. A lightly cerebral contest for extrovert teenagers.

5.45 ITN NEWS AT 5.45 with Alastair Stewart.

6.00 REGIONAL NEWS MAGAZINES.

6.30 PROVE IT with Chris Tarrant. Most ITV regions schedule this variety bill of undemanding novelty acts.

7.00 STRIKE IT LUCKY with Michael Barrymore. Plenty of lights on this set as three couples compete for a £3000 jackpot.

7.30 RISING DAMP by Eric Chappell. Most ITV regions show this repeat from the popular 1970s Yorkshire sitcom series, starring the late Leonard Rossiter.

8.00 THE BILL has an episode by Geoff McQueen in which Detective Sergeant Ted Roach gets the result and Detective Inspector Frank Burnside gets the credit.

8.30 THE RETURN OF SHELLEY, who faces a lonely birthday but makes friends easily. Hywel Bennett has the name part as ever, and the writer is Guy Jenkin.

9.00 BOON also has Hywel Bennett on hand, this time as 'guest star'. A new series for the West Midlands motorcycling cowboy played by Michael Elphick.

10.00 NEWS AT TEN with Sandy Gall and Alastair Stewart.

10.35 FIRST TUESDAY with Olivia O'Leary. Two films this month, one finding some excesses among evangelical Christians and one circling the problems of dyslexia.

11.35 REGIONAL VARIATIONS.

CHANNEL 4

9.30 SCHOOLS.

12.00 THE PARLIAMENT PROGRAMME with Alastair Stewart and Glyn Mathias. ITN reporting from both houses of Parliament.

12.30 BUSINESS DAILY with Susannah Simons.

1.00 TOURISM: THE WELCOME BUSINESS, otherwise an Open College lesson on what makes a good receptionist.

1.30 CATERING WITH CARE, which goes on about kitchen hygiene as thought desirable by the Open College.

2.00 THE IRON MASK starring Douglas Fairbanks. This 1929 black and white cinema feature is the sequel to *The Three Musketeers*.

3.20 THE THREE STOOGES with a Second World War farce called BACK FROM THE FRONT, also in black and white.

3.40 THE OPRAH WINFREY SHOW with another example of how Americans love to go to a television studio and tell all. Today husbands stay mum as their first and second wives air grievances at each other.

4.30 FIFTEEN-TO-ONE. A game show in which presenter William G. Stewart reduces fifteen contestants to one.

5.00 AMERICAN FOOTBALL including a main match in which Cleveland is at home to Cincinnati.

6.00 THE COSBY SHOW enjoys the generation gap in dance styles. Part of a repeat series.

6.30 DESIGN MATTERS: CITIES WITH A FUTURE? Another repeat series. This film considers the possibilities for the regeneration of Newcastle upon Tyne.

7.00 CHANNEL 4 NEWS with Peter Sissons and David Walter.

7.50 COMMENT with Jane Rogerson speaking from Edinburgh for impoverished students.

8.00 THE DIVIDED KINGDOM with Beatrix Campbell. Third in the documentary series in which presenters inspect the parts of the United Kingdom they do not normally reach.

8.30 4 WHAT IT'S WORTH with Penny Junor leading more consumer investigations.

9.00 THE OTHER EUROPE with Jacques Rupnik. Third in the documentary series turning a cold eye on the Soviet bloc countries of Eastern Europe. This week Rupnik examines the way the Communist party exercises power.

10.00 ST ELSEWHERE has to look elsewhere. Another series ends in tears as the Boston inner city hospital crumbles under bulldozer attack.

11.00 THE NEW STATESMAN by Laurence Marks and Maurice Gran. Rik Mayall is the eponymous backbencher who, in this repeat episode from the ITV sitcom series, is the well-whipped but ill-informed Tory spokesman for a by-election results programme.

11.30 AMERICAN FOOTBALL again. A repeat of the coverage seen in the early evening.

I
BREAKFAST TIMES
AND BEFORE

Midnight – 9 a.m.

1   IS IT ALWAYS LIKE THIS?

The first programme I watched was TV-am. I think TV-am is good for grown-ups. Most grown-ups like chat shows like TV-am. They like the happiness, the sadness, the good and the bad, and that is what TV-am is based on.

ZOË MASON, AGED 11,
GEORGEHAM, DEVON

> *The two minorities catered for at the top of every television day are first the insomniacs, and then the larks. At 2 a.m. on Tuesday 1 November 1988, there were 400,000 watching the ITN headlines on ITV. For the next three hours this number was reduced to 100,000 or less. At 5 a.m. the insomniacs were joined by the first larks of the day and the audience began to grow again. At the breakfast-time peak, around 8.15 a.m., the combined TV-am and BBC audience reached 3.8 million.*
>
> THE CASE OF THE WANDERING WET-SUIT
> *Few are at their best at breakfast. Some owls feel severely jarred by any kind of talk at all at this time. It is not surprising that, after five years of British breakfast television, the watching habit remains limited. Most still prefer the radio or silence. On-screen performers, and their guests, feel that they should give the appearance of being brightly awake. Off screen, broadcasters will admit that they would like nothing better than a return to reasonable working hours, preferably with no drop in salary. Some will put this more pungently. As, for instance, presenter-interviewer and One Day diarist Jeremy Paxman, who this morning presides in suit, tie and combative manner over the BBC1 Breakfast Time.*
>
> *'How long have you been in your present job?' we ask him. 'Too long', he replies. 'And how long have you worked altogether in the television industry?' 'Not long enough', he modestly adds. His diary now begins . . .*

Another of those ghastly nights when you wake an hour before the alarm goes, because you're afraid of oversleeping. At 4 a.m. it still sounds, and feels, like a pneumatic drill. Outside it is cold enough for still wet hair to freeze-dry on the bicycle ride to Shepherd's Bush. In summer the air can be positively sweet at that time, but now the only sensation is the cold.

The five o'clock briefing is more subdued, less profane than usual due to the presence of a Yorkshire Television documentary crew. There are no overnight news stories (our bread and butter), so we have interviews scheduled on the Government plans to abolish free dental and optical checks, the Chancellor's Autumn Statement, Israeli elections, the closure of the Gdansk shipyard, seal protection, dyslexia, as well as the inevitable animal and music items. There are a couple of good film features, and notably little sports news (they are reduced to giving a breathless nation details of Australian horse-race results). Discover to my horror that I have been assigned the cat item and am expected to hold one on my lap. I am allergic to cats. My co-presenter, the perfectly-formed Scottish intellectual Kirsty Wark, laughs vigorously.

The next hour is spent reading the newspapers and briefing notes left by my colleagues on the production team. I try to think of a new way of asking the Health Department's nominated flak-catcher, junior minister David Mellor, about the impending back-bench revolt over health charges. Advise Kirsty (allotted Israel interview) that it is a country in the Middle East. Jocular banter as she throws a copy of the *Scotsman*: she has a poor aim before 6 a.m.

At seven we go on air. The first half-hour goes swimmingly; not a single hitch. (One of our recent ones was a map to illustrate an Australian cyclone story, on which was superimposed a fading Daguerrotype of Charles Darwin. He looked slightly bewildered. Not surprising: the wrong Darwin.)

Sprightly interview with Sir William Clark and Tony Blair at 7.30. Sir William describes an error of £10 billion on balance of payments forecasts as 'more or less right'. Then chaos ensues. Susan Hampshire, due to review the papers and talk about her dyslexia campaign, gets into the taxi sent to collect her (*our* taxi) and says she's going to TV-am. Having arrived they invite her to be interviewed about dyslexia. Meanwhile in Shepherd's Bush, bedlam breaks out. To fill the space left vacant by Miss Hampshire, four design students are ushered in, to be interviewed by Kirsty about their designs for wheelchairs, display cabinets and wet-suits. The wet-suit has been mislaid on the way into the studio, and arrives only after the discussion has begun. I watch as the wet-suit, a curious confection in pink, blue and day-glo yellow, is passed from hand to hand behind the camera like some deranged, headless hippy. I laugh. Too soon.

Our night editor, Sara Nathan, whispers in my earpiece that I should introduce an item about seals next, and interview Britain's Head of Seals after a short film. The film runs. I look about for Head of Seals. He is obviously not in the studio, unless he is hiding inside the wet-suit. The film ends. I address the monitor, knowing that the Head of Seals is a Cambridge man. Perhaps he is in the Cambridge studio. To my horror my own face looks back at me.

At times like this one needs guidance. Unfortunately the talkback link to the control gantry has broken. A floor manager waves a sheet of paper headed with a number beginning in six and ending in zero. I grab a similar sheet from the desk. It seems to be a script about robots. 'Well, we're having some trouble getting through to Cambridge, so let's . . .', and I utter one of those banal 'links' for which television presenters are rightly reviled, 'let's talk about robots, which are also made in Cambridge.' There

Jeremy Paxman arrives for work 'cold enough to freeze-dry wet hair'

is blank incomprehension in the studio. I blunder through the few sentences on that piece of paper, which turn out to be a link into a standby film. At the end of the last sentence I realize that wherever that robot film is at the moment, it is definitely not standing by.

The floor manager is now waving her arms even more animatedly than the wet-suit of a few moments ago. I have read the wrong script – 640 instead of 680. With a laughing apology I begin again. 'Well, let's hear about something not from Cambridge', I say, grabbing the script. Oh no. It is an introduction to a film about dead babies.

As, finally, the film begins, I observe an academic-looking man slipping into the seat next to me, the Head of Seals. 'Is it always like this?' he asks, before someone takes his arm and leads him away to make way for David Mellor.

Mr Mellor says there is a woman with three cats outside. Is he expected to talk about them? I give him a bouncer first off: as custodian of the nation's health, has he a single piece of evidence that abolishing free checkups will improve our health? Like the practised advocate he is (QC in real life), he doesn't answer, and off we go for three or four minutes of

STOP! Regular visitors to the BBC Television Centre in West London know they must allow several minutes for front-gate negotiations before they are allowed through

knockabout. The Head of Seals looks on bemused. The wet-suit leaves the studio, narrowly missing a basket of three kittens arriving for their interview.

The rest of the programme I cannot really remember. Susan Hampshire did finally arrive, and talked about dyslexia while sitting on her mirror and hairbrush. The cats were highly eloquent. And at the end I talked to a couple of people about *One Day in the Life of Television*. Seemed more like a month to me.

JEREMY PAXMAN, PRESENTER

The couple comprised One Day project director Janet Willis and television presenter Phillip Schofield. The latter arrived at Lime Grove Studios five minutes late to discover that Breakfast Time is now produced at the Television Centre in Wood Lane.

I have a personal goal each time I go to the Centre – my normal base for television. That's to find a new and original way to persuade the chaps on the gate that I should park in the management car park and not the multistorey. I think they may have given up on me because I entered without hindrance . . .

At 8.55 I was interviewed (rather cynically) by Jeremy Paxman, who is an excellent presenter and journalist. I felt he pitched his interview perfectly, with humour, though I felt he had not been fully briefed on the subject matter . . . I think I put across the facts I had been asked to, so the rush was worth it. I couldn't ever present breakfast telly – it's all far too early . . .

PHILLIP SCHOFIELD, PRESENTER

Rather more aware of the confusion surrounding this particular Breakfast Time, a complicated two-hour live show at the easiest of times, was its night editor Sara Nathan.

When the day started I had already been at *Breakfast Time* for six hours and was well into preparing the Tuesday morning programme. The first draft of the running order was printing as the night team of director, production assistants and VT (videotape) operators drifted in for our production meeting at 12.15 a.m. It was obviously going to be a difficult night: what we needed were a couple of breaking stories; what we had were potential nightmares like four people in the studio with props talking about children's design and a former model promoting cat spaying, complete with two or three cats. Other minor worries included a dyslexic paper reviewer, an outside broadcast from the Commons on the Autumn Statement, and a studio that had been totally reset the previous day to accommodate the new *Newsnight*.

As the night goes on the scripts start to come through for approval, the first editions arrive but still no new story breaks, so there's a lack of freshness and excitement about the programme. It's not often that big stories really do break in the small hours, the last one was the Rome plane crash a couple of weeks back. Anyhow nothing tonight. Between 1 and 1.30 I view films, look at background scripts and embark on endless discussions with the director about the logistics of a one plus four [interviewer plus the four people mentioned above] and who is going to hold the cats. She seems to think that these items have been set up specifically to annoy her. The night shift is only occasionally pierced by journalism; most of the time is spent by the team worrying about graphics and whether their library material will ever turn up. Come 4.30 it's time to do timings, a rough approximation of how long I would like each interview to last, the usual dilemma about how long to give David Mellor on the health revolt as compared to a couple of journalists on the Israeli election.

At 5 a.m. I generally brief the presenters on the interviews they will each be doing: today there are six each and they have to be carefully juggled. Jeremy Paxman likes politics but is not so hot with children and terrible with pop stars. Kirsty Wark is generally flexible, maybe not as tough as Jeremy but should get a fair proportion of the heavy interviews. The briefing goes off reasonably well apart from Jeremy rebelling when told to have a cat on his lap: he claims an allergy and certainly has an aversion to looking cute . . . After the meeting, which has run late, I make another trek down the fifty-five stairs to the VT area and view the backgrounders; no problems there except some aren't finished and my confidence that the less experienced members of the four-man night team will actually get them done is a touch limited. Still, I get down to the studio at 6.50 with a reasonable hope that all may be well.

On air and into the news satisfactorily, but the dread tidings come that we have no contact with the OB [outside broadcast] due on the air at 7.30

The BBC Television Centre newspaper order. Never let it be said that anybody feeds off print

and that the paper reviewer hasn't turned up. The first half goes smoothly but the OB only gets going with 30 seconds to go, leading to the first panic of the morning. Then the trouble starts: the paper reviewer (Susan Hampshire) has gone to TV-am instead and now no one can find her, so there's an imminent five-minute hole. I move up a film and the design item and tell everyone we'll do the post-8 a.m. seals item just before the news. But the design item producer is trying to find Susan Hampshire and hasn't brought one of the vital props in, so one designer wet-suit circles the set in the hands of the assistant floor manager, who consequently forgets to get the guest in for the seal item. Neither I nor anyone else notices. We go into seals and the background piece runs but there's no guest. Jeremy doesn't hear the demand that he goes to a film standby and reads the wrong script, so no film comes up. Then he reads the right script and, oh joy!, we're back on course and have two minutes to recover.

After that, with the pack of cards well and truly collapsed, I have to brief the presenters, juggle the running order, get the comings-up altered and stay sane. Manage first three. Meanwhile Susan Hampshire has appeared on TV-am and got into a cab to come to us. Most unusually I get a charming call from the TV-am producer, who says he had no idea she was booked to be with us, as we were similarly ignorant about their

Even Sir David Attenborough needs editing. 'I know this room like a lifer knows his prison cell'

request. I can't believe it. We thank God it is only television and go back
to our respective shows. No other major traumas between 8.10 and the
end of transmission – even Miss Hampshire gets on the air – but we come
off with even more relief than usual.

I hold a brief post mortem in the lift back to the production office, and a
more detailed one over coffee and left-over buns amid total hysteria. The
night team are on again in nine hours so they drift off to get a few hours'
sleep. I slump over an elderly currant bun (the first food since beans on
toast at midnight) and at about 10 a.m. decide I can't postpone going home
to bed any longer. After the traumas of the night it seems unlikely that I
will be showing much more interest in television today.

SARA NATHAN, NIGHT EDITOR

*Any glamour attached to television work in the minds of outsiders
would not long survive conversation with reporter Mark Easton, who
produces short taped items for Breakfast Time. He sees his room, Edit
52, as 'a humming, airless broom cupboard'.*

I know this room like a lifer knows his prison cell. It has the childhood
smell of a train-set transformer. The floor is partially covered in scraps of
carpet that might have been picked off a skip. On the walls, more carpet
to absorb all the noise. In Edit 52 no one can hear you scream. Three
chairs, one too high, one too low and one broken, are squeezed in behind
the door like forgotten props from a television production of Goldilocks.
Against the walls, rickety benches support the editing machines –
thousands of pounds' worth of equipment resting on tables that seem
permanently on the verge of collapse. There are no windows, just a
flickering strip-light and a broken Anglepoise. The one reference to the
world outside is a clock which, fittingly, has stopped. It is here, in the
timeless place they call Edit 52, that I am destined to spend my day.

Today my editor is John. He's very good, but bored. He goes on holiday
tomorrow. The key to such situations is psychology. Some editors respond
to flattery. Some require an endless supply of coffee. John likes jokes, he
simply wants to laugh. The story itself is an unpromising candidate for
amusement. It concerns a Government scheme to recruit more cadets into
the Merchant Navy. Not many laughs there. Fortunately John has an
obscure sense of humour. He finds reporters hysterical. Now, I'm as
proud of the fourth estate as the next hack, but needs must. And so we
embark on a day-long demolition job of journalists and journalism while
at the same time creating a news story for tomorrow morning's
programme . . .

MARK EASTON, REPORTER

IS THERE HONEY STILL FOR BREAKFAST?
*The original TV-am, using the ITV channel but never accepted as a full
member of the ITV federation, was the company of the 'Famous Five':
Anna Ford, David Frost, Robert Kee, Michael Parkinson and Angela*

*Rippon, very different in their style and skill but all celebrated
television performers when the breakfast service took to the air in early
1983. Their celebrity, combined with the capacity of founding father
Peter Jay for sounding intellectually impressive, persuaded the IBA
(Independent Broadcast Authority) to reward TV-am with the breakfast
franchise. Jay promised not merely to avoid a 'bias against
understanding' (a catchphrase invented in 1975 with his then London
Weekend producer, John Birt) but also that he and his team would
embark on 'a mission to explain'.*

*The package proved hopelessly top-heavy. The lack of news-gathering
resources was immediately evident and the audience, splendidly
unimpressed by the grandeur of the TV-am presenters, stayed with the
BBC. By 1988 only one of the 'Famous Five', David Frost, retained a
link with the company. Under managing director Bruce Gyngell it has
travelled as far down market as the IBA would allow and consequently
attracted an audience double the size of that which watched the rival
BBC show.*

*A 1987 dispute resulting in the lock-out of its employees belonging to
the ACTT (Association of Cinematograph, Television and Allied
Technicians) brought severe technical problems, and more unwanted
IBA attention, in the early part of 1988. By 1 November the problems
had largely been solved to the satisfaction of the management, but for
One Day the ACTT picket line reassembled in full cry. However,
newscaster Gordon Honeycombe had no problem about passing
through.*

A voice tells me it's time to get up. LBC (London Broadcasting Company).
The radio has switched itself on. It's 4.25 a.m. . . . A disturbed night.
Woke at 2.35 a.m., dreaming of being chased up a stony hill by a young
lion. Later Mike Morris was being irritating, wanting to take some photos
of me. Can't remember any more . . . Lurch out of bed, feet in socks . . .
have chosen the suit the night before, transferred all necessary items to
pockets. Draw curtains, check that the car is below. It is, never fails now.

Ken, the driver, says there are pickets outside TV-am. What? Why?
They haven't been there for days. It's nearly a year since they were locked
out. Most have got other jobs now. Why today? There are lights, a TV
camera. About two dozen figures, well wrapped up. Some peer in the
window. We pass through easily. Get out of the car, say 'Good morning',
raise a hand in greeting as some pickets call 'Good morning, Gordon',
loudly, ostentatiously. What a way to earn a living.

No one in the office, the one used by Mike Morris, Richard Keys and
me. Head out along the first-floor open-plan deck around the atrium to the
big circle of computers, phones, papers and personal debris, backed by
maps and notices. Always slightly suspenseful, this moment. What has
happened overnight? What will happen this morning? I greet the night
shift, most of them have been on since 9 p.m. last night. At 4.55 a.m. I
punch up the bulletin list on the computer and then the top story . . .

BREAKFAST TIMES AND BEFORE

For the next thirty minutes I go through every story, initialling it GH when done, checking the facts, correcting any sloppy grammar, spelling and punctuation, removing unnecessary adjectives, adverbs, revising where necessary to suit the way I say things and to make better sense of an item, querying this and that with the writer or either editor. There's seldom a dispute, there isn't time. Depends who's on, and how belligerent, bloody-minded or brain-dead people feel.

The ITN [Independent Television News] bulletin comes on at 5 a.m. Half attend to it, to see what they're saying, what pictures they have. Brenda Rowe reading, fair performer . . . Then tea, coffee and toast arrive on a tray. Non-arrival of said nourishment can lead to friction and abuse . . . Martin is the bulletin editor, his first day as such on a weekday show. He seems calm, not a comedian like some. And under thirty, like most people here. I'm old enough to be everybody's father. Almost. Only Bruce [Bruce Gyngell, managing director] is older.

By 5.25 I've done what I can. Martin gets the stories printed. I head off to Wardrobe, where is Sue. I'm wearing the slate-grey suit (a different one each weekday – I've ten in all) and she chooses a lemon-coloured shirt, and, yes, I'll wear the gold tie. Next door to Make-up where Kathryn [Kathryn Holloway, co-presenter of *The Morning Programme*] and Carol [Carol Dooley, weather forecaster] are having their faces and hair enhanced and Keys [Richard Keys, co-presenter of *The Morning Programme*] is being noisy. He's joshing Gerry [*Good Morning Britain* producer]. Gerry goes and Keys subsides into his routine of washing his hair and shaving. The hairiest man on television, he is. Arms like a chimp's. 'Hallo, Honey', he calls. 'Hallo, Hairy', say I.

Gordon Honeycombe prepares to cast the TV-am news: 'Stuff one end of the ear-piece into my left ear, Lara clips the cord to the back of my collar, and I plug the other end into my desk'

Simon makes me up, borrowing bits as his kit has vanished on a van returning from the opening of the Birmingham studio . . . No gossip today. Some chat about the pickets. Not an average day at TV-am. And it's Anne's [Anne Diamond, co-presenter of *Good Morning Britain*] last day, the end of an era here. Star-set. Sad.

Into Studio B, sit at the desk. Victoria is at the autocue. Quickly mark up the bulletin stories, each on a separate yellow page. Stuff one end of the ear-piece into my left ear, Lara clips the cord to the back of my collar, and I plug the other end into my desk. Now wired for sound from the gallery . . . Check on a television monitor that my tie is straight, while on the other monitor the sun rises to music and turns into the TV-am logo. Keys and Kathryn, in Studio A, appear and do the introduction . . . Then Kathryn hands over with a 'Good morning, Gordon' and I turn to camera one saying: 'Hallo, good morning, the news from TV-am.' Read autocue and begin to tell a dozy, docile nation what the news is today.

So the first of seven bulletins goes out. Eye and dental charges lead the news and Gerry Foley reports on them. Says bulletin director Jill in my ear, of a female Tory: 'What is she wearing, looks like a dead cat?' Next is Tony Birtley reporting from Jerusalem on Israeli reaction and retaliation after the petrol bombing of a bus. Mother and three children die. Then sentence on Galtieri for his Falklands war crimes, and Adam Boulton in

Warsaw deals with Thatcher's visit to Poland. Finally, two men have stolen a simulated missile in Belfast. An unexceptional news, six minutes, and all goes well.

Anne [Diamond] arrives in a sweater dotted with pink koalas, looking well and smiling. Her last day on *GMB* should have been last Friday but she stayed on this week so that she could appear in the YTV film. Now her farewell appearance on *GMB* today, though few know about this or seem to care, will go unfilmed, though not unreported. She will soon be over the rainbow and off to Oz. Will she marry Mike there? Lips are sealed, but I think so . . .

Hand back to Kathryn at 6.35. Chris appears with tea, toast and honey on a tray, and unloads them on to the desk. As I butter the toast Bill Ludford (director of news and current affairs) makes a rare studio visit, says we said that Adam was our political correspondent. Should have been political editor. Oh, shucks. Correct script, advise Victoria. 'Everything all right?' enquires Bill and departs with a belch.

Follow him out, taking toast on a plate to our green room, the Pagoda. Glance over morning papers, mainly the pops, quicker to read. Take in the write-ups on Anna Ford, going to the BBC *Six O'Clock News* in January. Said variously to be paid £50,000, £60,000, £80,000 and £100,000. Probably £50,000. Twatchell [Nicholas Witchell, co-presenter of the *Six O'Clock News*] would be peeved if she got more than him. And she's only doing three bulletins a week. Very bourgeois of the Beeb to appoint her. Such impeccable tones and features so perfect are not right for the News, as wrong as spots and a squint. Interfere with the imparting of information. Few women get it right, though it's not their fault. Anna Ford apart, the wrong ones are chosen and then vanity obtrudes. As it does with some men. Angela Rippon was right, and Sue Lawley, and Moira Stuart. She should have got the job.

It's almost 7 a.m. On the monitor Keys and Kathryn hand over to Anne and Mike. *GMB* music and titles, those titles never bore. Anne and Mike do the menu for their part of the morning, then hand over to me . . . The main impact on me this time, while listening and watching and reading, is made by a grey-haired Israeli woman in glasses, denouncing, decrying, in close-up. What is she saying? Why such passion? No one explains. And a bulldozer vindictively knocks down a palm tree, a house. The news goes out without error. At 7.11 I hand over to Mike.

Over to the office to look through the in-tray. Keys at his desk. Exchange views on BBC presenters, newsreaders in particular. Keys derides new *Nine O'Clock News*. A failed format, he says. I agree. The newsroom background is a distraction and a mistake, as it was the last time they tried it. We agree that the opening music is OTT and old hat, RKO did it better, that the captions are not positive enough, and that the whole caboodle, like Smuggins [Martyn Lewis] himself, comes across as phoney and portentous. Gravitas contrived. Curious that the management can't see this. But self-important egos will admire their own kind and see nothing amiss.

Yet the *Six O'Clock News* has it absolutely right, were it not for the Poisoned Carrot [Nicholas Witchell]. We agree that [Andrew] Harvey and [Philip] Hayton are the best newsreaders they have. I remark on the ugliness of some reporters, a female with grisly gnashers who looks like the Alien's daughter, and a misshapen male who might understudy Frankenstein's monster. Good journalists they may be but good looking they are not.

And surely all reporters/presenters should fulfil the very basic requirements of looking good, speaking well, and to some extent being good as well. They're on television, after all. It's a visual medium and the viewers don't want to be faced with disagreeable persons beamed uninvited into their homes. It should be a maxim that visages arousing fear and loathing, that intrude their oddness, divert attention from their words, are out. And that includes beards and red hair. Both provoke a certain distrust. Keys says I should write about this when I leave. 'You could say a lot', he says. And he means also about TV-am. But if you wrote up everything that happened here, no one would believe it. 'It's unbelievable', Keys agrees . . . We agree that the Weather should be computerized, or made more interesting at least, less like something in a nursery. But where is the will to get things improved? A style-book was planned three years ago. Necessary and not hard to devise, but nothing's been done. And it's taken as long for the new News set to arrive.

The 7.30 headlines go out OK. Back to Make-up for a swift dust to dim the glowing dome . . . On the monitor is Susan Hampshire, talking to Anne about dyslexia. Susan starred in the film of my first novel, filmed in Jersey. I speed upstairs to the office to collect my autograph book, which is to be auctioned in due course or sold for charity. Susan H. comes out of Studio A, says 'Hallo'. It's fifteen years since *Neither the Sea*. So badly made, embarrassing, but she did her best. She's about to autograph my book when David our Greeter enters Make-up, smiling, says she should be at the BBC. She's been double-booked. 'Oh, my goodness', she gasps, scrawls her signature and flees.

Back into Studio B . . . The new set, when it arrived some weeks ago, turned out to be too big for the studio, and despite specific requirements being known, no spaces had been made for monitors, mikes, cables etc. It had to be rebuilt. It's said to have been a job lot. It looked like a section of the Roman Senate and some said I'd have to wear a toga.

The 8 a.m. goes out, our so-called flagship and the fifth bulletin . . . Much better now that we have our own reporters home and away. There was a time when nearly all the VTs came from CBS, ABC, ITN, and were merely voiced by our writers. Certainly the News has improved 100 per cent since I came here. Creditable now. I hand back to Anne, but Mike appears. The *GMB* gallery didn't tell us they had changed their minds. Damn.

Feel unusually alert this morning. Must be the unusual aspects of the day . . .

The sixth bulletin of the day goes out. Stay in B to hear Anne talk to

James Whitaker in Australia, in Perth, about the split between Jane and Alex Makim. He as if next door. What time is it there? 4.35 p.m. Maybe this time next year I'll be there. I won't be here for sure.

Back to the office. Kathryn pouring coffee for Keys, who's lying down across three chairs. He says the National Union of Seamen are outside. Who? Yes, standing by in case the ship sinks. Perhaps the pickets are about to board us from the canal. The lowest locks of Camden Lock are below our window. Daylight outside now, calm and clear and sunny. Open the few letters that have arrived this morning.

It's 8.55. Back to Studio B for the last News of the morning, the seventh . . . On the *GMB* monitor I see Anne has been given a bouquet of flowers by Gyles [Brandreth]. From TV-am. 'I shall be back I know not when', she says.

Up the spiral to the meeting in the dismal conference room by 9.32, twenty minutes later than usual . . . I skim through the typed and photocopied five-page list of viewers' phone calls . . . There are eighty-one in all. Two women from the South say they will miss Anne very much. Others complain about Carol standing in front of the South-East. Another asks: Is Carol one of the Dooleys that used to sing in cabaret? There are birthday requests, other comments, and questions about dyslexia. My son has it, my daughter. Most phone about the eye check charges, much concerned. Some respond to the Duchess of York's long stay in Oz, leaving her baby in England . . . After 9 a.m. callers complain that models are always tall. Why no small ones? Indeed. And who will take note of anything the viewers say? The meeting is soon over, some points are made. And that's the end of my working day at TV-am.

But there's more. I had organized snacks and champagne to be sent up from the canteen for a farewell presenters' breakfast for Anne in our office. Heard yesterday that the champers, as expected, had been banned by Bruce. Oh well, in the office are Anne, Jayne, Carol, Kathryn, Morris

Carol Dooley: new TV-am weather person, found standing in front of England's south-east

and Keys. Bruce turns up, and our secretaries, Gay and Suzanne. All quite cheerful but mellow, like the end of term . . . We're all going, going. Me in March when the contract runs out. Maybe Keys, aware the longer he stays, the less good he does himself. As with Morris. Both would fare better as sports presenters. Too many square pegs in round holes here.

A few people come into Anne's office to say goodbye. Officially she's off on three months' paid maternity leave. Before being driven home she is snapped by press photographers. She wonders if the photos will appear in the papers, thinks *Today* has decided to ignore her now, and the *Sun*. Since the court case she's avoided publicity, and the papers have got the message. Now the women in the news and the papers' pets are Lawley and Ford . . .

GORDON HONEYCOMBE, NEWS PRESENTER

> *At least one employee of TV-am was clearly pleased by her good fortune in being allowed to work for such a wonderful company. Telephonist Janet Harper rose at 5 a.m. having given an 'inordinate amount of thought and planning' to her dress. 'Mustn't be too hot/cold, tight/creased; must be smart but casual/brightly coloured/durable.' By 6.15 she is ready to be conveyed from her Islington home to Camden Lock.*

Grateful to sink into company car waiting to carry me in comfort to the studio. I feel cosseted and privileged as we slip through the quiet morning streets and through a small but angry line of pickets, still aggrieved by the outcome of their recent, much publicized industrial dispute.

Glass doors open and close, enveloping me inside the cloistered world of television. Reception looks immaculate as usual, aglow with lights and fresh flowers and with an open-plan backdrop resembling a tropical glasshouse. I ponder for a moment the devastation left at home but quickly dismiss such disturbing thoughts. Nothing must spoil the prospect of another day crammed with good humour and bizarre incidents.

I switch on my computerized switchboard and small television set simultaneously. Both work perfectly as always. Expectations are soon realized as an array of visitors, guests and regular staff begins to arrive. Most have quick wit and a ready smile . . . A telephonist's first duty is to attend quickly, efficiently and politely to all telephone calls. After that we must enjoy ourselves and be seen to be doing so. That's fine by me. We do it well, I think.

Noise increases and the good humour is infectious. The show is going out to millions and I am able only to snatch glances at it, always rooting for friends who have become celebrities and vice versa. The controversial matter of Government proposals to introduce dental and eye test charges is under discussion. This evokes immediate response from the public. At once every line is busy. All are dealt with as speedily as possible.

The pickets outside become agitated, their noise escalating with the arrival of management and senior staff. This serves only to reinforce the feeling of camaraderie that exists within the building. The adrenalin is flowing.

Nigel Dempster ambles amiably through, sure of where he is going. Susan Hampshire rushes up to us, not at all sure she is meant to be here at all. Within minutes she is on the screen. Someone walks by wearing a set of Dracula teeth and someone else is dragging a 30-foot-long tree past us, no doubt destined for the hanging gardens beyond. Nothing is surprising.

Reception is the hub of the building. We are the centre of information, purveyors of news good and bad, the answers to all questions: 'You need a sleep before you go on the show? Fine, we'll find someone to take you'; 'No you don't have to be disabled to use that loo'; 'Yes, stand still, we'll fix your suit with a safety pin, it'll never be noticed.'

Morning flies by in a haze of madness. Must pace myself. It's a long time until 6 p.m. Meal breaks are necessary but sometimes arrive too quickly, threatening to disrupt the fun of our tightly-knit group, working well together. I don't leave the building. The bright canteen overlooking Regents Canal provides all I need in the way of sustenance and social life. Not even the bright sunshine of this first day of November can draw me from the safety of our warm cocoon . . .

Chauffeurs arrive and depart. Bouquets of flowers are delivered regularly, adding to the colourful scene. Anne Diamond is leaving today. Mike Morris departs, his morning's work over, waving happily, and pausing for a moment to ask how we are feeling. Film crews gather and disappear and our own reporters phone in from around the world. What a strange and happily insular world this is . . .

By 4.30 p.m. the mind is willing but the body is weakening. Difficult to wind down, but at 6 p.m. glad to return home to loved ones and relative normality. So much to tell them. They cannot possibly understand how it feels to have been touched by the stardust of live television . . .

JANET HARPER, TELEPHONIST

Rather less touched by stardust was Diana Slade, secretary to the finance director, who struggled across London from Wimbledon and 'arrived late this morning feeling very nauseous, as I am five months pregnant'.

Even though I work at TV-am I haven't watched any breakfast television. It doesn't play any part in our lives since we don't have a television in the bedroom or the bathroom. Instead listened to *Today* on Radio 4 . . . My boss had 'flu. The morning was taken up cancelling meetings, informing various departments he would not be in, answering queries, opening post and taking advantage of his absence to do some filing . . . In the afternoon I had a problem with a laser printer, which probably won't be fixed until tomorrow. Everybody in the finance department is falling like flies: two cases of 'flu, one strained back and one case of shingles. Left work at 5.30 p.m. . . .

DIANA SLADE, SECRETARY

2 IT'S NOT WHAT YOU SAY

> *As viewers blink into consciousness it is evident that the presenters,*
> *whether perceived as likeable or obnoxious, make much more of an*
> *impression than anything they or their guests may say. The first batch*
> *of diary extracts suggests a preference for the BBC's breakfast*
> *alternative.*

I put the telly on at 8.25 a.m., about ten minutes after waking up. I was on
half-term holiday but had to get up anyway because I was going out.
When I'm around in the wee hours I'll always watch BBC *Breakfast Time*
rather than TV-am because the presenters come across as more natural
and friendly than those who perform for *Good Morning Britain*.

Anne Diamond really makes me cringe. Surely she must be acting as
she coos and grins through hours of tabloid-type Royal Family/cute
animal/heroic children stories which make it hard to hang on to your bran
flakes at the best of times. She's always accompanied by some dodgy
token male (who also happens to be a sports expert) and a liberal
sprinkling of total dimbos such as Gyles 'I write stupid puzzle books for
children' Brandreth and totally-out-of-her-mind Lizzy. Mix gently with a
lovable granny or two and a reformed music critic/patronizing kids' show
presenter named Timmy Mallett and after a bit of 'wot a scorcher' type
baking the end result is total nausea. As you may have guessed I used to
watch TV-am but have now seen the light.

And the light is *Breakfast Time*: re-vamped since it arrived with Selina
Scott etc. Now there's not a celebrity in sight. This has led to a much
more interesting and well-balanced programme which manages to appeal
to a wide range of viewers: unlike TV-am, which I feel is aimed at middle-
aged or older women . . .

When Phillip Schofield was on *Breakfast Time* talking about this
television day I couldn't help wondering what on earth he had to do with
it all. Apart from being adored by hundreds of little girls who would go
for anyone younger than Terry Wogan, Phillip Schofield is nothing
special. He loves himself too much already, so why did the BBC give him
more unnecessary air-time? It was probably his idea anyway (he seems to
have them in the palm of his hand) so that he could get himself squeezed
into the archives . . .

TOM BISHOP, AGED 15,
SWINDON

Pondered whether to put on *Breakfast Time* in the kitchen to see if Jeremy
Paxman was saying anything amusing to the politicians, but decided I
didn't have time. Arrived at school at 8.45 and was shown a picture of

Rowan Atkinson by a friend. I commented 'Oh' and thought that Tony Robinson as Baldric looked better, but realized in time it would be more than my life's worth to mention it.

During break talked about the *Smash Hits Poll Winners Party* and the wonderful, in my opinion, Phillip Schofield . . . Talked over lunch about *Whose Line Is It Anyway?* (Channel 4) and all agreed that it's a very funny programme. Also had a heated, but enjoyable, discussion about Phil Schofield and Rowan Atkinson, me defending P. Schofield . . . Finished homework quite quickly . . . put my video tape in the machine, and watched Phillip Schofield (surprise, surprise) on *Blue Peter* to find out exactly what I am supposed to be writing down now . . . I realized *A Question of Sport* was on next and, as I loathe this programme, I looked in the paper to see what else was on. Nothing good enough to watch, so put on a different tape in the video recorder and watched a bit of the *Smash Hits Poll Winners Party* and . . . PHILLIP SCHOFIELD!!!

**HANNAH SKEATES, AGED 14,
IPSWICH, SUFFOLK**

Twitching 'twixt the lightweights of TV-am and the pithier fare of *Breakfast Time*, and being particularly irritated by the self-important posturings of a junior politician who shouted down the interviewer (Paxman, no easy task) whenever he was asked to answer the question, I got the day off to a good start . . .

**L. J. F. SHEERAN, DESIGN ENGINEER,
WEYMOUTH, DORSET**

On 1 November I was a patient in the Wessex Nuffield Hospital, Chandler's Ford, hence the long viewing hours. Woke about 3.30 a.m. but three weeks' experience of Television South's all-night show has taught me that there will be nothing worth watching until 5 a.m. TVS greatly inferior to ITV London's all-night offering. At 5 a.m. watched *ITN Morning News*, an excellent hour. Will miss it when I am sleeping again at night. Particularly good coverage of US elections . . . At 7 a.m. BBC *Breakfast Time*. What an opinionated, boorish, self-satisfied presenter Jeremy Paxman is! Would I watch this if there were any alternative to television? Interruptions of hospital routine positively welcome, at least there is some human contact . . .

**B. C. W. HEARD,
BOLDRE, NEAR LYMINGTON, HAMPSHIRE**

Saw a bit of TV-am but there was Anne Diamond's smiling face so I switched to BBC1's *Breakfast Time*. Jeremy Paxman was in a belligerent mood, as usual, interviewing two politicians about the Chancellor's Autumn Statement. Also as usual he was more rude to the Tory MP, as has been noticeable with all television journalists: it's aloof 'Mr So-and-So' to the Tory and 'Tony', or whatever their Christian name is, to the Labour MPs. It's quite blatant how chummy they are with the Socialists, and stand-offish with the Tories. The television stations say they are impartial but it just doesn't hold water.

Comparing the two early morning programmes: TV-am is trivial and silly with too much attention paid to one personality, who is too overpowering; whilst the BBC is boring, aloof and self-satisfiedly smug, as presented by their journalists, who really believe these days that they are all-powerful, do nothing wrong and 'how dare anyone question anything they do or say'. Later Jeremy Paxman kept up his bullying mood, interviewing David Mellor. I've seen literally hundreds of these interviews and Labour MPs never get the same searching, hard treatment.

Yes, I am biased in my own views, but it must be said that television has now taken on the role of political opposition to this Government, a very dangerous move. Television journalists make quite plain their views, chat show guests are chosen to mirror what journalists want to say and put out. It could be said that as the Government moves to the Right television has moved to the Left to compensate, but this is so dangerous. Television is beamed into our rooms straight before our eyes and our children's eyes. People say 1984 (a novel by George Orwell) was about politicians gaining too much power, surely now we should question the influence and power of television on our lives, swaying our thoughts and opinions.

Back to TV-am only to find Anne Diamond glorying in her favourite topic, Royal gossip. Today about the Duchess of York's sister's marriage problems and the silly business of Fergie staying away too long from her baby. How on earth will the baby know? Of course Anne lapped it up, but newspaper items about the private lives of television personalities, like her and Frank Bough, are not discussed . . .

I strongly believe television makers badly need taking down a peg or two. They must listen to such criticism and take note of it, not dwell in their ivory towers ignoring the public's demands . . . Then they have the gall to get up in arms when Government tries to regulate some of their excesses, such as the interviewing of terrorists which the majority of the public do not want on their screens. At least a Government is elected, by however small a majority. The BBC and ITV are not elected in any way, and they want to remember that when they set themselves up as the arbiters of public taste, morals and opinion . . .

**PETER D. HOPPER, ARTIST,
LUTON HOO, BEDFORDSHIRE**

Despite it being half-term, which meant the children were not going to school, I still got up at 7.30, and went in to breakfast. We watch *Breakfast Time* every morning in our house. I think it is an excellent programme, I like the up-dating of the news, the local news from Northern Ireland, the weather, the papers and any reports on current issues. I would never watch TV-am, the BBC sets the right tone, and to me is much more up-market than the other channel.

It does, of course, have its disadvantages. For example Jeremy Paxman, who is rude, ignorant and extremely unpleasant. (After watching *Open Air* on 2 November I gather I am not the only person who feels that way.)

Oh for the days of Frank Bough and his team. But despite Jeremy Paxman I am not going to stop watching *Breakfast Time*. I keep the television on until just before I go to work at 8.50. All our family find the *Breakfast Time* clock invaluable. We catch buses, get the car out and leave the house using it. We would all be at a loss without it, and did not know what to do when the Olympic Games were on . . .

**ANTHEA SHACKLETON, HOUSEWIFE AND
PART-TIME DEVELOPMENT OFFICER,
BELFAST**

Jeremy Paxman's brilliantly incisive interview with David Mellor who, true to his calling, adroitly avoided answering the questions. Clip of Dame Jill Knight, rebel, a 'sensible' Tory. Northern Ireland news: surface-to-air missile nicked from Shorts of Belfast. 'In its present state it is no use to terrorists', said a spokesman. Who are they trying to kid? Jeremy's interview with Susan Hampshire about dyslexia, what a beautiful angora sweater, such soft blonde hair, so pretty. Wonder what he thinks, would he rather be attacking Mellor's waffle . . .

**MAY MILLIGAN, SUBSTITUTE TEACHER,
DUNGANNON, CO. TYRONE**

Until 8 a.m. I was in bed and only half-watching, well listening. Two very different styles of morning programme: TV-am offering informal chat with a special guest(s) of the day, mixed with serious news items; and *Breakfast Time* a much more formal, and high standard, news service.

I like all these presenters. Jeremy Paxman is accused by some of being

Breakfast Television: a
politician and his audience

aggressive, even rude, when he's interviewing. I'd say he was direct, and why should politicians, especially Government ministers like David Mellor, who he was interviewing this morning, be allowed to get away with not answering questions? Jeremy insists they do answer, to his credit. Besides he's got a lovely, wicked grin.

As a Scot I have a slight national bias towards Kirsty Wark. Perhaps she takes herself a little too seriously at times, but working alongside a wit like Jeremy I suppose somebody has to be serious. I tip her for greater things. The excellent *Left, Right and Centre*, a Scottish political discussion programme, and *Scottish Question Time*, which she also presents, will, I hope, make her the natural successor to the likes of Sir Robin Day, David Dimbleby and Sue Lawley on national television . . .

Whatever the gutter press say about Anne Diamond I think that she's the life and soul of *Good Morning Britain*. Her lively style and vivacious personality certainly brighten up breakfast television. She can be annoying on occasion but no more than everybody else. Mike Morris is my least favourite. He's not bad, I suppose, but he verges on the boring at times. He and the whole programme will suffer without Anne because it always loses its relaxed atmosphere and becomes more laboured when she is not there.

SHEONAGH MARTIN, POSTGRADUATE STUDENT, EDINBURGH

The presenters are laughing because the wet-suit was delayed. They seem like a club to which the rest of us don't belong. Their familiarity is deceptive. Jeremy is cross because his script has been changed, Francis is more poetic than ever, but I don't really know them, even if they are in the corner of my living-room.

VALERIE WHITMARSH, CLAIMANT ADVISER, FARNHAM, SURREY

A member of the Educational Institute of Scotland, I'm on strike today, protesting about the 'anglicization' of Scottish education policies. When I come through into the living-room at 7.45 a.m. my wife and two sons, nine and five, have *Breakfast Time* on, though they're not really watching it. I don't watch it, but I don't put it off either. As usual, the main items concern the Government's withdrawal from social and moral responsibilities in the name of encouraging initiative . . . I switch current affairs television off more and more now, because the news of what the Government's up to is so depressing.

BILL DUNCAN, TEACHER, DUNDEE

Paxman, he of the sloping sneer, in trying to be incisive, succeeds as usual in being hectoring, but with studious impartiality. Domestic and international political coverage leavened with the Design Centre awards. Kirsty Wark examines one of the winners with the intense interest of a Scotch terrier at a rabbit hole. As ever, takes words out of the mouth of interviewee, so betraying the fact that she hasn't listened to what he said in the first place.

The question, not the answer, is the thing. Why is it and what is it that the producer yaks into their earpieces that leads to this non-communication between interviewer and interviewee? Paxman interview with David Mellor determined to stick out for his set point. Jeremy attempts to haul him back to his. Deuce? Advantage Paxman, I think.

Resident weather man, Francis Wilson, back from sunny Spain. Lots of jolly banter to show how relaxed, friendly and well-integrated the team is . . . Even the local news has to be referred to as 'where you hang your hat' and 'in your neck of the woods'. Aren't we cosy? Why can't time allocated to items take account of differing nature and degree of difficulty, thus avoiding the irritation of being on the brink of something worthwhile only to be whisked away to a piece of trivia . . . Quick check on TV-am from time to time. Makes *Breakfast Time* seem a feast of intellect and presentation. Top marks for inanity to Gyles Brandreth. Is he real?

DR SARAH J. G. CALDWELL,
RETIRED LECTURER, DUNDEE

I start the day with BBC's *Breakfast Time*. I much prefer this to TV-am; in the short time I have in the morning I do not want to sit through the same few adverts day after day, nor to listen to Anne Diamond. It was refreshing this morning to witness (if not actually see, then be aware of) pandemonium in the *Breakfast Time* studio and to detect a glint of terror in the eyes of the presenter, who did not seem to be aware of what was going on . . .

I feel that it is important to voice my opinion that the output of British television is at present quite excellent on the whole, and the prospect of evenings such as that of 1 November becoming a thing of the past, due to the plethora of choice soon to be foisted upon us, is saddening. If my experience of American television is anything to go by we will be worse off. In Orlando, Florida, this year I had 35 channels to choose from and invariably there was nothing worth watching.

JONATHAN P. K. SMITH,
CHARTERED ACCOUNTANT, LEICESTER

Blearily switch on *Breakfast Time* at 7.30 a.m.; hubby likes it, and I find it cut and dried . . . Jeremy Paxman, looking like a moose playing Noël Coward, is cheerfully putting the boot into a politician as usual . . . Hubby off to shave, so switch over to TV-am. Mike Morris and Anne Diamond on their settee like a suburban father and daughter entertaining her fiancé's parents . . . Their weather woman has raided the kiddies' dressing-up box again.

Hubby back, so back to Paxman, all smirks, now leaning back (to have his tummy tickled?). Female song-writer gives unique interview, using the phrase 'kind of like' three times, and the word 'like' incessantly. Wonder what her lyrics are like? Phillip Schofield turns up to publicize diary day; short-haired, stubbleless, even the stone-washed denim looking water-

washed. Grannies could fancy him, let alone all those sent schoolgirls . . .
THELMA SUTTON, RETIRED SECRETARY, WOKING

> DIAMOND CUTTING
> *Of all the breakfast presenters on 1 November there is no doubt that Anne Diamond of TV-am's Good Morning Britain aroused the most emotion. Not all the emotion was friendly.*

See Anne Diamond is still presenting, prior to her *second* imminent birth as a single mother. I very much object to her high profile on television as it gives the young the idea that it is acceptable these days to have babies without the support of a husband and home.
TRUDY BARRELL, PART-TIME TYPIST AND CLERK, COLCHESTER

Always watch TV-am. Not so keen on Anne Diamond flaunting her pregnancy, even though she's not married . . .
GILLIAN McMONAGLE, HOUSEWIFE AND MOTHER, HALIFAX

I suspect that women who dislike Anne Diamond are either jealous or have Victorian moral standards. As a television presenter I find her charming and quite professional.
THOMAS RUSH, AGED 71, KIDDERMINSTER

Anne Diamond wasn't wearing anything particularly awful this morning . . .
ELIZABETH McFARLANE, GUIDANCE OFFICER, GLASGOW

My husband said: 'Have they sacked that daft woman yet?' He meant Anne Diamond.
PAM MALKIN, ASTROLOGER AND CLAIRVOYANT, MATFEN, NORTHUMBERLAND

I usually have TV-am on, but Anne Diamond drives me cuckoo. She insinuates that every item is the most serious since time began, making mountains out of molehills . . . She is just too irritating when you are eating bran flakes, but I don't remember if she was on this morning.
DAVID PARKER, TRAVEL AGENT MANAGER, WOKINGHAM, BERKSHIRE

I can't hear very well, but the bright face of Anne Diamond fills the room as I chat to my friends and munch my breakfast.
ELIZABETH YOUNG, RESIDENT AT CEREBRAL PALSY CENTRE, CROYDON

A hurtling squash ball has rendered my left eye useless and the whole world looks like a television screen with exceptionally bad reception . . . Find a very twee Anne Diamond. God knows how she sits there looking so perfect at 7 a.m. Maybe if I was paid her money I would make it my business to find out.

JOANNE TERRY, LEGAL WORDPROCESSING OPERATOR, ROCHESTER

> *Viewers of TV-am programmes have mixed feelings about its relish for gossip about the Royal Family and its attachments.*

I watched incredulously as Anne Diamond pursued the marital problems of the sister of the Duchess of York. Not only did she leave no stone unturned, she must have turned each one twice. Then we had another lengthy discussion as to whether Fergie should have left the baby behind or not. What on earth is this all to do with anyone but the people immediately concerned?

MAUREEN ROBSON, RETIRED SHORTHAND TYPIST, LIVERPOOL

I was interested in the live report from Australia about the Duchess of York's sister and the break-up of her marriage. We all enjoy Royal gossip.

SUE BARNSLEY, HOUSEWIFE, AMLWCH, GWYNEDD

I sit and want to have a good look at what Anne Diamond is wearing. How big is her bump? When she starts talking about Fergie's sister I am enthralled. When she is finished I turn the telly off, quite sure I now know why Fergie left her baby.

ANDREA O'KELLY, HOUSEWIFE, DUBLIN

> MORNING MARKET
> *Another matter of contention for TV-am viewers that morning was the toy advertisements timed for the Christmas shopping season then beginning. The commercials were especially well placed when many English schools were on half term, and Scottish schools were closed by industrial action.*

The advertisements after the news all geared to expensive toys for Christmas. Seems to have been going on for weeks now, and I abhor the excessive build-up and the emphasis on commerciality that goes on. And I pity the parents whose kiddies must be continually demanding this or that expensive item they've seen on the screen.

YVONNE RICHARDS, HOUSEWIFE, HEMEL HEMPSTEAD, HERTFORDSHIRE

So many of the adverts shown today were for children's toys. Of course, we are in the run-up to Christmas and the manufacturers' teeth are bared. But so many of these adverts seem dubious to me. At least four, during a forty-five-minute period, advertised toys costing more than £50; terrible amounts of money and yet both parents and children are put under enormous pressure to buy them.

So many of the commercials are also appallingly sexist. Today they included two little girls living in a pink and frilly world of combworthy ponies, and little boys encouraged to think of themselves as warlords with convertible fighting machines. One of today's commercials summed it all up. They were advertising a sort of children's modelling clay, stuff which has been around for years. Their particular gimmick was machines into which you place the gunge, which can then be squeezed out into different patterns and shapes. The little boys played happily with a lovely machine which squeezed out wormy heads of goo through monster heads. The little girls played daintily, squeezing their pretty coloured dough into flower baskets.

All I can say is that I know which one this lady would have enjoyed as a child, the monsters. Not because I am some sort of sexual deviant, but simply because I'm me.

**SARAH HELMY, TUTOR,
TEDDINGTON, MIDDLESEX**

Mike Morris does little to wake me up . . . I'm back with my tea and toast at 8.20 a.m. My three-and-a-half-year-old son is washed and dressed and watching more toy adverts. Of course he wants everything . . .

**JOANNE PIKE, PART-TIME SHOP ASSISTANT,
NEWTON ABBOT, DEVON**

Around 8 a.m. one of my children switched on TV-am. As usual I wasn't paying much attention, but I found the bombardment of adverts for expensive children's toys rather tiresome. I can just imagine millions of children across the nation clamouring for these latest, greatest gadgets and harassed parents being made to feel that their kids' Christmas will be miserable unless they spend their hard-earned cash on them.

**RAYMOND GIBSON, CIVIL SERVANT,
NEWTOWNARDS, CO. DOWN**

Pressure on parents. On 1 November advertisers are already pushing mothers and children towards Christmas excess

*Young people who wrote diaries were evidently less conscious of this
assault on their natural acquisitiveness than adults, so concerned about
parents less strong-minded than themselves.*

Put TV-am on, I prefer this because the BBC is a bit boring. That weather
girl wears much too bright clothes, it's too early in the morning for those
colours. I like Gordon Honeycombe, because he usually smiles when he
reads the news. I enjoyed hearing about reading difficulties, I'm glad I
don't have that problem.

**ISABEL WRIGHT, AGED 11,
EDINBURGH**

When I get up in the morning I watch a bit of TV-am to pass the time. I
think it is boring and I don't know why I watch it. I think it is boring
because all they do is talk to people who they've had on the show before,
about boring things like writing books or what that person has done years
ago.

**WESLEY JONES, AGED 11,
SANDBACH, CHESHIRE**

Watched TV-am news, Gordon Honeycombe going very bald. Anne
Diamond is very fat because she is pregnant. Mike Morris kept making
mistakes, and all they were talking about was boring old Fergie and her
baby.

**GORDON McHATTIE, AGED 12,
SHOREHAM, SUSSEX**

*While TV-am is, as shown by audience research, more watched than the
BBC it is not necessarily more loved.*

The BBC *Breakfast Time* was stilted and rigid to a degree. By contrast
TV-am was easy-going and free-flowing but not less deep in its view of
things. Good reporting mixed with gentle humour by excellent
professional presenters. They have the best newsreader on television,
Gordon Honeycombe.

**WILLIAM SIMMS, RETIRED MANAGER,
BELFAST**

The BBC *Breakfast Time* continues to be of a much higher quality, despite
all those IBA wrist-slaps of TV-am. Serious journalism rather than star-
studded banality.

**CLARE JENKINS, JOURNALIST,
SHEFFIELD**

I put on the gas fire and TV-am to see Anne Diamond talking to Susan
Hampshire about dyslexia. It looked quite interesting but Daisy, three,
was by now demanding breakfast so I had to go into the kitchen and try to
listen to it while preparing the meal . . . I wondered about Diamond and
Morris: they somehow come across as rather dim, yet of course they can't

be as they have to assimilate such a lot of information at such speed. They seem friendly enough but I've never felt they were speaking to me. I did used to identify with Frank Bough and Selina Scott.

**JUDITH TAYLOR, HOUSEWIFE,
STOCKPORT**

It is reassuring to discover that *Huckleberry Hound* is still alive and well. It appears that the years have been kind to him. A pity that the same cannot be said of the ailing TV-am . . . It came as no great shock to me, to find that anybody who is anybody has long since got up from that well-cushioned sofa, and moved on to bigger and better things . . . It is difficult to believe that at its launch TV-am was marketed as a magazine whose objectives were to cover as wide a variety of issues and areas as possible.

**LINDA ORWIN, TRAINEE PRINTER,
KING'S LYNN, NORFOLK**

I do wish Carol Dooley wouldn't block the South-East corner of the UK with her body and dangling objects; still, she's a new girl and she'll learn. As I can't hear what is being said I rely on vision almost entirely. Although I'm elderly I prefer the lighter style of TV-am and I enjoy Lizzie's smiling face and daily new clothes.

**I. GOLDMAN,
RETIRED EDUCATIONAL COACH,
EASTBOURNE, SUSSEX**

I am still boycotting TV-am because I dislike their behaviour to the unions, also I can't stand rubbish in the morning.

**DERA PEARSON, ACTRESS,
LONDON SE4**

It was 1.15 a.m. before I went to bed but I still awoke at 4 a.m. as usual. Thank goodness for all-night television. There's a limit to what you can do in the early hours for fear of waking neighbours. I very much enjoy *60 Minutes* (ITV, Thames), providing American news from 4 to 5 a.m. On TV-am there was talk of a possible means test for pensioners. I feel concerned. I have to get a new television licence this month, up £4.50, and the money is more difficult to find. However, I feel it is very good value at £62.50 and I'll go without anything rather than television . . .

Mostly I watch TV-am rather than the BBC at breakfast time, its subject-matter is lighter and better for that time of the morning. I think it would be a good idea to change the presenters more frequently. I'm not sorry to see Anne Diamond leave today. Her once-endearing pursing of the lips at the end of a sentence became irritating. So did her taking over from Mike Morris in the middle of an interview. That is the trouble. Mannerisms become noticeable until the viewer reaches frustration point.

**HYLDA DAVIES, RETIRED,
BASILDON, ESSEX**

My television day may well have started with a short burst of TV-am, although I don't remember for sure. They put out those wishy-washy programmes you have on to find out about the weather. The chat beforehand is so uninteresting that you leave the room to do something more exciting (like cleaning your teeth) and come back to find Gordon Honeycombe beaming at you. Yes, you've missed the weather.

GAVIN RICKETTS, STUDENT, FAREHAM, HAMPSHIRE

Stagger downstairs at 6.05 a.m. in a sub-human mood. Hello Richard Keys in your pink shirt, face to match and beaming smile. How he manages it at this time of the morning is beyond me. I haven't a clue what he's saying as I'm trying to feed the cat and get breakfast started . . . Why does Peter Coe wear those ghastly spectacles when he must earn enough to buy a decent pair? Goodbye Peter. Sorry, no time for Lizzie Webb's work-out . . . Down again with my brand-new face. Ten more minutes of Richard Keys and I'm just about human. I'd better be, I have to go to face the great British public and sort out their (mostly) self-inflicted problems all day.

YVONNE HOARE, CIVIL SERVANT, SALISBURY, WILTSHIRE

I am taking the girls to London for the day. While they got ready went into the lounge and turned on TV-am. It's the sort of thing I do on my own. It's like having the family there, background noise . . . It's all very innocuous stuff, all I can take at this time of the day before the caffeine works.

Anne Diamond sitting on the sofa, archetypal superwoman, confident, intelligent, sensual and pregnant. Beside her a poor example of male species, inept and chauvinist: I realize what centuries of women have put up with. Gordon Honeycombe restores male esteem with old-fashioned charm. The weather is no longer a serious subject in the hands of a brightly-coloured 'dolly-bird'. I hate myself for watching and soaking up inane gossip . . .

ELIZABETH DANCER, PSYCHOLOGY LECTURER, DURSLEY, GLOUCESTERSHIRE

CLOCK WATCHING

A few viewers found ways of using the television screen without turning to either the BBC or TV-am breakfast programmes.

Turned to teletext at 7.41 a.m. Yes, I page my Oracle. Read pages 221 and 223 on ITV as I do every day: 221 is the television news page, it used to be called *Chatterbox* but I think Aled Jones put them off; 223 is my favourite. This is *RSVP:TV*, Oracle's version of *Points of View*, but without Anne Robinson.

RSVP is a lot better than the BBC show for several reasons. If you write in, your letter is more or less guaranteed use; you can comment on any programme on any channel; you can telephone your views; possibly most important, there's a £10 star letter prize every Friday. The best way to start a controversy on *RSVP* is to write in and say how much you enjoyed the programme where the cat got microwaved, but your enjoyment was spoiled by the fact that there was a small green button the size of an atom on the microwave, which wasn't invented until 1992, therefore the microwave couldn't have been made in 1988, thus ruining the period feel of . . . blah, blah, blah.

SHARRON HATHER, STUDENT, WOLLATON, NOTTINGHAMSHIRE

I use breakfast television mostly as a clock to tell me when to leave for work and as background noise . . . This morning (being a chief sub-editor for 4-Tel, Channel 4's teletext service) I switched over to check our *On View*. It wasn't running so I rang work. My colleague already knew. There had been technical difficulties. A shame on this day.

ALEX WHITE, JOURNALIST, LONDON W2

Get up at 5.36 a.m. and switch on television to use up the backlog of programmes on recorded video. Yesterday's episode of *Neighbours* to start with, don't know why I watch it, it's sort of compulsive, relaxing . . . Zap through other channels, nothing, back to *Neighbours* . . . Fast forward rest of tape in case something else worth watching has been recorded by accident . . . I'm usually catching up on reading or administrative activities while watching television or video. Find it hard just to watch television. Today I'm jotting notes for this diary . . . Surveys of this kind must be careful of Heisenberg's uncertainty principle: 'You change things by trying to measure them.'

BRUCE LLOYD, FREELANCE MANAGEMENT CONSULTANT, LONDON NW6

3   EARLY BIRDS

Far from the domestic concerns of breakfast television many British broadcasters were either abroad, or on their way overseas, in the early hours of 1 November. Among their number, almost inevitably, was the nasal-toned, sixty-three-year-old veteran who has long enjoyed the title of television's most travelled man.

One minute past midnight and, as you might expect, I'm in a Boeing 747, 39,000 feet over Samarkand. Over Tamdybulak, if you must know, 120 miles south-west of Tashkent. On this very day I am starting to recce my next *Whicker's Worlds* for BBC1. No British television for me this month, but a new series for viewers next year.

Hong Kong, where I'm heading, has been a significant part of my television life. I first visited the Territory, then called the Colony, as a 1950 war correspondent on my way to Korea. It took three days and ten stops to reach Tokyo in a BOAC Argonaut. On my way back some months later, slightly battered and recently reported dead, I was accompanied by an equally weary Randolph Churchill, then on the *Daily Telegraph*. We relished our few days' rest and recuperation at the Peninsula. Later Hong Kong was the setting for my first full-length *Whicker's World*, in March 1959. A lot of film has passed through the projector since then.

In 1970 I filmed an oriental series for YTV. At home in Jersey last week I reviewed these past programmes and, as usual, now doubt whether I can ever produce anything as interesting again. I boarded this Cathay Pacific flight at Gatwick at 6 p.m. last night. I'd just judged some videos for the International Travel Market Awards at Olympia, and Hong Kong's entry was easily the best. This increases my sense of inadequacy.

Now, after Krug and an excellent dinner, we await the movie. At the back of the aircraft they're showing *A Fish Called Wanda*, which I long to see. What do we get? An early *Bergerac*. Much as I like John Nettles and enjoy seeing Jersey, with a murdered millionaire in every swimming pool, I regret for the first time that BBC Enterprises has at last started to be enterprising. Meanwhile, the champagne flows . . .

It is said to be quite wrong to party on an international flight, but since I never sleep on aircraft (despite forty years' flying, eyes clenched) and since I refuse to be bored by the thin-lipped Perrier-and-pills routine that earnest travellers advocate, I prefer to see my flights as enjoyable round-the-world adventures . . . and pay any penalties later. I'd rather be jet-lagged than pill-lagged.

At 1 a.m. everyone is asleep and I'm getting down to my research reading. It's always the same on these night flights: on this enormous aerial cathedral, there's one little pool of light in the darkness – and it's me. Everyone else is drugged stiff behind their eye-masks, or turning restlessly.

My pool of light is up front because I need to hit the ground running – researching or filming as soon as we land. I long since decided it's not possible to emerge totally shattered after flying through five time zones on some twenty-three-hour marathon to Melbourne in the back of a jammed jumbo – and instantly go about my business. The BBC of course sees this as utterly unreasonable and refuses to support so wild an indulgence. If they had their way, I'd be strap-hanging. So they supply a steerage ticket, and I pay the difference myself. It was never like this with ITV.

ALAN WHICKER, JOURNALIST

| *For ITN's Jon Snow the drink seems a bit stronger than champagne.*

Jon Snow of ITN, reporting from the well-lubricated 'flying pig'

It is just past midnight and we are 31,000 feet over Omaha, Nebraska. I am aboard the 'flying pig', the grotesque Presidential Airways 737 that has been home for the Dukakis Presidential bid for so many months that the plane's interior looks like the aftermath of a long and tragic hostage drama. Worse, tonight it's Hallowe'en. Masks of the unfortunate 'Duke' abound. ABC's Sam Donaldson stormed off the plane at the last stop, saying it had all become beneath his dignity . . . It has to be said that most of the crews and correspondents aboard this thing are pissed.

We finally land at Youngstown, Ohio, at 1.30 a.m., having started in Los Angeles, six hours ago. Initially the pilot had refused to set down, circling until the drunken brawlers at the back of the 'pig' sat down. Dukakis himself had temporarily gone to the faster back-up plane and landed somewhat earlier. Half an hour later myself, Jim (camera) and Pat (sound) arrive at the hideous Ramada Inn, last stayed in when Mondale came to Youngstown in the dying days of the '84 campaign . . . I swore then, never again. Room 79 provokes me to wonder whether I have been at this too long, as I clamber into the well-used sheets.

Alarm at 6 a.m. and thirty minutes later we leave aboard a bus bound for the Working Men's Club Question and Answer session, with Dukakis being beamed coast to coast by satellite. I detect some severe hang-overs. The 'Duke' is one of the least ducal figures I have ever encountered. Seems decent enough, clean, shirt-sleeved, small and suddenly a bit fired up after a flagging autumn campaign. I can't see him making the White House, though God knows Bush has to be one of the most unelectable figures that ever attempted it . . .

JON SNOW, DIPLOMATIC EDITOR, ITN

POL POT'S REVENGE
Jon Snow's discomfort would doubtless look like luxury to cameraman Henry Farrar and the Blue Peter team in Kampuchea.

Oxfam have been helping the Kampucheans to rebuild their country. I am in Phnom Penh to film their work for the BBC's *Blue Peter*, which is going to televise an appeal for aid. At 5.45 a.m. it is time to face the 'en suite' bathroom of Room 207 at the Sukhalay Hotel. The light is permanently on; where the switch should be is a cover which must hide wires that are twisted together. The sink has one cold-water tap. It also has a plug tied to a piece of string, but the water refuses to drain when the plug is removed . . . The toilet consistently overflows when flushed, the overflow mingling with the water from the primitive cold-water shower, swirling over the drain in the floor and refusing to go down.

At 6.15 a.m. breakfast is taken at a café full of pretty waitresses and noisy Chinese music. Producer Alex Leger says he is feeling better after two mornings of the sickness known to the crew as Pol Pot's revenge. Sound recordist Brian Showell is rather subdued, but presenter Caron Keating must be well. She nips into the café for a bread roll and spreads it with peanut butter.

We leave the hotel at 7.05 a.m., filming as we go. My only regret is that we do not have a battery light to balance the shadowy faces of Caron and Oxfam co-ordinator Bill Yates with the bright sunlight in the streets. We break the journey at the Russey Keo Technical Training School. Here Caron interviews a technician who survived Pol Pot's regime. He painfully relates how he escaped into the forest and lived for many months near to starvation as most of his family were caught and executed . . . An Oxfam member notices a funeral procession. Picking up the camera I hurry down the road to film it, wondering if they will object. The people in the procession seem not to notice as I take shots of the mourners . . .

The school took longer to film than planned and we arrive at the Oudong ferry later than expected . . . On the crowded raft Caron makes a hit with two children by taking Polaroid pictures. They can't have seen anything like this magic as life-like images appear on film. We reflect on what happy people the Kampucheans are as they burst into screams of laughter as the Polaroid is examined by everybody on the ferry.

One final request for a picture from the tugboat crew and we are safely across and into an area which was a Khmer Rouge stronghold. It is still regarded by the authorities as 'sensitive'. Driving off the ferry we are met by an army jeep containing our armed escort: six soldiers with automatic rifles. A seventh carries a loaded rocket launcher with four spare rockets strapped to his back. We are told not to leave the vehicles, which makes such an exciting journey difficult to film. Fortunately our driver manages to follow close behind the army jeep so that I can take shots of it through the windscreen.

The town of Skoun is regarded as a safe place to stop for lunch. Large black spiders, four to a bamboo skewer, is obviously the local delicacy, 'like eating crackling', Bill informs us. . . Caron decides to buy a straw hat to keep off the sun, which by now is getting very hot. I walk with her to the stall, followed by two of the soldiers with guns at the ready. Caron purchases four hats altogether, one each for Brian, John and myself. The bill totals 40 riels, that is about four pence per hat . . .

There is only time for minimal filming at the Kompong Chane ferry before dark. Then we take the short drive to the rest house. There are four rooms full of beds and very basic facilities. We sit on our beds drinking the last duty-free wine and whisky, discussing if it is worth erecting mosquito nets. A distant generator brings life to the strip light high in the ceiling and the decision is resolved as the room fills with a swarm of beetles. Some roll into black balls as they land on the mattresses; others leap around the room like tiny grasshoppers. As we leave for the dining-hall it is impossible to walk without crunching them into the concrete floor.

HENRY FARRAR, CAMERAMAN

AMAZONIAN TEETH
Things are not much more comfortable for BBC Natural History cameraman Hugh Maynard, perched beside the Amazon.

Amazonian snap: BBC cameraman Hugh Maynard recording the piranha life-style in a tank beside the Amazon

The day started as had the fifteen or so previous ones when I was woken at about 5.30 a.m. by the incessant calls of kiskadees, a type of flycatcher which inhabits the scrubland around my little rented house on the banks of the Amazon. Kettle on, a quick shower, a cup of tea and fresh fruit for

breakfast. It's hot and humid outside, even at 6 a.m., but makes a change from my little room with its rattling air conditioning unit.

A short distance away a huge rectangular hole, seven by ten metres and four metres deep, had been dug and lined with concrete. It was full of water, tree trunks, and about 150 piranha. I was there to film for David Attenborough's next series, and the piranha feature in a sequence on hunting techniques. Although there was a viewing room with a window through which I could film, there's nothing like getting in close for the real action, so it's on with the face mask, flippers and air tank cylinder. I tested the camera housing for leaks. A hurried emergence from the water, a few adjustments, a second test, OK this time. Luckily the piranha were more apprehensive than I was and had more interest in a fat bream-like fish than in me. In an explosion of scales, flesh and bones the poor fish disappeared down countless throats in a matter of seconds.

I surfaced, checked the camera, all OK, good sequence. Time for a small cup of very strong, very sweet coffee, Brazilian style, brought over to me by the maid; it'll never catch on in the canteen. I then moved to a much smaller tank containing a shoal of fish, each about six inches long, with a mouth full of long, pointed teeth. It is named dogtooth and has a beautiful slim body, just like a freshwater barracuda.

I positioned myself and camera to film through a window into the tank and had an assistant above me to push little grey fish down a tube to the waiting fish below, without disturbing them. The idea worked perfectly, the little fish were delivered just above the predators and swam slowly around. The dogteeth were not interested. We tried another fish, then another, then another. No good, no reaction. My assistant took the small fish out and left the dogteeth for another day.

Lunch was salad and a hard-boiled egg prepared by the maid, and then straight on to another tank with some more piranha. This time I stayed outside the tank and filmed through the glass to get real close-ups, the small sharp teeth and incredibly powerful jaws. I had to stop by mid-afternoon because the sun was now dipping down and casting long shadows across the tank. I stored my cameras in a cool room.

The fish scientist in charge of the whole establishment came over and we discussed draining the large tank, taking out all the piranha and replacing them with catfish. Half a dozen fishermen arrived, got their nets and lines ready and went out in their canoes for a night fishing trip for the required catfish. By now a few beers had been consumed as we watched the sun go down over the river.

I had previously taken some frozen meat out of the freezer, fried this in my primitive little kitchen and spent the next half-hour trying to eat it. I think even a piranha would have given up on that old cow. Time for an obligatory half-hour with my portable compact disc player, then bed under a mosquito net with a good book. Lights out early to the song of the rattling air conditioner.

HUGH MAYNARD, FILM CAMERAMAN

YES, PRIME MINISTER

On location in Dominica, West Indies, BBC Wales production assistant Val Turner is awoken by an unexpected telephone call.

We are half-way through a shoot for a film documentary about Eugenia Charles, the Prime Minister of Dominica, one of a series of six about women politicians for BBC2 transmission in 1989. I woke about 6 a.m., for a moment thinking a hurricane had started. A look over my hotel balcony reassured me that it was just the sea crashing against the rocks. I drifted off to sleep again only to be woken by the ring of the phone. Just the Prime Minister to say the Cabinet meeting we were meant to be filming at 10 a.m. was now scheduled for noon. I wonder if Mrs Thatcher makes her own telephone calls? . . .

VAL TURNER, PRODUCTION ASSISTANT

AFRICAN EPISODES

Mohamed Amin works out of Nairobi in Kenya as head of the Visnews African Bureau. After returning from the Seychelles yesterday he begins work at 4 a.m. today.

The lead story in Kenya's three dailies is about the massacre of five white rhinos in Meru National Park. These rhinos, the only five in the country's national parks, were penned and taken out to pasture every day under armed guard. Something has gone badly wrong. Must find out cost of air

BBC production assistant
Val Turner, woken by the
Prime Minister

charter to Meru and telex London to offer story. A crew can't get in and out by road in one day.

At 10.25 the duty news organizer calls from London to say it is a good story and we should go ahead . . . At 2.10 p.m. Shaffi comes through by

The white rhinos of Meru. Even an armed guard could not protect them

radio hook-up from the plane. The Meru Park landing strip is swarming with army men. The minute the plane landed the crew were hustled into the warden's office and told to leave the camera gear on one side . . . The warden told Shaffi the carcases had been buried, which is unusual. When Shaffi asked if he could film the graves he was told 'No'.

At 7 p.m. Shaffi and Jack return from Wilson Airport. They haven't got any footage of dead rhino, only wallpaper of surviving white rhinos in Solio ranch and rangers tracking. We'll have to do something to justify the cost. Naturally, having been assured by the Director of National Parks that we could film freely, I feel keenly about this. I had offered the story on the basis that we could film the carcases.

I think also that my major reaction this day was one of sadness at such wanton slaughter. I'm not only a television news cameraman but a wildlife photographer. The way that poachers are destroying this great natural legacy entrusted to Kenya not only makes me angry and disappointed but also very despairing of the future. I'm also very conscious when a story like this breaks, how much I am tied to desk work. Ten years ago I wouldn't have been sending out a crew on a story like this. I would have been there myself, and I find that particularly frustrating.

**MOHAMED AMIN, BUREAU CHIEF,
VISNEWS, NAIROBI**

It is one minute into 1 November. Another electrician and I are supplying the lighting effort and equipment for a BBC Bristol production called *The Great Rift*. The Rift is a particularly interesting geographical feature in Africa. The only thing is that we did not have to go to Africa. The place we are working in is the BBC studios at Elstree.

Our set-up is on the floor of a dusty prop store where various pieces of *'Allo 'Allo!* are stored. There is a model of Africa stretched over half a giant ball. A Chapman camera crane, with two seats, is being used to simulate an aerial pass over the aforesaid Great Rift. The light source has to be very carefully placed in order not to create 'hot spots' on this round model. Another problem is keeping strong light from the black floor surrounding the model.

We were promised a wrap at 10 p.m. the previous evening: that's showbiz, I suppose. The camera whooshes up in the air, whirring like a demented food mixer. 'No good', 'Cut', 'Come down', 'Turn over', 'Lift no good'. There is nowhere to get a cup of tea in darkest Elstree. At 3.30 a.m. it is a wrap, everyone suddenly pleased, floor getting thanks all round. Gather gear and make our way back to Ealing. Drive home as people are getting ready for work. Creep indoors and see a lot of envelopes in an armchair. It's my birthday, I'd forgotten.

**DENNIS KETTLE,
FILM LIGHTING ELECTRICIAN**

OUT FOR THE COUNT
Ann McGuire, a producer for the BBC1 Nine O'Clock News, is far from

The BBC's Keith Graves, a
commanding presence at
the Israeli general election

*studio comforts as she struggles to make her journalists heard amid the
hubbub of an Israeli general election.*

I wake at 6.30 a.m. after four hours' sleep on the seventeenth floor of the
Tel Aviv Sheraton. It's the ninth day of work on the trot, absolutely
shattered. Paranoia overtakes fatigue. Latest polls say Labour and Likud
neck and neck. Immediate anxiety: what can we say tonight that we
didn't say last night? At 9 a.m. Keith Graves, our Middle East
Correspondent, meets me in hotel reception. Feel rotten, clothes dirty and
creased, hotel laundry service intermittent.

Arrive Herzlia studios, ten miles outside Tel Aviv, at 10 a.m. Graves
says a Likud van has been attacked by a petrol bomb in Arab area of
Jerusalem, a woman campaign worker has been badly burned. From
London the *Nine O'Clock News* producer asks what I have in mind. I say:
the day's violence followed by polling scenes and, on a graphic, an
explanation of how the Israeli electoral system works. This is a massive
task, there are twenty-seven parties. How do I do this without it being
long and boring?

I continue monitoring pictures and interviews. The petrol bombing is
quite nasty; Keith and I decide some of the pictures of the injured woman
are too upsetting to use. At 5.45 p.m. London tells us there are some
pictures of an Israeli air raid in Lebanon. We should mention this in the
Nine piece.

At 7.55 p.m., London two hours behind, we decide that the *Nine* piece
will begin with the day's trouble. The petrol bombing of the campaign
workers' van, some stone-throwing in the occupied territories, then the
Israeli raid on an Arab village in Lebanon. We leave a black space for the
pictures of the raid to be inserted in London . . . By 9 p.m. I am starving.
Keith says it's my own fault, he had a nice steak at lunchtime.

We arrive at the Labour party rally in Tel Aviv at 9.45. Disaster. The
world's cameras have been jammed into a tiny enclosure. It is impossible
even to see ours, let alone reach it. The live interview looks severely
threatened. Heart starts pounding. Keith crawls through miles of cables
and elbows to the camera. Conditions not ideal, he sounds as though he's
in the gents. The live two-way with London still in jeopardy: I tell Keith
he must do a piece to camera on the latest from Tel Aviv as a stand-by.

At 10.40 we are back in the log-jam. We cajole, beg, plead, grovel our
way into the main body of the Labour hall – press not really allowed . . .
We have pushed our way to the front, Keith worried that with so many
people he will be jostled during the live interview. Or worse, if anyone
disagrees with him. Five minutes before the *Nine* we have a stroke of
luck. The crowd thins out a bit. Keith is able to stand on a chair in view of
our live camera. London can see but not hear him. Keith is told to keep
talking and sound is restored. I get the sound man to hold the chair Keith
is standing on, I have nightmares of him falling off it during the live
interview . . . We hear the piece we edited earlier being transmitted in
Britain. Michael Buerk, in the studio in London, asks Keith what's the

latest . . . We collapse with relief, slight hysteria, that was a close one.

We have an hour to prepare ourselves for *Newsnight*. Keith sees Labour's charismatic campaign chairman, Ezer Weitzman, who agrees to do an interview. It becomes my unhappy task to shadow this individual . . . We reach Keith at 12.27. He regrets that *Newsnight* has led its programme on another story. Weitzman storms off and I follow . . . Weitzman now talking to party workers, it's slow progress. At 1.16 he is settling into a radio interview. Keith suddenly screams, 'NOW, NOW!!' I grab Weitzman's arm and drag him to Keith. *Newsnight* cut live to him three seconds after Weitzman has uttered an obscenity. Keith asks him a question about Peres's future. It seems to inflame him and he walks out of shot. Keith thanks the empty space for the interview.

At 2.45 a.m. I am back in my hotel room. I order a toasted cheese sandwich but I have lost my appetite and seven pounds. At 3 a.m. I settle down for four hours' sleep, before it all starts again.

ANN McGUIRE, JOURNALIST

WHAT'S DUNN CANNOT BE UNDONE

Many broadcasters at home are also working some time before the breakfast-time segment of the television day is done. Among their number is Richard Dunn, Managing Director of Thames Television and Chairman of the ITV Association. Thames is the largest of the ITV companies, measured by programme output and diversity, revenue, facilities and staff numbers. It has broadcast in the London area since 1968, from Monday to Friday.

Richard Dunn, captain of the Thames ship

The Independent Television Association is the trade association to which all the ITV companies belong. On 1 November it is chiefly exercised about the Government's White Paper on the future of broadcasting, due the following Monday. The contents of this had been sufficiently leaked for ITV to know that it would be hard-pressed to survive in its present form. A problem for ITVA is to persuade its members to respond to the Government onslaught with one voice. Its chairmen and managing directors range from Thatcherites, people convinced that television should be ruled by market forces, to public service men (it is an all-male club) who consider that commercial practice should be the servant of programme diversity and excellence.

With qualifications, and due obeisance to his shareholders, Richard Dunn belongs to the second faction. He is also able to contain his hardness in argument beneath the manner of a diplomat. He has been chosen by his peers to speak for them at this time because they know he will always measure his words with care, and will not be undone. He is tall, silver-haired, elegant, and his outwardly calm manner is matched by the restrained opulence of his Euston office, all dark wood and black leather. It is characteristic of the Dunn style that he should refuse to use a desk that could stand between him and any visitor to his office.

On his way into the office on 1 November the Thames MD remembers first the reception he attended the previous evening at 10 Downing Street. He had asked Lord Young about the White Paper and the Secretary of State for Trade and Industry had replied: 'You won't be disappointed.'

Exactly what John Wheeler MP, chairman of the Home Affairs Committee, had promised me the night before. Later, at the same reception, Brian Griffiths, head of the Policy Unit at No. 10, told me in conspiratorial tones: 'You won't be disappointed.' Have they all had the same brief? It probably means they have decided not to hang us, after all. It's the firing squad instead. David Young and I also shared a joke about wishing we had never heard of Gibraltar.

Arrived at the office at 8.15 a.m. to deal with correspondence and board papers for the meeting tomorrow. I also read Martin Cave's *Conduct of Auctions for Broadcasting Franchises.* My junior secretary typing the fifth draft of ITV's guideline response to what I imagine will be in the White Paper. I worked on some submissions to the Windlesham-Rampton inquiry we have set up into the making and screening of our Gibraltar programme *Death on the Rock* . . .

Andrew Quinn (Granada managing director) rang me for a word about his *Game, Set and Match,* which was getting disastrously low ratings. My director of programmes (David Elstein) was considering moving its starting time from 9 to 10.30 p.m. on Mondays. Andrew wondered if it would be right to move it, specially at White Paper time. I said I thought we should leave it to our programme directors, knowing that Elstein had already begun to think it was perhaps best left where it was. 'I doubt,' I told Andrew, 'if we'll be able to carry such passengers in the new world.'

The post included a letter from the IBA's Director of Engineering (John Forrest) seeking my views on whether transmission should become a subsidiary of the IBA or completely privatized. Also some fabulous reviews of our *Jack the Ripper* mini-series from American newspapers and magazines. We had poor reviews in the British press . . .

Lunch with Roy Addison, chairman of the ITV network Public Relations Committee, Penny Marshall, the new media correspondent of ITN, and Nick Higham, the new media correspondent of the BBC. Wide-ranging discussion of all the White Paper issues, dress-rehearsing for the following week's show. On the way downstairs, I met Butch Stuttard, who has just produced and directed our *Witness* documentary on the social services in Bradford. A huge building site next door to Thames has just been demolished to make room for a major new development. 'Look,' I said wryly, pointing to the destruction, 'ITV.'

Granada's *Game, Set and Match* on location in Berlin. 'But who cares about ratings anyway, Ian, this is art'

Oracle informed me: 'Superchannel, Italians in control.' A Signor Marcucci of Betatelevision now had more than 51 per cent, to Virgin's 45 per cent . . . Liz Timms, ITVA press officer, phoned to say *Newsnight* was requesting an interview with me on Monday, post-White Paper, together with Rupert Murdoch and John Birt . . . Roy Hattersley's office phoned mine to cancel lunch on 8 November, the fourth time since April he has cancelled at short notice. He will no doubt rant and rave about the White Paper but he doesn't seem to be that interested in ITV's position . . .

The overnight ratings showed that *Game, Set and Match* was only getting a 16 TVR (rating) against *Panorama* with 15. In five weeks it has rated 20, 16, 13, 13, 16. Rang David Elstein, who said at least the rating was up so we should wait a week. The 'Top Ten' ratings then arrived, showing Thames with four of the places: *This Is Your Life*, *Jack the Ripper* and both episodes of *The Bill* . . . A letter from Lord Windlesham, who is conducting the inquiry into *Death on the Rock* from an office just down the corridor. They want to have the copyright of their report, but they also want Thames to indemnify them against any legal action arising. It's bad enough having this Inquisition, but we have to pay for it as well . . .

RICHARD DUNN, MANAGING DIRECTOR, THAMES TELEVISION

MADE IN MADAGASCAR
Channel 4 is the youngest of Britain's four terrestrial television channels and was due to celebrate its sixth birthday the next day. It is charged by Parliament to cater for tastes and interests not otherwise well served, and to innovate. Formerly the respected documentary head at Yorkshire Television, John Willis has recently become its controller of factual programmes, in charge of about half the output.

Work starts at 8 a.m. The large desk I inherited from Justin Dukes (former managing director) is groaning under the weight of programme proposals and cassettes. I sometimes feel that Channel 4 is a giant Hoover sucking up documentaries from all over the world.

As I plough through the proposals I also watch tapes. First one is *Come Back Africa*, an extraordinary 1958 film about life in the South African townships. Directed by Lionel Rogosin, it has recently been re-released in South Africa to great acclaim. It's a curious piece: new and powerful and with people 'acting' themselves in some key scenes. It is well worth showing but will need to be topped and tailed with a brief introduction from someone like Louis Nkosi or Donald Woods setting it in context. Decide to buy.

As I watch I answer proposals. This morning a typical Channel 4 suggestion, *Furniture Making in Madagascar*, is among the twenty or so I sort through. Overall I find the standard disappointing. Few are well tailored to C4's requirements and an extraordinary number of the documentaries are to be shot overseas, about eight out of every ten. A recent submission concerned a salmon-fishing river in Scotland. It ended with the sentence: 'We will then compare it to a river in Chile.'

Carole Sedler, my secretary for the last six years, arrives. Without her I would drown in paperwork here. Thanks to her I am able to take a quick walk into Soho, with Nick Hart-Williams (former commissioning editor, single documentaries), to see a film. A rarer treat than I would like. This is a Jane Gabriel documentary about the impact of tourism on Cyprus. Jane has run into trouble with an earlier C4 series about Greece, but this is a straightforward portrait of the conflict between the need to protect the human environment and the economic benefits of tourism. Nick and I make some (I hope) helpful suggestions and I agree to come back for a final viewing in a week.

Meeting with Rachel Krish about money. Just as dustmen have become refuse operatives so cost controllers like Rachel have become programme finance managers. She has not been here long but is refreshingly interested in the programmes as well as how much they cost. Our major problem is a film about nuclear scientists made by an American director, Karen Payne. She wants to edit the film in San Francisco. Judging by our one meeting she is a very pleasant but forceful woman. It is her first film and at some stage before I arrived Mike Grigsby was asked to help her out. Grigsby then fell by the wayside as did Karen's camerawoman. This may be no bad thing, to have two directors on one film is daft, but it does not increase confidence in Karen's ability to cut her own film thousands of miles away from our offices in Charlotte Street.

We discuss the economic and editorial implications and it is clear that although there is a danger that Karen is so desperate to cut in her home town that the project might collapse, the only way to ensure that C4's interest in a good film is preserved is to cut it in London.

Lunch with Alf Dubs, former Labour MP and member of the Broadcasting Standards Council, in the boardroom, with half a dozen C4 people including Michael Grade. It is a genial discussion. Alf is clearly feeling isolated on the Council as a Labour supporter. It is clear too that Lord Rees-Mogg has so much more time than the other members, to get to grips with the policy of the Council, that he will dominate their activities. We are able to express some of our anxieties about the Council and all in all it is a useful exchange of views.

Routine meeting with Bob Towler, commissioning editor for religion. Do we have enough religion at Christmas? Will John Wells and the Three Wise Men be serious enough? Perhaps too serious, suggests Bob . . . Later the Bob Towler budget meeting. This is the big one, which Michael Grade (Chief Executive) attends. All goes well. Bob knows his demands have to be modest, the two hours a week agreed with the IBA. The proposals are talked through and, apart from Michael's anxiety about an excess of Jewish programmes, everything is agreed.

Home from my daughter's Hallowe'en party at her school. She wins some Smarties. Joy all round. I watch *The Other Europe*. I inherited the series when I arrived. It is extremely well made and presenter-commentator Jacques Rupnik is a real discovery. It seems to have stirred up antipathy in some quarters for its Cold War tone. It's a degree or two too cold for me but, as television should, it has sparked off a healthy debate about the nature of 'Eastern Europe'.

Finally *First Tuesday*. This is the programme I started and nursed for six years. It is a solid rather than a vintage edition but I wish my old colleagues and friends well. I hope *First Tuesday* continues to thrive. It deserves to and, in an ITV system under siege, it is important that it does. This edition does what one key part of current affairs always should: reveals something new to the audience in a clear and accessible way.

JOHN WILLIS, CONTROLLER OF FACTUAL PROGRAMMES, CHANNEL 4

BEXHILL SHOOTING
All over the country broadcasters stir. The first we meet has his eye on another white house.

Wake up at 3.45 a.m., two hours before the alarm, cold . . . I've taken over shooting at Bexhill-on-Sea for the *Building Sights* series from another director, with whose efforts the BBC is not satisfied. An added responsibility . . . Reach the location at 6.55, on a beautiful morning. The De La Warr Pavilion, the subject of the film, looks absolutely brilliant. It's a striking white modernist building, we should have no difficulty in making it look amazing today . . .

Sophie Hicks, the presenter, arrives at 7.20 a.m. She was fashion editor of *Vogue* and is too much of a sophisticate to cast as an *ingénue*. What's more she's seven months pregnant and doesn't want it to show.

Sophie Hicks (left), former fashion editor of *Vogue* and 'too much of a sophisticate to cast as an ingénue', takes advice from *Building Sights* researcher Ruth Rosenthal

Researcher Ruth Rosenthal and I debate the importance of this. Sophie has no experience of presenting or of writing. I have to make her feel comfortable and look and sound enthusiastic . . .

NEIL CAMERON, PRODUCER

At 8.10 a.m. cycle to work through Kensington Gardens to Hill House, the largest private day school in Britain, the subject of our BBC *40 Minutes* documentary. The headmaster, eighty-year-old Colonel Stuart Townend, greets me in his second-floor study. He is in sparkling form . . . This is only day two of our shoot and I have never directed a film before. Very nervous . . .

**GRANT MUTER, PRODUCER
(ON ATTACHMENT)**

Early start, having to recce with technical crews for two half-hour episodes of Thames's *The Bill*. Left home at Wimbledon at 6.45 a.m. and arrived at location base forty-five minutes later. There is a crisis in casting. We need two coloured stuntmen for a car crash sequence and there is a possibility that neither of the two coloured men on the stunt register will be available to us. May have to 'black-up' white stuntmen. Not an ideal solution but as they will barely be seen at the moment of impact we'll probably get away with it . . .

At 3.30 p.m. stuntman situation still not resolved. Coloured actor flatly refuses to allow white stuntmen to 'black-up'. Threatens to walk off set if we resort to this. Seems a very arrogant attitude, we're trying our best. Will talk to him later . . . At 5.30 return to base. Casting report, coloured

Octogenarian headmaster,
Colonel Stuart Townend
prepares to sparkle for
BBC2's *40 Minutes*

Detective Inspector
Burnside (Christopher
Ellison) of Thames's *The
Bill* considers the latest
casting crisis

stuntmen now booked. God knows who they've found. I hope, whoever
they are, they can achieve the crash sequence without killing themselves –
or us, for that matter . . .

CHRISTOPHER HODSON, DIRECTOR

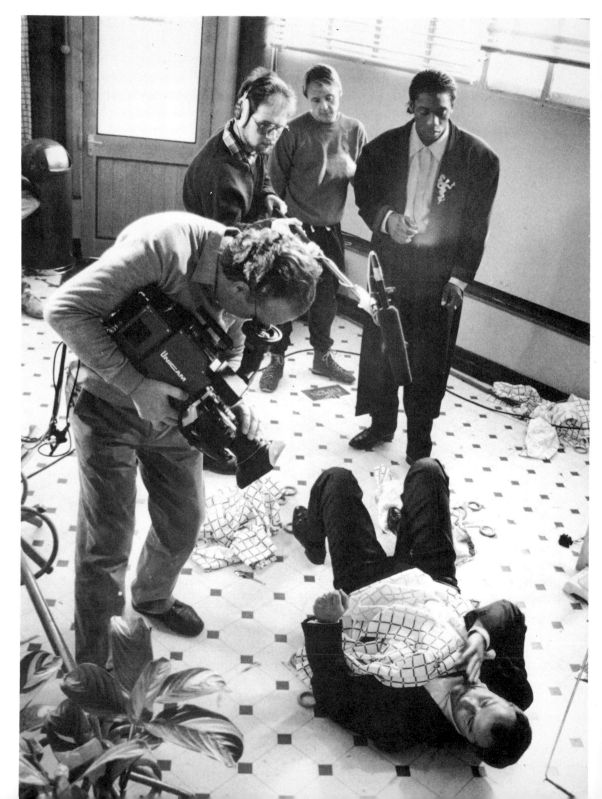

One fine day for BBC
weatherman Bill Giles.
'And that's just about it for
now'

The alarm clock screamed in my ear at 5.30 a.m. . . . Scraped ice off the
car windscreen, well at least yesterday's forecast was correct . . . In office
at Television Centre soon after 6.30, switched on power, booted up the
computers, instructed one of them to draw up the weather data received
overnight from Bracknell . . . Conference with London Weather Centre
and Bracknell, decided on the weather story for the day . . . Make-up lady
arrives, covers my shaving cuts beautifully. Lovely to see a cheerful face
at this time in the morning . . . Pressure building up, switch on lights . . .
At 8.59 a thirty-second broadcast into the South-East News followed at
9.02 with a thirty-second summary for the UK, fifteen seconds more than
normal . . .

BILL GILES, BBC SENIOR WEATHERMAN

It is 12.30 a.m. and I have been in bed, at my home in Chepstow,
Gloucestershire, for an hour. The telephone squeals at me. It's an
automatic call from my building management computer at Culverhouse
Cross. A failure has been detected in the air conditioning plant serving the
transmission area. I punch a few keys on my remote terminal in an
attempt to override the problem, but it refuses to accept my instructions. I
creep out of the bedroom and set out on the forty-mile trek to Cardiff . . .

At the studios I check the message and find it is an urgent call from
Bristol, HTV West. A serious flood has occurred in a plant room over the
sound control gallery serving the main studio. Water has broken through
the floor and the sound desk, new only last year, is saturated. I've had
workmen demolishing an old air handling plant, obviously they have
neglected to blank off the heating and chilled water services . . . I manage
to contact the workmen's employer who despatches two plumbers to
Bristol . . . Back to bed at 4.30 a.m., an alarm call at 6.45 and by 8 a.m. I
am at the Bristol office discussing the problems with the directors of
production and engineering. The desk could be out of action until
Christmas . . . I lie in wait for my demolition men's boss to appear on site,
to confront him with a possible repair bill of some £140,000 . . .

**DAVID PARNELL,
PLANT AND SAFETY MANAGER**

I arrive at BBC Pebble Mill just before 8 a.m. The day starts with the
normal opening of various doors . . . On the sixth floor I am greeted with:
'Can you open this door and can you open that door, the key I was given
has mysteriously jumped out of my tin and hidden itself.' I think to
myself, 'Why didn't you let me know before I came up here and save me
having to go back for the key?' 'Of course, my pleasure,' I say, with just a
hint of John Cleese . . . The Singlettes are beating out a rhythm that seems
rather unnatural at this time of the morning. But then so does being
awake . . .

GRAHAM KIDNER, SECURITY CHARGEHAND

Awoken by the radio alarm, and startled by Kylie Minogue blaring out, at
7.15 a.m. What a start to the day. The morning is white over with frost as

The Singlettes 'beating out
a rhythm that seems rather
unnatural at this time of
the morning'

BBC canteen workers,
'Well, it's surprising what
people eat these days'

I ride my bike to work at the BBC Leeds canteen. By 8 a.m. I am changing into my chef's uniform and making coffee to try and get some feeling back into my body. Then on to preparing the vegetables and making up the sweet which is on the day's menu . . .

CRAIG JACKSON, CHEF

Arrive just before 8 a.m. at the Scottish Television studios in Glasgow. By 8.30 equipment has been checked and we are proceeding to Govan and the early morning press conferences with candidates for the parliamentary by-election. A message on the crew car radio from the newsroom. We are to divert to schools to illustrate a story on the effect of the 'day of action' called by the Educational Institute of Scotland. At 8.40 we arrive at Dunard Street Primary School, where five children are kicking a ball in the playground. Cameraman shoots an illustrative sequence and I record ambient sound. The kids are pleasant and co-operative, and are interested in knowing when the story will go out . . . Visit four secondary schools in the district and find them all closed, no children around. We shoot a selection of film showing empty schools and at 9.20 return to base . . .

L. E. SOUTHAM, SOUND RECORDIST

Called at 5 a.m. and urged by reception to 'have a nice day now'. It is still pitch black outside but the clock face of the *Liver Birds* building, seen from my hotel window, confirms the time. With difficulty we get into the hotel conference room being used as the make-up room for the cast of *Bread*. (The top-rated BBC sitcom which won an audience of 17 million in the week of 1 November.)

At 5.55 we are preparing ourselves for the onslaught. The whole cast is filming today, as usually happens when the action is in Kelsall Street. For just the two of us to get everybody ready in time we should have started at 4.30 a.m., but we know there will be various odd times when we can do the finishing touches. Anyway the artists unfortunate enough to be done first would probably go back to bed and then need doing again.

At 6 a.m. Julie (Hilary Crowson) arrives to finish her hair. She hangs upside down in unbelievable contortions whilst drying it . . . We have now given up the battle of trying to make her look like the first Julie. As the present Julie admits herself, she has thin eyebrows and thick lips, where the previous one had thick eyebrows and thin lips. If they can get away with it in *Dallas* with Miss Ellie, then so can we in *Bread* with Julie.

Mrs Boswell (Jean Boht) arrives at 6.20 a.m. What a dear. She has put in her own rollers already, which we leave in as long as possible. We give her a quick foundation and leave the refinement until later . . . All this time my assistant, Polly, has been making up Aveline (Gilly Coman). This is usually done in three sessions; make-up first, then costume, then hair which is ornamented to match or clash with the costume. Her false nails are left to the last second before shooting starts, as it's impossible to do just about anything while wearing them.

Jean Boht as Mrs Boswell of the BBC's *Bread*, her rollers in by 6.20 a.m.

Polly makes up Joey (Peter Howitt) while Grandad (Kenneth Waller) takes my chair. He is still a young man really, so it takes all our skill to effect the transformation convincingly. Adrian's (Jonathon Morris) hair piece goes on. To suit his new artistic image, he has decided to grow his hair long enough to tie back into a pony-tail. Unfortunately, this cannot be achieved quickly enough by Mother Nature. We have had a back piece made for him, which we hope goes undetected by the viewers.

At 7.15 everybody boards the coach to take us to location. Trying to remember to bring everything with us is the main problem. At 7.30 it is breakfast time at the Gasometers. There's a Force Nine gale starting up, which makes it very difficult balancing a bowl of porridge in one hand and a cup of tea in the other. Most of it ends up on the pavement. Two small boys are trying to steal the caterers' generator, but they are persuaded against it by some of the larger members of the crew.

We arrive at location around 8 a.m. It is a line of tidy streets sloping steeply down to the Mersey. They act as wonderful wind tunnels. With that and the persistent damp the only way to keep everybody's hair in style is by using tons of lacquer. Thank goodness all our sprays are now ozone friendly. We do our last-minute finishing touches and then, right at the last minute, Grandad's moustache goes on, and Mrs Boswell gets her lipstick.

With turn-over imminent the wind is really getting up. A slate blows off a roof down the street and then one of our lamps is blown over. The first scene is a scuffle between Joey and Shifty (Bryan Murray). During take one a dog trots down from the top of the street and bites Shifty's leg before trotting off again. It turned out that the dog does not like, and will not tolerate, fighting. Shifty just manages to get to the end of the scene before almost passing out. An ambulance has drawn up a few doors away, and they whisk him off to hospital. By 9 a.m. it is clear that there has to be some massive re-scheduling . . .

PAULINE COX, MAKE-UP DESIGNER

II
MORNING TIMES

9 a.m. – 1 p.m.

4 'THE OLD GIRL'S NOT PAST IT YET'

Day-time viewing must be the most socially unacceptable mass participation sin of the 1980s. We all watch, we all pretend we don't . . .
DIANA HUTCHINSON, HOUSEWIFE,
STOURPORT-ON-SEVERN, WORCESTERSHIRE

Whatever else may be said about 'soaps', drama serials without end, it is clear that they win and retain larger audiences than any other form of television entertainment. After early hiccups the twice-weekly Brookside has always been Channel 4's top-rated show. In the week of 1 November the Monday evening episode was watched by 4.4 million and the Wednesday show attracted 3.9 million, both totals increased by the 2.5 million who saw the Saturday omnibus repeat.

Episode one of Brookside was shown on the first night of Channel 4, 2 November 1982. It was the creation of Phil Redmond, he who upset so many parents by drawing the veil off the comprehensive school with the BBC's Grange Hill. He, and his independent Mersey Television, turned their backs on studio-bound 'soap' and invested in a set of 'new estate' houses, outside Liverpool, boasting the latest electronic technology. The outside world is sometimes glimpsed, some characters have even been allowed overseas trips, but Brookside Close has remained the permanent set where most of the action is contained.

The realism of the set was matched, in the earliest episodes, by the realism of the characters. Some aspired to middle-class gentility, others were earthy dissidents armed with thick Merseyside accents. The young were uninhibited and disrespectful. There was a certain amount of 'bad language'. The censorious alliance of the right-wing press and Mary Whitehouse's clean-up lobby demanded change. Despite this publicity the audience fell close to the 200,000 mark.

Eventually some judicious mellowing of the characters, and well-placed positive publicity, brought the hostilities to an end. Brookside became an accepted institution and the national ear became attuned to the accent. Six years later it has its barren passages, and its sometimes tedious repetitions, but it remains the most realistic and socially aware of the 'soaps'.

CLOSE COLLEAGUES
The diaries of those who play Annabelle Collins, Billy Corkhill and Sheila Grant provide the starting-point for a tour of the 1 November television morning. Annabelle, otherwise actress Doreen Sloane, begins.

The alarm clock woke me at 6.45 a.m., just as I was putting on a Father

Annabelle Collins (Doreen Sloane) of *Brookside*: 'It's surprising, since I started having an affair my fan mail has more than doubled. I am amazed. So the old girl's not past it'

Christmas beard and moustache, already dressed in red trousers and jacket. What would Jung have made of that dream? . . . Drive myself to Brookside via Lime Street station to drop Sarah off. (My daughter, Sarah Noble, went to Radio Leeds today.) Arrived at 8.45 for my 9 a.m. rehearsal call.

The Close was a hive of activity. A BBC *Open Air* crew was already in action and about to interview Phil (Redmond) and the writers. At 9 a.m. Jim (Jim Wiggins plays Paul Collins) and Vinny (Vincent Maguire plays Brian) and I went over to the Collinses' house to rehearse. Only three scenes, two with Jim and one with Vinny. I'm going to enjoy these scenes. Paul hasn't found out about Annabelle's affair with Brian yet, but she's sailing close to the wind. Director Romey Allison is a joy to work with. She knows exactly what she wants out of a scene, but never forces you to behave out of character. One feels it's real teamwork and one can rely on her judgement. About 10.15 we discussed the scene we were rehearsing, because of doubts about whether it might give the storyline away. We broke at 10.30. I dashed to Make-up, didn't want to go down to posterity with a shiny nose. Vanity, vanity!

Back in the Close at 11 a.m. Outside the Corkhills' house to 'rehearse' a scene for *Open Air*. It was meant to be outside the Golf Club. The Corkhills' was chosen because it's the first house you come to at the start of the Close, so Phil and the *Open Air* crew wouldn't have so far to walk . . . Bang on cue came Phil. He was the 'go-between' with *Open Air* interviewer Pattie Coldwell in the studio in Manchester . . . When it was all over I felt a bit deflated, didn't think I was serious enough . . .

About fifteen minutes after *Open Air* finished I had to rehearse a scene with Steven Pinner and Jennifer Calvert for the other rehearsal crew, with Ken Horn directing. Again this is unusual, normally we are shooting two episodes and rehearsing the following two in one week, but because we have extra episodes to shoot for Christmas, we are having to add them to our regular schedule. It is a straightforward scene: Jonathan and Cheryl arriving home for Christmas, happy; Annabelle arriving back, unhappy, and worried about how Paul will receive her.

Finished rehearsing at 12.30 p.m. and collected my post from the administration block. It's surprising: since Annabelle started having an

Pattie Coldwell, the *Open Air* presenter of gut feelings

affair, my fan mail has more than doubled, and a lot of the letters are from young men and boys. I am amazed. So the old girl's not past it yet. Flattering! Joined Janice Troop (press and publicity officer) and Paula Trafford (*Open Air* researcher) for lunch in the canteen. Afterwards to the green room where I started watching a film, *The Importance of Being Earnest* . . . It was so hot that I fell asleep, and then woke abruptly at 3 p.m., when I was due at Make-up. I must have a built-in timeswitch.

Staggered, half asleep, to the dressing-room to change before going into Make-up. Gill Ion (wardrobe mistress) and I had a laugh about what I should be wearing for this episode. I'd had a message from Vanessa Whitburn (producer) via Andrew Higgs (director) that she wanted me in 'loose' clothes. What are loose clothes? Do Annabelle's clothes have to be 'loose' as well as her? In the end we decided loose means casual. We opted for beige cords, and beige and turquoise sloppy jumper.

Ready for work by 3.30 p.m. but the shoot wasn't ready for me. Back to the green room to wait . . . At 5.45 p.m. Mark and I were called to do our scene. It went well, finished by 6.15. Leaving only fifteen minutes to do the other scene. Vinny and I were not very happy at being hurried. We walked through for the camera and with five minutes to go, we were asked to shoot without a rehearsal. I said I wasn't happy with that, as I felt it was a difficult scene, so we had a proper rehearsal and then went for it with two minutes to go before wrap time.

It was going like a lead balloon. I was so worried about it, I dried. So in the end the clock beat us and we'll have to pick it up later in the week. I felt very cross with myself that I hadn't been able to rise above it and felt I'd let everyone down. But Vanessa met me as I crossed the Close and said I'd been quite right not to be rushed and that we shouldn't be asked to do a scene like that in fifteen minutes. I felt a lot better. Ego restored, I changed and went home.

Got home about 7.15 p.m. I wanted to see the first episode of the new series of *Boon* on ITV: Mandy (Amanda Burton, formerly Heather in *Brookside*) is now featuring in it much more. I can't help it, I just don't find it very interesting. I think Michael Elphick and Mandy are very good, but are struggling with a very mediocre storyline and scripts. So went back to the *Telegraph* crossword . . .

DOREEN SLOANE, ACTRESS

It proved a less satisfactory day for John McArdle, otherwise Billy Corkhill, who woke to find himself suffering from a sore throat, aching limbs and a headache.

I have a 9 a.m. call for rehearsals this morning. I don't think I can make it. It will be the first time in three years I have phoned in sick. Still, I am only in a couple of scenes and they can go on with something else. If it was a shoot I would drag myself in half dying. Phoned up work to tell them the situation. They were very understanding and said, 'Don't worry about it.' The doctor said it was a virus that was going round and gave me antibiotics.

I go with my wife Kathy to the *Manchester Evening News* theatre awards, even though I am not feeling too good. Feel really bad in Bolton, returning home to Cliviger near Burnley. Go straight to bed at 2.30 p.m. but can't sleep, so put on the portable. The *Oprah Winfrey Show* on Channel 4 has first and second wives having a go at men, seems to be making entertainment out of people's domestic lives or sex problems. The hostess is very competent and watchable. But all the afternoon shows appear to be aimed at housewives. With so many men unemployed there should be programmes to suit them . . . I get my call for tomorrow, a 9 a.m. rehearsal and an 11 a.m. shoot. I must go in even if feeling bad. One day off a twice-weekly soap in three years is enough . . .

JOHN McARDLE, ACTOR

For Sue Johnston, who plays the long-suffering Sheila Grant in the serial, it is a rare day off. For once she is able to go home and look at television after dropping her son at school.

Sheila Grant (Sue Johnston) of *Brookside*: 'Lines to learn, ready for the shoot tomorrow'

I love *Open Air*, I find it fascinating. This morning it's great because it's coming from *Brookside*, where I work. The first visit at 9 a.m. has taken the cameras into the writers' meeting with Phil Redmond. This is a rare insight for me as an actor, no matter what they are saying to the viewers: actors are never allowed to these storyline conferences.

At lunch-time I am presenting an award at the *Manchester Evening News* awards in Manchester. It's always an enjoyable affair. I meet my friend Ken Thomson (Channel 4 senior press officer) and we go in for the reception. I present the best production prize to *Don Juan* at the Exchange Theatre and Phil Redmond presents another award. I leave Manchester in the rush hour and the journey back to Warrington takes for ever. By the time I have collected my son from my mother's place we have missed *Neighbours*. A tragedy.

The television will stay on as background while domesticity takes over. I also have lines to learn, ready for the shoot tomorrow. So after my son is bathed and in bed the television goes off and the music goes on. At 9 p.m., however, I watch *Boon*. It stars my friend Amanda Burton, she's terrific. When the programme is finished I ring her. I have many friends who work in television and the great thing is the support we give each other. Mandy and I have a lot of news to catch up on, so the call is rather long, enormously long in fact, but a rather nice way to finish a very enjoyable day.

SUE JOHNSTON, ACTRESS

BROOKSIDE WRITER
Mother and writer Chris Curry woke at 6.15 a.m. in a mood of panic and guilt.

Panic because the *Brookside* story conference is being televised today. Guilt because I forgot to get the chicken out of the freezer and suspect I didn't relate enough to my kids yesterday. So, what's new? I drove the eighty minutes of motorway from Clitheroe to Brookside Close and arrived before the BBC. The 'pretend' story conference starts, going live soon. Will my daughter realize I've pinched her jacket? Must buy some clothes for myself for a change, but buying things for me brings an attack of guilt. Guilt is delivered along with children, but is it fair that working mothers are issued a double dose?

It is 8.50 a.m. and we keep being told we're 'going live' any minute and keep talking. It would be easier to keep talking if they didn't keep interrupting us to tell us to keep talking. Behave as normal. Normal is the usual dilemma of: Do I say little and seem uninterested or say too much and appear pushy?

We discuss the question of whether one of our sixteen-year-old girl characters would sleep with her boyfriend. I think about my daughter, who will be sixteen in six months, and feel very non-liberal about the issue. We must mention the issue of AIDS and the new morality. All the lessons taken on board by my generation, don't need to marry the first man you sleep with, etc., all out of the window now. And I thought things might be easier for my kids.

At 9.05 the television lights go off and we can start our day's work proper. Phil says he and cameras will return at coffee and toast time. Grab, munch, chew – scream our points of view. Some of the women writers, and some of the men, fall over backwards to put the feminist point of view. Some of the men writers feel threatened and think we women try to emasculate the male characters.

Will it ever be lunch-time? Forget I'm waiting for it as we get into yet another row about storylines. Makes me smile when people say 'soaps' aren't serious. If they ever saw the intensity of debate they'd wonder how it didn't all come out like a serialization of Dostoevsky. At 12.30 p.m. a plea for an early lunch is met with favour by our new producer (very reasonable person, female). Off to the pub for (mainly) liquid lunches.

The afternoon is more debate, more coffee, and some decisions on storylines. The drive back seems longer. When I get home I'll have a nice relaxing bath. Except it never is because I realize the towels want washing and I clean the bath while I'm in it. Resolution, must relate to kids more, must be better organized with housework, must stop feeling guilty all the time.

CHRIS CURRY, WRITER

BROOKSIDE BOSSES
Producer Vanessa Whitburn has been in charge at the Close for four months, too absorbed by her work even to find herself a proper place to live. On 1 November she arrives at 8.30 a.m.

Busy day involving the second of a two-day storyline meeting with thirteen writers and four production staff, held each month. This is always a demanding and pressurized session which is both exhilarating and exhausting. Ten weeks into a new job the particular kind of concentration required is still tricky. My mixed feelings of energy and anxiety remind me of early days as a producer-director in radio drama . . .

Today starts early because of our contribution to *Open Air*. Myself, the executive producer and six of the writers launch into a warm-up discussion about whether one of our younger characters will sleep with her boyfriend. The early hour doesn't cool the ardour of the conversation and we're off to a flying start . . . Once *Open Air* leaves us there is a brief break during which I go through some continuity points, brief one of the writers on a rewrite required on a second draft and chat to a director about cuts required after rehearsals have indicated that his episode is over-running. Amidst it all my secretary Lisa tells me my solicitor has phoned: I'm trying to buy a house up here and it's all stuck, no time to chase that one today, maybe tomorrow early.

Storyline session brings another animated discussion on sex. This time it is the question of whether our young police constable would prefer a new girlfriend to marriage. There was an equally passionate discussion yesterday, about religion. Sex and religion, still the two subjects which universally raise most energy and dissent . . . Lunch-time involves a quick look at the post, a few scribbled notes to remind me what needs following up and a leap over to the canteen to eat. Then I sit with the director shooting in the Close this week, and the director who is in rehearsal. Both bring me up to date with their problems. I can help with a couple, delegate one and sympathize with what is left.

Quick talks to two actresses, then back to the meeting. Things start slowly at 1.45 p.m. After a good morning the ideas make hard work this afternoon. We want some job-orientated storylines looking at the police force and the responsibilities of magistrates. Several writers offer to jump out of the window (luckily we're on the ground floor) when energetically presented ideas fall flat.

This is where I must have the confidence to let the conversation roll loosely as we go up several blind alleys, on the way to the inevitable dead ends, before we find the right idea, the one that inspires and grows and refines. I bury my head in my notes. Would some of my pre-prepared ideas help if I throw them in now? I do, one's for the window before me and one helps, good. Now I sit back, listen, absorb, encourage and pull out what is important and dismiss what gets in the way of the thought line. I'm amazed how quickly the time goes. We wrap up early at 4 p.m., it's been a good energetic session . . .

Home is a 'take-away' (I must stop this when I get my own house) and then I will watch *The Bill*, because I'm interested in its pseudo-documentary style; *South of the Border*, because I know the producer and it's 'off the wall' and unusual and young in feel; and *First Tuesday*, always good and this time they are covering dyslexia. I make a mental note of some of the points which might inform our portrayal of 'Growler', who suffers from dyslexia in *Brookside*. Then the television goes most firmly off.

A little time for late-night phone calls to patient and valued friends, decide I really must find that swimming pool for early-morning exercise up here, and what has happened to my personal life? Never give up, I know it will settle. And there's never a dull moment between Stratford-upon-Avon, which I love and where I still have a house, and Liverpool, and an exciting and demanding job on the most interesting soap around.

VANESSA WHITBURN, PRODUCER

> At 6.30 a.m. the founding father, Phil Redmond, is already reading the first draft for a new drama series. He is at Brookside by 8 a.m. In the morning, apart from the visit by Open Air, there is a meeting to discuss new Mersey projects for the BBC, Channel 4 and ITV with managing director Alexis Cross.

At the *Manchester Evening News* Theatre Awards lunch I presented the best actress award to Josephine Blake and Diane Langton, and took the opportunity to make the point that Sue Johnston is one of the best actresses in the country . . .

PHIL REDMOND, CHAIRMAN

> OPENING THE AIR
> Day-time programming, as it is known, is a relatively new development for both BBC1 and ITV. It meant transferring the obligatory schools television to BBC2 and Channel 4. It also meant finding money for television hours when, despite high unemployment, audiences were bound to be small. The BBC led the way in October 1986, and set the pattern of studio-bound audience, chat and game shows; old movies, American and Australian 'soaps'; relieved by its traditional strength in children's programmes.
>
> At this time the opportunity was also taken to correct a fault which had persisted since the earliest days of BBC Television. This was its failure to give viewers who wanted to complain or enthuse on air either a consistent slot or even a proper respect. Galvanized to some extent by Channel 4's highly regarded and weekly Right to Reply, the BBC resolved to do better. It instituted BBC Manchester's Open Air, generously allowed two editions and around seventy-five minutes each weekday morning. The programme was at least as much an advertisement for BBC programmes as a critique of them, but it was an improvement on the past. Today both editions attract an audience of 800,000, many of our diarists among them.

My diary will not be as I would have liked it to be as I work for an agency which sends me away for two weeks at a time to look after old people in their own homes. On 1 November I was in Richmond, Surrey, obliged to watch what my employer at the time, Mrs Bernard, chose, and hoping that my son at home was remembering anything I had asked him to video . . .

Why ever does she switch over to TV-am the second that *Breakfast*

Time finishes? I cannot understand how anyone could not be interested in *Open Air* . . . Oh good, Mrs Bernard is going out of the room, switch to BBC1 quick. Gosh! Marvellous! Just in time for a *Brookside* planning meeting. It is my family's favourite soap, so much so that every episode had to be recorded for my son during his three-month trip to the USA. How good it was to hear about the planning that goes into it. Why is it that *Brookside* is not very popular? . . . It has a variety of families, working and middle class, just as one could find on a modern estate. I find it easy to identify with . . .

So *Brookside* is going to be featured on *Open Air* at 11 a.m. also. I don't normally go out shopping until 11 a.m. but I must try to get out quick this morning. How lucky that it is my son's day off work. I must get to a phone and ask him to video it for me. No chance of seeing it here.

MONICA GROUCOTT, COMPANION-HELP, RUGBY

On *Open Air* lots of people complained about Paul Daniels. (*Paul Daniels: Live at Hallowe'en*, BBC1, 31.10.88.) At the end of the show he was put on a bonfire and it was set alight. I was very scared. I thought it was tasteless and they should not have done it at all. Whoever thought this up must be mentally disturbed.

TRACEY McCOY, AGED 13, WEMBLEY

The first thing I properly watched was *Open Air*, the early one. It was like it always is, some thought-provoking debate which is really very tedious.

Cheryl Baker, Mike Shaft and 'some rather pernicious-looking green balls' in the BBC's *Open Air*

The best bit was the thing about Paul Daniels trying to kill himself on a bonfire. Pity he didn't.

**TIM ALLMAN, AGED 12,
HIGHWORTH, NEAR SWINDON**

There is an *Open Air* discussion about the Paul Daniels show last night. I didn't watch the programme as I do not agree with the type of fear it instils in people. I did switch on at the very end and was horrified by the witch test. Despite complaints I don't think it will harm Paul Daniels' career, in fact it will probably enhance it. Other guests are Cheryl Baker, who is a total nut case and should be kept on children's television, and Phil Redmond, who looked half doped . . . In the main edition he showed us round the set of *Brookside* and looked more awake, as if he has had a litre of Lucozade . . .

**MARIA ELLIS, UNEMPLOYED,
LIVERPOOL**

I usually watch snatches of the early edition of *Open Air*, which would be so much better if it didn't fall into the trap of so many 'discussion' programmes by dragging some minor celebrity into the studio. What has Cheryl Baker got to say, I ask you? Please stick to people who matter: producers, directors, writers or tea ladies. Also make more use of the interestingly named Mike Shaft, who informed us this morning that he'd had lots of calls complaining about the weather. What's it got to do with him?

**PAUL WHITMORE, CHEF,
IPSWICH, SUFFOLK**

For me *Open Air* is a great show and one that's long overdue. Today a young viewer was invited to the studio to talk to Cheryl Baker, presenter of the Saturday morning 'cookery' show aimed at four- to fourteen-year-olds. Needless to say the whole studio got covered in parsley and peanut butter as Ms Baker demonstrated some rather pernicious-looking green balls that a four-year-old can whip up, no bother.

**MARIE HIGGINS, CIVIL SERVANT,
ST BOSWELLS, BORDERS**

Phoned *Open Air* with a question for Cheryl. It was: Who eats all the dishes she makes on *Eggs 'n' Baker* (BBC1, Saturday mornings)? An hour later I got on to the programme and put the question to her. It felt really strange, actually talking down the phone to a 'star', and seeing them look at you from the television and answer the question . . . If I hadn't been on half-term from college I wouldn't have been on. I videoed my phone call of course and tomorrow I'll be inviting my pals, who didn't see it, round to watch.

**MARCUS McCOLLUM, AGED 16,
BALLYMONEY, CO. ANTRIM**

Now it's *Open Air II* and Pattie Coldwell is saying, 'In fifty years . . .' for the forty-eight, forty-nine, fiftieth time. She is talking about ODILOT (*One Day in the Life of Television*) far too much. It reminds me of an argument I had on 'the process of observation may change the phenomena being observed' lines . . . Michael Grade came on and gave a brilliant joke. Good to know that the Channel 4 chief executive has a sense of humour. C4 hasn't tumbled in quality under Grade and why should it?

Now that the Government (known as Maggie to her friends) looks like it wants to milk television for more cash, I wonder what this means for 'our lovely Channel 4'. I don't know. I hate the alliance of Government and advertisers. They know bugger-all about television, except how to change buttocks and sell coffee, and they want to have all the say in how it is run. I mean the audacity of leaving *us* out of it.

No surprise really, this country can now hardly call itself democratic, but the danger is that if television goes the way of newspapers, or goes to all-entertainment like the United States, we won't be able to tell if the country is democratic or not. In fact no one will be able to say, debate, discuss or investigate anything. Then this Government will rule . . .

MICHAEL RILEY,
LONDON W12

Was first person to be interviewed on *Open Air* about *One Day in the Life of Television*. Quite enjoyable and it appeared to be acceptable . . .

MR M. MACPHERSON,
PRINCIPAL LIGHTHOUSEKEEPER,
SEAHOUSES, NORTHUMBERLAND

I was making notes in preparation for the writing of my diary when the telephone rang. Imagine my surprise when I discovered that the caller was from *Open Air*, asking if I was going to enter the competition by completing a diary. The caller asked if I would be prepared to take part later in the morning in a live interview. After a moment's hesitation I agreed and was told that I would be phoned about 11.30 a.m.

This had the effect of making me formulate some ideas about the programmes I had seen, or would watch, during the day, so that I would have something to say when the call came. The telephone rang at 11.30 a.m. as promised. After turning off the television sound, as instructed in the earlier conversation, I answered in what I hoped was my usual voice. I was immediately put at my ease and was told that I would be connected to the sound engineer, who would check the level of my voice. This was quite a painless procedure. I was then told that when I was named by the interviewer, who would probably be Mike Shaft, I was to respond as if talking to a friend.

While waiting I was connected to the studio and could listen to the programme through the telephone receiver. It was certainly different listening to a programme while unable to watch it. The time seemed to pass very slowly although the programme was interesting. Then the sound engineer's voice came softly over the line saying that I would be called in about two minutes. I listened with interest to Paul Daniels talking about his Hallowe'en programme the night before, and then suddenly Pattie Coldwell was telling the viewers that the programme had run out of time.

What had happened to my earth-shattering interview? The friendly caller, who had first contacted me, spoke again and apologized that some of the items had over-run, as happens on a live broadcast sometimes. I was thanked for waiting so patiently. I replaced the receiver with a feeling of disappointment . . . but soon recovered and continued to make notes on the rest of the day's viewing to complete my diary.

**SHEILA M. COLE,
HOTEL ADMINISTRATIVE ASSISTANT,
RAMSGATE, KENT**

KILROY WAS HERE

After feeling its way in its apprentice period Kilroy! *was now an audience show, for better or worse, assured in its style and well into its third season. The exclamation mark in the title had become just a little less ironical. The show was designed for an audience that was likely to be mainly female. The lean presenter, darting about the studio audience with microphone at the ready, had the kind of tanned and bland good looks which are admired in advertising agencies.*

Robert Kilroy-Silk, a Warwickshire lad now forty-six, began his career as a lecturer in politics at Liverpool University. He became Labour MP for Ormskirk in 1974, and moved on to Knowsley North in 1983. A fairly isolated figure on the right of the party, he resigned from the House of Commons in 1986 to become a television star. Though still capable of bad temper, when people in his studio spoke out of turn, he had proved adept at persuading guests to make private thoughts public.

On 1 November his subject was 'marital rape', attacks by husbands on their wives which were taken to range from sexual congress, achieved without willing female consent, to wife-battering with a sexual ingredient. A couple of men, allowed the privacy of dark shadow, were in the studio to confess. One or two others tentatively tried to enter a plea for understanding of male sexuality, but in general the programme was a vehicle for the expression of female hurt and anger. Here are comments from a few of the 1.1 million who watched that day.

This was a very taboo subject. The programme went into a lot of explicit detail and I felt that it was a bit too sensitive an issue to be tackled at 9.30 a.m., especially on a day when many children are off school and might watch it. Although the debate was very exciting my attention was divided between it and my diary writing . . .

**DAVID GREEN, AGED 14,
HOLYWOOD, CO. DOWN**

Kilroy! is a very erratic programme. The 1 November show was very good and, I think, dealt well with an unpleasant and disturbing topic. I have no patience with people who do not want to see this sort of thing discussed on television. The good thing about *Kilroy!* is that it does bring people of diverse opinions together and that makes for a lively and heated debate which makes the audience think.

I am not a fan of the man himself. I get the feeling that he is constantly grooming his own image as the bedroom-voiced confidant of the women in the audience. It is clear that most of them regard him with suspicion and quite often with outright antipathy. *Kilroy!* always provokes some sort of reaction in me but the producers should resist the smarmy host's attempts to turn it into 'tabloid television'.

ALYS THOMAS, POSTGRADUATE STUDENT, ABERYSTWYTH, DYFED

Kilroy gets straight into his stride, kneeling down by a woman who relates the full horror of acts perpetrated by a husband in an earlier marriage. Story told, discussion is thrown open, Kilroy darting hither and thither, offering the microphone to others wishing to relate similar experiences, express support or publicize a liberationist viewpoint.

As a male observer, one feels distinctly threatened by the avalanche of female condemnation being generated. A smattering of the male species, 'experts' in psychology and the law, offer muted advice on cue. Carefully choosing their words to avoid confrontation. The 40-minute programme ends abruptly, inconclusively. The expanding hot air balloon of discussion is punctured by the strains of the signature. Suddenly, it's 'Goodbye and see you tomorrow' from Kilroy . . .

JOHN TRUSTRUM, SINGLE PARENT, BRENTWOOD, ESSEX

I become instantly interested in the harrowing stories women are telling on the subject of 'marital rape'. It seems an experience far removed from my comfortable life. Then my throat chokes up and the tears flow when a plump, grey-haired, granny-type tells how her husband raped her just seven days after a hysterectomy. I thank my lucky stars for a loving, caring husband. One question: Why did the men in the programme remain in shadow while the women had the courage to appear openly? Still, on with the housework while thinking of what I have just seen . . .

CHRISTINE TAIT, LIBRARY ASSISTANT, FAREHAM, HAMPSHIRE

This is a programme which I sit down and watch whenever possible because it gives me an opportunity to exercise my thoughts on the day's topic, sometimes keeping my mind buzzing all day. I attempt to watch today as though I am an alien from another planet, with no knowledge of the human race, a completely open mind, no preconceived opinions on the topic in question. As an alien I conclude that 'rape' means sex without seduction. This saddens me. I wish that human married couples could learn to communicate better, and to enjoy seducing each other. Then there would be no need for this 'attack and defence' situation.

MARGARET SANDERSON, HOUSEWIFE-GARDENER, RUGELEY, STAFFORDSHIRE

As a sociology student I have come to analyse television in great depth and sadly find pronounced elements of sexism and racism. In *Kilroy!* this morning the point is clearly shown. Ancient, even Victorian-style opinions of women were expressed by some men. They felt they had the right to rape a woman, she has no say in the matter.

Women are sadly still not equal with men in the occupational field and thus not financially equal. One man, advancing what he thought was a rhetorical question, asked why women do not leave these violent homes. It was inferred that because they decided to remain there, whatever happened was their own fault. Does this man not know the economic position of so many such women? They simply do not have an ounce of independence, they are literally tied to the home with children. And no government is willing to cure the disgustingly low level of state child care.

Some people felt that the subject of rape was not 'nice' and should not have been chosen for 1 November. But it is a sick, shadowy aspect of 1980s society and it is only fair, and honest, to present this true aspect for future generations to comprehend . . .

MELANIE O'CONNOR, PART-TIME STUDENT, SOUTHEND-ON-SEA, ESSEX

Feelings were running high and I became emotionally involved. I thought it was cruel that a wife should not allow a husband to complete what he had started. My wife came into the room and was not interested, so I turned it off . . .

DAVID ROSS, ENFIELD, MIDDLESEX

Very interesting. While hoovering I stopped several times to listen to the various participants. I thought I knew everything about sex but several wives' experiences stunned me. I was left feeling that 'victims' are born as such. I wouldn't have stood it for one moment. I had five children but would still have left and kept my self-respect. . .

PAT STEPHENS, TEACHER, BOGNOR REGIS, SUSSEX

I'm still cleaning the kitchen. I have to have something going on, otherwise I would start to rail and seethe against the inequalities that have me working all hours to support myself and the children, while subsidizing a high-earning husband in his relentless financial investments and share ownership. Kilroy again comes to no conclusion. His programme is becoming more and more a television version of the *News of the World*, voyeurism and titillation. Still, it drowns the noise of the kitchen tap; having dripped for two years it is now running constantly. Will he ever fix it? . . .

MARGARET YOUNG, NIGHT-SHIFT CARE ASSISTANT AND FREELANCE ARTIST, BRIDGNORTH, SHROPSHIRE

Arrive at work in a London secondary school and half watch breakfast television, personalities chatting about their favourite subject, themselves, which somehow seems to highlight my own boring existence . . . Then, for the argumentative, comes the programme which enables them to shout at the television, whether it be *Kilroy!* or ITV's equivalent. These shows amaze me for their futility, their inability to change the horrendous things discussed. But I suppose they are the equivalent of a 'nice cup of tea' after some terrible accident, therapy for the masses . . .

CAROLYN SERTER, MEDIA RESOURCES OFFICER, LONDON SW16

Both my wife and I knew this character when we lived in Ormskirk, Lancashire. On one of his several 'walkabouts' he shook my hand and hoped he could count on my vote . . . He did not look like a politician, he was quite a 'dandy'. Suffice it to say that I disillusioned him as to my vote . . . When he appeared on my television screen he had apparently undergone the usual glamour treatment and I was quite put off. Possibly jealousy on my part . . .

JOHN DILWORTH, RETIRED CIVIL SERVANT, STORRINGTON, SUSSEX

I hate this programme. Perhaps I shouldn't watch it. To see Kilroy-Silk with his designer haircut and professional sympathy, skilfully provoking argument by exposing pain, may damage me as a viewer as much as it hurts those taking part.

Today's subject is rape in marriage. Women re-live their horror under merciless studio lighting and the cruel zoom of the camera. Men who admit to rape in marriage have their features darkened. In law there are neither criminals nor victims. Yet the men receive protection and are made to resemble what all women fear, the anonymous rapist of back streets and dark alleys . . .

KATHLEEN BELL, BIDFORD-ON-AVON, WARWICKSHIRE

MULTI-COLOURED BUS

The BBC has always been the strongest broadcasting organization in the area of children's programmes. It is a sign of this strength, perverse or otherwise, that it is willing to abandon such a venerable and widely loved infants' vehicle as Play School, and trade it in for the carefully multi-ethnic Playbus. This new five-days-a-week show had its first trip on 17 October and was still shiny new.

The 1980s fashion is that children's programmes should be presented by a young man, sounding ever so enthusiastic, and speaking from a picture-plastered small room. On this day Andy Crane, an elder-brother figure adored by girls on the verge of their teens, was on duty for BBC1. He is allowed the first say.

My day begins as normal. What to wear? The great question that starts each day. Guess right and nobody notices. Get it wrong and in come the letters. The decision made, it is over to the Television Centre for what turns out to be a fairly normal day. At the office by 9.45 a.m., to Make-up at 10 a.m., on studio floor at 10.10, transmission at 10.25. Birthday cards read before *Playbus*. The new programme is one to watch where *Play School* encouraged participation. Time will tell.

The mail sack arrives at 11.15 (ish). *Children's BBC* receives between 2500 and 3000 letters and cards a week, keeping Doreen and Jane fairly busy. My producer is at an edit so the office is fairly chaotic. The phone rings continually with messages. I am reading and answering mail, and signing pictures by the hundred for people who write in for them.

Preparation for the *Children's BBC* afternoon. The line-up includes *PC Pinkerton*, teaching children about the police force, and *Fireman Sam*, a similar show about the fire service. The latter is topical today because Bonfire Night is imminent. Then, after *Ratman*, comes *What's Your Story?* live from Birmingham. Viewers are invited to phone in story contributions. Great idea, great show, love it. Sylvester McCoy presides and it is nice to be able to exploit the 'liveness' of *Children's BBC* by having short exchanges with him at the beginning and end of the show. *Newsround* and *Grange Hill* excellent as ever . . .

I like my job very much. Live television gives one a great 'buzz' that is

Dave Benson and the Why bird: the BBC *Playbus* driver-conductor contemplates his route

hard to match anywhere . . . But what I do is not easy or glamorous, it is
hard work, rewarding but hard work. Afterwards I do not party my life
away at nightclubs or pubs. I do not stay up until all hours, whizzing
round the West End of London. I ended this day, as I end 99 per cent of
my days, by going to bed.

ANDY CRANE, PRESENTER

This was one of the better days on television for me. One of my favourite
television presenters is Andy Crane. I like Andy because he's funny and is
always full of laughs and jokes. I dislike the presenter of *Children's ITV*
because he treats everyone as fools.

**JOANNE GODFREY, AGED 12,
WITNEY, OXFORDSHIRE**

Today my daughter, Cathryn, celebrates her third birthday and we gave
her cards and sang 'Happy Birthday' . . . I set up the video to record
Playbus and the birthday messages read out by Andy Crane. We were
thrilled when Cathryn's message was read out, it was worth the effort of
painting Thomas the Tank Engine. It will be lovely to keep that on the
video so that we can see it any time. My mother had made a point of
watching to see if Cathryn was mentioned and she rang us to let us know
she had seen it, and to wish Cathryn a happy birthday . . .

**SUZANNE MILLS, PART-TIME
CRECHE ASSISTANT, FAREHAM, HAMPSHIRE**

The first programme I meant to watch, but missed, was *Playbus*. I hope
this is going to be the child's equivalent of my adult diet, as *Play School*
was. But I have my doubts. It looks like my two-year-old is in for yet
another 'snappy' (disjointed), 'relevant' (OK to talk sloppily, that's how
kids talk) format, when all we parents wanted was gentle *Play School*,
which actually left children time to think. At least ITV's *Rainbow* is still
left, though no doubt it too is for the chop.

   Anyway, as I said, we missed it. The trouble is that you have to be so on
the ball to catch pre-school programmes, they're so short and scattered in
the schedules that you blink and they're over. Unless of course you get
into a routine that includes them. If *Playbus* improves, perhaps I'll find
the motivation to get that routine going again . . .

**ALISON STANCLIFFE,
TEACHER NOW AT HOME WITH CHILDREN,
RYTON, TYNE AND WEAR**

Playbus is right for children at the age of three and four. I am seven but I
like it too. There are lots of different stops. Today it was the playground
stop. I like *Playbus* better than *Play School* because there are lots of songs
that children know, and it helps my little sister to read and count. My
Mummy videos the programme for us to watch when we get home from
school . . .

**AMY DUNN, AGED 7,
SUFFOLK**

At 10.30 a.m. I turn over for Anna to watch *Playbus*. The baby has gone to sleep, so I close the lounge door and go into the kitchen. I can sit down for half an hour with a cup of coffee and Sunday's paper, which I still haven't had time to read. I know I should be watching with her, discussing it etc., but I don't care. I deserve a little peace and quiet. Anyway I'm boycotting *Playbus* – bring back *Play School*! . . .

J. A. COUNDLEY, TEACHER TURNED MOTHER, TELSCOMBE CLIFFS, SUSSEX

I thought that Rebekah and I would sit down together and give *Playbus* another chance. I sulk about it more than the children, but losing *Play School* is like losing a tried and trusted friend. Hannah watched *Playbus* last Sunday (she's at school now) and instantly pronounced it second rate beside *Play School*. However, I concede that she may well have heard and seen my own sulkings and grumblings on the subject.

Not that we watch every day. We don't. We're too busy most days to watch television at all and, as I don't want Hannah to become a habitual after-school children's television viewer, we never automatically switch on. Reading together is of far more benefit, I tell myself, and her. Anyway, apart from *Play School* and *Rainbow*, I feel there is little else of any substance for younger children. I simply refuse to allow my children to fill their impressionable minds with programmes featuring 'He-man', 'She-ra' and the like. 'Mindless rubbish', I tell them, and get them to switch off. Children need stimulating stories with good diction and nicely worded scripts. Stories that can stand up without the need for 'other worldly powers' being called upon . . .

MRS L. J. MOORCROFT, ADULT EDUCATION TUTOR AND HOUSEWIFE, AYLESBURY, BUCKINGHAMSHIRE

I didn't watch *Playbus* properly myself, but the few minutes I did see made me think that one of its problems is that the presenter talks to children in the studio. It may work for other children but small children need to be addressed directly. Alexander can cope with this and says he loves all of *Playbus* but I don't think a younger child would concentrate as easily on it as he did on *Play School*, from the age of one . . .

CLARE STEVENS, PUBLISHER'S READER AND HOUSEWIFE, LONDON SE5

I sat down with my son to watch *Playbus* and was very moved by its impressive professionalism. I loved everything about it. I particularly liked the negro presenter. His lovable, malleable, expressive face moved me greatly. I felt he was made for the medium and this was reflected in his whole persona. Towards the end of the programme, when he did a rather old and hackneyed magic trick, it still had my attention because he won the hearts of the innocently starry-eyed children with his warmth, timing, professionalism and sweet voice.

It was particularly refreshing, too, to see a story item featuring a beautiful negroid puppet. I was enthralled to see that the BBC are advancing by strides in the direction of balancing the racial mix. I might add too that my son enjoyed the programme immensely and commented on the unusual puppet . . .

**DOROTHY COOK, TEACHER,
GRIMSBY**

> TIME FOR VERSE
>
> *All kinds of verse, let alone poetry, are rare on television. There is not much risk of BBC1's* Five to Eleven *taxing the nation's attention span. It lasts five minutes, time on this day for admired actress Patricia Routledge to read three salutary poems by Elisabeth Jennings about animals trying to come to terms with the human world.*

Catch the tail end of Patricia Routledge reading poems. It's a pity I missed most of it. I can't understand why so little poetry is regularly featured on any channel. Poetry is, after all, what Coleridge called 'the best words in the best order'. But one minor thing on Patricia's reading. Why hold a superfluous book in your hand and then read from the teleprompter? Whatever happened to people who read aloud from books before the age of television? . . .

**PAUL LESTER, UNEMPLOYED,
BIRMINGHAM**

Caught the end of a poem, written from the viewpoint of a stag and how it feels to be hunted. It was spoken so beautifully by Patricia Routledge that I was moved to tears, after just those few lines. Why can't *Five to Eleven* be extended to ten or even fifteen minutes? An extra five minutes a day isn't much to ask . . .

**MRS M. R. HOOD, HOUSEWIFE,
WALLASEY, CHESHIRE**

Well, it isn't a typical day. I wouldn't be watching much television on such a sunny day unless I had bronchitis, I'd rather be in the garden . . . Just before 11 a.m. I switched on and saw Patricia Routledge. She recited a poem about a ladybird. Maybe it's because I don't feel well, I'm not sure, but it moved me. It reflected the way I feel about society; money is paramount and people come a poor second, so there isn't much hope for mere insects . . .

**STELLA FOSTER, INFORMATION WORKER,
LONDON SW16**

I love the spoken word intelligibly delivered to camera with warmth, directness and control. It is still the most compulsive single image on television . . .

**MICHAEL RANDLES,
RETIRED SCHOOLMASTER,
ABINGDON, OXFORDSHIRE**

CHAT BEFORE LUNCH

The last BBC1 programme before lunch on weekdays is Daytime Live, *a
light and inconsequential talk show presented live from the Pebble Mill
studios in Birmingham. The presenters this day are Sue Cook, entrusted
with the more or less serious interviewing; bubbly Floella Benjamin, a*
Play School *old girl; and Alan Titchmarsh. We hear first from Alan.*

The day starts leaving home at Alton in Hampshire at 5.50 a.m. I arrive at
Pebble Mill three hours later and kiss Sue Cook and Floella Benjamin. I
feel no excuse is necessary as they are my co-presenters. I change into a
rather flashy striped shirt and tie, part of my now trendy image, before
getting down to toast, marmalade and coffee. I open the mail and find that
one 15-year-old likes my red sox (and body) and asks if I will show them
to her on screen (sox, not body). Resolve to do my best.

From 9.30 a.m. I am working with a researcher on an item about life in
the *Daytime Live* office. Secretaries and producers are surprisingly at ease
with cameras and lights hovering over their desks. Then rehearsals start
in office and studio. Guest Su Pollard is funny and loony. My interviewee
is an expert on office psychology. She is nervous and her chat is not very
meaty. I spend time trying to persuade her to be more exciting, though not
in so many words, and hope she is OK 'on the night'.

Just before noon I say 'hello' to the studio audience, very jolly. They're
all accountants in grey suits. What a surprise! On air all goes well. The
staff perform well, but fortunately not too well, and my interviewee
comes up trumps. Eight minutes in the talkback in my ear breaks down, I
have to rely on counts from the floor and fingers held in the air. It is not

Alan Titchmarsh: calories
for *Daytime Live*

always reliable but we soldier on. The Su Pollard bit is a hoot and her first boss, from the Co-Op, is a gem. I wrap up to a count from the floor, praying that it is accurate, and say 'goodbye'. It was a good show, faces in the office show that, and say so, too. If it's not good they avoid your eye and just don't speak, polite indifference . . .

ALAN TITCHMARSH, PRESENTER

> *His colleague Floella Benjamin was* in situ *to start her work at 8 a.m. with a briefing meeting on what was in the show that day.*

I did a voice-over for the top of the show and then got together my notes about Su Pollard, who I have to interview. At 9 a.m., after the arrival of co-presenter Alan, I ring home in London to make sure my kids are fine. I had spent the night away and my husband was with them. Reassured, I read over my notes on Su and start to plan interviews with her, Sylvester McCoy and Chris Pilkington. The latter two are involved with this new children's drama concept where the audience is invited to ring in and say how the storyline should continue.

At 10 a.m. I begin to read through letters from viewers. They are all complimentary, isn't that nice? After answering some of the letters I chat to Su about our babies, hers is six months old, mine is two months. Rehearsal begins at 11 a.m. The item about children's drama has not been cut the way I was briefed, so I have to change the line of questioning. To Make-up and Wardrobe, then I have a few quiet moments with myself. The show starts, going very well, and I do my interview in Studio A with loads of action going on behind. Su goes down a storm, she is quite a character. The show ends and I leave the studios with Sue Cook, just after 1 p.m., to catch a train back to London.

I watch very little television when I get home. I see *What's Your Story?* with my little boy Aston, the news and *Fawlty Towers*, which was a scream. I personally think there is too much unnecessary violence on television and that we have a responsibility to the public, especially our children. People are affected by what they see.

FLOELLA BENJAMIN, PRESENTER

> *There were no complaints about violence, unnecessary or otherwise, in Floella's show.*

Quite a good magazine programme with good presenters, specially Alan Titchmarsh and Floella Benjamin . . . Sue Cook, I'm afraid, just doesn't work. She comes across as having no sense of humour. She's getting better, maybe it's just nerves.

The producers must realize that we are not all middle-aged housewives, sitting there, knitting and having coffee mornings. I'm 23, with one child and married. I was a punk in my younger days and enjoyed programmes like *The Tube*. There must be many people like me out there. So could they make the schedule a little more diverse? We are not all sat there

cooing over Fergie and her baby, or worrying what the very irritating
Princess Diana is wearing . . .

**BELINDA BROWN, HOUSEWIFE,
BRISTOL**

The musical item better than the usual pop. They did at least finish off
properly. How does the audience know when to start clapping a group so
that they can fade themselves out? Does someone give them a signal?
What would happen if they didn't? I wonder what Sir Thomas Beecham
would have thought of the practice? I once heard him reprove an opera
audience for applauding before the final notes had died into silence. He'd
probably have said, 'Music? Bah! Unmitigated noise.' . . . Su Pollard
somewhat over-boisterous. Alan Titchmarsh looking more presentable
than recently, when he resembled the terror of 4C. Did he have to put his
finger on the iced bun? . . .

**CHRISTINA BABB, RETIRED TEACHER AGED 82,
ALVA, CLACKMANNANSHIRE**

It's television navel-watching. With Titchmarsh around Pebble Mill
studios: 'Here are the girls in the back room who . . .' This time last year,
when I was on maternity leave, I watched a lot of day-time television, and
most of it seemed to involve the scrutiny and dissection of television
itself. It seems neither healthy nor productive, but perhaps it's cheap. For
teachers of media studies it must be a godsend. I'm amazed the day-time
diet has changed so little and that Su Pollard can look so awful but be so
popular . . .

**HILARY MORIARTY, TEACHER,
MONMOUTH, GWENT**

The Channel 3 morning entertainment pattern is even newer than that of BBC1, and to some extent imitative. The network stays in the hands of TV-am until 9.25 a.m., when the ITV federation of companies takes over. Taking the 1 November audience figures as more or less typical, it can be seen that Channel 3 keeps its breakfast-time ratings lead until the position is reversed at lunch-time.

On this morning the biggest BBC1 audiences were 1.1 million for Kilroy! and 1.7 million for Daytime Live. For the opposition, TV-am's After Nine scored 1.8 million and ITV's imported soap A Country Practice, leading into the lunch-time peak, was watched by 2.5 million. As always both audiences slipped to the lowest point of the day in mid-morning, 700,000 for BBC1 and 1.2 million for ITV.

LARGER ISSUES
Our diarists attending to Channel 3 looked first at TV-am's After Nine, a women's interest magazine suggesting that any men still lingering about the house should find something to do elsewhere. On this morning fashion person Merrill Thomas was concerned about flattering the fuller figure and keep-fit zealot Lizzie Webb was, as ever, at war with surplus fat.

TV-am would have us believe that about 60 per cent of women are a size 16 or larger. No wonder dieting is such big business. They model clothes for the fuller figure, most of which are pretty flamboyant and definitely expensive, £75 for a pair of trousers! . . .
P. L. DUFFIELD, MOTHER, WESTON-SUPER-MARE, AVON

Was most interested in the feature on 16+ (size, not age). Somebody said: 'You can look wonderful at any size.' Thank you, ma'am, a thought after my own heart. Being big doesn't mean being unfashionable . . . Felt enlightened and inspired afterwards, the presenters were honest without being patronizing, and offered a refreshing approach. I was slightly annoyed that all the clothes were shown off with very expensive accessories. Why do fashion editors show an acceptable outfit and then pile on expensive extras? The average person does not have a great deal of money, especially students, to spend on little items that have no major function . . .
DENISE SMITH, STUDENT AND LIFEGUARD, TROWBRIDGE, WILTSHIRE

Wished hubby a happy birthday and got on with my morning chores. Our television is never switched off during the night. I sleep with the remote control under my pillow in case anything interesting is on in the night and I am awake . . . Skipped the bulk of TV-am and I didn't catch mad Lizzie, though her exercises are not taxing, more for the older woman, I would say.

Found Jayne Irving and Merrill Thomas, not my favourites, on today's fashion-scope for the larger lady. Great. My two girls moaned for attention but I had to watch this spot. The clothes and models were great, and the stuff was affordable and not dowdy. Being tubby myself I certainly benefited from the tips being given. Anyway men prefer ladies with something to hold on to, rather than a smile and a bag of bones. Usually Merrill Thomas comes on with *Vogue* magazine-type leggy stick insects and expensive, unwearable clothes that turn me off. Though I wish I was a little slimmer . . .

**MRS M. LUNAN, HOUSEWIFE,
LONDON E5**

After Nine is appalling. I am a woman at home with two children but I do not want to watch endless dross about fashion, make-up, babies and 'women's problems'. This morning they had outsize fashions. The two sylph-like presenters, Jayne and Merrill, sat extolling the virtues of the fuller figure, while models strutted around in £200 coats and £100 dresses. How many people do they think can afford such prices? . . . I feel these programmes are so out of touch with reality and the wants and needs of the woman of the 1980s . . .

**PATRICIA PAKNADEL, HOUSEWIFE,
LONDON N4**

SNAKES AND LADDERS

At 9.25 a.m. ITV launches into the first game show of the day. This is Lucky Ladders, *bought by Anglia Television from the independent*

Lennie Bennett of ITV's *Lucky Ladders*: 'You asked for promo shots, so that is what you're going to get'

*Action Time and now embarking on its second season. Host Lennie
Bennett descends the inevitable stairs, wearing the inevitable smile, to a
cluttered set which looks too tiny to contain him and the two competing
couples.*

I love Tuesdays. It's the best game show day of the week. There hasn't
been a game show invented which I don't enjoy. I suppose it's because
you see ordinary people winning lovely prizes, and I like pitting my wits
against the contestants. My day started with *Lucky Ladders*. Lennie Bennett
is an excellent presenter and the holiday prizes are all worth winning.

It's immediately followed by *Going for Gold* (BBC1) . . . the next
programme I saw was *Give Us a Clue* (ITV) . . . then there are the evening
shows, *Fifteen-to-One* (C4), *Blockbusters* (ITV), *Strike It Lucky* (ITV),
Telly Addicts (BBC1), and *A Question of Sport* (BBC1).

Unless you are caught in the poverty trap, you cannot imagine the joy at
winning. Otherwise you have no hope of ever buying anything for
yourself. When I once came away with £175 plus prizes it was a
wonderful feeling, knowing that you won't need to declare it to the DHSS.
They would have taken it all away, had I earned it. Competitions and
game shows are a means of survival to many of the hundreds of
housewives whose husbands are unemployed. Keep them rolling.

**MARGOT MONTGOMERY, HOUSEWIFE,
EDINBURGH**

I'm constantly being told off by my family for flicking through the
channels . . . I found *Lucky Ladders*. To me shows like these are very
boring and trying. The worst one I ever watched is *The Price Is Right*. It's
so bad they could use it for the Chinese torture. When *Lucky Ladders* is
finished and the people go home with their polystyrene prizes I flick
through the channels again and can't find anything, so I go and get dressed.

**ZOË REDDING, AGED 13,
BIRMINGHAM**

Lucky Ladders is a game show that is cheap television at its worst, but
watchable. The host Lennie Bennett tries hard to bring it alive, but as it is
solely concerned with word association one does get bored with it.
Bennett also seems obsessed with trying to convince his audience that the
show is live, when it is obvious that it is recorded in batches . . .

**PHILLIP WELLSTED, RETIRED,
BISHOP AUCKLAND, CO. DURHAM**

I have a special interest in this programme as my wife and I were
contestants last year. We did quite well but the holiday shown did not
materialize. Contestants are given £100 for each rung of the 'ladder', to a
total of five times. I suppose it's cheap to make and doesn't tax the
brain . . .

**GEORGE GILLEN,
KILBARCHAN, RENFREWSHIRE**

NOTTINGHAM THE PLACE

Another audience show depending on the ability of researchers to find articulate people open to self-exposure, The Time . . . The Place, is thought of as ITV's answer to Kilroy! The ITV show, which has been running since the start of its day-time entertainment schedules in September 1987, takes advantage of the federation's regional structure. Thames is in overall command but all the companies take it in turns to put the programme together. This can lead to tensions and does so today, when the show is with Central at Nottingham.

Here is Steve Clark, Central's Nottingham-based news supremo, 'popping' down to Studio 6 at 9.30 a.m. to check up on The Time . . . The Place. 'Today's show is about credit and debit and I've an uneasy feeling about it. I've resisted the temptation to overrule the producer on a subject which I think is tired.' At 10 a.m. he watches in his office 'as avidly as the telephone allows' . . .

I don't like it. The show is bland, slow and repetitive. If I was watching at home I'd turn over or put the kettle on. After the show I ring my wife, a typical viewer and the best television critic I know. She confirms it. She thought the BBC's *Kilroy!* was better. I call a meeting of the six-strong production team for noon. We can and must do better . . .

They expect straight talk so I give it. I hated today's show and say why. Apparently it wasn't entirely the team's fault. Thames had suggested the theme. In future we will politely listen to their ideas, reject them if we have something better, and press on. I resent Southern pomposity which implies that London knows best . . .

STEVE CLARK, HEAD OF NEWS

The presenter is the experienced Mike Scott, a Granada luminary who made his name as the linkman of Cinema in the 1960s and graduated to hosting audience shows, and then producing current affairs. He was

'Why not fly with me?' Mike Scott, veteran Granada presenter, attempts to get *The Time . . . The Place* studio audience airborne on the subject of credit and debt

*appointed the company's programme controller in 1980. Now he is
content to be back where he started, greying and mellowed. His first
encounter today is with Martyn Clayden, the Central researcher who
obediently set up the 1 November show.*

Groaned into work at 7.30 a.m. to prepare for the audience onslaught.
Mike Scott appears at 8.10, trying to look sprightly, managing a
comradely smile. I discuss the on-air promo for 9.25, which involves me
relieving most of the offices of their credit cards (including an American
Express gold card, which I eye with interest). Today's topic is 'debt', and
all of the office agree that they could contribute to the discussion.

The shovelling of unhealthy fried food is interrupted by the arrival of
some of the studio audience, looking half alive, comatose. By 9 a.m. I am
starting to move the audience in, the Women's Institute group jostling the
pin-stripe businessmen, and a sort of nervous excitement ripples along the
corridor. Mike does his promotion at 9.25 and the audience relaxes as he
flourishes his collection of credit cards. We are on air at 10 a.m. My mind
drifts in and out of the discussion as I also keep an eye on the extra guests
in the hospitality room.

Just before 10.40 the production assistant is counting down to the end
titles and then all is finished. A flood of participants pours out of the
studio, earnestly discussing, grumbling, sorting coats, wishing they'd said
their speech differently. At 11.30 the last of the guests has disappeared
from the green room and we are filtering back to the office with thoughts
already turning to tomorrow's programme . . .

**MARTYN CLAYDEN,
SENIOR RESEARCHER**

*The distraction of the researcher was matched by at least one member
of the outside audience, simultaneously working at her
wordprocessor . . .*

The Time . . . The Place burbled away in the background, Mike Scott
efficiently marshalling opinion as usual. The public are poor dupes of just
about everything (credit cards today), and men in suits attempt to justify
their positions of power. Nothing too heavy, though, heaven forbid that
we should ever get to the crux of an issue. (The word 'capitalism' seems to
be taboo.) Marvellously cheap television, a visual version of radio phone-
ins, in which members of the public offer up subjective views in
opposition to each other, and nothing is resolved.

As usual, I find the programme depressing. What on earth is it supposed
to be doing – educating, informing, entertaining? It doesn't seem to do any
of these. And who decides on the topics anyway? Is this people's
television? Broadcasters make the heavyweight, in-depth analysis.
Ordinary people are used for anecdotes and cautionary tales. And the list
of such 'human interest' programmes grows daily. The airwaves are
buzzing with the hum of ordinary folk telling us the sort of tale I can hear
any morning in my local shop.

I try to imagine what it would be like if other forms of communication were like this: if newspapers were all chat; if the stages of our theatres were filled with 'ordinary' people shuffling on and recounting what happened when the double glazing went wrong, or they couldn't pay their electricity bill . . . If all novels were written by the bloke next door, if the cinema offered an endless round of the inconsequential and the everyday . . .
LILIE FERRARI, WRITER-RESEARCHER, LONDON N4

Not a topic dear to my heart, but I admire the way in which Mike Scott handles the heated debates and find myself, as usual, joining in vociferously. I can't afford phone-ins but, if I feel strongly enough, I have my say anyway, then write in. I wonder how you get on this programme? I often think this, real audience participation! . . .
CAROL RILEY, DISABLED FORMER TEACHER AND CLASSICAL DANCER TURNED WRITER, NEWQUAY, CORNWALL

SHOCKING PINK
A newer feature of the ITV weekday morning is Granada's This Morning, *a magazine stretching over ninety minutes and presented from the rejuvenated Albert Dock in Liverpool by Judy Finnigan and her husband Richard Madeley. The fixed and advertised slots today include ten minutes of knitting advice, and a further ten minutes about teaching babies and young children. Here is Susan Brookes, the programme's food researcher/presenter/reporter.*

It's hectic but fun, as we're crashing out an hour and a half live, each weekday for 40 weeks. I call it Anaglypta television, as it's cheap and cheerful and covers everything . . . Today I am in London to record a story about Marks & Spencer recipe dishes, at their Marble Arch store, which I had set up for transmission the following Monday.
The most memorable things about the day were the stunning cleanliness of the M & S kitchens, and how many jobs I seemed to be doing. Is this the television of the future? I was producing, directing, researching, presenting and production assistanting. One has to log the shots; it makes for quicker editing if you write down the time code as you go . . .
SUSAN BROOKES, RESEARCHER-PRESENTER

Back in Liverpool it is the job of telephonist Linda Townsend to sound the right notes when viewers answer the invitation to talk back to the programme.

This week the issue of tranquillizers and their effects, particularly withdrawal symptoms, are being featured. Although this isn't a phone-in subject people were phoning all morning, often telling of their own, harrowing experiences when they tried to come off the drugs. I find this part of the job can be quite depressing if you let it get to you . . . Today

was hard because, although you don't want to appear cold or rude, you're
not supposed to spend too much time with each caller, and this can at
times prove very difficult.

I also had quite a few phone calls today from people who just ring up to
comment on the show. Some people love it and are so nice when they ring
up to wish you all the best . . . Others, thankfully not that many today, are
quite rude about it and usually put the phone down before you can reply,
which is quite frustrating . . .

LINDA TOWNSEND, TELEPHONIST

> *On air that morning the centrepiece is an interview with antique
> romantic novelist Barbara Cartland. 'Lucky Richard' has had a 'special
> invitation' to visit the 88-year-old book producer and is filmed, forelock
> brushed for touching, arriving at her Hertfordshire manor in a hired
> Rolls-Royce. She is arranged in pink and pearls, clutching a white
> pekinese dog and dictating her 477th novel from a chaise-longue.*
>
> *'What people want today is love, real love, not what you get in those
> filthy books published these days,' she opines. 'Princess Di has changed
> the thinking of the world like the ancient Greeks did, women were
> looking like pseudo men until she came along to restore the idea of
> womanhood . . . AIDS is a punishment for the permissive society . . . I
> prefer the company of men to women . . . nowadays it is smart to be a
> virgin . . . I don't believe in death, there is no such thing . . .' And so on.
> Nothing else in the programme impressed diarists so much.*

Barbara Cartland jumps out and moans about old people sitting in front of
the television waiting to die. She obviously has no idea that no one is
sitting waiting to die today. They're too busy typing diaries. She talks to
the smiling, scared-stiff face of the interviewer Richard Madeley. He is
rarely seen. In fact he might very well have gone home between shots, so
completely does Barbara hypnotize the vision mixer.

**IVOR LEASK, AGED 21,
LERWICK, SHETLAND**

Barbara Cartland seen dictating the saccharine ending of her latest pulp,
dressed in violent pink, stretched on a sofa and smothered in a sheepskin
and several pekes. 'How many words?' she snapped at the poor little grey
stenographer. Not my scene. . .

**SYLVIA BATES, RETIRED TEACHER,
CALLINGTON, CORNWALL**

The programme threatens to bore with Barbara Cartland's views on
virginity. She must have a good memory . . . decide to switch off and get
on with the morning ablutions . . .

**BRIAN GARDINER, UNEMPLOYED,
DUNDEE**

The Queen of the Romantic Novelists . . . the interview was well worth

watching . . . She is a wonderful person to listen to and when she dies it
will take at least three or four other writers to fill the void . . .
**S. E. CHAPMAN, HOUSEWIFE,
LONDON SE18**

| *Others did not find the Cartland appearance so important.*

I am recording *The Woolstrand* to make absolutely sure I don't blink and
miss it. It is the only programme the whole day that I don't want to miss
and you can guarantee that Hannah will want her potty at 11.01 a.m. Why
are there so few programmes for women like me? Here I am, stuck at
home with a toddler, eight months pregnant and all I ask is for
programmes about embroidery, making soft toys, tapestry, dressmaking,
knitting by machine, patchwork and quilting, and seasonal crafts like
cracker-making, Christmas decorations etc. . . .
**MARJORIE WRIGHT, HOUSEWIFE,
WIGGINTON, YORKSHIRE**

This Morning featured items on knitting, pregnant women swimming and
a consumer test on fireworks, all swathed in the pink glow of 'coffee-
time' guest Barbara Cartland. Cleverly accessorized by pet peke, Miss
Cartland confessed a preference for male company and virgins. The ad
man's designer jumpsuits and gurgling babies, which permeated the
morning schedules, appeared almost real by comparison . . . My viewing
was fortunately interrupted by several trips to the local tip, with my
husband, to dispose of a load of rubble . . .
**JULIE DARE, CIVIL SERVANT,
BLACKPOOL**

VENERABLE RAINBOW

Thames's Rainbow, *for the very young, has been running since some of their parents were very young. It has achieved well over 1000 editions since 1972. Today the great attraction was Geoffrey Hayes 'making some very funny noises'.*

Rainbow is my 2½-year-old daughter's favourite programme. Personally I think Geoffrey is a bit condescending, but from a child's point of view he probably appears nice and friendly. There is always a good theme to the programme and plenty of variety. Bungle, Zippy and George are firm favourites with my daughter. She likes to dance to the song . . .

**GILLIAN SHAW, STAFF NURSE,
PRESTON, LANCASHIRE**

I missed my bus to art college today and so I am at home watching television. What a shame . . . *Rainbow* is now on and Geoffrey is making funny noises, and Bungle is wondering what Geoffrey is doing. I have always liked *Rainbow* ever since I was little, but now of course I don't take it seriously and find it very funny. I find George very hard to draw, the others are OK to sketch down but George and his big nose is a

Thames's *Rainbow* favourites, George (left), Bungle (centre), Zippy and Geoffrey Hayes tuck in under indulgent eyes

nightmare. My sixth-form friends draw the *Rainbow* gang during lessons, they are getting very good at it . . .

MICHAEL CHESTNUTT, STUDENT, IPSWICH, SUFFOLK

> *After Rainbow, at 12.30 p.m., ITV became what is technically known as a 'split network'. Each company was free to schedule for its own region. The result was a variety of Australian soap serials including* A Country Practice, The Young Doctors *and* The Sullivans. *Meanwhile Channel 4 had begun its 1 November transmissions at noon with* The Parliament Programme, *the daily ITN report of activities in the Commons and the Lords, and had followed this at 12.30 p.m. with* Business Daily, *the television equivalent of newspaper 'City' or money pages. The 100,000 who watched the political programme grew to 300,000 for the business magazine.*
>
> *The morning schedules also included the usual mix of television for schools. On BBC2 the sequence was called* Daytime on Two *and ran from 9.30 a.m. to 2.15 p.m. Channel 4's alternative* Schools *ran from 9.30 a.m. to noon. The use of these programmes was not confined to the classroom.*

I am on half-term holiday and saw the start of *Treffpunkt: Österreich* (BBC2). It was thoroughly boring and I only watched it because we went there on holiday. Only understood the word 'allo'. I gave it up after five minutes . . .

SUSAN PRICE, AGED 14, HULL

I was feeling ill again. All half-term I'd been at home with something or other rosea. I was sitting down scratching my spots, trying to decide what to do . . . I watched some schools programmes from 10 a.m. There was one for German students. It was about some children going rock climbing. It was interesting and very educational. I could understand most of it because I have learnt German for a year, and I learned some more by watching it . . .

HEATHER BUTTIVANT, AGED 12, NEWQUAY, CORNWALL

I did not go to school today because I had a bad cold. I watched BBC2 from 10.45 a.m. when *Investigating Science* was on. I did not see all of the programme about a telescope being launched into space, to see how far away the further stars are from Earth. I did see all of *Seeing Clearly?* This was about how far away and how near you could see things clearly. Some children also worked out how well you could see things that were either side of you when you are looking straight ahead.

At 11 a.m. I saw *Watch*, which was about working out which fabric is warmer to wear in winter . . . Then I watched *Wondermaths*, about two children stuck in a maze, and *Making History* . . . there were some photographs of the presenter at different years in his life . . . the theme was family history . . . I enjoyed all the programmes on this morning, I enjoyed *Seeing Clearly?* the most . . .

**KATHERINE ELY, AGED 10,
ELY, CAMBRIDGESHIRE**

I do not go to school. My Mum teaches me at home. My Mum lets me watch *Look and Read* on BBC2 programmes for schools. It is a good show. The story of *Badger Girl* tells us a lot of things about animals. Also it is about pony rustlers, they have a little bit of the story every week. I like watching television. I watch it with my family and my Mum and Dad help me to choose the right shows for children.

**SARAH-JAYNE O'NEILL, AGED 7,
SURBITON, SURREY**

I don't go to school, I am being taught at home by my Dad. In the morning I watch some of the schools programmes which I personally like because they are interesting and they treat me according to my age, unlike some of the so-called children's programmes . . . I'm not sure whether the expansion of our television will be a good or bad thing. I hope they will still show the schools programmes . . .

**NEILL HARVEY-SMITH, AGED 11,
BRAINTREE, ESSEX**

Morning appointment with some English teachers who complain that children's loss of interest in reading in third and fourth years is 'because of television'. The knee-jerk explanation? Television is more popular with ten- to twelve-year-olds, and they're the ones who use the library, I am also told. Don't bother to argue, but would like to see a course of logic offered to these nice people . . .

**MAIRE DAVIES,
LONDON E4**

A TEACHER'S STORY

I am 40, six foot one in height, white, weigh just over 13 stone, have a wife, a daughter and an incurable illness. I have Motor Neurone Disease so cannot walk or write, am unable to dress or feed myself and rarely leave the house. [He typed his diary with the aid of a head pointer.] Television is now an important part of my life, many of its images reminding me of recent normality.

This morning I watched two programmes for schools, *Seeing and Doing* (C4) and *How We Used to Live* (C4). I taught between 1967 and 1987 in Ruislip, Woolwich, Dagenham, Harefield, Eltham, Hartcliffe, Long Ashton and Nailsea. In all those places I sat with M1 or Class 6 or 'The Special Class', a lion tamer with a captive audience, and watched similar programmes.

I wasn't a brilliant teacher, and during the last few years I was neither as energetic nor as enthusiastic as I'd once been, but I made most children laugh and some children happy. I could choose a story or a poem which would encourage someone to imitate Sendak or Zimnik, Causley,

McGough, even me! I invented Leg Cricket for children who couldn't play cricket, and didn't like football, and I made up maths games for boys and girls who said they hated sums or couldn't learn their tables.

Now that my speech is a dribbled slur it's hard to recall how I controlled or cajoled every freckled Claire and Katie, pretty Jayne and Julie, naughty Wayne and Jason, knee-grazed Keith, mud-crazed David, quiet Ruth and round-eyed Ronnie, just Louis, Simon, Tim. Being anchored alone to record today's thoughts contrasts starkly with playground duty days shared with runners, stone-throwers, tale-tellers, skippers, swearers, sweet-sharers, hand-holders, coat-pullers, criers, shoelace-tiers, toy-takers, chasers, screamers, climbers and squealers, fighters and loners. Who'd have guessed I'd miss them so much?

During the afternoon I watched *Championship Bowls* and quiz programmes. When I was teaching I enjoyed organizing sports and quizzes but now I am no longer coach or question-master. I am the spectator who always makes the best move or supplies the right answer . . . I was watching bowls when my daughter Eleanor, four and three-quarters and escaped from school, burst through the door clutching a crayon drawing of me in her left hand and a nearly-eaten Cornetto in her right hand.

I was enjoying a close game, so she went upstairs to watch children's television and my wife set the video to record Eleanor's Tuesday favourites, *The Sooty Show* and *Count Duckula* (ITV). At about 6 p.m. Eleanor returned to my room, took a large pillow from the bed and arranged it on my reclining chair, so that she could cuddle up between my knees and watch the recording of the same programmes she had seen an hour earlier. Before next Tuesday we will have viewed this tape at least four more times, Eleanor enjoying each incident as if it was brand new.

As I am now unable to take my daughter to a park, a swimming pool or theatre, since I cannot play hide and seek or push her on a swing, read her stories or sing her songs, I treasure these moments spent together watching television. Ros fed me and Eleanor fell asleep near the end of *Count Duckula II* . . .

I viewed *The Mind Machine* (BBC2) with mixed emotions, marvelling at the intricacy and energy of the brain yet being constantly reminded of my dwindling neurone reserves . . . I had intended ending the day sitting up in bed watching bowls, but as my wife manoeuvred me from my wheelchair I slipped and fell to the floor. Ros was unable to lift me, so she telephoned for an ambulance and I lay there listening to the bowls and looking at the wall.

Soon after the game ended two ambulance men arrived. I was heaved on to the bed, 'goodnights' were exchanged, the television was switched off, plugs were pulled, lights dimmed . . .

STEPHEN PEGG, RETIRED TEACHER, CLEVEDON, AVON

SCREEN AT SCHOOL
Some 193 schools in all parts of Britain volunteered to participate in the

One Day exercise. The perils and distractions built into and around television-watching are often in the minds of these representative primary, junior and middle school pupils.

If we can't decide who watches what we have a huge SCRAP! But Dad does weight training and he always wins. If Dad isn't home and we have a fight, and I win, we get sent to bed by Mum so she can watch what she wants to watch.

MATTHEW COOPER, AGED 12, DURRINGTON MIDDLE SCHOOL, WORTHING, SUSSEX

I liked *PC Pinkerton*, a good man – he saved an old lady, and *Ratman*, but then I had to go to mosque . . . At school Class 5 went to the library to watch *Look and Read* but the video didn't record it. Our teacher kept looking for it, but she couldn't find it and we had to have *Zig Zag* . . .

AZEEM FAROOQUI, AGED 8

I saw *Fireman Sam* before I had to go to mosque . . . After karate I watched *A Question of Sport*, when they were picking the numbers. Then I had to go to bed.

ZAKARIA ISLAM, AGED 8

BOTH SIR JOHN CASS PRIMARY SCHOOL, CITY OF LONDON

My Mum doesn't watch television that much, but she's the boss when I'm watching. When there's something really good on, she comes and turns to a cowboy film. I absolutely hate cowboy films because they are always the same. She always tells me to turn the volume up or down, or change the channel, as though I was a slave. Even when I'm in another room she shouts, 'Lily, turn down the channel.' I think we need another television.

LILY MALER, AGED 11, NEW END PRIMARY SCHOOL, LONDON NW3

When me and my sisters are watching a programme and my Mum doesn't like it she makes us turn to the news . . . Tonight I missed the beginning

Classroom watch, better than sums

of *Colin's Sandwich* (BBC2) so I was asking questions. Everyone was going 'Shhh . . . shut up!' and I said 'No, you shut up!' And we started to argue and in the end they pushed me out to the living-room. So I watched in there and talked and asked questions to myself.

SEANA GAVIN, AGED 11½, NEW END PRIMARY SCHOOL, LONDON NW3

If there were no telly I would be bored to tears, I would go out of my mind, I would scream, I would go mad, very very mad. And I would go to my next door neighbour's house.

LYNDSEY FRANKLIN, AGED 10, ST GEORGE'S PRIMARY SCHOOL, BIRMINGHAM

When I watch television on my own I only laugh out loud if something is really funny, and I will only cry if it is really sad. If I am with my parents or my sister I will (instead of keeping them inside me) let my feelings show or make some smart remark. If watching television at a friend's house, or with friends anywhere, I will laugh out loud at the slightest possible thing.

EMILY GWATKIN, AGED 11, ASHFIELD PARK COUNTY PRIMARY SCHOOL, ROSS-ON-WYE, HEREFORD AND WORCESTER

We are a weird family because we do not like *Neighbours*, but we watch most other things . . .

DAVID BROOKS, AGED 11, MUCH MARCLE CHURCH OF ENGLAND PRIMARY SCHOOL, NR LEDBURY, HEREFORD AND WORCESTER

Me and my Dad argue in the living-room . . . he plays his drums and it gets on my nerves. I told him off because I was watching *Beauty and the Beast*, which is my favourite.

AMELIA EVANS, AGED 8, TAN LANE FIRST SCHOOL, STOURPORT, HEREFORD AND WORCESTER

I went out to feed the bullocks, the cows, the calves, the sheep, the dogs and the cats. I got into the house and just about saw *Neighbours* starting. My Mum and Bryn, my brother, were watching. Afterwards I went out with my binoculars to look at the stars. I was looking at the stars for an hour. When I got back I wanted to watch *Pobol y Cwm*, but Bryn would not let me because he wanted to watch something else . . .

RHYS EDMUNDS, AGED 10, CLOCAENOG PRIMARY SCHOOL, CLWYD

I can watch television when I am reading a book. When I hear gunfire I look up and see what's going on.

ADRIAN HAWKINS, AGED 10, GWERNIFOR JUNIOR SCHOOL, MISKIN, GLAMORGAN

My brother wanted to watch *Knowhow* (BBC1) and my sister wanted to watch *The Sooty Show* (ITV). This argument was sorted out when my sister cried and my Mam said it had to be *The Sooty Show* . . . I think television is very good and I don't think life would be very nice without television.

SALINA SARIF, AGED 11, HEATON MANOR SCHOOL, NEWCASTLE UPON TYNE

I am at my Gran's. I can't enjoy the programmes as much as I enjoy watching them at home. If I am at my Gran's everybody's talking and I can't hear the television . . . I have learnt from the television not to take drugs, because it can kill you in some cases. I have also learnt that drink can make you act stupid and make you do very foolish things.

GAYLE FAIRBROTHER, AGED 10, SPRINGFIELD PRIMARY SCHOOL, LINLITHGOW, LOTHIAN

The household I live in is quite a talkative one. They always talk or argue. My Dad is a farmer and my Mum works in the house but sometimes you would think she runs a taxi service . . .

ALAN TORMEY, AGED 12, KILKEEL HIGH SCHOOL, CO. DOWN

7 MOURNING HAS BROKEN

> *Having crossed to Ireland we will stay there as the starting-point of a morning tour round the broadcasting map. Brian Black, who presents the weekly* Counterpoint *for Ulster Television, has a fairly unenviable assignment as we join him on location at Enniskillen, Co. Fermanagh.*

Our programme concept was to capture the mood of the town and talk to a number of survivors one year on from the IRA bomb attack on the people who attended the Remembrance Day service in November 1987 . . . It was frustrating to wait for the mist to clear before picking up the GVs (background shots) that were needed to give atmosphere and presence to the story.

Ulster's Brian Black (left) . . . an assignment begun with misgiving

I began the assignment with some misgivings because any anniversary brings with it a spate of media interest and it was obvious that this issue was going to get more than its share. We had covered the immediate aftermath of the atrocity and my feelings were still quite raw from that experience, the needless waste of life, the carnage, the broken lives. So I had little appetite for an assignment that inevitably had to re-open wounds for those who had gone through so much . . .

I made a phone call to the chief executive of Fermanagh Council, Gerry Burns. 'You know,' he said, 'there's a lot of stress in this town. It's not just the people who were injured who are feeling the strain, it's their wives and families, the people who haven't been in the public eye but who are suffering in their own way.'

That started a new train of thought: surely this was an important dimension that should be explored. Every paper that week seemed to carry a story about the victims, television programmes were harping on with 'forgiveness' and 'How do you feel now?' themes. Here was a fresh angle that seemed to carry an importance for a wider section of the community.

There and then we changed tack. With the guidance of a local reporter I spoke to a number of survivors and people representing support groups. Their stories were riveting . . . They identified a number of reasons for stress over and above the immediate cause of their grief. One was media attention . . .

Another element then emerged. The victims had received the best possible medical treatment, and that meant not just the repair and care of broken bones, but expert medical counselling that allowed them to 'get it off their chests'. Not so with the people who had not actually been wounded, but who had shared the experience or who had perhaps been giving support to the victims.

It became clear they had been putting on a brave face, wearing courage on their sleeves in order to support the maimed and the bereaved. They too needed support and understanding and had a clear need to talk things through . . .

Current affairs programmes must reflect the changes in society and that means moving rapidly week by week from one issue to another. On this occasion, the suffering and quiet courage of the ordinary people whose lives were shaped by that terrible bomb have become deeply ingrained in me. I remember that programme well, I hope I always will.

BRIAN BLACK, PRESENTER

BEYOND THE GOLDEN TRIANGLE
In Glasgow the combative Gus Macdonald, Scottish Television's director of programmes, is already provoked by English attitudes at 7.30 a.m. 'Watch BBC Breakfast Time. Angered by posturing mock-irate treatment of Labour's Tony Blair by Jeremy Paxman. He then respectfully questions Tory Minister David Mellor, who browbeats him. Action please, John Birt.'

At the office Macdonald is checking the final script of Monarchy –the
Enchanted Glass, *a republican critique by Christopher Hitchens for
Channel 4. The IBA, unusually, have asked for a preview. He arranges
to hand over a script to David Glencross, at the religious broadcasting
consultation being held in Ulster next day.*

The IBA is also trying to resolve the scheduling clash of STV's *Taggart* on
ITV on New Year's Eve and our *Steamie* play on C4. Michael Grade
refuses to move, even at Lord Thomson's request. Although *Taggart*
normally plays post the 9 p.m. watershed I must now consider a 7.30 to
9 p.m. transmission. It is typical of C4's metropolitan insensitivity,
bordering on hostility for Scottish programming. Greg Dyke, London
Weekend programme director, says we should insist that the IBA make
Grade move.

My managing director (William Brown) is worried that a switch to New
Year's Day 1989 will take *Taggart* into the next financial year. 1988 has
not been good as advertising revenue has flowed to the golden triangle of
the English south-east . . .

**GUS MACDONALD,
DIRECTOR OF PROGRAMMES,
SCOTTISH TELEVISION**

HYMNS OF PRAISE

*Fiona Armstrong, admired ITN newscaster, is grateful that she has been
able to escape from London studios to enjoy some fresh northerly air
with Border Television. She is presenting* New Country, *a series about
countryside changes, and has to report to the Carlisle studios for
hairdressing and make-up at 7 a.m.*

Our crew sets off with a second one, from Yorkshire Television, filming
us. We're also being put in the time capsule, which is rather nice. In 20
years' time when I'm (probably) a housewife I'll see a programme about
television in the old days, and may see myself. We are making a feature
about the Mountain Goat Bus Company, a group of businessmen who've
developed a small firm of Lakeland minibuses. And the day is glorious.

We meet up with one or two passengers. Oh, and Ted, he's a former
bus-driver, now 73, who met his wife Iris on a Mountain Goat bus.
They're a delightful couple. 'Was it love at first sight?' I ask. 'Oh no,' says
a serious Iris, 'certainly not. I came to the Lakes for a holiday on the
Monday, met Ted on the Tuesday and fell in love on the Friday' . . . The
high spot of the day is a stop at the Brotherstown Inn: the mulled red wine
is delicious . . .

We get back on to the bus in excellent spirits and travel on to
Wordsworth's house at Grasmere for lunch, a packed lunch of rolls and
cheese. Then we film in the gardens. Oh, the scenery, the lakes, the
mountains and the history. This is where William and Dorothy read to
each other as the sun went down over the lake. We count ourselves very

lucky to have such wonderful jobs. Imagine getting paid for seeing this beautiful area.

We finish with a team photo. I see the result later, 22 of us to make a film. Don't let Margaret Thatcher see this. It'll confirm her worst fears about television being overmanned, and overpaid . . .

FIONA ARMSTRONG, NEWSCASTER

Meanwhile Tyne Tees director Barrie Crosier, and his crew, are also hymning the satisfactions of rural life somewhere in Weardale.

'O God, Our Help in Ages Past', with full orchestral accompaniment, booms out. Not in the usual studio setting, but on a river bank high in Weardale. Locals from nearby farmhouses are attracted like bees to honey, cameras in hand, as the voice of Sir Harry Secombe achieves full volume. It is 10 a.m. on a cold but clear morning and another *Highway*, ITV's networked religious series, is in full production.

We are recording to playback (music and voice already recorded on tape). Sir Harry's lip-sync is good so we have a take. On getting a clear from me, Sir Harry enters into long-distance Goon-like banter with the locals across the river, before moving on to the next location. It is to be a long and varied day covering a fair distance. We are recording this first hymn in three different locations to make the most of the wonderful Weardale views . . .

At Stanhope we have to record Sir Harry letting us into the secrets of a 250-million-year-old fossil tree. I worry that we will all become fossils, waiting for a break in the traffic to record clean sound . . . After lunch at the Bonnie Moor Hen (no, we do not have eggs) it is down to the river. No traffic problems here, just aircraft. Weardale is a test area for low-flying fighter jets. Thank you, God . . .

The road-show moves on to Escombe, with the oldest standing Saxon

Fiona Armstrong with Border Television: 'Don't let Margaret Thatcher see this photo. It'll confirm her worst fears about television being over-manned and over-paid'

church as its centrepiece. Will the branches on the churchyard tree have
been chopped down? If not, the use of the tulip crane for Sir Harry's
closing song will be severely restricted. I should have had faith in the Rev.
Nick Beddow. He has been as good as his word and one of his flock has
done the business. It is a night shoot, so there is a big lighting rig with
generator vehicles, crane and tracks. The locals must have thought we
were re-making *Ben Hur*, rather than Sir Harry singing 'When You Look
Back on Your Life' . . .
BARRIE CROSIER, DIRECTOR

*For Sir Harry himself the lip-sync to the recorded music was not so
easily achieved.*

About 10.30 a.m. we went a few hundred yards down the road to the river
at Wearhead, where we started to record the first part of 'O God, Our
Help in Ages Past'. I was chilly by this time and had difficulty getting my
lips to work in sync with the music track. Much good-humoured banter
from the crew, to which I responded with a couple of irreligious
raspberries, which undoubtedly helped to warm up the lips . . .
**SIR HARRY SECOMBE,
PRESENTER-INTERVIEWER-SINGER**

GRANADA DRAMAS
*Granada, serving Manchester, Merseyside and the rest of the English
North-West, is the most enduring of the ITV companies. It is the only
network programme contractor, surviving as such, which was in on the
mid-1950s beginnings of ITV. It rejoices in the title, once applied by an
American magazine, of 'best commercial television company in the
world'. Just now it is in a spot of bother over its solidly made peak-time
spy serial* Game, Set and Match. *Producer Brian Armstrong is worried.*

This morning was a vital one for certain decisions about my series *Game,
Set and Match*. This 13-part drama from the trilogy by Len Deighton has
returned very low ratings for the first five hours. Last night episode six
was shown, and we are all anxiously awaiting the overnight ratings in the
London area. These must show an increase in TVR from 13 to 18;
otherwise the London company Thames will move it to a later hour and
substitute repeats of *Minder*. If Thames do this, others (Anglia, TVS and
perhaps Central) will certainly follow suit.

I arrive at Granada studios at 9.20 a.m. Steve Hawes, commissioning
executive for drama, is very kind about the show and urges an aggressive
response. It is all very well, but we really should be getting better ratings;
one episode was comfortably beaten by *Panorama* (BBC1) on the green
pound! I ring Sue Read in our London marketing office as soon as
possible: something of the gloom is lifted when she reads out the figures
for each of the four 15-minute segments for last night's episode – 14, 15,
17, 17 plus. Whether this will satisfy Thames's concerns no one can yet be
sure.

Next I have to get in touch with Andrew Lowry of BBC Manchester's *Open Air*. I have to appear in the programme on 15 November; the subject to be the setting up of one of these huge programmes, and how designers have to re-create reality in unlikely locations, East Berlin in Bolton, Gdansk at Victoria railway station, the Iron Curtain in Cheshire, and so on. It's my belief that ordinary viewers always find the making of television fairly interesting, it promises to be a revealing ten minutes.

After a canteen lunch of 20 minutes I spend an hour with the promotions department trying to work out a campaign to increase viewers' awareness of *Game, Set and Match* . . . In the growing exodus of long-serving staff from Granada are two more colleagues, I learn this afternoon: Andy Stephen, cameraman on *Game, Set and Match*, and Lars MacFarlane, production manager. Both sad losses . . . Go to bed reflecting that there was a time when I relished every single day of working in television; not any longer, I fear.

BRIAN ARMSTRONG, EXECUTIVE PRODUCER

Creative tension: director Christopher Morahan (in cap and long hair) organizes a 1940s railway platform sequence for Granada's *The Heat of the Day*

Meanwhile other Granada shows must go on. Presently on location in Cheshire is The Heat of the Day, *adapted from Elizabeth Bowen's 1949*

novel. It is directed by Christopher Morahan, he who made The Jewel in
the Crown. *The cast includes Irish character actor David Kelly.*

Our coach leaves at 8 a.m. for our film location, Combermere Abbey,
Whitchurch. Bitterly cold morning with brilliant sunshine. Pass through
dreary town setting, on to smart suburban one, and out into countryside.
Snatch glimpses of pretty period villages, early morning mist making
Christmas card views. Reach the great house itself at 8.30 a.m.
Combermere is a happy mix of bewildered architectural thinking. It
stands beside a great lake amid rolling green plains. There are great oaks,
swans, sheep, large Constable cattle and I count 24 pheasants before I
alight from the coach.

First coffee, then into my costume. I play Donovan, the family retainer.
I have a comfortable warm caravan to sit in while I wait to do our scene.
We film Patricia Hodge arriving at the house in a horse-drawn side car. I
help her down and usher her into the house, followed by two maids and a
friendly hen. The sun stays with us and we shoot the scene from several
angles by 11.30 a.m.

Free to relax in caravan, and in fact am not used again today. Through
my little window I see the sun leaving us, leaves falling like snowflakes,
Peter O'Toole's daughter Pat playing with a little black dog across the
fields. Lasting images. Augurs well for the film . . . Back in the hotel at
7.30 p.m. I realize that at this moment I am appearing 'live' on Irish
television back home: in fact an interview I recorded last week to be fed
into a live tribute to my friend the author James Plunkett . . .

D A V I D   K E L L Y ,   A C T O R

Being recorded in the Granada studios is the 13-part Children's Ward, *a
daunting project involving many child characters and over 30 extras.
Child actors require chaperones, taxis, even schooling. It is not easy to
keep everything running to schedule.*

By the time tea break came around today I had never had the chance even
to get a coffee, let alone snatch a quick bite. It is part of my job to inform
everyone of where we are up to, and the time they have to be back from
tea, so that rehearsing and recording can begin again promptly. No tea
breaks for me.

Well, it's 2.05 p.m. and I've just been on the receiving end of a torrent
of abuse from the floor manager, due to a couple of artists not being back
from lunch on time. I have the unenviable, superhuman task of rounding
up 35 adults and children, all in various far-flung parts of the television
centre, and herding them together so that they are in the studio
simultaneously. This involves running round the canteen, chasing up and
down corridors, hassling (ever so tactfully) make-up artists, and shouting
in the gents' loo . . .

**M A R I E   C A T T E R A L L ,
P R O D U C T I O N   O F F I C E   A S S I S T A N T**

The studio is slightly fraught, we're behind schedule. The extras, mostly children, seem to be under my feet all day. However, they are very good when actually told to do something. That is except the two three-year-olds, who are useless without their mothers. Complete waste of time, I just wanted to send them home there and then . . .

At tea break time, 3.45 p.m., we were asked to do an hour's overtime. Or, should I say, some people were asked, I was not. I had to act on the rumour. I had a problem with my two-year-old daughter. My husband could not leave work early so I left the sweet-talking of his auntie, the baby-sitter, to him. I rushed back to the studio to round up the principals for the next scene.

By 4.30 the young children were getting very tired and the extras were asking, 'When do we finish?' I got a bit ratty when one of the kids ran into my legs for the umpteenth time that day with a wheelchair. I snapped at him and it seemed the studio went all quiet. I regretted it immediately but

Patients of Children's Ward: *a rare moment of calm in a Granada studio*

the tension and adrenalin had been mounting all day and it was just
something that snapped in my brain . . .

It was a wrap at 6.20 . . . I gave all the artists their calls for tomorrow,
thanked the extras for a good day. As I was rushing to catch the train, the
producer stopped me and asked me to make sure the chaperones with the
young extras made it to their taxis. I spent 20 minutes sorting that out,
missed my train, had half an hour to wait for the next which was 15
minutes late. Auntie and uncle still waiting to go home, daughter to be
undressed and played with. No alcohol in the house, starving, tense, but
exhilarated as I know I was good on continuity today . . .

**DAYLE EVANS,
ORGANIZER STAGE MANAGER**

The girls shared one dressing-room and the boys shared one. When I was
ready I found Robert and went to Make-up. A lady called Tracy plaited
my hair and she put ribbons in my hair, and she put some make-up on me
to make me look pale. Then me and Robert went to the studios and did
some lift scenes, then we did some ward scenes . . .

LEYLA NEJAD, AGED 9, ACTRESS

I woke up at 7 a.m. in Sasha's Hotel, Manchester Piccadilly. The taxi
collected us at 8.30 to go to Granada, where I did my school work until
10.30 . . . After Wardrobe and Make-up I went into the studios and
worked on and off until 1 p.m. After lunch I started work again at 2 p.m.
We had a 15-minute break at 3.45 and went on working until 6 p.m. . . . I
felt very happy about today's work and highly interested as it is only the
second time I have filmed anything . . .

KIM BURTON, AGED 13, ACTOR

What an exhausting day! My first recording day and it went so quickly.
One whole episode is now in the can . . . Oh, I wasn't ready for today. The
set, the cameras, the number of people behind the screen, each with their
own important job, took me a while to adjust to. By the end of the day I
had settled down a bit and my nerves were calmer . . .

We didn't talk much in the taxi on the way to Granada. Me and Kate are
usually gassing away, but this morning I think we had a few butterflies.
At 9 a.m. went up to the green room for our lessons (cup of tea and a chat)
with our friendly tutor Bernard. At 10.15 in Make-up to plonk on the
punky face I wear for my character. Kate found my hair-style very
amusing until she discovered that her mass of hair had to be back-combed
as well. Then it was my time to laugh. She looked like Worzel Gummidge.

On the set I met Rod, the producer. He didn't like my make-up and said
it looked too old for 'Keely'. He asked my opinion about my face, and I
felt awkward . . . as if I was betraying Karen, the make-up lady.
Eventually I told Rod that I wouldn't go out looking the way I did, so he
told me to go and change it. I asked Karen to put more colours on my
eyes, and with a bit of teamwork we got it right. Everyone, including Rod,
was much happier . . .

After lunch me and Tim 2 (there are two Tims in the cast) went to play catch in the day room. He is really good for a laugh. In fact I like all the cast, we are all getting on well with each other. Up to now. Back to the set at 2 p.m. and back to true discipline. There is a lot of hanging about while filming but there is no time for a quick daydream. You must know exactly what you are doing all the time.

I must stop gabbling my lines. I have been given about three notes on 'clarity' today. When Nick told me to slow down a bit I realized just how nervous I was. Then I pulled myself together and tried to correct the notes he had given me. I hope it looks OK. It's also really hard ignoring the cameras. It's difficult not making obvious moves to avoid 'eye contact' with the camera, or even walking into one. Janette Beverley plays Diane, the nurse, and she is very good at being natural in front of the cameras. I've been watching her and a few others today so I will learn. I hope before the last episode . . .

All these things, though, have made the day good fun and very exciting. I know I've enjoyed it because I didn't look at my watch once . . .

**JENNIFER LUCKRAFT,
AGED 16, ACTRESS**

WELSH INTEGRITY
Teliesyn CYF, a Cardiff independent production company, is making a biographical film for Channel 4 about the Welsh television journalist John Morgan, who was later to die of cancer. Helen Garrard, working on the film as an assistant editor, is this morning working with colleagues in a cutting room at Production House, Bristol.

John Morgan developed cancer three years ago. He decided with colleagues, and encouraged by his doctors, to investigate the emotional aspect of cancer suffering, in the light of having had it and having been cured. The filming took place over a year, during which his cancer returned. Obviously the relapse affected the filming, as he became ill and unable to complete the project in the way intended. The producer and director had to film interviews which Morgan had hoped to conduct himself.

We found ourselves with material that fell into two halves: the diary of the personal and immediate suffering of a man with progressing cancer, seen through the objectivizing eyes of a journalist well-versed in his craft; and the retrospective and subjective views of patients, relatives, doctors, nurses, therapists and other carers . . . We reluctantly decided that the two sets of material did not enhance one another and sat uncomfortably together. John Morgan agreed and by 1 November we had assembled his diary of events, and the thoughts and feelings the events provoked . . .

From 10 a.m. that day we were viewing the cutting copy on the editing machine and making finishing touches: trimming shots; adding black spacing to act as time gaps between thoughts and events. Thus bringing the programme down to the required length of 51 minutes 30 seconds for an hour slot on Channel 4. (An hour filled out with commercials.) The material we have been working with over the last six weeks has left us with an overall feeling of great sadness for John Morgan's experience, and has proved quite difficult to live with from day to day . . .

**HELEN J. GARRARD,
ASSISTANT FILM EDITOR**

PRIVATE PERIODS

Returning to London we alight first in bleak Acton, where various BBC departments are banished, and where actors, starry or otherwise, are required to rehearse. Present today is Nigel Hawthorne, renowned for his performances as Whitehall mandarin Sir Humphrey in the superior Yes, Minister *and* Yes, Prime Minister *sitcom series. This morning he is embarking on his third day rehearsing David Mamet's* The Shawl.

It is a three-handed stage play which Bill Bryden is directing for BBC Scotland. It is a very difficult piece to do, with two men, Karl Johnson and myself, who pose as mediums to con a wealthy and distressed lady, Brenda Blethyn, out of her fortune.

Shortly before 1 p.m. a BBC camera unit arrives with a Yorkshire Television producer. They are recording rehearsals throughout the building for *One Day in the Life of Television*. I explain that a rehearsal is of interest only to the actor and feel that it is a private working period to which the public should not be admitted. The public should see a production when it is finished, and not be subjected to the flounderings and other creative 'juices' provided by insecure people in the early stages of discovery.

Nevertheless we go ahead and bluff it out for the camera. And, surprisingly, I feel we have learnt quite a bit about the scene by the time the unit leaves and we return to our rehearsal.

Rehearsing is a very painful business. It can be exciting, too, but most of the enjoyment comes from the chemistry of the combination of actors and director. Fortunately, in this case, the chemistry works admirably. Bryden gives out energy all the time and provides a stimulating atmosphere for invention. The play will be filmed in the studio with video cameras. This means that Bill will not have to retire to a gallery, thereby losing all contact with his actors, but remain on the floor with us. A most welcome bit of news . . .

NIGEL HAWTHORNE, ACTOR

The persuasive Yorkshire Television producer Ian Rosenbloom tells how he saw the rehearsal chemistry.

Nigel Hawthorne feels that rehearsal is such a private process that he will have difficulty participating in the film. I explain in detail what I would like to achieve. He asks why is a Granada crew filming a BBC rehearsal. I tell him it is a BBC crew and I am from Yorkshire. He asks me if my father works for Anglia. I reply that my father is not alive and was not involved in television. He ponders and says that he is now willing to take part.

The content of what follows is fascinating. One of those awful technical points: both Hawthorne and director Bill Bryden keep removing and replacing their spectacles. For the sake of continuity, when the film is edited, I ask them both to put on and take off and fiddle with their spectacles several times. At least they know why they are doing it. The general public think it is *Candid Camera* when you ask this type of favour . . .

**IAN ROSENBLOOM,
SENIOR PRODUCER-DIRECTOR**

Brian Glover dressed overall as *Campion*'s man. 'If we pull it off it will be turkey for Christmas'

Actor Brian Glover is spared a camera looking into his rehearsal attitudes. The BBC has given him a day off.

I join Entertainment Express, providing cheap rail tickets for the industry, and buy my return to Liverpool at a cost of £18. It is a decent profit on the BBC expenses. The show I am in is *Campion*, eight hours of television this time, and, with luck, another eight next year. I'm not required at the Liverpool location until tomorrow. I suppose they're looking for another *Miss Marple*, they really are very similar. I hope they're right. If we do pull it off it will most certainly be turkey for Christmas . . .

To Peter Jones in Sloane Square to buy the word processor I had been ogling on Saturday. It costs me £600 but I have to have it if I'm to join the technological revolution. I think I do as André (Molyneux) has been on to me (again) about *Shamrocks*. If it ever gets made it will be a television film, the brainchild of David Tucker, that I was commissioned to write last year. Unfortunately we encountered a few censorship problems from the Beeb's legal eagle, Glen del Medico, and the going has been very slow . . . I arrive home with the PCW 6512, it's an Amstrad, and spend the rest of the day attempting to work out how it works. The instruction book is quite thick, and very daunting . . .

BRIAN GLOVER, ACTOR-WRITER

BRONZINO'S WARNING
Bamber Gascoigne, formerly in command of the long-running
University Challenge *and now a still further up-market quizmaster, is spending the morning at the National Gallery enjoying the research for the 1989 series of his BBC arts quiz* Connoisseur. *He recognizes that in creating this game he has made 'a quizmaster's nightmare'.*

Contestants are allowed to say anything they want about the origin or content of a painting, scoring points as they give correct answers. I have to be well prepared with an up-to-date list of everything they might correctly say. And 'up-to-date' is the snag.

My main subject this morning is a superb painting which happens also to be in the National Gallery. Painted in Florence in the 16th century, it is by Bronzino. Its subject-matter ensures that no one passing through that room fails to notice it. Most of the canvas is taken up by an intimate embrace, painted with icy realism, between an adolescent boy and his mother, both stark naked.

They are Cupid and Venus, which perhaps makes it more respectable, but beyond that simple identification the meaning of the painting has long been a matter of bewildered dispute. And it is a startling new theory that I am trying to track down this morning. It concerns a tormented figure, tearing his or her hair, who is just visible beyond Cupid's provocative buttocks. This figure has usually been interpreted as Jealousy, envious at the delights of love.

I now discover the new theory, by J. F. Conway, that this figure suffers from all the symptoms, as recognized by doctors in the 16th century, of the scourge that had recently swept through Europe, brought by sailors returning from the newly discovered America, the scourge of syphilis. If Conway is right, the moral of this painting becomes a very explicit and topical warning – that however delightful illicit sex may seem at the time, there is a most unpleasant sting in the tail. It becomes a Renaissance precursor of our own AIDS ads. And, you may say, just about as incomprehensible – remember the iceberg and the monumental mason?

. . . With a few more chinks in my *Connoisseur* armour for 1989 safely plugged, other work calls . . .

BAMBER GASCOIGNE, QUIZMASTER

> *There are no AIDS problems among the characters assembled for the latest spat of Spitting Image, the Central puppet lampoon, despite the incontinent abandon of their actions. Cameraman Roy Booker arrives in the studio as a grotesque version of Keith Floyd, enthroned on a public privy, is noisily relieving himself of excess food and drink.*

The production team is at least two weeks behind schedule, as usual. While we shoot the Floyd sketch we are surrounded by chaos. Scenes and props are setting the next sketch and lighting are trying to light. Some of the camera crew are trying to position reverse-scan monitors for the puppeteers. Workshop assistants are up to their necks in spare arms, legs, eyes, heads, glue and other spare parts. Wardrobe are dealing with a mountain of clothes, hats and shoes. Puppeteers not in the Floyd sketch are looking at scripts and refreshing memories as to what comes next. As the fold-back speakers gush the indelicate sounds of Floyd excretion a huge fish tank arrives and is filled . . .

After the tea-break we are in the bedroom set. The Fergie and Andy (Duke and Duchess of York) puppets are in bed. There is a ship's wheel at the foot of the bed; and a kangaroo at the head, complete with hat plus corks on strings and cans of lager stuffed in the pouch. The quilt cover depicts Sir Francis Drake's voyage from 1540 to 1596 . . . Just before lunch we finish the bedroom set and move on to a Russian 'glasnost' sketch which goes OTT (over the top) as Gorbachev tells of his sexual performances . . . The puppeteers have spent the last hour lying down on the job in bed together. Just a thought . . .

ROY BOOKER, CAMERAMAN

FACTS OF NATURE
London is the centre of the British television industry and broadcasters who have absorbing work in regional centres must sometimes come to the capital, if only to be frustrated. Up from BBC Bristol today is Peter Salmon, editor of Nature.

The real heart of the day was a meeting to determine whether a complicated yet adventurous evening of television would go ahead next year. The BBC2 Controller (Alan Yentob) likes my suggestion for a whole night's viewing on the environment – a pot-pourri of information, music, performance and fund-raising. At Arts for the Earth, a charity attached to Friends of the Earth, we knock the concept round. I weave between elation and misery as great ideas are aired, then dashed, then swept into corners.

You spend every meeting like this, wondering what's in it for all concerned. Like every good television idea, for me, it just seems to snowball. What was alive in a conversation becomes a programme proposal, becomes a meeting, becomes an event, becomes a programme.

Secretaries are trained to say, 'He's in a meeting'. Sometimes he really is. Here the BBC television management are whisked through the morning agenda by MD Paul Fox (fourth from left). On his left are controllers Jonathan Powell (BBC1 and bespectacled) and Alan Yentob (BBC2 and bearded)

Somewhere along the line people have traumas, there are crises and
collapses but everyone stumbles by.

Jonathan Porritt, director of Friends of the Earth, questions whether the
BBC is getting a whole evening's viewing for free. I try and rally the
Corporation's cause. Though it's a holding position, I feel uneasy selling a
case I can only half defend. Yes, we're giving the event air-time and staff
but isn't BBC2 getting all these performers free? How much does an
evening normally cost and why isn't it being made available? I'm sure the
normal offering of Saturday night repeats are really pretty cheap . . .

The only stimulus for all this is the thrill of tackling the unknown.
That's the continuing ultimate challenge. Each new project provides new
frontiers and new hurdles. I always have mixed views; why don't I just
keep my head down instead of opting for Ulcerville? My meeting lasts for
more than three hours. I stumble across London for a 125 and leave the
big city and the bright lights behind. Any optimism that today would
provide the answer to the question, can we pull off the 'big night', is
dashed. You are never quite convinced, the delight of success is always
one more meeting away, the disaster you feared has been warded off.

PETER SALMON, EDITOR

> *David Boulton, the Granada man in charge of both art and religion, is in*
> *London for a meeting of ITV's Education and Religion sub-committee,*
> *sifting programme proposals under the supposedly even-handed*
> *'flexipool' system.*

The flexipool sub-committee system, introduced earlier this year, has
been a disaster so far. Each company's representative has an impossible
brief: to get as much of his own company's product through the system as
possible, while retaining enough objectivity to back the best regardless of
source.

We know that the IBA, fortified by the Central Religious Advisory
Committee, has knocked back Greg Dyke's demand that religion be down-
graded on Sunday in favour of higher-rating entertainment. With the God-
slots safe for another year we agree to commission a new Sunday midday
religious magazine programme aimed at younger viewers.

Steve Morrison (Granada director of programmes, in the chair) and I
have agreed that Granada won't pitch for this. He thinks it is politically
desirable that we award it to one of the smaller regional companies. We
do pitch for a six-part series called *Borderlines*, a documentary serial in
which a group of modern pilgrims tour the Irish border in search of peace
projects.

There is fierce competition, about 50 proposals for nine slots, and we
are driven down to a three-part series subject to confirmation at the next
meeting. This after a bit of horse-trading with Scottish Television (I've
told them privately I'll back their next offering if they'll back this one) . . .
Most of the day's decisions, I'm afraid, are made on a geo-political rather
than a merit basis: not the best programmes but a carve-up. The meeting

runs from 11 a.m. until 4.30 p.m., through lunch, and afterwards I rush for the 5 p.m. Euston to Manchester train to speed me northwards . . .

DAVID BOULTON, COMMISSIONING EXECUTIVE, ARTS AND RELIGION, GRANADA TELEVISION

> *Yorkshire's personnel boss is in London for meetings to tell his company's 160 metropolitan employees of the company's plans to be slimmer and stronger in the face of impending challenge. There are two conferences at the Institute of Child Care, each attended by the YTV executive directors and about 80 staff people.*

The morning conference went well but the audience was far more subdued than those in Leeds which, bearing in mind that they were predominantly sales managers and staff, was unexpected. Maybe much of what I had to say about our personnel strategy was deemed by them to be only relevant in Leeds: a 10 per cent reduction in managers and staff by 1 July next year, improvements in working practices to reduce costs, a ban on external recruitment. (Not feasible in London as all sales offices have a high turnover.)

The afternoon conference follows much the same pattern. YTV sales of air-time are not going well currently and we are losing ITV revenue share. That is a feature of the North/South divide with advertisers attracted more to the affluent South. I drove back from London to Leeds, leaving at 6.30 p.m., and, as always, was delighted to leave London behind . . .

JOHN CALVERT, DIRECTOR OF PERSONNEL, YORKSHIRE TELEVISION

> *Among those in attendance is Barbara Hosking, the retired information head of the IBA, now advising YTV on matters political.*

I'm not too pleased to be going to the Yorkshire teach-in as I'm not staff. But I was told that everyone on the payroll must attend. It is very thorough. First a well-made video about the industry and its likely future. Then talks by each of the executive directors about their new, semi-autonomous departments. Rapt response from the London staff, broken during questions when John Fairley (Director of Programmes), standing at the back of a darkish room, failed to recognize one of his own staff . . .

BARBARA HOSKING, POLITICAL AND MEDIA CONSULTANT

> AROUND THE ROCK
> *Much in need of Hosking skills, the ability to win friends and influence people in unfriendly political places, is the Thames head of factual programmes and editor of* This Week, *Roger Bolton.*

Awoke with a black cloud above me. This particular black cloud has been there for rather a long time. It is the inquiry into *Death On The Rock*. It began in late September, is expected now to report in December [it actually reported in late January] and is unprecedented. I believe it to represent an extremely dangerous tendency developing in Britain today, the intimidation, by accident or design, of television journalism. However, as there is no 'smoking gun' they can't find one . . .

View an almost final cut of *Greyhound*, a network documentary scheduled for transmission in December. It's good. Try to tactfully make some suggestions. The hand has come out of the glove at an earlier viewing. Will these sorts of documentaries survive the White Paper? Will *This Week* survive? I am suspicious of some of the programme controllers!

Back to the office to meet producers of *This Week*, who are working on other projects, and offer advice. We are making a programme for nine days' time about the Protestants in Northern Ireland. The Sinn Fein ban will affect it. Another political hot potato.

Must keep my bosses, the IBA and Ulster Television, informed, as well as guide and protect the poor bloody infantry on the ground. My team is not that experienced in Northern Ireland affairs, although the researcher on the project is Irish. I have an awfully long memory, however, as I started making Irish programmes in 1970 . . . Lunch in the canteen at Thames. Try to smile and be confident as people make remarks like 'How are you?' in a tone that refers to *Death On The Rock* . . .

ROGER BOLTON, HEAD OF NETWORK FACTUAL PROGRAMMES, THAMES

Thames's Roger Bolton views 'an almost final cut' of a network documentary and tries 'to tactfully make some suggestions'

CLIENTS AND SPONSORS

Judy Franks, who administers the television business of the Leo Burnett Advertising agency, is the kind of person who matters more than programme directors like to admit.

I am not someone who potters around in the mornings, so I get washed, dressed, made up and straight to work on the Jubilee Line, reaching the office at 8.15 a.m. . . . Sent a letter to Frances de la Tour's agent, together with her cheque for a new commercial we have just produced. Today was the air date and therefore use fee was due . . . Equity don't seem to have received our cast lists for several commercials produced in the last few months. Another one for the post strike. Mind you, I would love to know where they get some of their information from. We would never have sent any details for *Olympics*, as the entire cast are babies. We assume they do not have to be Equity members . . .

Today's disaster. Yesterday was the first day of split copy transmission arrangement with TV-am. They transmitted the wrong copy. Not only that but it was seen by the client. Not only that but the client has decided he doesn't like it anyway and wants it taken off air completely. Numerous meetings now follow. What copy do we send to TV-am now, and will they be able to get it on air in time for the remaining spots booked? What to do about TV-am? What different copy can be run on TV-am, ITV and Channel 4 for the burst commencing on 7 November? What replacement copy should be substituted on the media plan for future bursts? Phone calls to recall copy from all stations already supplied. That way no one can make a mistake . . .

More discussions about more sightings of the TV-am incorrect commercial. Now someone's saying they saw it on London Weekend, or was it Thames? All 'sightings' are checked into . . . Order up electronic verification data especially urgently. This is the only way we are going to be 100 per cent positive about what actually happened. Things now getting silly. Client's wife says she has seen the commercial on air, but the date she says she saw it was before we even supplied it to the station . . .

**JUDY FRANKS, HEAD OF
TELEVISION ADMINISTRATION**

TOMORROW'S SPACES

Out to West London again, where one of the many problems being tackled by the BBC on this sunny November morning is the guest list for Tomorrow's World.

Arrive, after cold cycle ride from W2, to bad news. Central won't give permission for a *Spitting Image* puppet to appear on the *Tomorrow's World* Christmas show. The list of rejects grows longer by the day. Most celebrities we would like are either busy, out of the country or don't seem to realize what a tremendous boost to their career it would be. Joan Collins would have loved to have done it but is filming something called *Dynasty* . . .

Meet with Jane Aldous, who's now helping with the show. Her list of rejects is even longer than mine. Search through *Radio Times* for more stars to contact . . . We're trying to persuade the Palace that Prince Edward should do a turn on the show. Write memo explaining the format. It would be a great boost to his career. Find note from Richard Reisz (executive producer) hidden in desk debris that the eminent and fun scientist who was on last year's panel won't work on Sundays. Yet another rejection . . . Harry Enfield and Hale and Pace say 'No'. They seem to be in good company. David Bellamy says he'll be at the North Pole. In December? . . . At least we've got a warm-up person booked . . .

CYNTHIA PAGE, PRODUCER

| *Her presenter appears more optimistic.*

I discuss our Christmas programme and potential guests with members of the team; and my item on 'social cigarettes' with the producer of this week's programme. It is claimed that this cigarette does not produce smoke to harm others, or tar to harm the smoker. I am sceptical, and need to find out more about this weird-looking cigarette, which is now being test-marketed in America . . .

Uncelebrated warmth. The anonymous warm-up man, this one working for Thames, attempts to arouse the studio audience before the show begins

I find it much easier to remember my words, and deliver them with conviction, if I write them myself. For that reason I rarely fix other engagements for Tuesday: I am happier spending the day at my desk . . . Having written them I always read the words aloud. That is the best way, for me, of making sure that they work. People who see me doing this, and do not realize what job I do, often think I must be mad . . .

JUDITH HANN, PRESENTER

STATIONS ANCIENT AND MODERN
Enough of London for the moment. The morning tour that began in Ireland must now move on to its conclusion in the English South-West. Enjoying a day trip to the Devon and Exeter hills, robustly equipped with walking shoes and orotund grammar, is the IBA 'site finder'.

I visited the Pensylvania area of north Exeter where there is a known deficiency in terrestrial television services due to the local topography, and lack of signal penetration from existing stations. My mission was to locate a suitable site for a relay transmitting station . . . I was looking for high ground in the vicinity of the target area, but no higher than absolutely necessary, with easy access and an electricity supply within reasonable distance. It appeared that these conditions could be achieved at Stoke Hill . . .

I had a meeting with the Exeter City Planning Officer for informal consultations and was advised that a tall structure in this sensitive environment would undoubtedly cause concern, and that I would be expected to reduce any impact on the landscape by careful siting and use of background trees in the hope of best reconciling the technical and amenity aspects . . .

At approximately 12 noon I returned to the site area and made a number of local enquiries, to finally discover that the area of interest was part owned by Bovis, the national builders, and part owned by a local farmer, a Mr John Clark, whom I met at approximately 1 p.m. . . . Since Mr Clark's land appears promising technically and certain features of it provide more scope for blending in a site with the environment, I decided not to pursue the Bovis land, bearing in mind that a national builder only acquires land for building development, often on a long-term basis, in any event . . .

**J. S. P. BURTON,
SENIOR ESTATES OFFICER, IBA**

Meanwhile, armed with more informal usage, local architectural guru David Young was filming for Television South West at the city's cathedral.

'Lord, let the sun shine today on your beautiful Exeter Cathedral, we can't afford five grand to light it properly.' The first prayer of the day is answered as I open the bedroom curtains of my Axe Valley home, to be greeted by glorious sunshine . . . Having just completed an A to Z series of my favourite towns in the South-West, for TSW's *Today* programme, I am about to start a short series on West Country cathedrals and cathedral cities . . .

We arrive at the cathedral in good time. I am to start the day interviewing the Dean. His schedule is tight, he's only available between 10.15 and 10.30 a.m. 'You folk are never usually on time,' he remarks as I usher him towards the crew (John Graham, Ray Hendrickson and David Penny). The Dean is great, his concern regarding the maintenance of the fabric matches my own. We both feel quite strongly that entry money should be charged, as in France. Tourists are happy to pay quite enormous sums to enter our stately homes, surely a quid a head would not be asking too much . . .

A delightful, unplanned situation develops as an old lady, pushing an even older bicycle, festooned with plastic bags, is quite suddenly shrouded by pigeons and seagulls. Unconcerned, she scatters bread amongst them and the green Cathedral precinct becomes a living grey and white carpet, undulating around this ancient velocipede. John has captured it all, could be the highlight of my film . . .

DAVID YOUNG, PRESENTER AND WRITER

III
LUNCH TIMES

1 p.m. – 2 p.m.

The television is on all day from 7.30 a.m. until bedtime. During the day we find it is the only way to keep the dog occupied while we are at work. He used to chew the house fittings, now he leaves things alone . . .

**IAN VICTORY,
EDUCATION WELFARE OFFICER,
MILTON KEYNES, BUCKINGHAMSHIRE**

In the television industry, particularly that part of it which is in proximity to the West End of London, the news of who is having lunch with whom is a matter of great interest. Each executive assignation can be seen as some kind of political straw in the wind, even if the 'working lunch' is really no more than two old friends exchanging gossip. Or two new friends in the throes of a love affair.

FOOD FOR THOUGHT

Not every industry diarist was precise about where, and with whom, he or she had lunch on 1 November. Many did own up, one being the ITV Association's director of programme planning, Paul Bonner. He is a large and cultured man with a reputation for improvisation in organization. His 33-year broadcasting career has taken him from the BBC to become Channel 4's first programme controller. Now he has the harder task of being even-handed between companies much more concerned about their progress and survival than about the ITV system as a whole.

He has spent the morning at his office in Knighton House, London W1. On the walls is evidence of his accomplished interest in photography, but there is also a feeling of the temporary, of impending change. This morning he has listened to BBC Radio, read the Independent, run with his dog on Wimbledon Common, started writing a paper on programme guidelines to be adopted by the new Broadcasting Standards Council, consulted about ITVA's new computer system, telephoned about agreements reached during the ITV strategy conference at Turnberry the previous week, and about the joint ITV and Channel 4 film purchasing posse to descend on Los Angeles the following week.

Now it is time for lunch with Raymond Snoddy of the Financial Times. Thanks to the combination of a newspaper that knows how to use his enthusiasm and skill, and his own unrelenting hard work, Snoddy is regarded as the most effective print reporter of television politics now at work. Industry leaders tell him things and also learn from him.

Paul Bonner in his Channel 4 tie, which he has now cast aside to try and co-ordinate the ITV federation

I want to talk over his view of the possibilities for the White Paper and he will doubtless pump me for ITV concerns. It's the usual deal: off the record unless he declares an interest in publishing, and then I have to reconsider my words.

He starts by surprising me with the news that the White Paper may be published on 7 November. This is earlier than anyone expected; the Thursday was held to be more likely. There is a National Health Service demo planned for Monday. The Government could use the White Paper to keep that out of the headlines, Monday might be on I suppose. Ray is witty and revealing on industry gossip (and gets some from me) but nothing else is news . . .

**PAUL BONNER, DIRECTOR, PROGRAMME
PLANNING SECRETARIAT, ITVA**

Perused the papers to see what pronouncements Michael Grade had made about the future of the industry, or whether Paul Fox (Managing Director, BBC Television; recently Managing Director, Yorkshire Television) was telling us about the superiority of the BBC output over that of ITV . . . Had to sign far too many taxi and car vouchers currently being used on our productions . . . Walk to the Savoy Grill for lunch with James Kelly of IMG. Interested to see Raymond Snoddy hovering in the foyer, waiting for his lunch date. Goodness, it's Paul Bonner, singing for his lunch. No major demands are made on me, thank goodness. Walk back to Bedford Row via Kingsway and meet London Weekend producer Robert Randell in cheap suit shop. Either they don't pay well at LWT, or his alimony is stiffer than anticipated . . .

**VERNON LAWRENCE, CONTROLLER OF
ENTERTAINMENT, YORKSHIRE TELEVISION**

THE FOOD OF POLITICS
Melvyn Bragg has had a morning at home, working through scripts submitted for London Weekend's The South Bank Show. *Now he is wearing his hat as Deputy Chairman of Border, his local ITV company.*

Lunch at Locketts with Chairman and three senior executives of Border to talk to all the MPs in our area about our view on the imminent White Paper. They are an impressive bunch, very bright but only patchily informed. It is difficult to get over the argument that Channel 4's financial separation from ITV would kybosh the five smaller regional companies. It is also difficult to spell out that a quality regional service is expensive, and well worth having and paying for. There is a lot of misplaced suspicion that we are afraid of losing the monopoly . . . A wonderful Manuel-type waiter threatens to ruin the entire (separate room) rather posh lunch, with his clattering and chuntering. It is difficult not to collapse in mild hysterics at times . . .

**MELVYN BRAGG,
DEPUTY CHAIRMAN, BORDER**

Preparing for visit to New York to cover the United States elections . . .
Lunch with Peter Brooke MP, Conservative party chairman, and New
York producer Sue Tinson . . .

**SIR ALASTAIR BURNET,
ASSOCIATE EDITOR, NEWS AT TEN**

CUTTING CHOPS AND BAD BACKS

*The London Weekend Director of Programmes, Greg Dyke, is the guest
of Independent Broadcasting Authority Director of Television, David
Glencross.*

Lunch at the IBA with David Glencross. A convivial discussion about the
forthcoming White Paper. We talk about where the IBA and ITV
companies got things wrong. I argue that the IBA's obsession with
minority programmes had led to ITV turning away from popular
programmes. The result was an enormous increase in the price of
advertising and pressure from advertisers on Government for change. We
both agreed we were witnessing the end of an era . . .

**GREG DYKE,
DIRECTOR OF PROGRAMMES, LWT**

Elsewhere there is fraternization between the IBA and the BBC.

Lunch at Aquaviva with Peter Rogers, IBA director of finance. Aquaviva
is a Charlotte Street hostelry full of advertising agency and Channel 4
people. It's always vital (not to mention good value) and cheers me up . . .
Peter speculates about the new chairman of the IBA, post-White Paper,
when Lord Thomson retires. He has heard that Jeffrey Sterling is back in
the frame. The prolonged uncertainty is bad for his colleagues at the IBA.
Peter would like to be sure of the shape of the future and then get on with
it. He doesn't share the gloom of some in the ITV system . . . I have been
working with Chris Irwin on performance statistics to help the BBC
monitor programme costs and deployment of resources. I pump Peter for
some information that will help me make comparisons with ITV. He
fences elegantly . . .

**PATRICIA HODGSON, HEAD OF THE
POLICY AND PLANNING UNIT, BBC**

*There is even a kind of fraternization between the BBC and the
Government.*

Agreed with Paul Fox that he should ring Peter Weil to tell him that we
had appointed him Topical Features head at yesterday's board, and ring
John Morrell to offer him the deputy head post. I would then ring the
unsuccessful candidates . . .

    To lunch at Clarke's with Professor Brian Griffiths, head of Mrs
Thatcher's policy unit and her adviser on broadcasting. The White Paper,
due next Monday, he said, would set ITV franchises at ten years and they
would be renewable. This was new to me. No other surprises. The BBC

should not feel required to chase the ratings. I told him why we must reach a wide audience.

I asked Brian what were the next important issues he was looking at. Top of his personal list, he said, was homelessness. I said that one of our producers, Louise Panton, had just made one film on the subject and was now making one about the young homeless. He was keen to hear what she had discovered and I said I would ask Louise to ring him, which I later did . . .

**WILL WYATT, HEAD OF FEATURES
AND DOCUMENTARY GROUP, BBC**

> *While her presenter, Murray Sayle, escapes for table talk with the BBC
> Deputy Director-General, John Birt, producer Victoria Wegg-Prosser has
> a more difficult time.*

Murray Sayle has lunch with John Birt, an old friend of his, at L'Escargot. (Food to photograph, not to eat.) Gossip from the lunch included Birt's real concern about the impending strike of journalists, over the censorship of terrorist spokespeople in Northern Ireland, and his plans to open up an office in Japan. He would stay with Murray when setting this up in Tokyo . . .

The new production assistant had to start the standards conversion of *The March of Time* tapes without me. Assuming all was well I left to deposit New York representative Neal Hornstein with series director James Barker for lunch. Disastrously and for the first time ever, a master tape was wiped and I am faced with repeat telecine costs and a real sense of embarrassment . . . Important appointment with osteopath at 1.20 p.m. Three years ago I fell out of my roof store of videotapes and since then have needed treatment at least once a month. It's a real help as usual . . .

**VICTORIA WEGG-PROSSER, PRODUCER-
DIRECTOR, FLASHBACK TELEVISION**

Lunch with Martin Sorrell, chairman of WPP, which includes J. Walter Thompson, to brief him on the importance of BSB to the advertising industry . . . Afterwards medical treatment for a bad back . . .

**A. SIMONDS-GOODING, CHIEF EXECUTIVE,
BRITISH SATELLITE BROADCASTING**

> FALLEN FRIENDS
> *There is no such thing as a free lunch, it is said, but sometimes the
> debts being paid off are entirely human.*

Drive to St John's Wood to take Derrick Amoore to lunch. He was my first editor (on *24 Hours*) when I came to London in the late 1960s, and we started *Nationwide* together. Then he hit bad times and ended up as manager of Radio London. Earlier this year I had to tell him that early retirement was to be his fate, following the new plan for Greater London Radio, not easy.

Yet he is still the best of company and it is such a waste that his talents are not any longer being used properly. We talk of former colleagues and the state of the BBC now. Derrick is very cynical of the new-style BBC and I get the uncomfortable feeling that he, and many of his friends, have been the inevitable victims of some of the changes. The place is a lot more efficient but a great deal less fun . . .

KEITH CLEMENT, HEAD OF BROADCASTING, SOUTH AND EAST REGION, BBC

> *Distinguished drama director Roy Battersby has also had a rough ride at the BBC, at one time black-listed for his leftish political affiliations. Now he is back, making Richard Langridge's* The Act, *a 75-minute studio drama, and reflecting that 'we all still work here for the lowest wages in the industry because it's committed to excellence.'*

Lunch at Television Centre canteen with W. Stephen Gilbert, writer, producer, critic . . . Talk about his meeting with Mark Shivas (head of drama group) that morning and Steve's desire to produce again; about a Les Smith script called *Bodycount* which Steve and I have tried to get made, as a 50-minute Vietnam-set film; and about my growing conviction that we shall have to do cottage film-making with friends if we're to make anything difficult in the coming period.

Steve and I did *King of the Ghetto* together for BBC2 in 1985–6; written by Farrukh Dhondy and all shot in the Bengali community round Brick Lane. It was the first single-camera video, all-location serial (four parts) and my first job at the BBC in 11 years. Stephen invited me to do it at short notice when a previous director left the project. Black-listed himself since 1979, for fighting to make an Ian McEwan script requiring a penis in a jar on a mantelpiece, he came under great pressure not to hire me. He stood firm, with Jonathan Powell's support . . .

ROY BATTERSBY, DIRECTOR

> WINE AND WOMEN
> *Edward Mirzoeff, editor of the BBC2* 40 Minutes *documentary strand, had a good film but a difficult lunch on his hands.*

A viewing has been arranged of a forthcoming film of ours, *Greenfinches*, about the women of the Ulster Defence Regiment. The top brass of the Ministry of Defence is turning up, to check that there are no breaches of security. Anyway, that's what the agreement says. The Director of Public Affairs for the Army, a forceful Brigadier, and his deputy eventually arrive rather late and without the third member of their party, the man from Northern Ireland, who has been fogbound in Belfast. I and my producer (Stephen Lambert) give them some quite good wine, a little BBC finger-food, and settle down to watch the cassette . . .

40 minutes later . . . The men from the Ministry have been making minute notes on what appears to be pieces of cigarette paper. Rather a lot of notes. It begins to seem ominous. They make a few small points; we

had expected these to come up, as the film had been checked out this morning by the Editor of News and Current Affairs, Northern Ireland, and he pointed out a couple of very minor security risks. Of course we agreed to these obvious changes.

And then the thunderbolt, which we had also, partly, suspected. One of the women in the film makes what could be seen as quite a strong point about why Protestants join the UDR. Or at least how some people in Northern Ireland perceive this. 'I'm not prepared to live with that,' says the Brigadier. But surely this isn't a question of security? 'Yes it is, the IRA will use it as propaganda.' But surely it is one person's personal point of view, and anyway she's just wondering if other people don't think this. 'It doesn't matter, she's not allowed a point of view, it must be cut out.' I suggest that this is an editorial matter. The discussion becomes heated.

Will Wyatt, my head of department, arrives late on; he hasn't seen the film yet, but is shown the relevant bit. He's quite supportive. The Brigadier becomes more insistent. A classic case of who, ultimately, has editorial control. We leave it unresolved, promising to think about it overnight. I think it would be wrong to give in under pressure. The Brigadier leaves, threatening escalation 'all the way'. How firmly will the BBC stand? We shall see in the next few days.

**EDWARD MIRZOEFF,
EDITOR, 40 MINUTES**

Edward Mirzoeff of *40 Minutes* (far left), defending the line against the Ministry of Defence

Virginia Nicholson is working on a documentary series, shot in a variety of locations around the world, about the extent of Christian mission work. 'I am rather critical of the series as a whole, as I think there isn't enough thought going into what we are really trying to say

*through the subject matter; but for me it is an interesting project to
work on . . .' A morning spent telephoning missionary groups in Japan
leaves her reflecting on the world she lives in and its contrast with the
world of evangelical Christians. 'What does our society really believe in
and how much value do we place on belief? In the world of television,
very little. Cynicism prevails. Perhaps we denigrate idealists too glibly.'*

*She is also six months pregnant and 'there seems to be a ripple effect
in Kensington House at the moment, though perhaps that is just
solipsism of a rather specialized kind on my part. Three ladies at this
end of the corridor alone, and at least three or four others in the
department.'*

Lunchtime is time for the pregnant mothers' convention. Three of us
decide to walk down Shepherd's Bush Road for lunch at a bistro where we
can talk uninterruptedly and without inhibitions about analgesia, cervical
contractions and partner participation in Childbirth Trust classes. The
third member of our group is due to give birth in the New Year; she is
beginning to get pretty tired, and a month away filming in Russia and
Italy for *Timewatch* has taken its toll. Now, at the cutting room stage, she
wishes she could stop but has four weeks' editing still to go.

Sue is plotting whether to take on a demanding film in the New Year
involving late night fly-on-the-wall filming in inner-city Glasgow next
February. She will be five to six months pregnant. I advise against it, but
she says she would rather take on something new and exciting than sit
around getting bored, which in any case wouldn't be fair on the BBC who
are her employers. She has a point.

VIRGINIA NICHOLSON, RESEARCHER

CURRY AND CHATS
*Farrukh Dhondy, multi-cultural guru of Channel 4, is thinking about a
new chat show for the Asian community.*

To lunch at Gaylord with Bheroze Ghandy and Rosie Thomas. We are
discussing a late night chat show. We are trying to get the format right
before I consider commissioning it. They are full of ideas. I suggest the
show ought to tell the British public what Asians discuss, and cause
conversation that would not happen without the assistance of television.
We come up with the idea of doing a pilot programme on homosexuality
in the Asian community. I outline the steps they should take towards my
commissioning it. Neither of them have produced a programme before . . .

**FARRUKH DHONDY,
COMMISSIONING EDITOR,
CHANNEL 4**

*More nebulous is the meeting of writer John Bowen and Anglia drama
people Graeme McDonald and Brenda Reid.*

Lunch in Soho with Graeme and Brenda, both old friends. I had wanted to talk about ideas for the future, theirs and mine, but really this was a 'Let's give John a good lunch because we haven't anything for him' occasion. So we talked about the future of television instead. Also flexipool, the system by which the ITV heads of drama, each with an allocation of drama hours mainly taken up with staples, chaffer and shift alliances in an attempt to get a few extra hours for what they really want to do. Towards the end of the lunch I do talk about an idea for a film which has been nagging away at the back of my mind for nine months now, and Brenda says warily that she will brood over it . . .

JOHN BOWEN, WRITER

Robin Carr, London Weekend comedy producer, has rebelled against the gathering of 200-foot cranes disfiguring the London skyline as seen from his office window, as well as the pile of unfunny, unsolicited scripts on his desk. Instead he spends the morning at the Brixton rehearsal rooms, working on the Christmas edition of The Two of Us. *Here actor Nick Lyndhurst apologizes for being ten minutes late and explains that he has been 'geezered'. His word for the many strangers who approach him with: ''Ere, aren't you that geezer . . . ?'*

Nick Lyndhurst, 'Sorry I'm late guv, but I was geezered'

Nick and I go to lunch with two writers, Paul Minett and Brian Leveson. They have written a comedy pilot for Nick, which he will make next March–April. It's a great script and everyone is very enthusiastic about it. It's Paul and Brian's first sitcom although they've spent years writing the bulk of Russ Abbott's material.

Nick hasn't met either of them so it's important for me to see some sort of rapport begin to exist between writers and star. Too often the writer is treated as a second-class citizen and, being a writer myself, I naturally refuse to let this happen on any shows for which I have responsibility. I worry needlessly. Within minutes they're old friends swapping jokes. Nick tells one about Simon the Fence Builder which causes Paul to choke on his chicken. They decide it's too rude to include in the script. It takes me longer to decide not to include it in my diary . . .

ROBIN CARR, PRODUCER-DIRECTOR

SLIMMING COURSES
Michael Morris, the Independent Television News personnel person, has spent the morning in the boardroom of the Guardian under the chairmanship of editor Peter Preston. With other members of something called the Core Committee of the International Press Institute, they have been discussing the Government gag on Sinn Fein. Afterwards:

Find my way to L'Amico in Horseferry Road where I meet ACTT shop steward Larry Dyer and shop chairman David Randles. They are a tough and professional team and let nothing past them. However, we have good personal relations. Occasions like this are vital to avoid misunderstandings at a time of rapid change.

They have asked for this lunch to find out what I learned on my recent tour of local television stations in the USA. The message is not an easy one: Americans make television with far fewer people than we do. Larry and David are also concerned about plans for the Grays Inn Road building. We agree that the most efficient technology must be installed and that we must continue to work together to ensure a smooth transition without compulsory redundancy. They ask for the earliest possible involvement in our thinking and I agree. I slip them a copy of the report I wrote on my return from America. The key is redeployment, training and the absolute minimum of new recruitment.

Larry has to dash back to the House of Lords for prayers. He is a cameraman there. David and I linger on for a few minutes to discuss the layout of the new building. He has strong views on how the input side should be configured. At 2.30 p.m. I leap into a taxi for the journey back. The bill for three at L'Amico comes to £80.10 and, in terms of clearing the ground for the future, it's money well spent . . .

**MICHAEL MORRIS,
DIRECTOR OF PERSONNEL AND
INDUSTRIAL RELATIONS, ITN**

We break for lunch. Elliot (my replay colleague), Jim (an editor) and I go to an Italian restaurant which has been recommended. As we begin eating we see three other ITN people, two union officials and a senior manager, eating together. They all look fairly amicable so things must be OK. We briefly discuss ITN staff who are taking up jobs at Sky, and those we wish were . . .

TIM BOURNE, TRANSMISSION POOL OPERATOR

> FOOD OF LOVE
> *Some supplement, or substitute, their eating with sounds more or less musical.*

My lunch break as usual was spent locked away in a sound-proofed voice-over booth. This is one way I escape from the 'hustle and bustle'. You may wonder why. I practise my saxophone regularly at work. Long shifts such as those worked at ITN can restrict hobbies, etc. So, with a bit of effort, I ensure some outside interests, my main one being music . . .

JO TURNER, CAMERA OPERATOR-STILLSTORE OPERATOR

Two BBC Information Division staff are getting married on 4 November: Gary Double, publicity officer for television sport and events, and April Hodson, assistant to the news and current affairs publicity team. This is their last day at work before the big day. Colleagues gather in my office at 1 p.m. to toast their health (in Australian Chardonnay or Perrier) and present gifts and a card. They're an attractive and popular couple. Much joy all round. Informal photographs. I play a brief snatch of the Wedding March on the trombone. It echoes round the Television Centre courtyard . . .

KEITH SAMUEL, HEAD OF TELEVISION PUBLICITY, BBC

> THE WAY TO THE STARS
> *Charles Denton was an accomplished ATV documentary-maker before he became Central's programme controller. Margaret Matheson won recognition as an up-market BBC play producer before taking charge of Central's drama output. Now they have both spun off into the Zenith group, a production cluster which, by dictionary definition, takes its name from 'the point on the celestial sphere vertically above the observer's head'. They hope that their product is not above viewers' heads, however little can be made of the mysterious initials hovering about.*
>
> *Before the morning board meetings Denton was asking himself why September had not been more profitable.*

Run through the current Zenith debtor schedule, assessing which (if any) debtors might be in real trouble, and which playing the delaying game. Not an academic study, as current debtors total more than £10 million . . .

(At lunchtime) opened a bottle with SL, RH and MN. Discussed the possibility of taking on XYZ as a senior producer to get us into the non-game show entertainment area. Agreed RH would make the approach. Sandwich! Agreed with Margaret Matheson that Zen North should (when appropriate) contribute its production fee to budgets, where doing so makes the production happen, providing we are not fooling ourselves. Zen North will clearly need to take risk deficit positions to build volume, but is growing well . . .

**CHARLES DENTON,
CHIEF EXECUTIVE, ZENITH**

> *Also concerned about profits and losses is the chief executive of the Cable Authority.*

Embarrassment! Men from the Inland Revenue arrive to collect PAYE, which they say has not been paid. In the absence of our accountant and secretary I see them, and am able to find a cheque stub indicating payment. The variety of a small organization . . .

Lunch at a City stockbrokers. I have had plenty of grillings over City lunch-tables about the prospects for cable. They have tended to become more friendly. But there are still misconceptions that have to be put right, and some scepticism not easily removed. Very different from my American visitors, but still enjoyable and stimulating . . .

**JON DAVEY, DIRECTOR-GENERAL,
CABLE AUTHORITY**

> *Tony Currie, his programme controller, bravely offers himself up to a BBC Scotland radio discussion about the future of television.*

Early lunch with the producer of the BBC World Service's brand new media programme. We discuss the progress of cable and speculate on White Paper proposals. Then off to Broadcasting House for 1.30 p.m. and the Jimmy Mack Show. BBC Scotland's head of television is on first, but I can't hear him as they 'forgot' to book a line from Glasgow to London. By the time it's connected I'm on. Jimmy asks a few questions, I try to cover the interesting points. By 2 p.m. it's over and I'm on the way back to the office . . .

**TONY CURRIE, CONTROLLER OF
PROGRAMMES, CABLE AUTHORITY**

> *Roma Felstein, planning women's programmes for British Satellite Broadcasting, has been attempting to persuade programme boss John Gau, and others, that large chunks of the output should be transmitted live.*

John has his own ideas and is not convinced . . . I argue my point, trying, probably in vain, to win him over. John has many years' more experience than I do in the television industry and thus it is hard to push one's ideologies, even harder when one is a woman in a very male-dominated industry. However, we are making programmes for women and it is very important that for once women decide what women want to watch, and when they want to watch it . . .

At lunch-time I indulge in a walk through Harrods Food Hall. I used to smoke cigarettes when I was anxious. Now I eat Harrods chocolate chunk cookies. Instead of lung cancer I will probably die of chocoholism . . .

**ROMA FELSTEIN,
CONTROLLER WOMEN'S DAYTIME, BSB**

NARNIA'S BEEF

Outside London the choice of eating places is more limited. If you are a make-up assistant on location in the Forest of Dean, on the go since 5.30 a.m. in the cause of the Narnia Chronicles (a BBC Sunday tea-time serial adapted from C. S. Lewis), almost any food would be welcome in theory, hard to deal with in practice.

At last lunch. It's been a long and busy morning and breakfast seems a long time ago. We all trundle over the planks which mark the route back to base, most of them embedded in the mud due to the heavy traffic of crew and artists. Lunch for us is always an indigestion-making rushed affair because we have a make-up check to do on all the artists.

The dwarves' beards and moustaches have to be re-stuck as, more often than not, they are removed for lunch. False facial hair is very fragile. It doesn't remain stuck too well when the wearer is munching his way through a three-course meal of soup, roast beef, Yorkshire pudding and sherry trifle. Mr and Mrs Beaver are not allowed to remove their prosthetic (foam latex) snouts, so they drink through straws and have restricted their eating down to a fine art. It's that or starve . . .

PETRONA WINTON, MAKE-UP ASSISTANT

Down in Plymouth, local presenter Rene Wyndham has had a busy morning researching for her community programmes.

Lunch with Glyn Worsnip to discuss a series on cancer that I am helping with. He says he almost envies the patients who have more certain knowledge of their death. What depresses him is the uncertainty of the slow degeneration of his speech and mobility caused by his incurable illness, cerebellar ataxia . . .

RENE WYNDHAM, PRESENTER-REPORTER

At Norwich lunch is a nervy meal for three young people competing for a job as an Anglia announcer. Before being tested in the studio they are looked after by presentation head Granville Jenkins.

I meet the announcer candidates in reception. I take them to the restaurant, where I buy them lunch and brief them on what will be happening during the afternoon. We auditioned three male candidates yesterday and today we have two female and one male. One of the females is nothing like the photograph sent with the application but she does seem to have a good voice. The other female is currently working for BBC Radio Cambridge and seems promising.

The male candidate lacks any real personality as we talk, and even at this stage I feel convinced he will not be suitable. I'm aware that at least two of yesterday's candidates were very good and at this stage I reckon we will have three worth Steve West, Philip Garner, Jim Wilson and myself considering . . .

**GRANVILLE JENKINS,
HEAD OF PRESENTATION,
ANGLIA TELEVISION**

Producer Sally Doganis and researcher Sacha Baveystock have caught the 8 a.m. from Euston in the hope of persuading the Greater Manchester Constabulary to be filmed by the BBC. The two are duly impressed by the Rape Referral Centre, the force's showpiece, and endeavour to turn the scepticism which greets their plans.

After the introductory chat we go down to lunch, and the point of the meeting, a request for access to film police operations. Our hosts air doubts about the filming of victims and investigation details. Sally does some fast talking. We discuss the possible parameters we should work within, and the question of editorial control. By the time the Assistant Chief Constable leaves we are quite hopeful of access. We dine in the bigwigs' dining-room – soup, salad and cherry crumble. Sadly Chief Constable Anderton's table is empty today . . .

SACHA BAVEYSTOCK, RESEARCHER

In Newcastle upon Tyne the local BBC Television boss has a relatively calm morning at the 'Pink Palace', so called because it is 'built of steel sheets coloured with a subtle shade of pink'. He has had meetings about the impending Gateshead Garden Festival, and children's programmes. Just before lunch:

I am picked up by a septuagenarian Rotarian and driven, terrified, to a Rotary lunch in Gateshead. I talk about the White Paper, the changes we expect in broadcasting and our plans for the Pink Palace. They seem impressed . . .

**MIKE READ, HEAD OF TELEVISION,
BBC NEWCASTLE**

CHIPS WITH EVERYTHING
Most had less serious business this lunch-time.

All the Channel 4 secretaries were called to a meeting and had a very pleasant surprise, that we were going to get a salary increase. Afterwards, in my lunch hour, I picked up some holiday brochures from the travel agent and then bought some chips . . .

VERNA JAFFE, ACQUISITIONS SECRETARY

Meeting with David J., chemistry lecturer at Open University . . . Lunch with him always fun. We analyse the fate of a producer colleague who has just had a nervous breakdown, and another who recently died.

DR DAVID JACKSON, PRODUCER, OPEN UNIVERSITY

Lunch-time provides a quick dash into Cardiff for a birthday present for my daughter, two days hence. Recognition from people who recognize you from 'off the box' is commonplace, but for once a really odd one. A middle-aged lady says I'm Alan Brown and wants to know why I changed my name to Rustad. She refuses to believe me, says she watches every night and knows I'm Alan Brown who used to go to Cathays High School. I apologize profusely – why, for God's sake? – and explain that I'm of Norwegian descent, born and brought up in the Home Counties . . .

ALAN RUSTAD, JOURNALIST-PRESENTER, HTV WALES

The path of true lunch never runs smooth. On the way to local hostelry hub-cap of hire car falls off at traffic lights, passenger in back seat says she doesn't mind rising damp but she is slightly anxious about the pool of water in the back of the car. I know it's called the 'well' of the car, but really . . .

NICOLA HUTCHINSON, ASSISTANT PRODUCER, BBC, RESEARCHING IN SUFFOLK

When life looks like the back of a bus: Thames toilers eat right on to the end of the road

Lunch in the canteen with a colleague who's just come back from China. Our canteen is divided into two: the push-a-tray department which costs about a quid; and the restaurant, where you sit at tables covered with

hideous pink, white or grey paper tablecloths with matching paper napkins, and are served by very nice waitresses. 'What's the fish like today?' you ask. 'It doesn't look very nice', they reply. We are very rude about our canteen food, but really it's very good compared with British Rail . . .

KATE KNOWLES, ASSOCIATE PRODUCER, THAMES TELEVISION

Went to lunch. Couldn't decide between the steak pie and the macaroni, so had both. Shared a table with Marie, Sharon and Gail –very pleasant. Julie joined us later. Discussed the play we saw in the theatre last night, *The Relapse* by Sir John Vanbrugh . . .

ANTHONY LANGTON, TECHNICAL SUPERVISOR, GRAMPIAN TELEVISION

Invasion of the canteen by *Grange Hill* cast so did not linger. It was not all bad news, though, because I renewed acquaintance with an OB cameraman whom I'd first met on Ben Nevis, during an outside broadcast of an ice climb . . .

IRENE HAHN, RESEARCHER, BBC ELSTREE

Lunch with the secretary to the producer of *Casualty*. Go to the tea bar for diesel oil coffee and rubber sandwiches . . .

ASMAA PIRZADA, PERSONAL SECRETARY, BBC TELEVISION CENTRE

Russell, a fairly new member of the office who has the most extraordinary cheeks, resembling those of a well-fed hamster, arrives . . . Shortly after this we all trundle down to the canteen for lunch. Signs of the Hallowe'en Lunch of the day before lurking in the pudding section – dyed green custard and dyed red apple pie . . . The canteen is pretty good really, we all moan about it but then I guess we're expected to . . .

TERESA WATTS, PRODUCTION SECRETARY, BBC BRISTOL

We open the restaurant at 12 noon and immediately we have a queue. We feed 1500 people in the building, and most of them descend on us at 1 p.m. We are really busy today with a programme called *Umbrella*, and the orchestra are in. 45 kids charge in from *Umbrella*. They have every permutation of food with chips. Chips and gravy, chips and egg, chips and sausage or just chips. It doesn't seem to matter what nationality they are, chips are universal . . .

LIZ THOMPSON, CATERING MANAGER, BBC MANCHESTER

FOOD FOR WORRY
Lunch is also a time when the insecure look for reassurance about work in progress and future prospects.

Lunch in the canteen with Jane, Karen and Robin M. We get on to alternative medicine, again. It's certainly popular at lunch-times. But can I make a programme about it which people will understand? It's very hard to explain what I'm getting at. A moment's panic. I've not done the right research. I've missed things . . .

**HILARY HENSON, PRODUCER,
BBC LONDON**

Prepared a memo to the executive producer expressing my willingness to review my six-month contract. I'm hoping it will be extended to a year, though the insecurity has become part of life. None of my friends outside the industry can believe the precarious state of my position. And so to lunch in the BBC Club bar . . .

**SUSAN WESTERN, RESEARCHER,
BBC NATURAL HISTORY UNIT, BRISTOL**

Over lunch in the canteen, there were the usual rounds of tea at the film unit table and discussion of problems facing us as staff. BBC Wales is planning to lose 113 posts (including 30 per cent of film unit, though it has vacancies). There is also the possibility that we will lose our 'irregular hour working' allowance, which is worth 15 per cent. Add to this worries about independent producers and the future of public service broadcasting, and you have a fairly disgruntled bunch of people . . .

**PHIL CROXALL, ASSISTANT
FILM EDITOR, BBC WALES**

Chips with everything:
Umbrella participants
enjoy the delicacies of a
BBC Manchester canteen

ABOUT 15 MINUTES

Paul Fox, managing director of BBC Television, is not a presence easily missed. Yet even as an elder statesman of the industry he moves about it with leaps as private as they are prodigious. In 1973, when he was a notably combative and effective BBC1 controller, aged 47 and due for promotion, it was unthinkable that he would turn up next day as Yorkshire Television's director of programmes. In early 1988, when his influence in the system far exceeded his position as YTV managing director, aged 62 and heading towards retirement, it was beyond the bounds that he should suddenly return to West London, in command of BBC Television.

After a career in sport, news and current affairs, which began with the early 1950s stirrings of BBC Television, Fox is enjoying his return to 'the cornerstone of British broadcasting'. He somehow looks too big for his present office and furnishings, his style is at once resolute and guarded, his emotions near the surface, his loyalty to those close to him absolute.

This morning he has kept to his usual pattern. He has glimpsed the BBC's Breakfast Time before leaving home in Hertfordshire. By the time he is installed in his office he has flicked through the Guardian and the Daily Mail, The Times and Today, and has heard some of Radio 4's Today in the car which met his train at Cricklewood. From his desk he is faced by a battery of four monitors, silently flickering out the pictures of the four terrestrial channels.

Nothing keeps his attention for long. At the end of the day he notes in his diary: 'Total viewing during the day, about 15 minutes'. On the other hand he is constantly on the look-out for News, old habits do not die. 'After various meetings, back in office and see BBC1 out of the corner of an eye . . . Watch One O'Clock News, also ITN News at One, nothing fresh. Why do newsreaders do political interviews?' he asks himself before disappearing to lunch.

SMALL EARTHQUAKES

Doubtless unaware of this implied criticism from on high, One O'Clock News editor Mike Broadbent has been planning this edition, off and on, since the previous Thursday. Today it became clear that the Chancellor's Autumn Statement was likely to be the main story.

The biggest problem, as often at lunch-time, was how best to anticipate the Parliamentary stories which would happen after the *One* was off the air. Long experience shows there are few ways over this problem, so I settled for a preview by our business editor, plus political interviews . . .

In the office by 7.20 a.m. for the first row of the day; an increasingly common dispute about whether big Parliamentary occasions such as the Autumn Statement are the province of the political or specialist correspondents. In this case I won with my original allocation of Daniel Jefferies (business editor) to the Chancellor and Mike Baker (political correspondent) to the eye and teeth test charges . . .

With my deputy at 9.45, composed the running order for the *One*, putting it into the computer system so it can be called up throughout the building. We allocate estimated timings for each story, which are constantly up-dated as more information comes in, so we always have a rough idea of our likely overall length (normally between 26 minutes 30 seconds and 28 minutes). This is known colloquially as the 'fool's tot' . . .

The first hiccup at 10 a.m. The cameraman due to cover the Cabinet arrivals at No. 10 reports that *he* arrived too late. After a brief exchange of views he is ordered to stay put and, on pain of something awful, *not* to miss their departure. These are boring pictures, but the only coverage available to illustrate important decisions on our two main stories.

Then the man who runs our small film unit reported, rather late in the day, that he was offering a film on witchcraft – worries about children becoming involved in the occult. Warning bells always ring about this type of subject, especially in day-time news programmes, but I do recognize that it is a subject we should not ignore, so I put it on the running order, pending viewing. When I did view it, I felt it fell between two stools; it is an important subject but had to be sanitized before it could be transmitted, losing much of the effect. I felt it was more a subject for a *40 Minutes* film or an Esther Rantzen *Childwatch* special. I dropped it . . .

Discussed the stories to be headlined with the presenter Phil Hayton and the studio director . . . Recorded a good interview with Sir William Clark (chairman of the Tory back-bench finance committee), which I decided to give a little more time than intended; then a not so good one with Alan Beith (Democrat finance spokesman), worth only one minute, which also suited the political fairness we try to achieve . . .

At 12.50 p.m. everything was going so unusually smoothly that I had time to fiddle with the wording of one of the headlines when my computer terminal jammed. As I tried to fix it, I discovered that other terminals were going down one after the other. A big problem as, so close to programme time, there isn't time to bring in emergency procedures (typewriters); many scripts were locked in the computer, which also automatically transfers them to the Autoscript from which the presenter actually reads.

One of our three computer banks had gone down, but frantic work by our computer experts managed to release the Autoscript so that we could actually get on air, and other facilities gradually came back on stream. The only on-screen effect was a split-second blank screen after the final headline film. Apart from that, few problems on air . . . As expected, Gordon Brown (Labour finance spokesman) overran his time, but I dropped only a couple of minor foreign stories to come in on time.

While on air, I try to keep one eye and one ear on ITN's *News at One*. Today they astonished me by leading with the committal of a man charged in Belfast with murder at the funeral of the three IRA terrorists shot in Gibraltar. He was in court only six minutes and no evidence was offered. It seemed more evidence that the editor (an old BBC colleague,

Andrew Tilley) is trying to overcome the 2–1 audience ratings in the BBC's favour by unexpected lead stories . . .

Home after 5 p.m. . . . Watch a video re-run of the *One* to get the overall feel and catch up on the parts I missed on air through distractions in the gallery. The interviews worked well, rather less boring than I had feared. Similarly with the extended interview with the Master of the Rolls. After that, relaxed with *Neighbours*; I know it is rubbish, but undemanding rubbish and just what I need to unwind . . .

MIKE BROADBENT, EDITOR

WAITING FOR MRS MANGEL

The figures confirm Mike Broadbent's claim about the audience for his One O'Clock News as against ITN's News at One. On 1 November the ratio was 4.5 million to 2.2 million, the first segment of the day where BBC1 has a lead over ITV. This is probably not so much a judgement on the two news programmes as on what follows them. The ITV companies schedule old cinema films and hold their audience steady at 2.2 million. The BBC places the first of its two daily showings of Neighbours, *the cult soap of the moment, watched this afternoon by 6.3 million.*

Try to ignore the *One O'Clock News*, I don't want to hear about rising interest rates and new charges for eye and dental checks, which have been free until now. But I am a glutton for punishment so I watch . . .

**H. MORTON, HOUSEWIFE,
NEWCASTLE UPON TYNE**

Nigel Lawson was due to make his autumn budget statement this afternoon but 12 minutes of guesses and predictions are not NEWS so it really should not have been the first item. In contrast the South African Government's banning of a newspaper was given 30 seconds. The item on failed appeals to the Lords was succinctly submitted by Lord Donaldson, a pleasure to listen to. As for the Scottish teachers' strike, heaven preserve us from 'Anglicization'. There must be a phrase that would save us from that tongue-twister . . .

**MARJORIE DANKS, HOUSEWIFE,
WALSALL, WEST MIDLANDS**

What a consistently boring programme the News is, on all sides. All sides seem to focus on politics, foreign news and finance. Very rarely do they show happy or good news, people are interested in the happy things that go on . . .

**GLENDA SPRATLING, HOUSEWIFE,
SITTINGBOURNE, KENT**

Charming Philip Hayton couldn't lessen the despair that this half-hour of gloom and doom induces. Anyone looking at our news programmes in 50 years' time could be forgiven for being surprised that the entire human

race had not committed suicide at our total lack of anything uplifting . . .
**MISS R. E. TAYLOR, RETIRED,
DULVERTON, SOMERSET**

Most of the News was spent trying to explain to my talkative 2½-year-old
son, Richard, why Philip Hayton was reading and not Michael Buerk.
Richard first assumes that Buerk must be on holiday and then decides he
must be reading the IMPORTANT News later on . . . It is hard to explain
to a 2½-year-old about the world's conflicts, today illustrated by a car
bomb in Israel. Sometimes I wonder if I should let my children see the
more violent and horrifying items . . .
**CHRISTINE STONE, HOUSEWIFE,
SHEPTON MALLET, SOMERSET**

Where does this blind fascination with money markets come from? There
seems to be an established wisdom that what is good for bankers,
stockbrokers, commodity dealers etc. is necessarily good for the rest of us.
But is this really true? If our news reporters suddenly decided that what
was good for, say, trade unions, was also good for everyone else, then I
am sure there would be uproar in the corridors of power . . .
**SIMON BRACEGIRDLE, UNEMPLOYED
GRADUATE, ABERYSTWYTH**

Found myself mentally switching off when there was yet another item
about Ronald Reagan. Coverage of USA affairs is excessive even allowing
for the so-called 'special relationship'. I would appreciate more coverage
of, and comparisons with, other countries, especially in Europe . . . Glad
my student son was not here watching. His dogmatic comments on
various BBC pronouncements are not conducive to good digestion. Hastily
leap to switch off before *Neighbours*, which none of the family can
stand . . .
**LAURIE HALL, HOUSEWIFE,
HITCHIN, HERTFORDSHIRE**

Set is activated for the *One O'Clock News*. My wife seems to enjoy it,
even thinks it is important, whereas I let the *déjà vu* pass by whilst we
consume a snack . . . Bill Giles told us about the weather. It left me cold.
Because I think my wife likes it, and she thinks I do, we watch
Neighbours. Like smoking, it's a silly addiction . . .
**JOHN C. HACKETT,
CHARTERED ACCOUNTANT,
KIDDERMINSTER, WORCESTERSHIRE**

In the television soap area, it appears, craze serials flare and fade, and durable *Coronation Street* glows on forever. During one tedious summer, before which somebody or other shot JR, plastic *Dallas* was all the rage. When they were new the nation, or the nation's young, enjoyed a brief honeymoon with the abrasive *EastEnders*.

By 1988 the cult for bland *Neighbours* had swollen to craze proportions, the show transmitted on BBC1 each weekday lunch-time and repeated in the early evening. 'Yes, you've guessed it, and I know it's a silly habit, but I am a fan of . . . well . . . *Neighbours*', apologized mothers. 'We all go to the common-room for a good laugh', claimed students. 'I have to record it for my daughter', explained fathers. Others, from schoolgirls to grannies, teenagers of all ages and sexes, unashamedly relished the daily dose of clean and comforting suburban sentiment.

Untroubled by social issues, the classless families of Ramsay Street, a secluded Melbourne cul-de-sac, are subject to nothing worse than the occasional misunderstanding, quickly eased and as painless as a pinprick received under anaesthetic. The unfailing sunshine, the well-tanned poolside bodies and complexions, the smooth-running mod cons, the familiarity of the language and attitudes, make for an escape to a glossy brochure that is at once homely and yet fetchingly distant.

The Grundy Organisation's original *Neighbours* opened on Australia's Channel 7 in 1985, and flopped. It was converted and lightened for Channel 10 and then arrived on BBC screens in October 1986. In early 1988, after ace scheduler Michael Grade had moved the repeat from 10 a.m. next day to 5.35 p.m. the same day, it won its place in the British Top Ten. The cost to the BBC was £27,000 a week, compared to £40,000 for a single episode of *EastEnders*.

Among the fathers who indulged their daughters on 1 November was entertainer Roy Castle.

Worked on rockery, helped by my son Daniel, clearing columbine roots. Heavy-duty digging, moving stones, lifting bulbs (daffs, narcissuses, bluebells and crocuses) and replacing. At 1 p.m. caught up with the news (again) and *Neighbours*, in order to tell my daughter what was happening in Ramsay Street . . .

ROY CASTLE, ENTERTAINER

Madge Mitchell minces Mrs Mangel, or was it the other way round? All I know is that with 16 million others I am hooked on *Neighbours*. I even say 'G'day', and expressions like 'What a wombat' have crept into my vocabulary . . . Voices floated back to me this morning in the street from two fashionably jean-clad teenagers: 'Are they going to get engaged, Jane and Mike?' At church on Sunday the sermon was all about neighbourliness. The priest had no trouble illustrating his theme from the serial. As a French teacher, I use it too. Exercises on the future tense are a doddle when the question is: 'What will Mrs Mangel do next?'

Everyone watches, young and old alike. Everyone is portrayed. Nellie Mangel invited Harold to the church dance today and neither could be considered spring chooks. Young Lucy loses her mice and Helen gives Scott advice on budgeting. Daphne, expecting a baby, is not too well as she manages the coffee shop. Willingly or not, happily or not, these people are part of a community which makes up its differences and where no one is lonely . . .

**JOSEPHINE MAY, TEACHER,
HENLEY-ON-THAMES, OXFORDSHIRE**

Best time of the day, at least on the box. Yes, you've guessed it, I'm a *Neighbours* fan. I'm not ashamed to say I'm hooked. I know it's a lot of nonsense, but it's good clean entertainment and it doesn't make you depressed like *EastEnders* . . .

**ELAINE HINDLE, HOUSEWIFE,
PAISLEY, STRATHCLYDE**

It's 1.30 p.m., yes, you've guessed it, on goes *Neighbours*. My husband likes to watch it but doesn't like to let on that he likes it . . . It's got the old formula of *Crossroads* when it was brilliant, the sets move, people

Finger wags: Mrs Mangel and Harold discuss a point of diet in the 1 November episode of *Neighbours*

have silly things to say, even Lucy has trained her eyes to move while her head is still . . . Yes, OK, I'm a fan, but don't tell anyone . . .

**MARY SCOTT, HOUSEWIFE,
KENLEY, SURREY**

Like all soaps it's highly addictive but has the bonus of showing what appears to be a very pleasant lifestyle in Australia. I already find myself using Aussie expressions like 'shot through' and 'galah' . . . It is nice to be able to exchange television gossip with relations living in Tassy (Tasmania) . . .

**ROSALYN ROBERTSON, HOUSEWIFE
AND PLAYGROUP LEADER, BRISTOL**

As an Australian I am deeply embarrassed by *Neighbours*, it seems to be acted by kitchen staff . . .

**MISS F. E. ROWE, RETIRED,
LONDON WC1**

I find *Neighbours* light-hearted and pleasant, the Australians are so classless . . .

**RACHEL MINSHALL,
RETIRED SCHOOLTEACHER AGED 81,
MOUNTAIN ASH, GLAMORGAN**

I watched with my mother. It was a conciliatory, coming together gesture after we had had an argument. Asking me to join her was an oblique apology on her part . . .

**SARAH TURNER, UNEMPLOYED,
ALDENHAM, HERTFORDSHIRE**

Lots of babies love the theme tune. 'They' say it's because before they were born their Mums used to watch it and they could hear it inside the womb . . .

**MRS B. MARCHANT, HOUSEWIFE,
BROMLEY, KENT**

Has to be the best soap on British television at present. Even my son Richard, who is only nine months old, loves it. He stands in front of the television and dances, and kisses the screen, when the title music plays . . .

**TRACEY COLEMAN, HOUSEWIFE,
RYDE, ISLE OF WIGHT**

Half the hospital ward gather round the television set, something's going to happen. Aghhh! *Neighbours*. That theme music with its sickly-sweet nuances, how safe, how bourgeois. Oh Lord, how they love it. They can't wait to find out who's fighting with who, who's going out with who, and, ah, I see, the bottom line, who's sleeping with who. That's what they really want to know. Or do they? . . .

**MR S. SHARMA, CIVIL SERVANT,
WORCESTER**

I have three friends who phone for details if they've had to miss an episode. I'm glad to see that Mike has had his hair cut and I wish Scott would get one . . .

**JOHN HALL, ANTIQUE DEALER,
LONDON SW6**

I do enjoy *Neighbours*. Daphne used to be my favourite character but now I much prefer Madge Mitchell, I love her 50-fags-a-day voice. A lot of students watch. When it started our Students' Union bar lost so much money at lunch-time, with people going home to watch, that they installed a television screen . . .

**CAROLINE DAVIS, STUDENT,
STOKE-ON-TRENT, STAFFORDSHIRE**

We went to the students' union in Cardiff for lunch. In the canteen they have television sets which are turned on for two 25-minute periods a day so that everyone can watch *Neighbours*. As we entered the canteen the theme tune started, and the students' eyes turned to the screen as automatically as Pavlov's dogs used to salivate. There was no way either of us could have sat through lunch with 'that programme' within earshot. Normally, I have lunch earlier so the problem doesn't occur. Today, though, we had to buy lunch somewhere else . . .

**MARK CHILDS, STUDENT,
CARDIFF**

Today at St Edward's School in Oxford the first programme that I watched was *Neighbours*. Virtually the whole of our house (Tilly's) comes to watch. It is my favourite programme and I wish that on Sundays the BBC would show a run-through of all the week's episodes. To watch *Neighbours* I miss lunch each day to get a decent seat in the television room. I think it's worth it . . .

**JUSTIN DELAP, AGED 14,
OXFORD BOARDER**

On my return from a lecture at Queen Mary College, where I am a student, I switched on *Neighbours*. I was a devotee long before it gained the massive popularity it now enjoys. Back in its cult days many of my fellow students would dash back to my place at lunch-time, as I lived the nearest. Now it has become so popular I feel less inclined to watch it.

Having spent last year living in France, I have lost touch with exactly who is who, who is married to who, etc., although I was sent regular bulletins by friends during the year. One friend in particular used to keep me up to date by sending audio tape recordings of selected episodes to prevent me from going 'cold turkey'. Moreover, old loyalties die hard, and I still watch it.

In any case, I have to report the day's events to my flatmate, when she gets back from work. She is an absolute hard-core addict. She even phoned sick on the day of Scott's wedding, so she could watch it. It was at

this point that we decided to go to DER and rent a video . . .
**WILLIAM ROBERTS, STUDENT,
LONDON E2**

Neighbours was completely fabulous, as usual. I am deprived of it in the
day, being in that centre of academic excellence that is school. Naturally,
I am able to watch it at 5.35 p.m., but Mum, being the nice person that she
is, records it at lunch-time just in case the bus breaks down, the bus
doesn't turn up, the bus has a crash, it snows, etc. . . . Poor Mum has been
known to sit through it three times a day: once 'live' at lunch-time; once
'live' at tea-time with me; and once, on the video, when Dad comes home,
if he has missed it at lunch-time . . .
**HELEN R. AYLIN, AGED 17,
SOLIHULL, WEST MIDLANDS**

I have seen *Neighbours* a few times before as my nine-year-old sister is an
ardent fan. She refuses to come and eat her dinner until it is finished,
which may often provoke shouting matches from one side of the house to
the other. Who would have thought that a sanitized, polystyrene soap such
as this would cause such a rumpus? Today it was a laughable 22 minutes
of over-acting, 'cliff-hanging' on typical domestic crises, improbabilities,
and an ending which caused me to have mild hysterics on the sofa . . .
**SARA SMITH, AGED 17,
TAYPORT, FIFE**

Today I was unfortunate enough to miss both editions. Even when I
watch *Neighbours*, though, I spend a large chunk of the 25 minutes
fidgeting with anything available. I don't watch it to see what happens. I
couldn't care whether Charlene and Scott are wed, or whether Mrs
Mangel sues Des and Daphne, I really couldn't give a monkey's. I watch
Neighbours because I watch it, every day . . .
**SIMON HOWAT, STUDENT,
SWANSEA**

I used to be an addict but, thankfully, am no longer hooked. Would it be
possible for a 'Helpline' to be set up for people who wish to be cured?
**JULIE SPROULE, UNEMPLOYED,
BANGOR, CO. DOWN**

STUDIO TURMOIL
At ITN preparations for News at One *have met their share of minor
problems. We meet first the head of operations who has spent the later
part of the morning in the master control room.*

I am trying to discipline myself to do what the American management
specialist Tom Peters calls 'management by wandering about'. In my case
this has to be by blocking off dates in my diary and sticking to them as
much as possible . . . At 12.50 p.m. a dramatic cameo of the turmoil
unseen by the viewers but which ITN engineers have to overcome.

A live temporary link to bring in a report from the Stock Exchange is delivering only a snowstorm of shash on the monitor in MCR (Master Control Room). The programme editor comes in with brow fevered. At 1.08 p.m. the picture materializes, followed a minute later by the sound. At 1.10 p.m. the report is transmitted without a hitch. The engineers and riggers have dragged cables and equipment up 18 floors and made the air with seconds to spare. We all take it for granted, we make it with seconds to spare most days . . .

**DEREK TAYLOR,
HEAD OF OPERATIONS, ITN**

Into the studio for a token rehearsal before the programme. Newscaster (Julia Somerville) having a mild panic about her lack of scripts. A couple of teleprompt changes. Heaven help us if the teleprompt ever went down during the programme. Julia looks tired; probably her new nipper keeping her up. Far be it from me to suggest it, but a new hairdo always perks a girl up. Programme pretty straightforward . . .

**DEBORAH LORENZ,
SENIOR FLOOR MANAGER**

| *The punters apparently do not mind the hairdo.*

I prefer ITN to BBC national news, more timely, higher factual content, less doctrinally 'liberal'. Today not wildly exciting and my mind wanders . . . I become mildly impatient with business commentators talking as if 'the City' is a homogeneous entity rather than a conglomeration of diverse interests. Also that, like an old-fashioned schoolmarm, it rewards unequivocal correctness and punishes undoubted delinquency . . .

**T. E. LLOYD, RETIRED,
MEXBOROUGH, YORKSHIRE**

News at One is somewhat lighter than the BBC show. Julia Somerville is ideal for me to watch while I eat my lunch . . . Afterwards a dreadful film, but I manage to stick it long enough to miss *Neighbours* . . .

**LESLEY SPARSHOT, MOTHER,
SELSDON, SURREY**

Although *News at One* is on in the background as I do my hair into a bun, I am contemplating the psychologists' remarks, in *Daytime Live*, about managers and secretaries. When they talk about getting on with colleagues at work, and acceptable leadership styles, it sounds so easy . . .

**ANNE-MARIE MOYES, CLINICAL NURSE,
MANAGER OF SURGICAL UNIT,
WORTHING, SUSSEX**

| DISTANT LOCAL NEWS
| *After* News at One *the network splits into its regional components, which first present local news and then an old cinema film of their own choosing. At Thames there is a minor problem.*

DISASTER!!! It is 12.40 p.m. and ⌐

Mayor of London. This involves recorᴅ.

adding pictures, with their accompanying sυ.

tried this myself, and I get a little confused abouᴛ

on which sound track. Before I know it I have erased ⸝.

commentary, which means that she has to record it again. ⸝.

bulletin is getting near, I decide it is prudent to ask editor Mike ⸜

take over. I apologize to the reporter, Gail Goodwin. Fortunately shᴇ ıs

very nice about it. After watching Mike sort things out, it's time for

lunch . . .

**MARTYN FOX, SENIOR ENGINEER,
TRAINEE FILM EDITOR**

If it wasn't that I travelled to Handsworth most weekends, the Central
local news would have little relevance for me, living here on the edge of
the known world . . . Shots of 'rural areas' look like the far-flung
territories of the Birmingham Parks Department and bear scant
resemblance to the craggy peaks outside my front door.

What must the local hill farmers think as they watch Midland news?
They know murder and mayhem go on nationally, but in Gladestry? And
do the waxed jackets and green wellies of roving reporters make it any
more relevant to them? Here, where electricity came 30 years ago and
30-year-old tractor drivers still wear flares and platform soles for family
weddings or funerals, I sometimes wonder . . .

**SYLVIA HAYWORTH, UNEMPLOYED
EX-TEACHER, PRESTEIGNE, POWYS**

STEAMING AND FRYING
*Channel 4 occupied the lunch-hour with adult education about touring
and catering. Some zapping viewers found their way to the Catering
With Care programme about kitchen cleaning.*

This advocated that everyone should continually drown everything in
disinfectants. I almost expected the catering staff to jump in a huge bath
of bleach themselves. I can't help thinking that the amount of chemicals
they were using to keep their kitchen 'hygienic' would do more harm than
a few friendly bacteria . . .

**MARTIN BUCHANAN, ACTOR-PRESENTER,
EAST GRINSTEAD, SUSSEX**

Others, rejecting anything on air, played back tapes or made their own.

In the lunch break replay *This is David Lander* (Channel 4). Only laughed
twice; and groaned at simple error that wouldn't have occurred in the
Radio 4 original – a solo councillor can't grant planning permission. Why
are television versions of radio originals almost inevitably coarser, thinner
and much less funny than on radio? . . . Is this because the controlling
people in television are essentially visual, cut-price amateurs, who hate

writers and are tone-deaf to boot? Shouldn't moan too much. In the post-nanny broadcasting era no one will employ the real Roger Cook or successors because either the Government or the advertisers will zap them . . .

**IAN WELLS, INFORMATION
CONSULTANCY JOURNALIST, PRESTON**

With 59 other girls I am in a boarding house at Sevenoaks School . . . At 1.30 p.m. three of us meet to continue work on a video for the Voluntary Service Unit in the school. We are editing together film from a carol service and children being taught craft. We also decided to take a camera and film some sixth-formers taking a games lesson with local primary school children. It is very difficult to keep the camera steady, particularly when it is heavy, but despite that we got some good shots which we will be able to use in the future. When I watch television I always try to work out how it is done; camera angles, cuts, special effects etc. It has always fascinated me that we only see a tiny part of what is really going on . . .

**HELEN OSTLER, AGED 16,
SEVENOAKS, KENT**

CLIPPED SEX

The Channel 4 premises in Charlotte Street have this morning and lunch-time been the venue for some mild and muddled promotional activities. Print journalists who write about television have been invited to preview the opener of a new food series, Scoff, *and meet its presenter and associate producer, Dawn French. Less expected is the simultaneous preview of* Sex on Television: What's All the Fuss About?, *to be shown the following evening in the* Signals *arts slot. As a researcher records, the sex show is still an uncertain feast.*

The programme tells how the BBC and IBA have regulated themselves over the past 40 years, what television scenes people have got upset about in the past and what may happen to sex on telly come deregulation. Will Patrick Malahide's buttocks be banned for ever more, will we be inundated with soft porn from Belgium? . . . We have a lot of clips, used centrally to the line of the argument.

We use *Body Heat*, for instance, to show how the ITV companies cut films so they're suitable for television viewing. Ken Fletcher, who has the onerous job of deciding where to apply the knife, is seen watching *Body Heat* and saying things like: 'It's obvious what's happening here . . .' (as we see Kathleen Turner's head, we assume she's being laid) '. . . this will have to go.' Anyway, the crisis of the day has been that Brian Hambleton of Warner Brothers called to say we could not use any clip from *Body Heat* . . . Less than 36 hours to transmission we are trying to recut a one-minute sequence so the offending material can be removed . . .

C'est la vie, it's not particularly surprising to me, although we have to stick to the line that we thought we had clearance all along. I knew it would be shaky, but our old BBC reporter (Michael Cockerell) likes to sail close to the wind and left it in, against all advice from his researcher and his PA . . .

SELINA MACNAIR, ASSOCIATE PRODUCER

> *Meanwhile John Archer, associate editor of* Signals, *is in a state of some anxiety.* Sex on Television *is the first programme he has produced outside the BBC, and he is still feeling his way in the independent sector.*

Carol Millward in the C4 press office phones to say that a press viewing is on. As she has seemed to block this, even asking whether Mrs Whitehouse has seen the programme in her 'official capacity', I'm relieved it's on but worried whether anyone will have been invited.

Selina Macnair phones me to say we don't have clearance to use the extract from *Body Heat*, a key sequence in the ITV censors' section. Initial annoyance at not being told of any doubt soon followed by practical considerations. First consider pleas to Warner Brothers who, despite selling it on its sex when it first came out, don't like that image of the film now. They won't budge. Ask Michael Cockerell and his film editor to prepare a substitute piece from the rushes.

Tell Andrew Holmes, executive producer, of the *Body Heat* problem. He says *Signals* is 'almost definitely' to be recommended for another series and, yes, he'll phone Warner Brothers' contact. This doesn't change

Hotbed of hacks. Gentlemen of the press (from left) Charles Catchpole (*News of the World*), Roger Taverner (*Daily Express*) and Tony Purnell (*Daily Mirror*) search for televised sex in a Channel 4 viewing room

their minds . . . Walk to Channel 4. Journalists begin to arrive for viewing, including raincoated man from *News of the World*. Seedy scene in viewing room, male dominated . . . *Daily Mirror* journalist irrationally cross over use of 'ordinary viewers' to discuss sex on television.

Discussion with journalists on programme with Roger Graef, series editor; Lucy Hooberman, assistant producer; and Pam Mills, the audience researcher who led our viewing groups. Give them Broadcasting Standards Council number to check the accuracy of Lord Rees-Mogg's opinion poll figure, saying 70 per cent of viewers want more control of television. Worried how the programme might come over in the papers tomorrow . . .

JOHN ARCHER, ASSOCIATE EDITOR

| *The newspaper people had their own perspectives.*

Off to Channel 4 to see *Scoff*. Fume in traffic jam for 45 minutes. At Charlotte Street ignored by Dawn French. Could this be because I once said she and Jennifer Saunders would never be the new Morecambe and Wise, because no one would be able to tell which was the one with the short, fat, hairy legs?

With brilliant timing, C4 have also organized a screening for *Signals*, their new arts programme, at precisely the same time. Abandon *Scoff* for *Signals*, in which Lord Rees-Mogg reveals he would have allowed Patrick Malahide's buttocks to be seen in *The Singing Detective*. Wow! Photographed watching *Signals* by a photographer claiming to be from *One Day in the Life of Television*, but who I suspect may be from the *News of the World*.

Lunch is three pints of Sam Smith's Brewery Bitter in the Fitzroy Tavern, Charlotte Street. Bar full of trendy television folk discussing up-coming 'indie' (independent) productions, deregulation etc. Am I the only person in W1 who doesn't have his own production company, and doesn't have an opinion on deregulation? . . .

CHARLES CATCHPOLE, TELEVISION CRITIC, NEWS OF THE WORLD

Heavyweight presenter Dawn French is an obvious foodie choice as presenter and she makes food interesting in both the UK and USA. Unfortunately I didn't have time enough to interview her. All the tabloids milled around her while I am freelancing for *Slimmer* and *Healthy Living* magazines. Maybe I'd catch her eating that mammoth cake, as big as a car seat, and iced with the word *Scoff*. We ate it, Dawn vanished . . .

PEGGY TROTT, TELEVISION AND CINEMA REVIEWER-INTERVIEWER

Soon after 8 a.m. I am rummaging around in the office at my home in Brighton trying to find any press clippings about Margi Clarke and Dawn French, who I hope to interview during the day. As a freelance I don't enjoy the luxury of a cuttings library on tap . . . On the train I bump into a friend of mine who is making a new music series for Channel 4 and we drink some BR coffee . . . We discuss television and drop names. A woman is feeding her young daughter Coke from a baby's bottle. For a second I feel superior but then I hear our conversation the way she must be hearing it. I realize she is firmly convinced that she is sitting next to a couple of prats. I also know she is right . . .

I arrive at Channel 4 half an hour before starting time. Dawn French is already there, but I don't want to talk to her until I have seen the programme. After 15 or 20 minutes a woman from a Birmingham paper announces that Dawn French is not staying after the programme has been shown. She overheard her talking in the corridor.

I must earn my crust, I want to write a piece about Dawn for the *Yorkshire Post*. The interview centres round food and who does the cooking in her house. It's Lenny and he makes a killer chilli. We sort of discuss dieting. As I look like a Sumo wrestler who has been on a less than successful diet for a couple of weeks, I don't feel bad about asking these questions. Dawn gives every impression of never having worried about her weight. I envy her that.

A number of journalists turn up just as Dawn is about to leave. You can see their self-assurance being replaced by either disgust or controlled panic, depending on how badly they need to talk to Dawn. A couple of colleagues borrow my tape recording of the interview and take notes from it . . .

Dawn hot pot. A minimum of salivating by Mrs Ann McCormack (left) as Dawn French mixes something nourishing for Channel 4's *Scoff*

Sometimes I think I live my entire life vicariously. Because much of what I write about is drama, and not necessarily high drama, I often find myself daydreaming about a life of excitement where handsome men with chiselled chins whisk me off my feet and make mad passionate love to me in five-star hotel rooms.

Then I meet the same men in drab preview theatres and all they see is a pen and a possible headline. All I see is an ego and a possible story. That's not true, I see other things. Some of them are just genuinely nice chaps. Their lives pulse with no more excitement than mine does. Other times I might as well be holding an autograph book as a reporter's note pad. I know it's unprofessional but I feel you can tell such secrets to a diary . . .

ANNE CABORN, JOURNALIST

IV
AFTERNOON TIMES

2 p.m. – 6 p.m.

I welcomed with open notebook this chance to fill in a television diary for one day, and I was quite surprised to discover that almost a third of my day was spent in front of the television set. It is worth noting that humans spend a third of their lives asleep. Therefore it seems that two-thirds of my life is spent either unconscious, or mind-numbingly wasted.

ROBERT KINNEAR, AGED 17, DONCASTER

STREET SCENES

In and around Coronation Street it is just another working day, as it has been for nearly 30 years now. It was December 1960 when the lugubrious signature tune, illustrated by as unpromising a row of terraced houses as could be found in Manchester, first signalled the arrival of Granada's all-conquering serial. More than any rival, this is institutionalized soap.

The original grittiness had long since mellowed, but the audience renewed itself and stayed loyal. In the week of 1 November it remained, arguably, the most popular programme on British television. The Monday episode was watched by 16 million and the Wednesday show by 16.9 million. Both these figures were comfortably above that for any single showing of the BBC soaps, EastEnders and Neighbours.

Several members of the cast kept diaries. We hear first from Nigel Pivaro. He plays Terry Duckworth, the beefy and wayward son of Jack and Vera, a would-be tearaway. He had been on a night shoot until 11.30 the previous night and went into his morning rehearsals worried about not knowing his scripts as well as he should. At lunch-time he had escaped to the Ramada Hotel to present the prize for 'the year's best fringe production' at the Manchester Evening News Theatre Awards.

Nigel Pivaro plays Terry, the wayward son of Jack and Vera Duckworth, in Coronation Street

I didn't enjoy the meal because of the knowledge that I had to present the award and make an impromptu speech. There were many people I knew at the reception from the world of entertainment. I was also solicited by several journalists . . . I smiled for photos and gave some worthy comment to keep them happy.

I spoke about the fringe being the testing ground for writers, directors, actors etc., and the need for the more established side of the business to contribute more to the fringe. I rounded off with: 'Let the beneficiaries become the benefactors and let us give back to the fringe what it's given to us.' This got a round of spontaneous applause which threw me

completely and made me shake with nerves so much I could hardly read
the nominations . . .

NIGEL PIVARO, ACTOR

> *Barbara Knox plays Rita Fairclough, a red-headed widow who has
> survived the lower reaches of showbiz, and marriage, and now presides
> at the Kabin newsagent's shop with nicely turned common sense.*

Spent all Monday evening learning my current lines. We have only two-
and-a-half days to put an hour's television together. If we were doing a
60-minute play, rather than *Coronation Street*, we'd have at least two or
three weeks' rehearsal and several days in the studio recording it. Hey ho!

We also have to cope with the most hideous pop music BLARING out
under our rehearsal room windows, courtesy of Granada Tours. It is
almost impossible to hear ourselves speak. We have complained and
asked Equity to have it stopped. So far, nowt . . . Wardrobe department
up to discuss our costumes for this week's episode. I have had some of my
jumpers for donkey's years, it is time a few were thrown, but our budget
is tight.

Have just discovered I've left my second episode script at home. Never
done that before, think I picked this flippin' diary up instead, now that's
really thrown me . . . Went round the rest of the cast and managed to get
several scenes from other actors . . . A lovely moment. Howard Baker is
acting producer this week, Bill Podmore away, and just complimented me
on the last two weeks' episodes. 'Outstanding acting.' Well, that's praise
indeed.

Received my first Christmas card today, from a dear old fan. Some fans
write to me and become like family, telling me all their problems. Traffic
choked as usual. Took over an hour tonight, slightly foggy. The tricky
scene in Kabin keeps going through my head. Long warm bath, supper
and then retire early, with script. Which, let's face it, is an actress's
dream. Thank you, God.

BARBARA KNOX, ACTRESS

> *Intelligent and articulate Thelma Barlow plays muddled and mousey
> Mavis Riley, lately returned from a Parisian honeymoon with Derek
> Wilton.*

I am just back at work after a holiday in Sicily and there is always a
feeling, in these circumstances, that one needs to readjust to the demands
of the job . . . I live close to the studio, so walk to work in beautiful
sunshine, cold and bright . . . The pressures of a programme such as ours
do not lessen with the years and there is an enormous amount of work to
be crammed into the available rehearsal time.

At lunch-time a meal in the canteen and then a quick walk through town,
collecting books that were ordered. Shopping, or any public airing, always
means that one has to allow extra time, as members of the public stop us

to chat about the programme or ask for autographs, photographs etc.

An hour for lunch hardly allows for much public relations work, but the afternoon rehearsals go well. I have enquiries for two interviews, but the press have recently been misleading their public by writing about a personal relationship. Totally untrue, as usual, confusing fact and fiction. My acting colleague and I refuse a trip to Paris, including a handsome fee, offered by a newspaper. One would like to do it, really, but have no control over the copy . . .

THELMA BARLOW, ACTRESS

Bryan Mosley plays staid and rotund shopkeeper Alf Roberts, a solid citizen three times married.

Rehearsing in the morning and afternoon, fairly simple and quite funny . . . I should mention the working symptoms that crop up. The anxiety of getting the words right, of making scenes work, of relationships with other characters. The sometime frustration of not knowing if inter-reactions between us will be lost for the sake of 'shots'. The underlying uncertainty of the value of some scenes or parts of a scene, and whether all the work will be wasted or cut. Not feeling 'right' in certain positions, not having the props until the actual day (very important to me) of recording. The various odd worries about, for example, the noise of the shop till and where to place it between the words. The incredible frustration of knowing that much time will be spent (wasted) over technical matters (reflections, refractions, boom shadows [God, how we hate them], tea break, noises, etc., etc.) that diminish performances . . .

BRYAN MOSLEY, ACTOR

Widower Bill Waddington, once a top-of-the-bill comedian in army concert parties and variety halls, plays the barrack-room caretaker of the community centre, Percy Sugden. He has not greatly enjoyed his canteen lunch.

Would prefer to pay more for really decent food. I live alone so it would be a great boon for me anyway . . . Had four calls for me to do charity work all next week. I will do two. It never stops, one really is public property and doesn't want too much of these 'dos'. Read notice board re begging letters for all charities, impossible to respond to all the worthy causes which there are . . .

Just one more scene to do before I leave the studio and get back home, where I really learn my lines without interruption. I've installed an answering machine, so I've no need to pick up the phone until I have a break . . . Some of the scenes I have to learn can be boring and sometimes, like one this week, written not well at all. This has needed a bit of rewriting, which I have done. I am the one who will get the raspberries if it comes over badly, not the writer . . .

BILL WADDINGTON, ACTOR

Peter Baldwin plays the mother-pecked Derek Wilton, whose tentative courtship of Mavis Riley has just been blessed.

Have been playing the part on and off for 12 years, so know the character and have not to go through that process. Not too many words this week but am in eight scenes. Mavis and Derek have just returned from honeymoon in Paris. The scenes include congratulations from some characters and, very rare in the Street, a scene in bed, ending in 'a passionate kiss'. Much of our material (Thelma Barlow and me) is comedic, but don't think we can play that for comedy . . .

Go into Granada studio building. Standing outside is one of a few devout fans at the Street, who are nearly always there. Bit cold for him this morning. A pretty girl comes out, says 'Hallo'. No idea who it is. Granada is full of pretty girls. Rehearsals begin. Through the day we go over the script, scene by scene, each group of actors being called into the main rehearsal room by Shirley (Dynevor), the OSM (Organizer Stage Management) this week. In the green room, groups or pairs go over lines. A television set is on, don't know how anyone can work with that constantly pushing out day-time programmes.

Rehearse coming home from honeymoon scene. Overdo the acting with

Rovers Return: all
Coronation Street
generations assemble for a
group picture in their
favourite meeting place

cases and duty-free bags etc. Carry Mavis over threshold of flat . . . Lunch in canteen with Thelma, and Alan Hunter who is in for three weeks . . . Rehearsing continues until about 5 p.m. I go to the Old School, the Granada club, for a Scotch, and a turn on the fruit machine. Then back to the flat. Catch a bit of television but it all seems to be game shows. Turn it off and go out to eat at a newish restaurant-club not far away, with Thelma, and eat and drink far too much. But it was delicious . . .

PETER BALDWIN, ACTOR

| *Shirley Dynevor is this week's shepherd for the cast.*

The working day on any Tuesday is tightly structured, first episode in the morning and second after lunch. Every scene is rehearsed and timed three or four times in detail. It's the only day in the Street week when actors can explore the situations the writer has dreamed up for them . . .

At 10.30 a.m. I've got my stopwatch around my neck, script in hand, and I call the actors in for the first scene, in the Kabin. Thelma and Barbara know their lines already. The director slowly knits the scene together. I time them, prompt when necessary, adjust my plans and call the actors in for their next scenes, trying to keep a good fast flow. Watching the actors struggle and search, and then consolidate their moments, my concentration is intense. I feel their frustration and share their elation when the moment is found . . .

We rehearse Mavis and Derek, back from their honeymoon in Paris, and there's a tender bed scene after all this time. We all giggle a lot. Peter Baldwin and Thelma are amazing clowns, in and out of their characters. The rehearsal bedhead keeps slipping around. Sarah and Nick, the floor manager, discuss the bed and headboard at great length, it must be firm and padded. The thought of Mavis in a double bed makes us all chuckle and, when Peter leaps astride Thelma, on the creaking bed, at the end of the scene, we are all helpless with laughter . . .

The afternoon is very noisy, from the next door rehearsal of *My Secret Desire*. We have to persuade them to rehearse more quietly. We carry on, Peter and Thelma in the Kabin flat . . . 3.30 p.m. and the tea trolley arrives in the green room from the canteen. *Coronation Street* teas are wonderful – fresh sandwiches made with granary bread, filled with prawns, chicken and salad. Bowls of fresh fruit and platters of cheeses, a high spot in the day for everyone.

Five minutes and off we go again. Nigel Pivaro is back and can do his own Terry. I have been reading his part, now I can concentrate on my timings. We're a minute over. We'll probably tighten up quite a bit, but we can't hurry the kisses. Glo (Gloria Todd) and Pete have quite a lot of smoochy acting to do in Glo's flat. They practise a lot and we giggle a whole lot more. They have to consolidate the scenes today because Sue Jenkins has to go to a funeral tomorrow. Heavens, that means I shall have to stand in for the technical run. At 5.30 p.m. rehearsals finish. A quick chat with Sarah, what a good day it's been, a lot seems to have been achieved. It's so controllable in the rehearsal room . . .

Programme makers have a huge responsibility to the public. I hope they will continue to make programmes that do not pander to an audience of 'little brains' but will assume that viewers are intelligent and compassionate. Television should not be a time-filler, it should ask more of us and give more accordingly.

**SHIRLEY DYNEVOR,
ORGANIZER STAGE MANAGEMENT**

Sarah Harding, returning to Coronation Street *direction this week after maternity leave, is also enjoying the day.*

Tuesday is my favourite day on the Street. It's the one opportunity for me to work on the acting, interpretation and focus of the scenes . . . Our problem is that because of the speed of work and the amount of lines that have to be learnt weekly the scenes tend to go at an overall 'Street' pace, a rather breathless Northern rhythm. This can make for monotonous pacing, so I try to find the true pace of each scene in rehearsal, to provide slow and fast movements within the episode. I encourage the actors not to be afraid of pauses when appropriate but also not to make a meal of something which should be relatively light and throwaway . . .

This week's scripts, by Brian Finch and Barry Hill, are mostly about sex, which is fun . . . This morning we spent time with Mavis and Derek, establishing first that we see them in love and second that, although Mavis has become rather bossy in her new role as Mrs Wilton, she enjoys playing the 'little woman' so that Derek can be 'masterful'. These scenes have to show the ground rules of their marriage. After a stormy courtship we need to create a haven for them, establishing a real affection and passion between them to provide a good basis for whatever happens to them next. We must not play their bedroom scenes as purely comic . . .

SARAH HARDING, DIRECTOR

Barry Hill is normally a Coronation Street *scriptwriter but is just now working office hours as a stand-in storyline maker, while Tom Elliott has a break. With Diane Culverhouse he spends the day working on a pair of storylines that will be screened at the end of the following January.*

First, a summary of the story points to be included, as agreed at a conference of all the writers ten days previously. Then the task of working out the cast list for the two episodes – who do we really need? Who can't we have because of holiday commitments? From whom can we get best value in peripheral incidents?

A rough list is drawn up, followed by a run-down of the sets we will require. Would we get more value out of Brian Tilsley's garage? Perhaps we might get more use out of Alf Roberts' shop? A few minutes' discussion with Diane resolved it, we would go for Jim's Café . . .

The place is the Rovers living-room, as I slip easily into the world of Alec and Bet Gilroy and their problems. The pencil skims over the paper. Pause for thought. Another cup of coffee. Delete the first thought. Start again. Perhaps we can use Betty in this scene? Forget it. What would Betty be doing in the Rovers living-room at this time of day? Good thinking. Onward . . . onward . . . Quickly into the living-room of Sally and Kevin Webster, at the stroke of a pencil. From there to the Kabin. Back to the Rovers bar, pausing only briefly to call in and eavesdrop in Jim's Café. They said there would be opportunities for travel when I took this job . . .

After lunch it is time to get to grips again with the problems of Derek and Mavis, of Alec and Bet, of Alan and Rita, *et al.* Problems solved, new ones posed. They may be fictitious characters in the strictest sense, but to me they are as real as close relatives. I know them better, I see more of them, they are part of my life. And they have the added advantage that I can always shut them out when I have had enough . . .

BARRY HILL, WRITER

Diane Culverhouse, one of the two permanent storyline writers, woke that morning at her Bolton digs after a story conference nightmare.

The writers were all seated round the table, exchanging priceless gems of witty banter as usual, but I was involved in seemingly futile attempts to extract bundles of pink scripts out of a front-loader washing machine. Does this say something about the need to clean up *Coronation Street*? Surely not . . .

Thinking about writing this diary, I ponder upon the nature of this job, and conclude how lucky I am to spend my days in happy contemplation, deciding the fates of the 30 or so characters that inhabit the Street, and get paid for so doing . . . Today I am preoccupied with Storyline 1903, transmission on 23 January 1989, the third episode in a batch of six that we have to concoct over a ten-day period . . .

At the office, armed with a cup of decaffeinated and lighting up the first cigarette of the day (a cigar in Barry Hill's case), we swap notes on recent events in our somewhat different domestic lives and then turn our attention to last night's *Street* episode. How well did the actors perform, and how cleverly did the director interpret the written word? How well written was the script in the first place, and how will the audience react?

Today was really one of those noses-to-the-grindstone days, helped by the unusual lack of interruptions which are normally part of our daily routine. Members of the cast frequently peer into the office, on the pretext of asking after our well-being. We know they've really come in to glance at Tom's chart on the wall, which reveals all about who is booked for which episode . . .

During the canteen lunch Denise regales Barry and I with an extraordinary tale extracted from the *News of the World*, which is unrepeatable here and nigh puts us both off our hot-pots. Bill Waddington then joins us with the latest news of his pride and joy, racehorse Lucy Lastic, and a series of entertaining three-line gags, and it's time to be getting back to the mill . . .

At 3.45 p.m. a very nervous stage manager pokes her head round the door with a query: she would like to know whether Mavis's budgie, Harriet, would become a greater or lesser part of Mavis's life if she was married. We attend to this with due seriousness, and unanimously decide that Harriet would feature more so, she being the ultimate confidante to Mavis in times of trouble . . .

**DIANE CULVERHOUSE,
STORY ASSOCIATE**

BEGINNERS, PLEASE

Meanwhile this was also, potentially, a historic day in the upper reaches of television drama. Our most considerable television dramatist, a figure who stood out even in the golden age of the single play, was moving towards a new career, as a director. A production assistant at the BBC Television Centre records the moment of arrival.

Dennis Potter, television drama laureate – his first day as director and no black eyes yet

After lunch our production team returned to the office to wait for the arrival of Dennis Potter. *Blackeyes*, a serial based on his novel, has finally been given the go-ahead and Dennis is going to direct it himself. Today is his first day in the office and he felt very strange and rather nervous. It is the first time he has worked with a team.

Before we throw ourselves into casting etc., we must make him feel at ease in the office environment. Our designer popped in for a brief chat about our sets, to be built on the stage, and both producers, Kenith Trodd and Rich McCallan, came in to welcome Dennis. Rosie, our production manager, explained the first draft film schedule, but it is only a draft until we get into casting. There are many difficulties about fitting everybody in over a six-month film schedule. All dispersed about 6 p.m. and I went to play tennis . . .

**MAGGIE STEVENS,
PRODUCTION ASSISTANT**

Valerie McCrimmon is not a name which would normally be set beside that of Dennis Potter, but this afternoon she has every reason to feel as nervous as he does.

Today I have a BBC Board for an attachment scenic properties buyer. This is my second attempt. I failed the last one in March, so I have put in a lot of homework for this one. After my son goes to school I settle down for two hours' revision with all the books I have taken out on furniture, silver and pottery from the 17th to the 20th century. The Board is not until 4.45 p.m. so I have all day to worry about it.

At lunch-time we go to our local for a glass of wine and a prawn sandwich, hoping it will relax me. It doesn't. Then I dress smartly and make up carefully, feeling pleased with the result . . . I drive to the

Television Centre and make my way to Room 303, PBAX Block, for the dreaded interview. I arrive at 4.40 p.m. but find they are running late. The candidate before me has not gone in yet. He is a young, fair-haired man, not very smart. I spend the waiting time writing notes and chatting to the clerks in the office. It must be boring for them, having nervous people around all day . . .

At 5.25 p.m. I am summoned to the Board. Four men. There should be at least one woman. First question: Why did I apply again? 'Because I want the job', I said positively. Then I tell them why I think I would be good at it. They are not as tough as last time, I am almost enjoying it. Then the pictures of furniture and period settings, my swotting has paid off. I've got them all right bar two. Food mixers were around in the 1930s. I didn't know that, but I can see they are impressed.

Then I'm asked to identify two objects in the room. One is an old BBC mike. The other looks familiar but I've gone blank, so I say a ship's instrument. Right, it's a ship's sextant. At 6 p.m. it's all over. I'm feeling

Cameraperson in control: sometimes, even at BBC Cardiff, a male preserve is breached

very relieved. It went much better than my last Board. I am 50, so my age is against me, but I can't do anything about that . . .

**VALERIE McCRIMMON,
ASSISTANT FLOOR MANAGER**

POSITIVE DISCRIMINATION

In television, as in British life as a whole, ageism is rampant. What of sexism? Surely that has been so heavily stamped upon in recent years, women can now advance shoulder to shoulder wherever they want to go? The fact is that there are several departments, from management to engineering and camera operation, which remain virtually male clubs. Other jobs still appear to be thought of as damaging to male esteem. This thought occurs to an Anglia schedules officer as he looks about for freelances to cover for sick staffers.

I need to find one cameraman and one autocue operator for Friday. I look at my list, running my eye along the names. Who have we used recently, who knows this programme, who would the head of cameras prefer? Oh yes, he'll do . . . Next, autocue. There's a strict rotation of the three experienced local women. Must get it right. Phone the first, she's busy. The second will do it if she can arrange a child minder. She'll phone me back this afternoon. Yes, it's a sexist business, television. Our departments are strictly segregated; apart from mould-breakers like myself in schedules, a freelance woman in despatch, one female director and two women editors. The production and ownership of television may be changing but other areas of life are a little slower . . .

JON BALL, SCHEDULES OFFICER

While these thoughts preoccupy a Norwich mould-breaker, the female-dominated HTV wardrobe department in Cardiff wonders if male efforts to jump the barriers are so welcome.

Born to shop. Start the day the valium way with a quick blitz to Miss Selfridge to buy up little black numbers to fit men. Kevin may be six foot four but I'm sure he'll look elegant in this stretch lace v-neck job, and I can afford it on the budget. Everything in triplicate for the Bananarama take-off sketch . . . Why is HTV so obsessed with transvestism? They could just employ real women, I'm sure there are actresses who could do with the work. I was really incensed when 'yBrodyr Gregory' dressed up as cinema usherettes. Now our relatively 'right-on' youth magazine *Stid*, which keeps my week balanced, is donning the frocks as well . . .

Decide against lunch in the canteen, it's a choice between stodge and soggy veg or a chance to chat to the production team. There's no calories in chat . . . Argh . . . they're advancing Paul and Adrian, collectively known as 'yBrodyr Gregory', two tiny Brynamman men who like to think they're pop stars. They're not joined at the hip but they do tend to use the Royal 'we'. I want to dress them as co-ordinated people, not peas in a pod. They're brothers, not twins. The producer reckons that the target audience is women between 25 and 50. I was insulted again. I'm 28 and I find the material dated, sexist and unoriginal.

It's 6.10 p.m. and I'm still in Top Man, digging out all my identity cards, credit cards, AA membership card, driving licence, birth certificate, anything that'll allow me to write a cheque for the next eight carrier bags'

Dressing down: concentration in the HTV wardrobe

worth of trendy-skinny-man clothing and get back to base. The sty on my eye is getting sore and throbbing and I'm tired . . . Caffeine, nicotine, alcohol, anything to get me away from these thin men who whinge about pretty clothes. I know when they get to wear them next week they'll say the whole image was their idea . . .

**EDWINA WILLIAMS-JONES,
ACTING WARDROBE SUPERVISOR**

IMPORTUNATE CLAIMANTS

Nobody is more important in large broadcasting organizations than the planners – the men (usually men) who know about money and resources and are able to tell lesser mortals what they can and cannot afford. At the BBC they loom large at all times, and particularly so in November. This is the month of the 'Star Chamber' meetings, at which each department must report to the managing director on its financial performance and forecasts. It is also the time when departments offer controllers the programmes they would like to do in the next financial year, and are cut down to what the budget allows. Among those at the summit is the general manager of programme planning, a man who goes home to a house at Great Missenden in Buckinghamshire, called 'Chart'.

One of his morning meetings concerned the financial difficulties of the plays department. 'It appeared that the only way of achieving their financial target was to drop plays on BBC1, which I did not believe would be acceptable to the Channel Controller. This he confirmed. Then went to see Head of Costing Services and spoke to the Manager of Drama, Plays, to make suggestions as to how they could make the proper financial savings without affecting BBC1. The financial problems appear to be on BBC2 . . .'

In appropriate chart form, here is his afternoon timetable. The number of broadcasters' lives to be changed, for better or worse, as a result of each of his meetings can only be guessed at.

12.15 p.m. Lime Grove for Programme Managers' lunch

2.30 p.m. Still at Lime Grove, visited the new offices of BBC2 late night arts show

3.00 p.m. Meeting with Manager, Schools, about audition for new presenter

4.00 p.m. Discussion with Independent Planning Unit and Planning Resources about how independent producers might use BBC resources in London and the regions

5.00 p.m. Meeting with Director of Resources to discuss the finance case for the Independent Planning Unit, and the Regional Planning review of capital development in Manchester

5.45 p.m. Meeting with Controller, Resource Operations, about the proposed reductions in staff and resource levels in 1989–90

6.15 p.m. Meeting with a senior member of one of the resource departments about restructuring within the area

6.45 p.m.   Drink in the bar with Light Entertainment producer about an
independent production . . .

**K. D. ANDERSON, GENERAL MANAGER
PROGRAMME PLANNING, BBC**

> *Planning started early on 1 November. Stuart Dewey, at present in
> charge at BBC1, had an alarm call at 4.30 a.m. so that he could catch a
> train from deepest Oxfordshire and be at an 8 a.m. Television Centre
> meeting about the drama series and serials offers. Whatever the
> difficulties of this they were slight compared to the afternoon problems
> of conducting a light entertainment offers meeting, while being filmed
> by Yorkshire Television.*

Jim Moir (Head of Light Entertainment Group) has arrived with cohorts
Tony James (Manager Light Entertainment, Variety – sporting an
enormous calculator) and John Bishop (Jim's deputy). Jim discusses
camera angles with the Yorkshire cameraman. Ready to roll – no, Jim has
no glass for his Highland water. I rush off on this important errand. After
shouting match with hospitality I return with tray and glasses held aloft,
trying not to fall over film unit detritus scattered across the floor.

The meeting gets away at 2.15 p.m. The problem is to keep secrets with
the film crew present. It is impossible to refer to programmes without
mentioning the star. Jonathan (Powell, BBC1 Controller) decides to use the
numbers on his briefing document ('suppose we have ten of number five,
and only six of number three' – I wait for someone to say 'with fried
rice?': they don't). The problem is that Jim and company don't have this
document, so there is some doubt as to whether we are talking about the
same programme. Mutter of 'GW, GW' from Nigel Pope (Planning
Manager, Resources) puzzles me, as I think we are talking about *The
Generation Game*. Then I turn the pages and realize that we have moved
on . . .

The crew leaves the room at 3.45 p.m. Everyone relaxes and checks that
we've understood the coded remarks. Jonathan suddenly freezes and holds
a finger to his lips, pointing to his radio microphone. Furious unplugging
ensues. The meeting ends amicably, having achieved far more than
expected . . .

**STUART DEWEY,
ACTING PLANNING MANAGER, BBC**

> *Another planner who attended these meetings was switched by them
> into Pepysian mode. His first encounter was also the breakfast one with
> the head of drama, Mark Shivas.*

Attended in the Annexe with Mr Controller Powell, Mr Dewey and
Mistress Wright, the keeper of the BBC1 Accounts, a meeting with the
Theatricals. Much discourse with Mr Shivas who is mightily
discontented, I found, about the wages, victuals and materials his players
are provided. Mr Controller Powell did listen to these pleas and did

determine new dispensations with great judgement . . .

Among other business transacted this morning with my Lords in many Departments are questions about the entertainment to be attended by Her Majesty at the London Palladium on the 21st of this month, the nature and hours of the plays to be performed by the Scottish troupe in March next year, and the sporting events to be approved by Mr Controller Powell as suitable for the people this winter. He being not in favour of the bear baiting, instead he approved the propositions from Sir Jonathan Martin regarding the football, prize fighting and horse racing . . .

Thence to lunch with Mr Controller Powell where we read Mr Moir's propositions regarding the revels he seeks to organize next year. But Lord, how sad a sight is the countenance of Mistress Wright when she tallies up the many millions of guineas Mr Moir and his clowns and tumblers seek from the BBC1 Exchequer for these entertainments.

At two o'clock Mr Moir and his Clerks are summoned to the Annexe where we hear his clamour for more money, and he shows us his reckonings by which he hopes we shall be persuaded of the truth of his arguments. But Mr Moir is yet a wise man and not seeking a great conflict. He knows that Mr Controller Powell's Exchequer has already been much reduced by the claims of other importunate claimants viz. the Theatricals, the Children's Entertainers, and the Common Provincials, so he lessens his demands by over one million guineas to the pleasure, and indeed surprise, of Mr Controller Powell. So after long discourse at four o'clock in the afternoon some matters are agreed while others are put off for another time . . .

**ROGER MACKAY,
HEAD OF TRANSMISSION PLANNING, BBC**

THE IMPORTANCE OF BEING TRAINED

Of more obvious use to programme makers, in theory, are those who train them. Kathy Chater finds documentary stories, archive film and stills, or anything else that may be needed by BBC television trainees.

Find a couple of useful addresses for my forthcoming publication, *The Television Researcher's Handbook*. I've written all the How to Find Facts, People, Film, Sound, etc., and am now gathering useful addresses and telephone numbers. When I first thought of the handbook, I assumed it had been done before, but no. Even *Newsnight* didn't have a data base of experts in different fields to call on, so I think this book should be a little winner. Fledgling researchers will buy it for the useful tips and even the ones who despise my methods will get it for the addresses. Currently, I think I've got about 1000, of which 700 still have to be checked out properly . . .

Although some of the directors arrive on the training course with their own ideas, most draw on the list of 40 or so stories we keep on file. Part of my job is to update and add to this list. Ring a dealer in antique cars who collects old taxis as a hobby. Out. Ring an artist I met at the weekend to get more information about a theatre group for able and disabled children that her daughter is in. Out. Ring a couple who own miniature horses which they are training to use in their magic act. Out.

Type up the notes I made on Sunday when I visited the oldest house in London. The film's only worth making if one of the owners, a Royal Shakespeare Company actor, will be free to be interviewed and talk about his house. This story could easily turn into the worst kind of *Nationwide* item – gosh, wow, the oldest house in London, this is a very old beam, this a very old beam, too, and this is another very old beam . . .

After lunch, drop in on the demo shoot as this is a new exercise and I like to know what's going on. One of the directors asks me about mental health stories in the area. She wants to do something on people who hear voices, but has a rather misty Joan of Arc idea about it. Tell her that that's schizophrenia and there's nothing romantic about it.

Tell her that I'm really not keen on exploiting people to no very great benefit for them. Training is not the place to make searing exposés of social unhappiness and injustices, as the films are not transmitted. Those who take part will have been put to some inconvenience and trouble with no publicity for their cause or solution to their problem. She's not convinced, I can tell. On every course there's one hack who wants to make a film about something deeply disturbing and sneers a little at our list of generally upbeat stories . . .

Watch the last 15 minutes of *The Importance of Being Earnest* on BBC1. This is followed by Rob Curling looking *Behind the Screen*, sweet boy but no contest. Wonder if the director of his programme is one of our graduates. If so, has learned nothing. A series of really bad shots that plainly have taken a lot of thought, as you cannot, without some planning, get the worst possible angle for every single shot. Not interested enough to wait for the credits to see who was directing.

The difference between the film and the programme was simply one of gusto. Enjoyment of the craft of film-making dripped from the screen in *The Importance*. The programme was a dispirited plod through something that the director had no faith or interest in, and not enough technical ability to hide this. Have always thought that I don't have enough visual ability to be a director but now think again . . .

Leave early to go to the Waldorf Hotel for their 80th anniversary party. Drink far too much champagne and eat far too much delicious food, and wonder why I can't have a job that lets me live like this all the time. Chat to some of the guests, all regular clients of the Waldorf, and realize I couldn't stand the boredom. These are the people for whom most television programmes are made. They watch, as I discover by subtle questioning, most of the programmes I hate. The problem with television is that you do have to be bright to work in it but you're making programmes for people who, by and large, have a different intellectual background. This sounds patronizing and it is . . .

Home at 11 p.m. and think again. Decide it's not just me who's patronizing about the viewers. The planners could put much better quality programmes on during the day but they dismiss those viewing then as just housewives, the retired and the unemployed. Have no ambition, however, to be Controller of BBC1 or BBC2. Perhaps it should be done in rotation, so that a representative of every social group gets a turn. That should make for some very interesting scheduling.

**KATHY CHATER, RESEARCHER,
TELEVISION TRAINING**

> *At BBC Elstree the senior instructor is indulging his film direction students, and to an extent himself, in the making of commercials. His lunch at the Club Bar has consisted of sausage rolls, alcohol and 'character assassination'.*

Have promised trainee to make film sound track for him. The commercial's storyline is about an unfaithful husband surprised by the return of his wife. The wife is really only interested in getting home for her Open University course on television. OOV (out of vision) sound track for orgasmic pants, followed by panic noises.

I have picked my supporting actress with care, K. from Planning Office. K. playing with department computer which is not working properly. It has not been working properly for two years now. Things work best when it is not working at all. K. and I go to the new Sypher Suite. 'Sypher' is the BBC engineering term for hideously expensive toy for doing things you don't want badly, while not doing things any film dubbing suite does cheaply and well. Sypher looks like the control of a Space Shuttle. No engineers in sight. We find one attached to a soldering iron. He agrees to help.

We throw ourselves into our roles. The window of the commentary box steams up. Life is not all a vale of tears in television training. We ask for playback. The machine fails. There is nothing on the tape. We embark on take two. Suddenly we witness a population explosion of engineers. Where have they come from? . . . K. and I shudder as we hear the unfamiliar speech patterns on talkback and observe the swivelling eyes and prognathous jawlines . . . A dozen of them ruminate collectively. A green light appears. I suggest we improvise dialogue lines. K. cries, 'I can't find my knickers.' This girl has not been totally frank with me . . .

PETER JARVIS, SENIOR INSTRUCTOR

> SPACE SELLERS
> *More seriously concerned about commercials are those who sell air time on behalf of the ITV companies. Fergus Lawson works in London for Television South West.*

Tuesday is normally a pretty horrendous day. Were it a Tuesday later in the month then my assistant, Bill, and I would be inundated with phone calls from buyers at the agencies we deal with. It is the day the 'Green Book' comes in; buyers check through their campaigns, cost them out and phone up with 'Where are my fucking ratings?' Today we are spared this chorus as it's only 1 November and it is much more difficult, so early in the month, to gauge whether a campaign is on line to meet its rating target, or not.

So, I arrive knowing that this is going to be one of those days when I can get quite a lot of work done, with the minimum of interruption . . . I manage most of the groundwork in preparation for the 1989 negotiations with my two biggest agencies, McCann Erickson and McCormicks. In brief, this involves looking at their spend on TSW, and what share of their business we take at what price, with a view to winning an increased share at a higher price in 1989. Doing this, by agency and by product, takes up most of my day.

To end the working day, some of us watched a *This Week* edition which one of our group managers had videoed. The subject matter was the future of television, something that is uppermost in the minds of those of us who work, and see their future, in this industry . . . That was the only television I saw, except for my usual ten-minute stint at breakfast time. I don't watch a great deal of television . . . Trips to the cinema, and watching videos, normally take preference. Why? Because, although I believe British television is good by comparison with other countries, it mostly bores the hell out of me. And, I expect, will do so even more in the future.

FERGUS LAWSON, SALES EXECUTIVE

Working life appears to be more hectic for Joanne Beckett, an Anglia salesperson stationed in the London office.

My assistant and I have gone through how much money we booked the previous day and how much we need today to keep on line for our weekly targets. I then divide between myself and my assistant the campaigns that we will work on to reach our pledges. Before the phone starts ringing, and new problems occur, I option up a package of air-time for a campaign due to advertise in December. This involves checking the campaign results to date, checking records and calling up information on the computer.

I've nearly finished this when the phone starts ringing. A buyer, whose campaign ends this week, believes he's not receiving the value guaranteed by Anglia. I know that if he's correct it will be a very time-consuming, difficult job to put it right. It will also delay me from booking money in. I assure the buyer I will attend to it as soon as possible. I check on the computer and find that there is no problem. I phone the buyer straight back but he's engaged. There's no time to hold, so it's on to the next thing . . .

Another buyer wants a heavier weight of advertising this week. I check the details and manage to move a spot and take some extra money from him. It's a good feeling . . . As I have fairly recently moved into a new portfolio of agencies my senior executive takes me out to lunch. She talks about the section and the way she wants it to run, and the media industries in general.

At 2.30 p.m. I assess what money has been booked. Frustratingly enough I've actually booked the amount I pledged, but new spots have been pre-empted. This means I have lost money and need to book the same amount again to meet my target. I pledge to do this . . . I manage to make all phone calls brief as none are high priority, but at 5.50 p.m. I am still struggling to turn the last money I pledged around. The buyer is in a meeting, so I can't pursue this any further. Even though I haven't cosmetically reached my target, I have booked more than double my target in real terms. I feel satisfied at this and confident about justifying my 'shortfall'. Finally my assistant updates me on his progress and we discuss a plan of action for tomorrow.

JOANNE BECKETT, SALES EXECUTIVE

> *However successful Joanne Beckett and her fellow toilers may be, no commercial can be shown on ITV or Channel 4 if it offends against strict rules. At the Independent Television Association the copy group head, and his colleagues, have spent the morning viewing 44 finished commercials and reading a large number of scripts.*

I also put my name to about 50 scripts that were being returned to various agencies, having been processed and either approved, enabling them to shoot the commercial, or rejected. Among the topics discussed by our group before lunch were such weighty matters as whether rodeo horses had their testicles tied up to make them jump, whether two old French people looked happier after the ingestion of alcohol, and whether we should allow kids to abseil down a cliff in a chocolate ad.

During the post-lunch peace and quiet I reviewed the advertising of a well-known battery manufacturer at a colleague's request, and viewed a rough copy of a bath cleanser ad for an agency who unwisely seemed to value my opinion of it. I looked at the afternoon's new script arrivals and moved amongst the group dispensing comments on the previous day's scripts. The fairness of the system is that within 24 hours of receiving a new script at least three members of staff offer a view of it . . .

A. KINGSBURY, COPY GROUP HEAD

> *All advertising on its two television channels has to meet with the approval of the Independent Broadcasting Authority regulators. Today the controller has a racial problem.*

A 9 a.m. session with Pam, my secretary. Dictate a note of my meeting yesterday with the Board of Deputies of British Jews, to discuss a controversial Midland Bank commercial alleged to be anti-semitic . . . At 1.30 p.m. nip downstairs to buy sandwiches. Eat them at my desk while watching the last few minutes of a Central discussion programme about whether alcohol advertising should be banned.

Kevin Gavaghan, marketing manager of Midland Bank, rings to tell me that the Midland are 'pulling' their controversial commercial as from today. This follows a number of conversations over previous days, when we registered mounting concern over public reactions. We discuss the lessons to be learnt from the case. I then quickly inform people who need to know, our Press Office, and my own case officer. I dictate a letter for the Chairman (Lord Thomson) to send to a complainant about the Midland case . . .

**FRANK WILLIS,
CONTROLLER OF ADVERTISING, IBA**

11   WORDS BETWEEN THE
LINES

The four terrestrial television channels all transmit teletext to those who have sets equipped to receive these pages. The BBC networks are fed by Ceefax and the IBA channels by Oracle. Sub-editors putting the words together are expected to work long hours. Miranda McIntyre started her morning shift at 6 a.m., suffering from a cold which causes her day to be 'observed through a veneer of self-pity, blocked nose and aching head'. When the editor asks her to cover the Chancellor's Autumn Statement she is less than enthusiastic.

Seven hours, and then some more, at the terminal. Miranda McIntyre keeps words succinct for the BBC's Ceefax

I am thoroughly bunged up with cold and by the time Lawson starts speaking will have been working for nine-and-a-half hours. I don't suggest that the editor gives me a wide berth for this reason, but I do point out that I'm fairly experienced at Budgets etc., and wouldn't it be better

for one of the acting chief subs, who are working this afternoon, to cover the statement, to get experience, with me acting as back-up. Unfortunately he doesn't appear to take my point, perhaps I put it across wrongly, and he retires apparently somewhat miffed.

The duty editor seems to think my idea is a good one. The roles of the editor and duty editor do tend to overlap, which makes it difficult to know where the buck stops, and when, but generally it is not a problem . . .

At 1 p.m. two major stories break practically on the dot, so that my handover to the 1 p.m. chief sub appears woefully unfinished. This so often happens. Everything is shipshape until 12.45 and falls to bits at 1 p.m., making the afternoon chief sub feel that one has been twiddling one's thumbs and failing to get on top of the stories. It leaves me rather depressed. I've been at the VDU terminal for seven hours now, with a few glances at newspapers but no other break. Mostly it's just tiredness.

Lunch is a BBC salad in the rest room. Then I return to offer my services to the 1 p.m. chief sub. The 9 a.m. sub is also hanging round, ready to write news, so there are plenty of willing hands. Things remain quiet until the Chancellor's speech. Then Kath, who has been doing some shifts as chief sub, handles the statement with back-up from the 1 p.m. chief sub and myself. She does excellently, proving my theory that the experience would be useful, but there are too many chief subs back-seat driving, or trying to, and I pity the poor girl.

It is all wrapped up by about 4.15 p.m. or so. By this time the 6 a.m. chief sub is usually fairly bleary-eyed and I am no exception. I do one final read through the afternoon's output, as this can be helpful for the afternoon team, but all seems to be well and there are no literals. I leave at 5 p.m. The shift is supposed to end at 6 p.m., but very few stay that long . . .

**MIRANDA McINTYRE,
CHIEF SUB-EDITOR, CEEFAX**

Carrie Harvey works for the Oracle opposition, preparing subtitles for the hard-of-hearing. Today she is working, with one colleague, the 1.30 p.m. to 8.30 p.m. shift.

Our output is very restricted at the moment. We have said goodbye to two subtitlers and seen no replacements. People are generally very committed and conscientious in our department, but even with everyone pulling out the stops, we cannot maintain our original level of output. Some programmes have had to go by the board. The posts will be filled, subtitling is seen as a boom area, but not until our union, BETA (Broadcasting and Entertainment Trades Alliance), agrees to fundamental changes in our contract.

We are all preoccupied with these conflicts of interest, which inevitably sometimes find expression at a personal level and which shape our working day at present. (Union meetings, whispering in corners, chatting over coffee and icy stares . . .) I have been doing the job for three years now and have put a lot of energy into it. In my more reflective moments, I wonder if it was worth it. The people are lovely, the work is fun, but management are reneging on my contract and the nature of my job will change considerably. It doesn't help to know that this is happening in all television companies. We are demoralized. And, although we have voted to reject the new contract proposals, we feel that the model set by other managers within the industry, over the past few months, shows that resistance will be fruitless. I am thinking of moving on, or rather out, since advancement for women in the industry is still very difficult.

All this and more is passing through my mind as I take the lift to the fifth floor, hang my coat up and settle down with a coffee to carry on subtitling *Blind Date*. I have already broken the script up into subtitles, partially edited, and stored them on disk with time codes. But the dialogue is fast and needs more work on it. The skill in subtitling lies in editing the text down so that it is barely noticeable. All the information must be there, together with the daft jokes and cheeky innuendoes. As many users of the service are hard-of-hearing, rather than deaf, and follow the sound track to some degree, the editor mustn't stray too far from the original text.

Blind Date is riveting stuff, although few people will go as far as to admit they watch it. Cilla Black's in her element this week. One of her guests is a Scouser and she's getting full value out of it. I wonder how

Betting men: satellite television adds to 1988 betting shop facilities

many sub-standard *Blind Dates* will grace our screen when television is
deregulated . . .

I break for coffee and chat with one of the 'checkers' (quality control)
about loss of morale in the office, and the inevitable effect this has on the
service. It's hard building up a good team, and tragic if it's not properly
valued . . . At 7.50 p.m. the news subtitlers emerge, looking rather
frazzled. Their live subtitling for Channel 4 was being taped for posterity
and the system crashed, causing a total breakdown of the service. This
happens from time to time . . .

CARRIE HARVEY, SUBTITLER, ORACLE

MESSAGES FROM SPACE

*Although 1989 was to be the year when satellite television began the
attempt to win itself a mainstream market, some use was already being
made of space technology in 1988. Among other things Satellite
Information Services provided pictures for betting shops. Joe McNally
courted bookmakers in Scotland and the North of England.*

Rose at dawn to a silent house. Headed north on the long drive to Dundee.
It is 54 shopping days to Christmas or, maybe more relevant to this diary,
55 viewing days until we see *Oliver!* again . . . I reach Ed Barrett's house
at 10 a.m. Two video cameras watch me as I come up the drive and pull
in. A very security-conscious man is Ed. He's got a lot to protect. The
house must be worth a hundred grand which, I know, would only buy a
three-storey kennel in Knightsbridge, but in Dundee it's the Ponderosa.
Ed's gardener is there again, working in the rockery. We say 'Good
morning'. A big guy, he looks out of place in his old clothes, but
contented. He used to be a Beatles bodyguard. So Ed told me. I believe
him.

Ed comes out to meet me, moving slowly. He's still recovering from a
hernia operation, of which he gives me graphic details when we get
inside. He's Dundee's biggest independent bookmaker, with eight shops.
He takes our live racing service in all of them bar one – a long-standing
problem shop and the main reason I've come to see him today.

Our satellite is 22,000 miles up and 27.5 degrees west of south. Each
reception dish needs to 'see' the satellite to pick up the signal. The line of
sight from Ed's shop in Alexander Street is from the centre front of the
building and would be perfect if the council hadn't built a 300-foot tower
block right across the road. We're trying to get a dish on the roof of this
block (our highest installation so far in the UK) and run cables down and
through ducting under the road into the shop. Negotiations for permission
from the council have been protracted and delicate and we're now close to
reaching agreement. But Ed's temper and patience are at breaking point.

I spend two hours with him . . . He's big, forceful, serious-looking, a
sort of Lon Chaney type, only more handsome. He has a 'pocket' cigarette
case as big as a Filofax and he smokes six during our discussion. In the
end he accepts that we're not to blame for the problems with his shop and
that we're doing all we can to sort things out . . .

It was after 1 p.m. when I left for Glasgow. Ten minutes down the road the car phone rang. I answered it . . .

'Hello, Joe. It's George Truesdale.' (He has 11 shops in Ayrshire.)

'Hello, George, how are you?'

'Not too good.'

'What's wrong?'

'Remember the wall I had to build in the cellar at Mossblown?' (I remembered. It was to strengthen the supporting wall above, which was to bear the main weight of the dish. I guessed what had happened.)

'It's been built in the wrong place', I said.

'It wasn't my fault. Wrong information from the surveyors, they sent the wrong drawings.'

'I'll have to get full details on it from them, George. I'll come and see you on Thursday morning.'

'Phone first. I might not be here.' (He always says that, but he is always there, six days a week. George is one of the hardest-working bookmakers in the country. He never misses a trick.)

'OK, George, I'll phone.'

'Right, 'bye.'

I pushed a cassette in and sang along with Billy Joel and Paul Simon most of the way home to Glasgow . . . From the window we overlook the Clyde and the lights are coming on now in the streets, and on the bridges crossing the river. I sit down with Brian to work through the switch-on list of shops for the rest of the week. Every shop has to be checked on switch-on day, so we draw up a journey plan . . . The phone calls die away after 5 p.m. as the racing finishes and the shops close. Around 5.30 Lesley and Angela go home. Brian goes at 6 p.m. I switch off the whirring fans and the photocopier . . .

JOE McNALLY, AREA SALES MANAGER

Also up and running, and visible to the few in Britain who were in the right place with the right equipment, was the European channel of Sky Television. Its schedule consisted of English-language general entertainment programmes, mostly bought from North America. John Rowe is in command of the station's own production.

In my office at 9.15 a.m. I check Sky output to make sure we are still on air. The programme is a pop video show which we buy from Much Music in Canada. Dealt with our transmission of the 1988 Miss World, which we take on a 30-minute tape delay basis. Spoke with our Scandinavian office about the possibility of making a series of country music programmes. A sponsor has pointed out that Norway and Sweden is the largest market for country music in Europe.

Had a meeting with Mars Pet Foods about a series of eight 30-minute programmes that Sky will be producing on their behalf. Through Mars our production team can be put in the right direction for all research, vets, locations, etc. Lunch with the music executive producer to discuss a format for new titles to one of our sponsored music shows, *The Nescafé UK Top 40*.

Afternoon meeting with a director to discuss a new series of pet programmes. Production heads assemble for weekly meeting to discuss future and on-going output. Meet with representatives of Reg Grundy Productions to discuss heads of agreement for two new series we have commissioned, *Pot of Gold* and *Sale of the Century* . . .

**JOHN ROWE,
HEAD OF PRODUCTION, SKY**

THE DYNASTY AND THE GAG

At this pre-historic stage of their existence the satellite services were not much concerned with the issues concerning mainstream broadcasters. As, for instance, the recent order from the Government gagging the voices of political violence in Ireland. Among those ruminating, as ever, were the two sons of what has been called the First Family of television. In the BBC's monochrome era the Richard Dimbleby commentary solemnized great national events, and he presented Panorama and general election marathons with magisterial command. Now his sons David and Jonathan maintain the broadcasting dynasty.

Younger brother Jonathan has had a breakfast meeting with David Aaronovitch, his editor when he presents the BBC's On the Record at Sunday lunch-time. During the morning he has presided at Thames over a showing for newspaper previewers of one of his Witness documentaries, this one considering social work.

In the afternoon a call to Carole Stone about *Any Questions?* (Radio 4). Last week was in Northern Ireland, the first live programme after the Home Office ban on Sinn Fein/IRA interviews. There had been much anxiety and press comment: how to stop a Sinn Fein demonstration or speech? When to cut it off? Should we record the programme? But if we do, then all programmes would have to be recorded, as the risk does not only lie in Northern Ireland. There were camera crews and journalists in Antrim to greet us. But the programme passed off without incident. Relief all round. No rent-a-quote opportunities for those MPs who take any chance to try and dish the BBC. Evidently everyone is impressed by how smoothly everything went.

Karen de Young rings from the *Washington Post*. She is writing a piece about the ban. What do I think are the problems? Not so much the news as current affairs, documentaries and television history. All those programmes that give background, context and analysis: the information that the public needs to appreciate the complexities that bedevil a solution . . .

JONATHAN DIMBLEBY, ANCHORMAN

Meanwhile older brother David is himself in Washington, preparing to anchor the BBC's US election results programme. During the afternoon he enjoys exchanges with respected BBC reporter Kate Adie.

Pause for cup of coffee and fiery argument with Kate Adie, about whether the BBC should be prevented from showing IRA supporters on screen. I take the Government's side, for the sake of argument, though I am uncertain what I really think is right. Share horror at IRA being given time to justify their bombings, but that has hardly happened for years now.

I don't, in truth, see it as an attempt to further damage the BBC, or as a sign of an authoritarian government. The damage to the BBC is to be achieved, or attempted at least, in a far subtler way. By casting doubt on the licence fee, and opting, at some point, for subscription, which no one thinks will really work. Much will depend on whether the satellites are a success. What is worse? Too much television, too much of poor quality, or good television, such as the BBC on the whole provides, in the control of a few people? . . .

DAVID DIMBLEBY, ANCHORMAN

Dynasty head David
Dimbleby presides over
Washington election
results for the BBC

*Kate Adie politely excludes David Dimbleby from her diary, but the
underlying anxieties in their conversation still exercise her.*

The BBC's Kate Adie: ace
reporter facing up to a
bleaker broadcasting future

BBC Washington office crawling with election specialists . . . Have drink
with radio correspondent Peter Ruff. Discuss life, the universe, the state
of the BBC. The last two years have been just one long, on-going, soul-
searching progress about whither journalism and whither broadcasting.
Journalism is being more constrained, yet tabloid journalism is rampantly
mendacious and sensational. Broadcasting is very probably to be thrown
to the commercial wolves, under the false name of 'breaking the UK
duopoly'. Deeply pessimistic that More means Worse.

I am confirmed in this view after having seen acres of US television,
and also European satellite services. Unlike MPs, who rarely view, and
anyway consider television a political football rather than a service. All of
us are fearful that commercial pressures will lead to tabloid rubbish,
sensationalism, trivialization of social affairs, deference to government,
diminution of credibility. Not all is pessimism though: large numbers of
people are determined to grit teeth and soldier on in defence of
independent broadcasting, and honourable journalism . . .

KATHRYN ADIE, SPECIAL CORRESPONDENT

OURSELVES ALONE

*With public opinion either indifferent or sympathetic to the
Government ban, with little support from the press and not much more
from the industry mandarins, there was not a lot the broadcasting
journalists could do apart from huff and puff. On 1 November the idea
of a 24-hour strike, or 'day of action', by the National Union of
Journalists, was finding some favour. Others thought it illogical to
protest against one gag with another, self-imposed, gag. These included
the bullish industrial relations supremo at Thames.*

A 4.15 p.m. conference call with ITVA and other companies to hear that
NUJ leaders are proposing a one-day stoppage on 10 November.
Companies' representatives received this information virtually without
comment, perhaps out of stunned disbelief. Despite all the Government
anti-union legislation and the dire threats to the industry's future, unions
still cling to old-fashioned ideas of industrial action that we will have to
stamp on. Unless the union changes its mind, it seems inevitable that the
company will have to seek an injunction in the High Court . . .

Later informed by Thames News manager of the vote at the NUJ chapel
meeting held this lunchtime. Of 70+ members only 26 turned up, mostly
from Thames News. The vote on strike action was 13 for and 13 against.
The FOC (Father of the Chapel) put his casting vote in favour of action.
What a brilliant example of the use of non-democratic methods to
provoke a demonstration over democratic rights. No wonder the
Government thinks its view of television and television unions is right . . .

**J. DAVISON, INDUSTRIAL RELATIONS
EXECUTIVE, THAMES TELEVISION**

| *Attitudes at Ulster Television were rather less confrontational.*

Ten minutes late for an NUJ chapel meeting, to discuss our attitude over the Government decision to ban Sinn Fein from the airwaves. We were unanimous that we would not agree with our national officers to take any industrial action. It seemed pointless and would only further the public's view of the NUJ being in sympathy with terrorist organizations. Instead we agreed to stay on air during the so-called day of action, explaining to our viewers why we feel it important to disagree with Thatcher's decision . . .

GERRY KELLY, REPORTER-PRESENTER

PROTECTING THE CHILDREN

Colin Adams, head of network television at BBC Pebble Mill, last night attended a Broadcasting House dinner and so awoke this morning at the next door St George's Hotel. Over breakfast he studies the Independent *newspaper.*

Breakfast on the 16th floor overlooking Broadcasting House. Reading analysis of the Government's new restrictions on broadcasting interviews with Sinn Fein, the UDA and their like, prompts thoughts of past political storms that have broken over the bows of Broadcasting House. The building itself still looks solid enough, but what of those on the bridge? . . .

Tube to Television Centre. Visit TK 45, where a complicated technical exercise is under way on another film in the Pebble Mill series *Protecting the Children*. These observational programmes – about the work of the NSPCC in the field of child abuse – have produced more than their fair share of legal and technical problems.

One film remains the subject of a restraining injunction, and I view some work that has been carried out to try and further mask the identity of the children featured in the programme, which contains some of the most harrowing, and important, material I have ever viewed. The level of commitment and support from technical colleagues in the BBC is, as ever, tremendous, but will it be enough to persuade a High Court judge that the film should go out in the public interest? It remains doubtful . . .

Attend editorial policy meeting, under the chairmanship of John Wilson . . . There is a very full discussion of what the Government's new prohibitions on free reporting in Northern Ireland really mean. The Belfast-based programme *Spotlight* has recently broadcast an interview with a member of one of the proscribed organizations. Sub-titles were used to give a verbatim account of his words. Given the undoubted public support for the Government measures, will they also recognize its farcical implications? . . .

Lunch and a discussion with Samir Shah (Deputy Editor, News and Current Affairs) about capital punishment, prompted by our NSPCC series, *Protecting the Children*. Should child abusers pay the ultimate penalty? As we move on to discuss the new restrictions in Northern

Ireland, and the threatened strike by BBC journalists, it prompts reflections on how out-of-tune programme makers often are with public attitudes. Striking in defence of freedom of speech does, though, seem profoundly illogical.

Phone the BBC Solicitors' Department and speak to Sean McTernan about the work on the NSPCC programme I had viewed that morning and the possibility of it leading to the lifting of the injunction. I tell him that the cost of the technique we were considering will be prohibitive. We will have to find another way. We discuss the timescale and the likelihood of success. I reflect that you cannot call a series *Protecting the Children* and then complain when the courts frustrate your intentions, in the interests of the children . . .

COLIN ADAMS, HEAD OF
NETWORK TELEVISION, BBC PEBBLE MILL

Sally-Anne Lomas, assistant producer on the series made with an NSPCC Child Protection Team in Lincoln, is on a day trip from London. On the train she has been reading the Guardian, *the* Independent *and the* Financial Times.

Reading newspapers is part of my job, the television feeds shamelessly upon the print medium . . . I find a report on a sexual abuse case in which Mr Justice Brooke, in jailing a man for two and a half years, has said: 'There is very considerable and widespread public concern today that children should be allowed to grow up without being interfered with sexually by adults, and the courts, in the sentences they pass, have to record that concern.' I find this strange reading. Is he reluctant to sentence? Only one per cent of abusers are sentenced as it is, even with 'considerable and widespread public concern'.

There are two interesting articles in the *Guardian*, one about the need to counsel sex offenders, the other discussing the feminist premise that all men are potential abusers. The journalist Paul Fisher questions the implications this has for his own relations with his daughter.

I am glad to see questions like this being raised in the press. Gender issues, the wider context, prevention of abuse, what the incidence of abuse says about men and society in general, are the important concerns which have been absent from the debate. There has been much concern over procedures and management but none on prevention. I suspect next week's studio discussion programme will repeat this emphasis and be dull.

I arrive at Lincoln and get a taxi to the NSPCC family centre. The social work team are rather jittery as their practice has been criticized in *Social Work Today*. We sit down to watch the final programme. It has hardly begun before Pat Fines, social worker, says it's boring. Cathy, the playgroup worker, contradicts her, saying: 'No, I think a lot of people will identify with this.' Pat is so negative at the moment. The final team response is positive, I report this back to base and there are great sighs of relief.

I drive out with Dave Pettit, social worker, to pick up Mrs S. She has redecorated her lounge since we filmed there. I compliment her on the wallpaper. 'So, you like my yuppie wallpaper, do you?' she fires at me, putting me firmly in place, no chance of buttering her up. She has another boyfriend and is in love. She is chatty and seems relaxed about the programme. I'd forgotten what huge eyes she has, a very attractive woman.

Dave leaves us to watch the programme together. Mrs S.'s five-year-old daughter was found having oral sex in the Wendy house with two little boys at school. Dave tries, rather clumsily, to see if the girl has been sexually abused and to teach her appropriate defences. Watching the programme with Mrs S. is tense, some very critical comments are made about her and her parenting.

Most parents, watching these films, have barely concentrated, fixing on the trivial. She watches in a focused way and picks up every word. In the end she accepts the programme as a fair picture of real events but asks that all names are removed, to further prevent identification. She is worried that her daughter may be recognized, and this will lead to more trouble at school. I think this is a reasonable request, though it means a lot of extra work.

I phone the producer, Tamasin Day-Lewis. As expected she goes barmy on hearing of the mother's request but she agrees to comply. 'We've just cancelled all our dubbing dates', she says. 'We'll have to do it all on VT, you know it's a day's work.' I do indeed, but we have agreed a process of consultation with the families and I am aware of how easy it is to walk all over them, use our power and their powerlessness. I think we have a duty to behave well by the brave people who agree to participate in programmes like this . . .

Driving to the station with Dave, I talk to him about my current frustration with television, how after working for a year on this project, becoming in television terms a child abuse expert, my knowledge and understanding is still superficial. One remains an observer, not a participant. I feel so limited by television's inability to intervene directly. Stuart Hall says that television is the nation's conversation with itself, but I am sick of letting other people talk, creating the space for the debate. I want to talk. I want to know, to believe, to have opinions, to act, not just watch. I'd like to speak out, but there doesn't appear to be a space for people working in television to do that. I shall have to leave in order to speak. Poor Dave, after that diatribe, I think he was glad to drop me off at the station . . .

Over a bowl of carrot soup at home I watch *Divided Kingdom* (Channel 4). Bea Campbell looks great, I like her voice and commentary, her television style is getting better. Yet the programme is dull . . . compared to the richness and subtlety of Bea's writing this seems very bland. But here we are at the limits of television. One simple idea is all it can handle . . . Looking at Tuesday's viewing I did feel that something was rotten at the heart of broadcasting. I think the spirit has gone out of it. Those of us that care are bailing out. But then, maybe, if it had been a Wednesday evening I would have felt differently . . .

S A L L Y - A N N E L O M A S,
A S S I S T A N T P R O D U C E R

> *Although her Child Line idea is not universally admired, Esther Rantzen, television celebrity, has at least been trying to give practical help to abused children. She has thoughts for them today, amidst the trauma of the first responses to her latest exercise in popular television, unveiled the previous weekend,* Hearts of Gold.

Central Television ring, a psychologist has attacked Child Line. I try and respond, we have counselled 40,000 children in our first two years. The biggest single problem is still sexual abuse. The children carry an intolerable burden of pain and guilt. We believe them, we tell them they are not to blame, we try and find someone in their families to confide in. They dread the intervention of the police because they think they will destroy their family. If only all of us working to protect children could

BBC presenter-producer
Esther Rantzen surrounded
by youthful *Hearts of Gold*

unite to make the law more child sensitive, and therefore more effective . . .

The *Daily Mail* ring and ask if I will defend Child Line against the psychologist. I do my best, again, wondering of course how and if they'll quote me. The *Mail* is so anti-BBC and pretty anti-Child Line, on the grounds they'd much rather child abuse didn't exist – wouldn't we all? But shooting the messenger may not be the answer, and the abused children ringing Child Line desperately need us to pass their message on . . .

So many hopes for *Hearts of Gold*, ambitions of creating a Good News programme riding on it. Too early to know yet if viewers liked it. The critics had a field day at my expense, predictably. All but one, Maggie Forwood of the *People*, and she cares about popular television. She liked it, maybe the viewers will . . . Paul Fox rings to say 'pass on congratulations to the team', and to say they have appointed a new head and deputy head to our department. I say how much it means to the team that he thinks the show works. Everyone walks taller after a bouquet from the bosses, back at the office faces brighten . . .

At home in the evening everything stops for *Fawlty Towers* . . . How can the politicians, the public, accept the idea of destroying the BBC/ITV competitive partnership that has created this kind of programme? Tuck the children in, discuss the infinity of the universe with Emily. Just as baffling as the deliberate destruction of the BBC. New head of department rings. He sounds very enthusiastic. I decide not to ask him either about BBC destruction or the universe, make lunch date instead . . .

**ESTHER RANTZEN,
PRODUCER-PRESENTER**

FOSSILS, ASSASSINS, REACTORS, ANTIQUES

Outside London other documentary makers were not invariably finding it easy to gather the material they wanted. Typically far from base was the agelessly enthusiastic Sir David Attenborough, a reluctant mandarin who was well on the way to becoming BBC Director-General when, in 1972, he opted to return to natural history.

There are six of us – cameraman, assistant, recordist, producer, production assistant, expert guide and myself – and we are working on a four-part series about fossils. It is neither an easy nor an obviously popular subject. I proposed the idea, so I have only myself to blame. I believe it to be a fascinating aspect of the natural world that so far has been virtually ignored. We have come up to the northernmost coast of mainland Britain, a few miles west of Thurso, looking for 400-million-year-old fossil fish. November is hardly the ideal time to be here, but the first location we chose to film this particular segment of the script, earlier in the year, proved to be no good, and as we have to finish the series before the spring and the arrival of warmer weather, we might as well do it now.

The morning conditions are as unfit as we might have expected, lowering clouds and driving sleet. Stan, our guide, says that fossil fish are amazingly abundant here. It doesn't seem that way . . . we rather lose heart. At 1 p.m. we retire to munch sandwiches, and drink chocolate and coffee from a thermos, optimistically crawling for shelter in the lee of some seaweed-covered boulders. To make matters worse, the tide is coming in and steadily covering the rocks which might contain the fossils we are looking for.

It is Mike, the director, who finds the first really recognizable segment of a fossil fish. We start excitedly but carefully splitting the boulder to expose more of the fossil; and we reveal not only it but two more fish lying in the same bedding plane alongside the first. They are almost complete, but not the spectacular specimens I had been visualizing when I wrote the sequence. Still, they are much better than anything we've found so far, and they might just serve the purpose. What is more, there are snatches of weak, rather bleary sun. So we film it all in thorough detail with careful continuity and only stop when evening begins to rob us of light.

We trudge back, carrying the gear, as the wind gets up and big waves

Another on the slate. Fossil hunters Sir David Attenborough (left) and Stan Wood contemplate a 280-million-year-old amphibian

start crashing up the shore, feeling a little more cheerful than we thought, at lunch-time, we would be. If the footage is really good, we might have about 45 seconds more of the completed programme. But it still might be that the day (and yesterday when we travelled up here) will have produced nothing at all that will get on the screen . . .

DAVID ATTENBOROUGH, CONTRIBUTOR

> *Some way to the south, at Tarves near Ellon in Aberdeenshire, works producer Simon Welfare. He freelances for Yorkshire and runs his own independent company, Granite. This morning he looked out from his study window to Grampian fields, cows silhouetted in the rain. He is setting up a 1990 history of the Soviet Union, made with archive film never previously seen in the West.*

I start this afternoon, like most others at the moment, with a call to John Lord, co-producer of the series and my guru in all things Soviet. John lives in New Jersey: this is one of the more complicated projects. We discuss the quality of Soviet film-makers, recognized this year by the award of the documentary Prix Italia, music for our series and the progress made last week towards raising the dollars needed from the American end . . .

I am reading Robert Conquest's *The Great Terror*. It is getting even darker outside. My desk lamp casts the proverbial pool of light. A cat wanders in and sits beside the word processor, basking in the heat of the lamp. I read of the event which gave Stalin the opportunity to kill, repress and traumatize so many millions of his countrymen.

'On 1 December 1934, at about four o'clock in the afternoon, the young assassin Leonid Nikolayev entered the Smolny, headquarters of the Communist Party in Leningrad. The few hours of the city's thin winter daylight were long over, and it was quite dark . . .' Kirov is about to be assassinated. In Moscow, two months ago, I saw archive footage of the aftermath. Kirov lies in his open coffin, his wife approaches for one last kiss. A few feet away stands Stalin, the man now thought to have arranged the murder. In my mind, a sequence begins to take shape. I enjoy the moment, the reality of the cutting room is always far less fun . . .

SIMON WELFARE, PRODUCER

> *Charles Stewart (cameraman-producer), Malcolm Hirst (soundman-producer), John Dinwoodie (editor) and Sally Hilton (assistant editor) have been working for Partners in Production on a Channel 4-commissioned observational film about nuclear power. The working title is* Nuclear Power in Action *and it is being edited behind British Nuclear Fuels security at Risley, outside Warrington. No material will be released until everybody is sure there has been no breach of national security. There is a worry that the film will be too 'objective', too much like a BNF commercial. John Dinwoodie remains decently sceptical.*

Before I could fully scan the daily papers for tales of nuclear woe it was time to depart for Risley. The car park for visitors is the only one I know

where you need a token from security to get out again . . . The film is a
76-minute documentary about Sellafield we are thinking of calling *Death
in Cumbria*, with no particular political or ideological slant. Unless
they're putting something in the kettle. There's plenty of material, 173
16mm camera rolls, and more to shoot . . .

Charles Stewart's languid and acute style of camera is a challenge and a
pleasure to cut. This sequence depicts the last opportunity BNF day
employees will have to enjoy egg, beans, bacon and toast to a traditional
oil-based BNF recipe. The breakfast has been 'bought out' to increase
productivity. Only one member of the queue wears a black armband . . .
Next we see a House of Lords delegation visiting the reprocessing plant;
then the plutonium finishing plant, which they are not shown. Quite a lot
of Sellafield is 'invisible' for reasons we're not allowed to mention.
Neither are we allowed to mention the fact that we're not allowed to
mention it. Rather like cutting for the BBC, in fact . . .

Channel 4 have insisted on editorial control over this production, which
is why it's being edited under high security. The accommodation is very
comfortable and spacious, two rooms, two Steenbecks freighted in
specially, but no alcohol permitted on the premises. We are perhaps a
touch too near the guardroom. BNF appear to be paying for the phone so,
of course, we will be bending over backwards to give them a fair crack of
the whip, and to remain impartial . . . One feels slightly beholden, but
justice will prevail . . .

JOHN DINWOODIE, FILM EDITOR

> *More fortunate in his location is Christopher Lewis, executive producer
> of BBC Bristol's* Antiques Roadshow. *The last recording of the year is
> being set up in the Devon town of Tavistock, on the western edge of
> Dartmoor. The stone-flagged Pannier Market has little comfort and less
> heating, but is considered preferable to the anonymous sports halls
> normally used. Also approved is Keith Spiers, the 'Market Reeve',
> manhandling chairs in braces and then putting on a tidy jacket to
> transform himself into an official council flunkey. Then comes the
> afternoon crisis.*

Expert Henry Sandon tells me he has just called on a local auctioneer, to
get their latest catalogue, and been given a leaflet inviting him to their
own valuation event timed to coincide exactly with ours. The leaflet
announces: 'Our show is truly on the Road'. Worse, the organizer, a tall
man with a patch over one eye, pictured in the leaflet, proposes to plant
two girls outside our event handing out his leaflet to our customers. 'Ah
yes,' says the Reeve, 'I've been meaning to have a word with you about
this. It's all most embarrassing, not least because he's a member of the
Town Council.'

Convulsions. We never allow commercial activity of any kind to ride on
the back of the show. It's one of the reasons people come to us, and trust
us . . . On the telephone the man with the eye patch is smooth, smarmy,

urbane and tricky. He shifts his ground as I attempt to describe my objections. He wasn't really going to have girls outside our hall, he was only being supportive of our event, he personally knew many of our experts, he used to do public relations for the BBC. He agrees his intention is to profit from the *Antiques Roadshow*'s drawing power. He sees nothing improper in this. For 45 minutes the argument rages. It ends when he starts to tell me about BBC policy. I hang up.

I ring the BBC solicitor's office. The line is pretty bad. I'm put through to the 'sister's office', which causes some confusion. ('Are you a solicitor?' 'Yes, I'm a sister.' 'No, a SO-LIC-ITOR . . .') Finally I achieve the home number of the duty solicitor, who tells me there's nothing I can do. I can, however, make announcements on the public address system, dissociating the *Roadshow* from any local auctioneer and recommending caution to anyone considering selling. Well, it might be something. I genuinely hate the idea of our vulnerable customers being picked off by greedy entrepreneurs who've seized an opportunity. Tavistock is the last place in which I would have expected trouble. The Reeve puts it this way: 'Fleas on a dog's back', he says . . .

**CHRISTOPHER LEWIS,
EXECUTIVE PRODUCER**

Mind my chest! The BBC's *Antiques Roadshow* visits Tavistock in Devon

And so to consider the actual afternoon schedules offered for the delectation of viewers on 1 November. The immediate post-lunch period is mostly taken up with old cinema films. Channel 4 ran The Iron Mask *(1929), the final monochrome Douglas Fairbanks spectacular and a sequel to* The Three Musketeers, *from 2 p.m. until 3.20. ITV companies showed a variety of films and soaps from 1.30 until 3 p.m. BBC1 substituted a trash movie and made an occasion with yet another transmission, from 2.15 p.m. until 3.45, of* The Importance of Being Earnest *(1952). For many this was the highlight of the day.*

Channel 4 revives the last of the Douglas Fairbanks spectaculars, *The Iron Mask*

As far as I'm concerned, television exists solely so that I can watch masses of movies gratis, in privacy and comfort, away from smelly and expensive picture palaces and their disgusting audiences. I saw cinemas

The Most Dynamic and Colorful Star in Screen History!

DOUGLAS FAIRBANKS

THE IRON MASK

Further Adventures of D'ARTAGNAN and the THREE MUSKETEERS

Narrated by RICHARD LEWELLYN
Spoken by DOUGLAS FAIRBANKS, Jr.
An Odyssey Pictures, Inc. Re-Presentation
Released by Lippert Pictures, Inc.

come, and now I've seen them go. In the whole of the Isle of Wight there is just one cinema left, and I don't shed one tear for their passing.

Since retiring, I've had the opportunity of watching television all day long, from *Breakfast Time* and TV-am right through, and my considered judgement is that, although many people claim we have the finest television service in the world, it is basically a flood of utter crud, redeemed only by the free movies it brings into my home . . .

At 1.30 p.m. my wife and I sat and watched the TVS film, *You Can't Escape Forever* (1942), a Warner Brothers newspaper-and-crime story with George Brent and Brenda Marshall. OK. At 2 p.m. our first VCR was switched on to record *The Iron Mask*, and at 2.15 p.m. I dashed upstairs to switch on *The Importance of Being Earnest*. I had recorded that twice before in the past, but Bo in Sweden had wanted the first copy, and a German friend had wanted the second, so I hadn't one of my own. After the film we had tea and then returned to our downstairs set to watch the slickly made John Landis comedy-thriller *Into the Night* (1985), which the BBC had shown on Sunday night, while we were watching *The Jigsaw Man* . . .

**PETER SEWARD,
RETIRED INFORMATION OFFICER,
SHANKLIN, ISLE OF WIGHT**

I searched the Tuesday schedules for something that, I thought, would be difficult to produce in 1988 and I came up with *The Importance of Being Earnest*. I felt that Wilde's witticisms would not be appreciated by the present generation. If the play was put on in its true Victorian atmosphere (and it was) the younger generations would probably think it over-acted. I have read the play and seen it acted, many years ago. Then, it seemed very scintillating, but now I don't think it got across as presented . . .

**MR L. E. TREMAYNE, AGED 92,
LUTON, BEDFORDSHIRE**

I told a friend that I had recorded *The Importance of Being Earnest*, because I know that she loves it. A comment she made, 'In those days men were real men and women were real women', sparked off a discussion about the general lack of good manners amongst young men today, and for this we blamed feminism. We came to the conclusion that, although women are now supposed to be equal, we have in fact never had it so bad. We have even lost the few advantages we had in the past, while ruled by male chauvinist pigs. Carol even went so far as to point out that if it wasn't for women (the liberated ones) harping on about equality and female mega-achievers everywhere, her husband would not be so irritating and unreasonable as to expect her to find a part-time job. The conversation became so heated that I nearly missed *Floyd on Britain and Ireland* . . .

**WENDY DADGOSTAR, MOTHER,
SUTTON COLDFIELD, WEST MIDLANDS**

**AFTERNOON
TIMES**

Far from seeing herself as a mega-achiever, Alison Fell watches this afternoon at a very low ebb. The supreme sweetness of the previous week had turned sour.

I watched television this afternoon and I had the sensation that my world was collapsing. To be more specific, as we watched *The Importance of Being Earnest*, my heart was shredded to ribbons. The end of love is rarely an occasion to be cheerful and this was no exception. The only redeeming feature of the event was that Colin looked particularly unattractive, sporting an horrendous new haircut and the remains of a big red scar across the face (last night's Hallowe'en fancy dress party). But pain overwhelmingly reigned.

A handbag? Michael Redgrave and Margaret Rutherford consider their past in *The Importance of Being Earnest*

The Importance of Being Earnest is a play full of discussion on love and marriage, which is just what Colin and myself had been delightedly

talking about last week. Those stupid women, fussing about whether their men should be called Ernest or not. I would marry Colin tomorrow, even if he was called Ernestina. (Heaven knows, Colin is a bad enough name.)

The declarations of love made us both wince. Very familiar phrases, and yes, we said them too, only recently, but it seems ages ago now. We did not say very much today, as we watched the play. Television frequently erases the need to speak. This brilliant, polished gem of a work laughed at our misery from behind the glass. Love must be a ludicrous thing, making a rational person like me give such promises of love and devotion to someone bent on cruelty. My senses are on fast forward, my brain on pause, my heart stopped. Have I been rejected, or ejected?

ALISON FELL, UNEMPLOYED, SHEFFIELD

HEAR NO EVIL, SEE NO TELEVISION
Alison Fell is 24 and unlucky in love. Others are older and plain unlucky.

Woke up very early (I won't even say what time, it was that early) and realized it was Diary Day. I felt uneasy, and this gradually built up to a feeling of intimidation. Must I really bare my relationship to that little silent box in the corner, even to myself? So I didn't, as I normally would have, switch on when I found I couldn't go back to sleep, to see what ITV was on about. The operative verb is certainly 'see', because I can't hear . . . Turn to teletext, which is my best access to news, and skip through the pages. ITV teletext news is usually more lively than BBC, but isn't today . . .

Through the morning the picture has just been ornamental. Switch on again at 3.30 p.m. to find the BBC has *The Importance of Being Earnest*. Some time last year there was a subtitled version that I enjoyed. This one was not subtitled but it's lovely to see these superb actors in their prime again. That's one inestimable gift of television, to bring back the past by showing old films. Margaret Rutherford, a joy! Because I know the story I watch longer than I should. Anthony Asquith was a director who knew his medium . . .

Through the rest of the day television is my closest companion and easiest access to my native language (when subtitles make the lip-reading easier). I look in on *Colin's Sandwich*, and find it funnier than I expect, but the phoney relationships (of which I have my fair share) are really no joke. At 10.55 p.m. delayed drowsiness overtakes me. I switch off. I hope I've shown how closely television is woven into the fabric of my life, however flimsily I gather its threads.

DOROTHY MILES, WRITER-PERFORMER, LONDON WC1

All set, pen poised, anxiously aware that the most important part of the day, for television viewing, was yet to come. We left the house for a short while between 2 and 3 p.m. and were burgled. The robbers stole our two television sets and video recorder. Needless to say this was a very untypical day in our household. And I'm sorry to say there is no postscript. We have borrowed a black and white set but the children, who normally enjoy most children's television, continuously switch from one channel to another, believing there is a fault . . .

SUSAN DUFFIELD, LECTURER, MIDDLESBROUGH

ALL BOWLS
It was not a big day for live sport. There were three BBC2 helpings of Championship Bowls, the first two at 2.40 and 3.30 p.m., but even in Sir Francis Drake's home town viewers apparently regarded the coverage, of the CIS UK singles at Preston, as less than lively.

I have no great interest in bowling, but today it was the least objectionable television. My attention was only partly on it, since I was completing a crossword puzzle and having tea. In fact I doubt if I watched at all, it was background . . .

MAIR WRIGHT, RETIRED LECTURER, MARKET RASEN, LINCOLNSHIRE

Today's television, if truth be told, is cast in a depressing mould, and most of us suspect with sorrow that it will be as bad tomorrow . . . Though most of us are patient souls who make no fuss o'er games of bowls I'd say three lengthy slots a day must make us yearn for 'rain stopped play'. . .

BERNARD CAMPION, NAVAL-SECRETARIAL OAP, PLYMOUTH

At Preston there is rather more concern, and commentator Jimmy Davidson got some satisfaction from his day.

The game at 2 p.m. was a second-round match between the Scottish champion Colin Sommerville and the 21-year-old Edinburgh postman Richard Corsie over the best of five sets, of seven shots. The game lasted three hours three minutes, and it is always a little wearing to commentate 'as live' for that length of time. There was a lot of personal satisfaction in seeing young Corsie win 2–7, 7–2, 7–4, 4–7, 7–2. When I was Director of Coaching for English Bowls I coached the then 17-year-old Richard for an intensive week . . .

No real meals, just snacks after breakfast. I find that while commentating live on television, concentration on what is happening and what might happen is so intense that I forget, immediately after one game, who played in the previous game I covered. Like everybody else I have to have a period of winding down to 'normal'.

JIMMY DAVIDSON, COMMENTATOR

PARKY GRINS AND BEARS
By mid-afternoon ITV has recovered the ratings lead it lost at lunchtime. The audience for The Importance of Being Earnest *on BBC1*

*descends gradually from 2.5 million at 2.15 p.m. to 1.8 million at 3.30.
By contrast the ITV audience climbs steadily from 1.3 million at
1.30 p.m. to 3.3 million for the second half of the Thames celebrity
charade show* Give Us a Clue, *shown from 3 p.m. to 3.25. This is the
opener of a tenth series for the male versus female formula, first seen in
1979. Michael Parkinson, grinning uneasily as his guests show off, now
presents in place of Michael Aspel.*

Give Us a Clue, give us a rest from this piffle . . .
**LEON PAICE, RETIRED
CIVIL SERVANT, BRISTOL**

Watched *Give Us a Clue*, video recorded from ITV. What a pity the
programme is spoilt by Lionel Blair's cheating. He mouths the words to
his team. And why is Michael Parkinson so biased for the men's team? He
gives them extra points for no reason at all. These two people spoil a very
entertaining programme . . .
**MR H. G. REDGRAVE, RETIRED,
HEMEL HEMPSTEAD, HERTFORDSHIRE**

Disharmony in the Oprah
house. First and second
wives were brought
together by *The Oprah
Winfrey Show*

INTO THE OPRAH HOUSE

The Channel 4 schedule has followed The Iron Mask *with a 1943 black
and white short from The Three Stooges. Staying with American
culture it embarks at 3.40 p.m. on* The Oprah Winfrey Show, *bought
from Chicago. This is the eighth of a first run of 40, for these audience
participation shows, on C4. During its 50 minutes the audience at home
more than trebles from 600,000 to 1.9 million. The black presenter,
sensible and sympathetic amidst the general clamour of confession and
confrontation, has persuaded first and second wives to sit in proximity
and air their grievances.*

Went to buy the evening paper, came back and started to glance at *The
Oprah Winfrey Show* while reading it. Mum was watching. A black
American woman hosting a chat show. It'd be the biggest breakthrough in
Britain if that ever happened here. A black British woman hosting a show,
tell me about it in, say, 20 years' time . . . It was quite amusing but a bit
overpowering, divorces and such like, the Americans do tend to be a bit
loud . . .
**MARVERINE COLE, AGED 17,
BIRMINGHAM**

Recently I have found afternoon programmes which bring me in from the
garden. Today's was *The Oprah Winfrey Show*. What a wonderful name.
She was talking to first and second wives, and the problems the condition
brings. Miss Winfrey is attractive, fluent, thinks on her feet and is kind.
She can also make jokes, which were needed in the war of the wives . . .
**SHEILA HANNAM, COMPANY DIRECTOR,
SKEGNESS, LINCOLNSHIRE**

Oprah Winfrey's is the only one of those studio participation and problem programmes I find watchable. A few minutes of *Kilroy!* was enough to show me that it was as heavy as a suet dumpling, only not so sustaining. But there is something enormously winning about Ms Winfrey's air of bemused common sense, in the face of the outrageous behaviour surrounding her . . .
**CLAUDIA GOULD, LECTURER,
CRAWLEY, SUSSEX**

The Oprah Winfrey Show is the finest chat show at present on television. It does not have the pretentiousness of *Kilroy!*, nor the patronizing pomposity of David Frost, nor the inanity of Parkinson, nor the blandness of Aspel. The questions are followed up by further questions, as would be the case if the average viewer was doing the questioning . . .
**MR A. C. TAPSON, RETIRED,
BRIXHAM, DEVON**

WESTERN APPROACHES
In addition to the efforts of 7000 or so school-age people who wrote television diaries of 1 November, associated projects were run out of 12 universities, polytechnics and other institutions of higher education. Representing the 250 and more students who were involved, here are four from the radio journalism course at the Falmouth School of Art and Design in Cornwall. They investigated viewing habits in various South-Western extremities, including the Isles of Scilly and the Lizard Lighthouse. Jane Carr and Matt Hall took a trip to the islands which lie 28 miles beyond Land's End.

Their first interviewee was Helga Williams, who runs a guest house on St Mary's.

Well, I do watch quite a lot, the television is on all day because I just . . . well, we get up every morning at six o'clock, and the television goes on, and we watch morning television. Whatever's on I watch. If it's something I don't like, I switch it over to another programme. Today I watched . . . that American lady . . . what's her name? . . . yes, that's right, Oprah Winfrey . . . then *Fifteen-to-One*, then from there I took it over to ITV and watched *Blockbusters*.

Fisherman Peter Honeychurch is more selective.

Our boy comes home at twelve, and the first job is to put the television on before anything else. Sometimes there's something of interest on, obviously you might sit down there and catch it, but breakfast television, as far as I'm concerned, is immoral. How anyone can watch television at that time in the morning, I am not sure.

The researchers come to realize that television is more important to islanders than to mainland viewers. The nearest cinema is across the

sea in Penzance, the arrival of newspapers and mail depends on the
weather. Storms, as Margaret Perkovic explains, can also blacken off
air television.

When we had the very bad weather a couple of years ago, of course all the
televisions went off . . . you know, the transmitters, they can't work . . .
then video is marvellous, you can bung a video in, watch it, and pretend
the weather is great.

*Fellow students Gillian Sharpe and Joanne Cutler visited Edward Street,
lighthousekeeper at the Lizard. He had been watching through the night
and was asked if he did this because he liked the programmes.*

No . . . the programmes that are shown from one o'clock to five o'clock in
the morning are of appalling quality and so you just watch for something
to do. I wouldn't deliberately stay up to watch a programme being
screened at that time of night, they're not worth it . . . In the day, well, I
presume someone at the BBC is being very, very clever. People are writing
their diaries and they have got *The Importance of Being Earnest* on, which
I presume 90 per cent of the population will watch . . . This evening *The
Cosby Show*, which is possibly the funniest show on television at the
moment, maybe *The New Statesman* . . . oh . . . *Fawlty Towers*.

*Edward Street was asked how he saw the impending changes in British
television. He was not in favour:*

Because the fear that I personally have, and I think a lot of people have, is
that there won't be much of a choice, there'll just be lots of the same old
rubbish. As more channels compete for a set number of viewers the
quality of programmes will fall rapidly, while they just try to pull in as
high a number of viewers as they can. They will cater to the lowest
common denominator. So stations like Channel 4 will become starved of
cash and we will lose out. We will just be watching American and
Australian-type rubbish 24 hours a day, on 20 different channels.

(*Interviewer*) Now you move around in your job . . . you do relief postings
. . . so you've seen a lot of different regional type programmes. What do
you think of, say, BBC South West?

(*ES*) They're all much of a muchness really, apart from the Channel
Islands, but I do enjoy watching the BBC South West programmes, the
local programmes, mainly because I know who they're talking about, or
the areas that they're talking about. They also have a high quality of
presenter.

(*Interviewer*) Do you think there could be more regional programming?

(*ES*) It would be nice to see more regional programming, but outside the
news shows they tend to concentrate mainly on fishing or gardening and I

don't particularly want to see more on those subjects. If the BBC could make local programmes of wider variety, then, yes, I'd like to see that.

(*Interviewer*) How important is television out on a rock lighthouse?

(*ES*) Working out on a rock lighthouse, television is about the only recreation you've got, unless you are an avid hobby fan, unless you're making ships in bottles or something like that. And what I have found when on those places is that you can home in on very strange interests, you suddenly become captivated . . . like when we all got into the *Crossroads* syndrome and just could not stop. I was on one particular lighthouse where the three things we watched without fail were *Crossroads*, *Emmerdale Farm* and the *Financial Times* index. For some reason we'd become totally besotted with the FT index and so everything would stop as we sat down at the end of the midday news just to find out what the index was doing. It was marginally more exciting than *Emmerdale Farm*.

13 WILLINGLY OUT OF SCHOOL

> *The largest number of pupils who wrote of the television experience as part of their school work were at the middle and secondary school stages. Here are a few of the many.*

The household in which I live is a female orientated one with one female adult (my mother), three teenage girls, one under-ten male and one under-ten female . . . The decisions about television programmes, and what should be watched, is generally up to the individual and who can get into either of our television rooms first . . . We are very democratic, there is no 'higher authority' who decides what will be on. While 'watching' there are various activities that I might be engaged with, such as homework, reading, eating, listening to music, talking to people on the phone or sitting with me.

I think that the circumstances in which I watch make a big difference to the enjoyment that I have from the programme. When the whole family is watching, people feel that they have to give their opinions on the various points in the programme. In comedy programmes someone usually points out the jokes at the end of each sequence, which I find infuriating. If it is a programme that I find particularly interesting, or one where I need to concentrate to get into the plot, I find that I would rather watch on my own, in the dark, in the smaller of our television rooms, sitting on a bean bag with my face level to the screen. This helps create a little more 'realism' for me and I do not like to be interrupted once I am absorbed in a programme or film . . .

HANNAH PHILLIPS, AGED 15, TANBRIDGE HOUSE SCHOOL, HORSHAM, SUSSEX

The *First Tuesday* kind of documentary, about the so-called 'Restoration Church' and its 'leader' system, interests me for two reasons. The first is that I take a deep interest in all religions and cults, as I find them and their effects on people interesting. The second reason is that, when my grandmother died, my grandfather let the 'church' take her place. He is obsessed with it. He has given up tennis, his life-long hobby, as he believes that it takes his attention away from the 'church' and is, in effect, 'against God's will' . . . Then there was my father himself. In 1979, when 'Evangelism' really seemed to get a grip on Britain, my father became totally wrapped up in a church rather like the 'Restoration Church' featured in *First Tuesday*. This nearly resulted in a divorce between my parents at that time, and it really was an evil influence on their marriage, whatever it called itself . . .

I suppose that the best place to watch television for me is my own front room, with its comfort, cats and relaxation . . . But, of course, who can resist popping out in the middle of any programme for something to eat? Well, I certainly can't. I am forever eating while I watch; to watch without a bite to eat on the side is like tea without a biscuit . . . When the process of deciding, eating and watching is over, the people with whom I talk most about what I have watched are my friends at school. When you really did enjoy something, like the fantastic *Jack the Ripper* recently screened on ITV, it really gives you this kind of great feeling of mutual admiration and taste, if all, or at least one or two, of your friends have seen and enjoyed it too . . . I would say that 30 per cent of my everyday conversations, if not more, concern television, video or some form of mass media information . . .

**SALLY LESLIE, AGED 15,
GARTH HIGH SCHOOL, MORDEN, SURREY**

Between 4 and 5 p.m. I watched *Miami Vice* recorded from a week ago. This is the best series in the present day. The mixture of action and music, and the quality of filming, makes me tape every episode. I don't understand why certain bits have to be cut. It is the way of life in Miami and should be shown. Of course *Miami Vice* is glamourfied but I still find it enthralling . . . and I have seen more violence on the *Nine O'Clock News*. This issue really annoys me as watching violence does not turn me into a psychopath, it just informs me about reality.

Another thing that annoys me is the cutting of nudity in programmes. We are all human forms, so why can't they be shown on television? I think that if children are shown nudity they will become less curious and less vulnerable when older. I think they will become more mature and less shy. I know my views are totally opposite to that of a normal BBC manager or censorship worker but I think I have a good point . . .

**MATTHEW VALENTINE, AGED 17,
WEST KENT COLLEGE, TONBRIDGE**

Unfortunately our family does not own a television set because we feel our time can be spent more creatively than sitting in front of a television all day, watching the junk which currently occupies our screen. We have been without a television set since July 1987.

**LAURENCE BECKETT, AGED 17,
CITY COLLEGE, NORWICH**

I've just come in from school and turned BBC1 on. That *Doctor Who* bloke, Sylvester Whatsisname, has just come on with that new programme *What's Your Story?* Well, I don't think I go a lot on that. A good idea I suppose, different anyway, a bit far-fetched though. Oh dear, this isn't much better. By the way, I'm watching *Knowhow*. It is an interesting way to learn things. I just can't stand Johnny Ball. Roll on *Grange Hill* is what I say . . .

I've just seen another *Grange Hill* repeat. I wish the Beeb would put a new series on. This definitely isn't the best series I've seen. Great, here comes Andy Crane. I think he's really ace, though he's not as good-looking as Phil Schofield. Hooray *Neighbours*, my Dad's just left the room in a hurry . . .

LISA DOWSING, AGED 14,
BENJAMIN BRITTEN HIGH SCHOOL,
LOWESTOFT, SUFFOLK

I switch the television on when I want and I turn the television off when I want. Sometimes if me and my sister are fighting over which side we want to watch my Mam turns it off . . . By television I have learnt how very dangerous fireworks are. I have also learnt a few answers for some questions what I never could have known. I also learnt how to make things like cakes and pies by watching cookery programmes.

Without television I would never have thought that someone could kill another person, or that there could be a ferry disaster or a car crash that could happen to a close friend or even me. If there was no television I suppose I would be pretty bored but I suppose I could find something to do like draw or listen to the radio . . .

NICOLA JOHNSON, AGED 12,
WESTERN MIDDLE SCHOOL,
WALLSEND, TYNE AND WEAR

I live with my parents, sister (who's eight), a dog, two gerbils, four fish and three television sets, two of which are in working order and one of which lies disembowelled in the corner of my room . . . I find the only really worthwhile viewing nowadays is probably making its second or third lap of the repeats circuit, although I do quite enjoy the really bad transmissions, ITV sitcoms and so on, with *Never the Twain* being a personal favourite. The decisions on what is watched and what is videoed or missed in our house are settled by, in reverse order of effectiveness, pleading, shouting, sulking, bribing and threatening with violence, and it's usually my sister who wins. I try and stay out of the battlefield, because I'm perfectly happy to watch a recording later or slink off to the neon-blue comfort of my portable . . .

Far from television promoting or furthering the art of conversation in my household, it's actually slowly killing it, and we've long since learned not to tempt the awful wrath of my mother by offering an opinion, or attempting to share a piece of observational wit, during *Neighbours*. Again the best solution is isolation, and it's off to my room again. If I talk about television at all, it's with fellow pupils, some of whom have got pretty much the same bad taste as myself . . .

NICK DIMMOCK, AGED 17,
NORTHAMPTON TRINITY SCHOOL

We live in a house called Maes y Coed by Menai Bridge in North Wales. With me lives my mother and father (who are doctors) and my little brother . . . I sometimes watch programmes while playing snooker . . . If my mother wants to see something and my father and I want to see something else, then we go into the snooker room. If we object my mother is sure to complain and look for excuses . . . so it's better if my father and I go to the snooker room . . .

Today I watched in college and at home. At college I saw a video of *Boys from the Blackstuff*. The character Yosser Hughes has become popular for his line 'Gizza job' and his head-butting, especially in schools. However, today I watched it in a different manner than I did when I was 12 years old. It held my attention today because I realized the true intention of the programme, which was about high unemployment on Merseyside . . . The programmes which were just going on in the background were the two soap operas, *Neighbours* and *Pobol y Cwm*, and the video of *Doctor Who* . . . With *Pobol y Cwm* I watched it because my father had written the script for today's episode, but I also watched it to hear what my mother and father said about some of the actors . . .

The thought that occurred to me today was why should people have to suffer and not have what is important to them (after watching *Boys from the Blackstuff*); and how small is the number of Welsh-speaking people and Bible readers in Wales. I was glad that this wasn't shown in a morbid or dull manner in the programme *Cyfieuthur Gair*. It was shown by using songs and acting, which made me feel quite happy, as humour sometimes gives a message with more impact . . .

Many pebbles on a Celtic beach: a gathering of the BBC's *Pobol y Cwm*

**RHYS WYN HUGHES, AGED 17,
GWYNEDD TECHNICAL COLLEGE, BANGOR**

I like watching plays on television but those which appeal to me rarely seem to be shown. I think that plays written for the stage should be performed on television as they would be on stage, without complicated visual effects or amazing scenery . . . Today *The Importance of Being Earnest* was not the most entertaining television I've seen, but enjoyable to watch. I do not like most modern plays shown on television and, in particular, the 'screenplays' written specifically for television. They seem to be too involved with moral issues or domestic upset, forgetting wit and ingenuity and the importance of entertaining . . .

It's much easier to remember something you've read rather than something you saw on television . . . I could never form any opinions of a work of literature from simply watching 'the series (or the film) of the book'. Television could never imitate or replace the unique pleasure of reading.

If I had taken too much notice of the dull, depressing, drab suits and grimaces in productions of Dickens' works, which were spoonfed to me by the BBC just about every Sunday tea-time throughout my childhood, nothing could have made me attempt to read any of the books, least of all *Great Expectations*. The very mention still instils severe and unremitting depression and an air of inevitable gloom (particularly in the form of dusty rooms and brown woolly suits) into my soul. The worst aspect of them was that, at the age of six, the only thing you could understand about them was that everyone was very hard done by and always very pale . . .

**FIONA GELL, AGED 15,
RAMSEY GRAMMAR SCHOOL, ISLE OF MAN**

The only thing you can learn from television are accents, for example, Australian. Most of the good programmes in which you are likely to see and learn something educational are on either early in the morning or late at night : . .

**JANET McALLEN, AGED 15,
KILKEEL HIGH SCHOOL, CO. DOWN**

If I had the power to change things on television I would scrap programmes like *World in Action*, *Panorama* and anything to do with Margaret Thatcher or any other politician. I would do this as all these things are boring, and are aimed mainly at an adult audience. I would also include more comedies and more sport, especially football. I would introduce different channels for different tastes . . .

**DONALD MACVICAR, AGED 13,
PAIBLE SECONDARY SCHOOL,
NORTH UIST, WESTERN ISLES**

I rather enjoyed the lesson when we talked about television. I would call myself a television fanatic, so I had a lot to talk about, and argue about. We came up with quite a few facts that you might find interesting. For example, did you know that the majority of people in our class (of 21 children) have two televisions? Eleven children have a habit of channel hopping. Eight have televisions in their room and three have videos.

Nobody watches *EastEnders*. Eight watch *Neighbours* . . . I think that I've probably said all there's to say about television . . .

**MUNA WEHBE, AGED 13,
LYCÉE FRANÇAIS CHARLES DE GAULLE,
LONDON SW7**

CHILDREN'S HOURS

Released from school, many return straight home to choose between Children's BBC, *which occupies BBC1 from 3.50 p.m. until the arrival of* Neighbours *at 5.35, and* Children's ITV, *which stretches from 4 p.m. until 5.15. Through this period on 1 November the ITV audience grew from 2.6 to 6.3 million. The BBC alternative started with 2.7 million, a figure which dipped below ITV to 2.4, before climbing again to 8.9 million. Introduced by Andy Crane, the BBC effort begins with instruction from the* PC Pinkerton *cartoon and the* Fireman Sam *puppets.*

When I got home from school I watched *The Young Doctors*, it's so boring, it's so sixtiesish, eugh, but I always seem to watch it . . . It's time for *Fireman Sam*. It's really funny how their bodies are so mechanical and how their mouths are closed when they speak, when suddenly their mouths make an OO shape. There's always a moral in the story. I like the clingfilm water spurting out of the cup . . . Andy Crane is sick. He's so plastic. I much preferred Phillip Schofield . . .

**ALISON HUNTER, AGED 12,
LONDON N8**

Then Andy Crane's knee made an appearance. He was also there, somewhere behind it, but it was extremely difficult to take one's eyes off the offending joint, peering menacingly from behind a designer rip in his jeans. Why is it felt necessary for children's presenters to dress themselves up as members of Bros, to enthrall the younger mind? Phillip Schofield's cheeky boy-next-door was nauseating enough, but if somebody doesn't style Andy's hair and iron Caron Keating's clothes soon I swear I'll scream. Whatever happened to John Keates, Brian Cant or Derek Griffiths? Children's presenters have certainly deteriorated, or perhaps I've just grown up . . .

**SALLY BLAKEMORE, AGED 17,
BOLTON**

The first programme I watched was *PC Pinkerton*. I thought it was quite good. It shows young children why to contact the police and not to make false calls. My second programme was *Fireman Sam*. It was OK, but I do not see much point in showing it. My favourite programme is *The Sooty Show* (ITV). I thought it incredibly funny. I would recommend it to stay on in the future, permanently . . . I do think there should be a channel for children. I did not watch much television today because Mummy said I watch too much . . .

**STEPHEN MUTTON, AGED 8,
STUDLEY, WARWICKSHIRE**

My three-year-old son, Liam, and I are at our weekly Tuesday afternoon social gathering of female friends and their various children . . . The children, aged between two and six, are already getting excited about *Fireman Sam*. None of the children get to watch a great deal of television, so they get particularly excited by it. We six mothers tend to video acceptable (to us, that is) children's programmes and play them back when the child needs a rest, or we do.

It seems safe to leave a young child in front of *Playbus*, *Jimbo*, *King Rollo* etc., as far as violence or swearing are concerned, but we are all appalled by how sexist most children's television still is. Where are the interesting, positive female characters for the girls to relate to? What damage is caused through our boy children constantly being faced with wet, boring, silly female characters in *PC Pinkerton* (his wife), *Fireman Sam* (every woman in sight) . . .

JACKY DEMPSEY, MOTHER-HOUSEPERSON,
BOURNEMOUTH

Ratman was not very good because it was so daft. Well, I mean, flying pizzas hitting important people isn't very good, is it? Anyway *Ratman* is Roland Rat in crime-fighting disguise. He has three assistants: Leekman, who's Welsh; Haggis Man, who's Scottish; and Pink Bucket Man, who's English. Chameleon Girl was the culprit, she's a master of disguise. I'm beginning to think this programme is a bit childish . . .

MATTHEW WILSON, AGED 11,
SHEFFIELD

Today *Ratman* was about low flying pizzas. I don't like Ratman himself because he thinks he is so clever. I like Pink Bucket Man because he thinks of everything and I like the way he speaks. I get bored when I watch *Ratman* because it's always the same plot . . .

LYNSEY HOSKINS, AGED 9,
WICKHAM, HAMPSHIRE

THE BRITISH TELECOM BENEFIT
This week actor Sylvester McCoy, the current Dr Who, is at BBC Pebble Mill with a group of actors, subjecting themselves to the dangers of a live (not recorded before transmission) eight-day serial. The storyline is being evolved with the assistance of telephoned suggestions from the audience. The script editor wrote overnight and the team has been working on the result since their 7 a.m. hotel breakfast this morning. Producer Christopher Pilkington has had little time to draw breath.

Whose idea was it to do a daily live drama with phone-in audience participation? Blast, it was mine . . . Before moving into the studio, re-check through over 500 good ideas from children following yesterday's transmission. Find some excellent detailed observations we can include . . . Painters look very tired, after working overnight to re-build and paint five new sets, but rather pleased that we are all so impressed . . . Our cast of seven have to learn dialogue and moves for the 4.15 p.m. transmission. We want to rehearse with them, but Make-up need them for wig fittings, etc. Tension . . .

We must fight for quality, contrast and challenge. This series throws the initiative straight back to the audience. If they respond we have a show. If they don't I have nothing to show for seven nights. But I know how inventive children are – I know they'll take this challenge. They will push us to realize their wildest imaginings. We must and will keep up. That's our challenge, artistically and technically. This is a brave experiment, there should be more . . . Great news. Just been told we had over 50,000 calls in one hour to our phone-in number. That beats all British Telecom figures, I knew the audience would respond! . . .

Talk to phone-in boffin about clogging of phone lines. Telecom promise to help, they underestimated the children's response . . . Running behind schedule now, dress run is 15 minutes late, must push on. So little time for coherent notes for the artists to digest and make their own . . . 15 minutes to transmission. One of our cast is really unhappy. His instinct is to play the role one way but script editor Peter Corey sees it another. Too late to alter it now. Must support him through what we have and encourage him to push it a bit harder . . . Five minutes to transmission, tension tightening now, adrenalin pumping, everyone is flat out . . .

Instant drama: a moment of apparent relaxation as Christopher Pilkington's BBC Pebble Mill team assembles its daily live serial, *What's Your Story?*

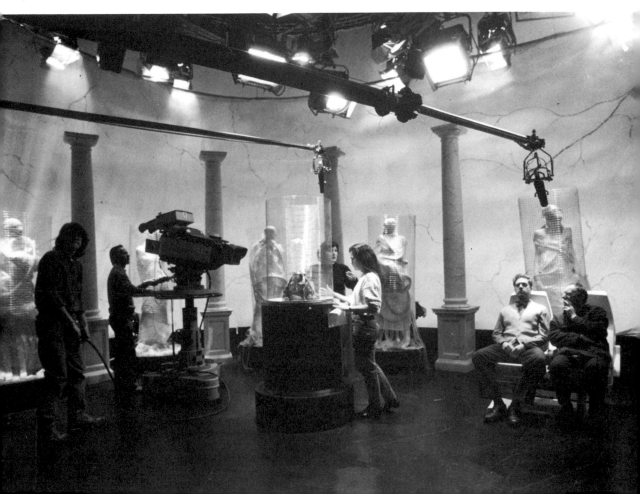

Off air at 4.30 p.m. Marvellous, touch static, but so classy and moody. Congratulate team, run down to artists, lovely sense of release. Magical sound as our 20 phone lines leap into action. Phone people answer and log down viewers' response about what should happen next. I monitor response and feed Peter with good ideas. He selects and outlines the best, these ideas flood in . . .

CHRISTOPHER PILKINGTON, EXECUTIVE PRODUCER

| *And how did it go for the audience?*

I watched *What's Your Story?* through curiosity, after hearing about it from a school friend. I think it is a very good idea to have the viewers writing the script, but only about ten ideas are ever used and I expect thousands ring in. Sylvester McCoy is a very good presenter. He hosts the programme sensibly and doesn't patronize the viewers. He also doesn't have hundreds of screaming ten-year-olds in an audience. This is the annoying part of shows like *Beat the Teacher*, where you have to keep the sound turned down all the time . . .

STEPHEN FOGARTY, AGED 15, NEWTON-LE-WILLOWS, MERSEYSIDE

My Mummy recorded some of children's television . . . I like *What's Your Story?*, it's exciting and adventurous. I like the actors and the man who tells the story. I tried to ring the number to add to the story. I would like to talk on the telephone, one day perhaps I will be lucky.

LEO BECKHAM, AGED 6, CHARMOUTH, DORSET

What's Your Story? was good and I phoned up about 50 times, but didn't get through. I'll try tomorrow. I was excited when the wall got warmer and warmer, I was amused when the aliens turned off the man next to Quint, and I was curious to know about the aliens themselves, and the old man in the cell with the children. And why on earth does Quint keep changing his name? If I don't find out soon, I'll explode . . .

ALISON WEATHERLEY, AGED 12, LOWESTOFT, SUFFOLK

I rang in last night after part one of *What's Your Story?*, but after an hour of trying I had still not got through. Unfortunately the same happened tonight, and I spent over an hour on the phone. I think the show is a brilliant idea, because it gives children the chance to have a say in the drama they see, but it can be very frustrating when the line is always engaged . . .

DAVID GREEN, AGED 14, HOLYWOOD, CO. DOWN

I hate this programme. I have tried to ring and it's always engaged. There should be more than one number and more people taking calls. I don't believe they listen to people anyway, I think that they have already written the stories. On the screen they put the names of people who have given ideas, but I think they are simply people who happen to have had the same ideas as the writers. This programme is stupid!!! . . .

**CLAIRE BRADBURY, AGED 15,
STAFFORD**

I watched *What's Your Story?* to see what it was like but I was not at all impressed, and I think that they should not have children using the phone, to say what they think should happen next in the story, as this may encourage young children to use the phone whenever they like, and may lead to high telephone bills . . .

**CLAIRE MOORE, AGED 12,
BANGOR, CO. DOWN**

Carrying a cup of tea to younger sister in the lounge I find I am watching *What's Your Story?* As my imagination goes into action I am wishing I were young enough to ring-in with my ideas. At last, it seems that someone has realized that children's creativity can go beyond washing-up-liquid bottles and sticky-backed plastic. So many children watch unconsciously as image after image passes on the screen, here at last is one programme which stimulates a response and encourages active participation . . .

**HOLLY CRICK, AGED 18,
LEICESTER**

After thinking up a major novel, on how the story ended, I considered phoning in myself. I decided against it when I realized that the names of the contributors appeared on the next show. I thought of what would happen to my reputation in the sixth form if I was found out collaborating in a children's show . . .

**RICHARD HEATH, AGED 16,
LEEK, STAFFORDSHIRE**

The children all love *What's Your Story?* and dash to the phone immediately it's over, only to find the number engaged, as it continued to be until 6.30 p.m., when the number closed down. Their father had been trying to ring us during that time, so was not amused. (For the rest of the week the children and I became more and more frustrated by the continued invitations to ring in each day. The number was never, ever, not engaged. The insistence that the children could influence the story was, in our case, patently not true.) . . .

**PAMELA BURCHILL, MOTHER,
LEIGH-ON-SEA, ESSEX**

GO KART, KNOW HOW?
After What's Your Story?, *the sequence of* Children's BBC *continued with* Knowhow, Newsround *and* Grange Hill.

I watched *Knowhow* mainly because my school (Shepshed High) was participating in it, doing a feature on their kart club. I think it is useful if children are involved. People tend to listen a bit more if the conversation isn't over their heads too much . . .

**RACHEL SIMMONDS, AGED 13,
SHEPSHED, LEICESTERSHIRE**

My Daddy taped *Knowhow* so I could see it after I finished my Chinese lessons. I like it because it is educational and also, sometimes, funny. The 1 November programme had lots of interesting ideas and information. It showed a whale and said its tongue weighed as much as an elephant. I had seen the whale before once, when I visited the Natural History Museum in London . . .

**SING YU JACKSON, AGED 6,
POOLE, DORSET**

Caught the middle bit of the *Knowhow* serial called *Hyperspace Hotel*. It was worse than *The Sooty Show* (ITV). Naff acting, washing-up bottle props, and a lack of properly spoken English (e.g. vac-you-um was meant to be vacuum). Even my four-year-old brother didn't like this. It made me feel angry that people think children like such things. Why don't adults ask children what they want to watch? . . .

**LAURA FLORENCE, AGED 14,
CROWBOROUGH, SUSSEX**

I learnt about aquatic creatures in relation to humans . . . The karting bit was really interesting, they should have more child presented slots. What was that stupid cartoon? Couldn't they have made the plane safety bit more interesting? Details kept me on the verge of my seat with excitement. Fireworks are brill put to music. The whole show was spoilt by corny jokes and presenters acting stupidly . . .

**ALEX HARDY, AGED 11,
STOWMARKET, SUFFOLK**

I saw the first part of *Knowhow* and I am now going about boasting, pretending I'm really clever, and saying a blue whale has a tongue as heavy as an elephant, blood vessels through which an infant could crawl, and a heart as big as a refrigerator . . .

**ELIZABETH PENDER, AGED 9,
GLASGOW**

Claudia, aged 14 months, climbs on my lap to watch the whales in *Knowhow*, and seems positively disturbed by the human presenter. Though she doesn't often watch for longer than a couple of minutes she stays for the item on go karts, and the space playlet, which I don't understand . . .

**JACQUI ROWE, TEACHER,
KING'S NORTON, BIRMINGHAM**

I would have gone to the television room when I got back from school at

4.30 p.m. but I had to practise for my saxophone exam. Annoyed that I was finding the scale of A flat minor very hard, I switched on and found myself watching *Newsround*, on the subject of Russian being taught in schools. Although *Newsround* is not one of my favourite programmes, I have always thought that it is very good . . . The programme's adult handling of young people impresses me . . .

**TOA FRASER, AGED 13,
BURITON, HAMPSHIRE**

I came racing down the stairs, missing the odd few, to see what was on. It was *Newsround*! Why had I rushed? I find it rubbish because they seem to belittle the younger viewers. We aren't as thick as you think we are, you know. It finished at 5.05 p.m., thank goodness . . .

**RACHEL LOWE, AGED 14,
ECKINGTON, DERBYSHIRE**

I feel that *Newsround* is understood by young and old. We, as a family, are Italian. My parents, who do not understand English well, find the programme easy to follow . . .

**AMANDA PERDONI, AGED 15,
LONDON N14**

The first programme I watched when I came home from school was *Grange Hill*. I have been a fan of this marvellous comprehensive school story since it began in February 1978, and have not yet missed an episode. The episodes now being shown are repeats but that does not make them any less appealing . . . The actors are all very convincing and I know from experience that their success and fame has not gone to their heads. I have written to each member of the cast and received lovely letters back. I have also met one or two of them . . .

**KATHERINE GRADY, AGED 15,
LIVERPOOL**

I watched *Grange Hill* which I think is good because it has all the problems that kids have in high school. But also it might frighten some children, that they will get beaten up at school . . .

**HELEN KIRKPATRICK, AGED 10,
SHREWSBURY, SHROPSHIRE**

Grange Hill was on next. This is one of my favourite programmes. The acting is very good. It deals with some of the problems that could happen in school. My favourite character is Gonch, because he's always got some idea of making money, but in some way it always doesn't work out quite right. Some parents think that the programme is bad for children to watch and that it may lead some children to turn bad. Well, I think that's wrong, because it's only a programme and the children know it's not true . . .

**KAMALJIT KAUR, AGED 12,
DERBY**

I watched *Grange Hill* because, although my school is not quite like that one, I think that some schools are. Although people say *Grange Hill* gives a bad impression to young people, and they then copy what happens, I think young people have their own minds to choose whether to behave in an acceptable manner or to run riot in a bad, unacceptable way. Usually the people who behave in the way they show on *Grange Hill* behaved like that years before they watched it. I think this good television programme shows youngsters what will happen if they act in a silly and naughty way . . .

**REBECCA BAGNALL, AGED 12,
CASTLE CARY, SOMERSET**

The happiest days? A group of staff and pupils from the BBC's *Grange Hill* comprehensive

It is a programme I watch quite regularly and like but there are faults. For a start if they used language used in real schools it wouldn't be allowed on television, so parents needn't complain. I also don't think that there are many teachers left like Mr Bronson, well, at least in comprehensives. He

is horrible, strict and I don't think he likes kids, but many teachers aren't very strict now . . .

**NATALIE DUNCAN, AGED 16,
SUNDERLAND, TYNE AND WEAR**

Listened to *Grange Hill* from the kitchen. So much like the school where I work that I could write an episode from my experiences . . .

**J. R. GODDARD, SCHOOL DINNER LADY,
NEWBURY, BERKSHIRE**

Grange Hill is BANNED. As a mother and as a teacher I find it a very disturbing programme. Many children in my experience are terrified of going to secondary school because of the bullying depicted. It is no good producers etc. saying the bullies always get their punishment in the end, the bullying still happens. Very worrying for primary age children . . .

**ELIZABETH SHAW, SUPPLY TEACHER,
KINGSTON UPON THAMES, SURREY**

I have banned *Grange Hill* because of the way the children speak. Also my son will soon be starting school and I don't want him to be put off the idea. He might think all big schools are like Grange Hill, with lots of bullies, boys who only seem to think about how to make money, and girls who only think about boys. Having said this, I used to quite enjoy the programme when I could watch it on my own . . .

**SUSAN SKINGLEY, WIFE AND MOTHER,
ORPINGTON, KENT**

I watched *Grange Hill* on my own because the rest of my family went out shopping. If my parents were in they would not approve of me watching it because they think it has a bad influence on me . . .

**SALMA PATEL, AGED 14,
LEICESTER**

I have always liked this show as it reminds me of how funny (and cruel) life was for me at school. The programme had just begun when I left school in 1978. Things have changed though. AIDS wasn't around then, and the idea of a girl getting a tattoo and of a grown-up seducing a young girl, would probably have caused a scandal. But that's *Grange Hill* for you, always keeping a lead in serious social issues as it did in 1978 . . .

**WILLIAM McLAUCHLAN, CHEF,
PAISLEY, RENFREWSHIRE**

Grange Hill, more school. The kids are much too well-washed and well-dressed. I refuse to believe that a large school is entirely populated by good-looking pupils . . .

**MR C. J. BUTTERY, TEACHER,
BEWDLEY, HEREFORD AND WORCESTER**

I LIKE FUNNY THINGS . . .
On this day Mark Granger presented the 75-minute sequence of

Children's ITV. *The favourites here are the Thames contributions,* The Sooty Show *and* Count Duckula. *Louise Black, the youngest diarist to contribute to the One Day project entirely in her own hand, switched over after seeing* Fireman Sam *and* Ratman *on BBC.*

The Sooty Show is my favourite programme because Sweep makes a lot of noise. I like their house and their Daddy. My little sister likes it too. *Count Duckula*: I like cartoons because if they are scary I know they are not real. I watch television after school and at weekends. I like funny things and stories about children.

**LOUISE BLACK, AGED 5,
ST BOSWELLS, ROXBURGHSHIRE**

Count Duckula is a brilliant cartoon, with the voices of all the British experts, in fact even my Dad likes it. The end cartoon animation is good. It is one of my favourite programmes. Sooty is a very funny programme for younger viewers, in fact it has me in stitches. I always feel sorry for Matthew Corbett, having to go through it all . . .

**KIERON CLARK, AGED 10,
RETFORD, NOTTINGHAMSHIRE**

Melanie, my nine-year-old daughter, likes cartoons. I think the adverts aiming at young children a bit unfair for unemployed people. We like Sooty. I used to watch the show when young. I think Sooty is less violent now. He used to do some mean things. The puppets seem more friendly and I would say the programme is more educational, however I wasn't a bit keen on today's show. Silly Melanie liked it. When *Count Duckula* came on I switched it off. This is a terrible cartoon, especially at the beginning where it shows occult images. I object to the theme and we turned over to *Knowhow* . . . Melanie watched *Newsround* with interest but the part about the whales upset her. She shouted at me when it came on as if I didn't care about the whales, and that I should be able to do something to help. Melanie often gets frustrated about nature programmes, if men are killing or harming animals. Children care but their voice is never heard . . .

**KIM PAYNE, HOUSEWIFE,
NUNEATON, WARWICKSHIRE**

The younger two watched children's television together, as usual. I feel absolved from watching with Jessica, four, when Levin, 11, is back from school. Preparing tea, there is still a pang of guilt. Sometimes she is frightened by one of the cartoons. She always comes running. Perhaps that's enough? Today there were no fears, lots of laughter.

I don't decide what they watch, but I do switch on in the first place. If I call them for tea, television goes off, not without arguments. They both picked out *Count Duckula* as the best programme; they both appreciate the silliness, especially of Nanny, a much loved character. Jessica: 'Nanny does silly things, like when she pulls someone up with her arms

Above: The BBC's Robert Kilroy-Silk: a toast for the tanned presenter

Left: Scottish exercise: TV-am's Lizzie Webb runs a mass workout in Prince's Square, Glasgow

Below: TV-am reception, the 'immaculate hub of the building'

Right: Phillip Schofield (left) and colleagues. 'I could never present breakfast telly – it's far too early'

Far right: Philip Hayton: the charm of the BBC newscaster set against the 'gloom and doom' of the news

Below: Out of the closet: Mr and Mrs Beaver, Peter and Lucy, in action for the BBC's *The Lion, the Witch and the Wardrobe*

Bottom: The BBC's Andy Crane on the day the balloons went up

Below right: Yazz and all that jazz: recording for the BBC's *Top of the Pops*

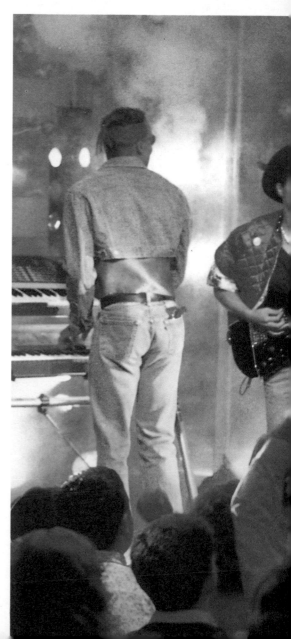

Left: Northern games: a scene from Grampian's *Pick a Number*

Below left: Whatever else *The Price is Right*. Excruciating pleasure as presenter Leslie Crowther massages our universal love of money

Right: Charlene and Scott of *Neighbours*. The wedding of the soap year between would-be pop stars Kylie Minogue and Jason Donovan

Below: Beale appeal: *EastEnders* stalwarts Kath and Ian share a scene

Left: Royal togetherness: the Duke and Duchess of York, in Australian kit, are reunited with baby Bea by Central's *Spitting Image*

Right: 'Is there much more of this?' Eddie Large appears too large for his party dress

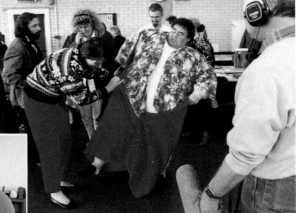

Left: Weighty entertainment: David Jensen (left), Eddie Large (centre) and Tony Blackburn (right) represent the full figure and Sid Little is amused

Below: 'This thing is bigger than both of us...' Thames scene painters in action

Left: Alabaster plaster caster. A ballerina emerges from
the BBC's sculpture department

Below left: A hairy moment. A variety of styles in the
BBC's wig department

Below: All of human life matched here. The world of the
property buyer in the Birmingham studios of Central
Television

Right: Peter Davidson, the BBC's *Campion*, is a detective who sometimes neglects to watch his back

Below right: 'You folk are never usually on time.' The Dean of Exeter emerges from his cathedral to talk to Television South-West presenter David Young

Below: American football finds an uncertain British following on Channel 4

Opposite above: Eyes on the monitors: transmission control at Central's Birmingham studios

Opposite below: Eastern colours. Sitar and tabla players at Central's Studio 3, *Here and Now*

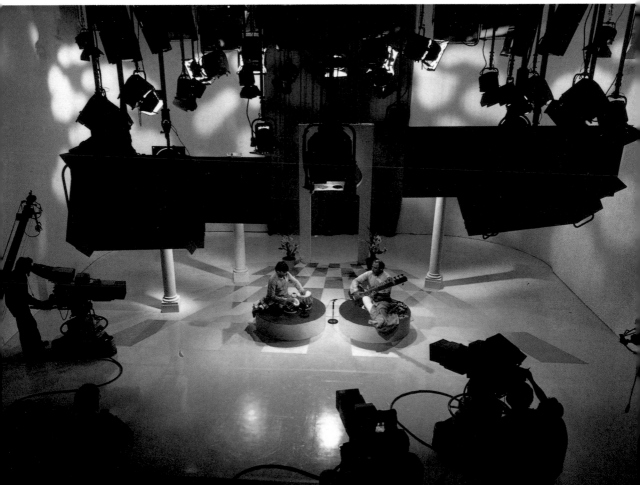

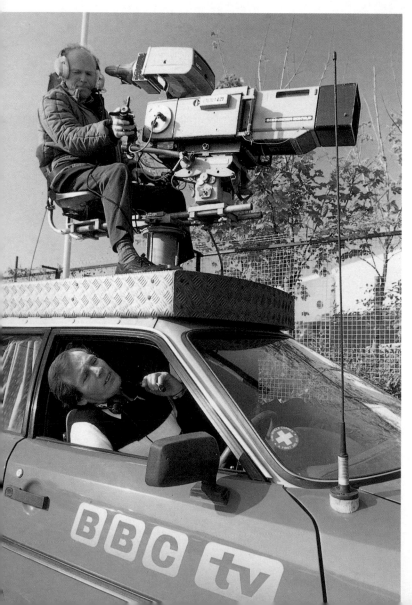

Above: Guernsey snapper:
camerawoman Rosemary Anne Henry
records 'the ridiculous position of the
new customs shed'

Left: Following the leader: the BBC's
colour roving eye is used for horse
racing and other fast moving events

Right: Waiting for the PM. A BBC Wales
crew is in wet Dominica for a series
about women politicians

Overleaf: Central photographer Nick
Lockett was in Australia on 1 November,
gathering material for an exhibition
about Aboriginal Television

Right: 'It goes something like this...' The BBC's *See Hear!* presenter, Clive Mason, makes four vital points

Below: A taste of television: another programme chewed over and inwardly digested

round them and falls over.' Levin (a bit more sophisticated): 'It has such good ideas. Nanny's ever so funny. The Vampire's vegetarian because, in the ritual, Nanny poured tomato ketchup over him, instead of blood, when resurrecting him.'

Jessica often recounts storylines: good practice, I think, for future creativity. (Dad's a writer.) Levin, the strong, silent one, not very often do you get much comment from him on a programme, despite the fact (or perhaps, ominously, because of it) that he is, by far, the biggest television viewer of the family. Boys can be a problem over television viewing, I've heard it said time and time again. There seems to be little discrimination. We have to impose restrictions or he'd cheerfully view for hours on end . . . My husband and I often wonder if he gains the sort of joyous escape in television that we used to in books, as children. Not that Levin doesn't read, he does. Not just the easy stuff either. Last book was *Dr Jekyll and Mr Hyde* . . .

**MAL JONES, TEACHER,
TELFORD, SHROPSHIRE**

After tea *Count Duckula*. I know it's for kids but I love it, though I certainly wouldn't admit to watching it . . .

**GEOFFREY SWANNEY, LECTURER,
CLEETHORPES, HUMBERSIDE**

God! Another day in the life of a teacher over with. Well, at least the part during which I have to be in school . . . Right now it's tea-time, so the television goes on. Why is children's television so patronizing? I don't know which side I'm watching, but it's a young bloke saying 'Hi!', 'OK' and 'Right'. He sounds like I do on a bad day. I teach the people that these programmes are aimed at, I know how they resent being patronized. Why do they do it? Is the motive political? Is the intention to keep tomorrow's social troops at bay? To stop them being adults? . . .

**MICHAEL GRIFFITHS, TEACHER,
WREXHAM, CLWYD**

REVIVAL OR REDUNDANCY?

Before leaving the area of children's television, here are some words from two who toil on these slopes in Manchester, both of whom would be hurt by thoughts that they might be patronizing or retarding their audience. At Granada producer Martyn Day is concerned about Dexter the Cat, puppet hero of the ITV series labouring under the punning title Tickle on the Tum.

Back to work and the problems of relaunching Dexter. I was disappointed to hear that, due to slipping ratings, the series is not to be repeated next year. It has been decided to lift Dexter from *Tickle on the Tum* and try to relaunch him in a new vehicle. Although puppets are popular with children there are certain limitations in their use. You cannot show them (hand puppets, that is) full length. You cannot have them talking to

Still animation. Cosgrove
Hall, the Manchester-based
Thames subsidiary, has a
reputation for finished
craftsmanship, both in
model and drawing forms

camera for too long, simply because their repertoire of facial expressions is limited. They are not very good at handling small objects; you could say that Dexter is not very dexterous. They work best when reacting to humans. So the object this afternoon is to create a fresh format within these limitations.

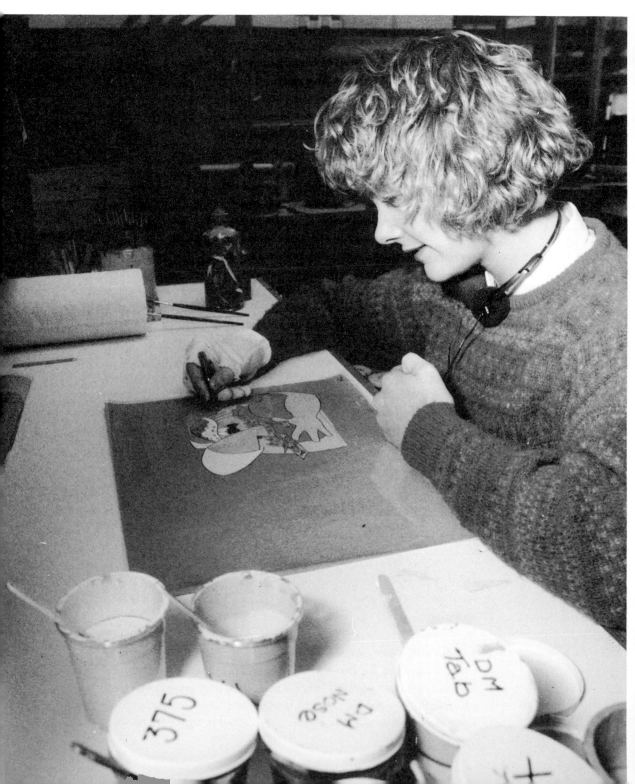

Two nights ago, in the early hours of the morning, I awoke with an idea, a cat chat show, a junior *Johnny Carson Show* featuring our furry friend, Dexter the cat with the chat. The idea is taking shape on my typewriter, a chat show introduced by Dexter and featuring guests with 'child appeal' – Frank Bruno, Kylie Minogue, the cast of *The Bill*, Bros and so on. The advantages of using a puppet as a host are that he can get away with being cheekier than a human and that with a young puppeteer (Dexter's talented operator, John Eccleston, is only 22) the puppet will be sympathetic to the audience's interests . . .

One of the departmental secretaries drops in with the rumour she's just heard, that the company is looking for a further 300 redundancies, and that letters to this effect will be coming round later this month. Although it is only a rumour I do feel some disquiet. I am now 43 years old and a staff member for nearly ten years. They talk about shedding old wood. Is 43 old? I know that I am hard-working, imaginative and enthusiastic as ever I was, but do 'the men in suits' see me this way? Is there any value today in being a 'good and faithful servant'? Is redundancy the kind of spur I need to kick me into a new and productive middle age? Such are the questions I ponder as I check my diary for tomorrow . . .

MARTYN DAY, PRODUCER

> *Not far away, at the Stretford premises of the Thames animation subsidiary Cosgrove Hall Productions, Hilary Wyatt is also concerned about the future, as well as the present* Count Duckula.

Today has consisted of final preparation of the sound tracks for one episode, *Prime Time Duck*, which is 20 minutes in length. As assistant editor I have been responsible for laying sound effects . . . For this film alone there are 13 reels of sound effects, three reels of music and four of dialogue. I spent most of the day charting the music and dialogue tracks with the editor, in preparation for the dub on Thursday, where all the tracks will be mixed down into one final reel.

Cosgrove Hall is generally thought to produce good quality animation, both model and drawn. In looking at comparable series on television, I am appalled and disheartened by the quality of animation shown (and quantity – most of it American). There appears to be a dearth of originality in programme ideas. Much is badly drawn and technically poor, and it's obvious that music and sound effects have been minimized in order to churn out as much as possible with the smallest possible outlay.

I'm also dismayed at how some of the series appear to be merchandising vehicles. This state of affairs seems to be a sign of the future under the proposed 'deregulation'. Television companies, run it seems by accountants and not programme-makers, are now debating the need to provide pre-school programming, once released from the IBA commitment. Instead of supplying this useful service we are likely to see slots filled by yet more foreign soaps, in an effort to deliver larger audiences to the advertisers, viewers with more spending power than the under-fives . . .

The present uncertainty in television is a product of the Government's deep-seated hate of the media unions, and the television companies, including the BBC, who do not toe the Government line as assiduously as most of the tabloid press. The plan for British broadcasting does not form a constructive course of action, which aims to better suit the needs of the viewers, divergent as these are. What is even more worrying is that those viewers do not seem aware that this is happening. It seems that British television is another area of British culture endangered by the present mood of philistinism . . .

**HILARY WYATT,
ASSISTANT FILM EDITOR**

> *On innovating Channel 4 there is a 30-minute interruption of the flow of United States material in the shape of* Fifteen-to-One, *a general knowledge quiz show produced and presented at Regent Productions by William G. Stewart. Dark-suited, middle-aged, bespectacled, mildly enthusiastic Stewart ensures that by the end of his half-hour 15 contestants have been reduced to one. If this show appears a bit foreign to the network's afternoon viewers, relief is at hand. The schedule returns across the Atlantic at 5 p.m. for an hour of* American Football, *in this case Cleveland v. Cincinnati, followed by* The Cosby Show.

I used to like *Fifteen-to-One* being, like millions of others, a lover of Trivial Pursuits-type games. (I can remember when it was called general knowledge, am I getting old?) Now the inherent unfairness annoys me. Contestants can win by tactics and/or luck rather than knowledge. Although it is only a quiz game I find it sad that contestants have to pick on others in order to win. Is it the first Thatcherite quiz game? . . .
**ALAN SHAEFER,
BELPER, DERBYSHIRE**

I almost dislike myself for watching this programme as I absolutely loathe the presenter. There has to be a deep psychological reason why so many of us get hooked on quizzes. Could somebody please tell William G. Stewart not to hiss 'No' with such contempt when contestants get the answer wrong . . .
**PEGGY GOULD,
LITTLE GADDESDEN, HERTFORDSHIRE**

The distinction between quiz games and panel games is sometimes not stressed enough. This programme, relatively new, is an admirable example of the former. Were it not it would be less easy to justify the turning on of the television set at a time very close to mid-afternoon on a glorious day, with the birds singing, the beach deserted and inviting, and the lawn appealing for attention. The two great assets of *Fifteen-to-One* are that it is based on general, if at times, trivial, knowledge; and that it has a presenter who does not act like a music-hall prima donna or, perhaps even worse, a 'superstar' concerned only with the way the audience receive him. William G. Stewart is a credit to his profession and long may his programme thrive . . .
**KENN PEARSON, FINANCIAL CONSULTANT,
ISLE OF WIGHT**

This is the best quiz on television. Fast moving, a good cross-section of contestants, a wide variety of questions. I like to keep a tally of my personal score. The only quiz I can recall that has included disabled people without fuss and sycophantic overtures. Good on the producer, may others take an important leaf from his book . . .

**JANET M. CARTER,
REGISTERED DISABLED,
TUNBRIDGE WELLS, KENT**

It's a good quiz, but what a lot of male contestants seem anti-female. It's a wonder at times that any woman gets on the board. Some of the men immediately and continually pick on the women . . .

**JOAN COMER, RETIRED POLICE CLERK,
EXETER**

A dully presented quiz, which is good for my ego. I always feel more confident that I am keeping senility at bay when I know most of the answers. Criticism: some of the questions are so easy it isn't true, with some of the others I am sure some of the contestants don't know what the hell he's talking about. My main interest is watching the unpleasant traits it brings out in people, male chauvinism for instance. There are only a handful of women competitors each day, but the men gang up on them and very few reach the final. That steely look appears in their eyes, as they look around the circle – who is the weakest? This applies to both sexes in the later rounds, I must confess. Lovely stuff . . .

**MAX DUNSTONE,
RETIRED CUSTOMS OFFICER,
FOLKESTONE, KENT**

I decided that the time was right to educate my 14-month-old son, Daniel . . . I turned to *Grange Hill*, safe in the knowledge that Daniel would, by 5.30 p.m., be a rebel without a pause. He let me down by playing with his bricks for ten minutes, before going upstairs to find his Mum. I waited till the end (cos I like the credits) and then channel hopped. I saw a bit about how to erect a garden fence (BBC2), two minutes of *Neighbours*, usually enough (BBC1), news headlines (ITV) and then found *American Football*.

Dan and I play a game called 'Touchdown' during this, so I went and got him back again. He runs up and down the room and every time there is a winning play I pick him up, throw him on the settee and shout 'Touchdown'. It gets very frenetic during the ten-minute run-down of the week's best scores . . .

**ROB WATLING, SELF-EMPLOYED,
SWANSEA**

EMBRYO YUPPIES

Between Children's ITV *and* News at 5.45 *the ITV network deploys* Blockbusters, *a quiz for teenagers made by Central. Presenter Bob Holness does not disguise his feelings for contestants he dislikes, generally those who are insufficiently extrovert.*

The television is on in the living-room and the cassette player is playing in the adjacent kitchen. One of my favourite programmes is on at 5.15 p.m. and I try my best to concentrate on *Blockbusters*, amidst the barrage of questions, people arguing, and shouting at someone to shut the door. I live with four, sometimes five, other students (or ex-students) and the cooking and talking causes quite a racket. Then the telephone starts ringing . . .

I love watching *Blockbusters* because getting the questions correct is due to a skill acquired from watching the programme repeatedly and not from a vast general knowledge. The 'easiness' and 'hardness' of questions goes in patterns and depends on the rhythm of the game, and also how badly a contestant is losing. For instance, you know that the answer to 'K', a picture card in a pack of playing cards, is 'knave' and not 'king'. This will give the slower contestants a chance to win a point because the quicker competitor will immediately guess 'king'.

As with most of my experience of watching game shows (which I do rarely) I shout insults at the television, regarding the contestants. The schoolchildren on the programme are invariably those types who are considered 'characters' or what a school report would describe as 'outgoing'. On television they appear obnoxious and embarrassingly precocious, as emphasized by their cuddly mascots. I am further aggravated when Bob asks them questions about themselves, especially when they say they want to go into advertising. When I was at school, people wanted to be teachers and nurses and footballers, but now everyone wants to awaken to a Maxwell House 7 a.m. shoot and be a media person . . .

NICOLA IRVINE, STUDENT, BIRMINGHAM

Blockbusters gets on my tits. It's all right sometimes, but I wish they wouldn't put it on so much. Once a week is enough . . .

LORNA HARRIS, HOUSEWIFE, NOTTINGHAM

I find Bob Holness makes my skin crawl. He obviously affects some of the more intelligent teenagers the same way. He is patronizing and rude and my 19-year-old son goes out of the room when he's on . . .

HAZEL KEMP, BISHOP'S SECRETARY, PERTH, TAYSIDE

ADVICE AND INSTRUCTION
Having completed its afternoon bowls coverage from Preston the BBC2 schedule moves into a cluster of home-made programmes where instruction has a higher priority than amusement. There are 30 minutes for the City Technology College at Solihull, and then five minutes for the Yorkshire artist David Blackburn. Half an hour of consumer advice is followed by a 30-minute lesson in garden fence construction.

I wanted to see *The College*, dealing with the new city technology colleges. Normally I choose particular programmes which confirm my own views and opinions. On this subject I'm undecided. Are these new colleges good or bad? I went to a secondary modern and so I've hated elitism since I was a child. I am also a university graduate, so I suppose that makes me a member of the elite, even though I am unemployed. The pros and cons in this programme were marshalled as one would expect. What infuriated me was that the contributors were interviewed separately on location and then edited to give the impression that they were addressing each other in normal debate. What I longed for was a face to face confrontation by those for and against. As it turned out I wasn't swayed either way, and I'm still undecided and pondering the matter . . .

**PETER STOCKILL, UNEMPLOYED,
MIDDLESBROUGH, CLEVELAND**

Figures in a northern light: David Blackburn (third from left) has a view for the BBC crew filming for his *Northern Lights* portrait at Slaithewaite in West Yorkshire

Ridiculous only giving five minutes to *Northern Lights* on David Blackburn. It was the most nutritious programme of the afternoon. Beautifully presented, both artistically and photographically, but, like most good things, too short. I don't know who decides on the time given to programmes. I suppose somebody sitting in a thickly carpeted office

who can't do a thing for himself but maintains he is terribly busy . . .
**MARISA CHATER, RECLUSE,
EDINBURGH**

Depressing, 'socially aware' (ugh!) information slot called *Advice Shop*.
Search for alternative viewing. There is none. Read book. Back to gloomy
Advice Shop. Proves to be largely incomprehensible except, I would hope,
to those poor souls it immediately concerns. Aerial view of
Middlesbrough interesting through personal nostalgia. Incredibly scruffy
interviewees derided by viewers present. Read a book: Jeffrey Archer's *A
Matter of Honour*, now that's entertainment. *First Time Garden*, a noble
effort to erect a fence through a slimy quagmire results in humorous
criticism from viewers, but a worthy programme for beginners. Continue
with book . . .
**GERRY DOUGLAS-SHERWOOD AND
TONY ELVERS, LIGHTHOUSEKEEPERS,
NEEDLES LIGHTHOUSE, ISLE OF WIGHT**

Is *Advice Shop* a propaganda programme? Who is it aimed at? One
assumes from the title it is to advise these millions of spongers about how
they can grab more free maintenance. It is an absolute scandal and an
affront to normal working people, who manage through their own efforts
to maintain themselves, but do not have anything to spare. Our taxes are
going to these spongers who are told that it is 'due to them'. We all would
like grant money free from a social fund. If people are homeless and have
no means to live, other than claiming all these benefits, they certainly
have no business being able to afford a television (plus licence) to watch
this programme . . .
**ANNE FOSKETT, HOUSEWIFE,
LONDON N11**

A milestone in television history. The co-presenters, Hugh Scully and
Helen Madden, deal weekly with subjects of vital importance to the sick,
the elderly and the unemployed. The inadequacies and unfairness of the
State benefit system are highlighted, alongside its redeeming features, to
provide a balanced advice service. This is just one of a few notable
examples of how television in the 1980s tries to educate rather than just
entertain. It is now common practice to supply us with helpful addresses
to contact, via captions on screen and so on. Viewers can send for
programme notes or fact sheets. Let's hope that such ideas are not
dispensed with when there are more channels . . .
**STEPHEN LAWSON, UNEMPLOYED,
DARLINGTON, CO. DURHAM**

First Time Garden was my Mum's choice, she's quite keen on gardening.
Personally I don't particularly like pottering around in a vegetable patch,
or declaring nuclear war on the greenfly infesting our rose bush.
Gardening programmes always show such beautiful flowers, which is
great, but it only fuels that 'maybe this time it'll be different' feeling that

creeps over you at the Co-op seed stand. Which in turn leads to frustration, anger and tears when the plant dies after three weeks . . .

ANYA PEARSE, AGED 16,
BUCKLEY, CLWYD

> HERE WE GO AGAIN
> *Between 5.30 and 6 p.m. the BBC1 audience rises from 8.9 to 10.4*
> *million, while the ITV following can only stretch from 8.5 to 9 million.*
> *The reason, of course, is the repeat showing of* Neighbours.

I don't think Mrs Mangel has got any Christian compassion now that she has lost her memory. Even though she had very little Christian compassion before she lost her memory. She doesn't even make an effort to be nice now. I think it was extra hilarious when Madge told Mrs Mangel to cook Harold Bishop a nice juicy steak, cooked rare. Madge used a very slimy, mysterious tone of voice when she was talking to Mrs Mangel, which added extra atmosphere. I must admit that I think Mrs Mangel was a bit hasty when she put the damages money down to a thousand dollars, but then, she is a bit like that anyway. I think Harold was brave telling the old battleaxe, Mrs Mangel, that she had no Christian compassion . . .

MARTIN WARD, AGED 11,
ENFIELD, MIDDLESEX

Neighbours is great because it is filmed in Australia, and you get to see if Australia is nice or horrid. They have brilliant characters like Jason Donovan and Kylie Minogue . . .

BETHAN LLOYD, AGED 8,
ABERGELE, CLWYD

I really enjoy *Neighbours* and watch it every day if I can. I find it refreshing to watch something that is situated somewhere else other than England. I also find it good to have something that is on every weekday, and at such a convenient time, when most people are just in from work or college . . .

SARAH HORLOCK, STUDENT,
ST PETER PORT, GUERNSEY

Come home from work. Hide in car for ten minutes to avoid watching *Neighbours* . . .

ALAN DUNN, COMPANY SECRETARY,
CARLISLE

Just after 1.30 p.m. this afternoon, Nell Mangel served up underdone steak to vegetarian Harold, and Lucy lost a pet mouse. In other words, because I have a board meeting of Sussex Opera this evening, we were watching the early showing of *Neighbours*. Why do more than 15 million of us switch on to this fairy story five days a week, ten if you're hooked on the repeats?

It can't be its credibility. Some characters go off on quite ordinary journeys and never come back; others come back being played by different actors. The storylines are crammed with incredible incident – a tracheotomy on the kitchen table, a hijacked wedding party in gorilla suits and so forth. I think what it has is charm, a prevailing good humour of the sort that is not present in Albert Square. It has the human appeal of *Coronation Street*, without the Street's enduring cardboard quality. It is not bad enough to be a cult *per se*, and not good enough to win any award I've ever come across . . . I suppose what we are beguiled by is its prevailing 'niceness', in the nicest possible way . . .

BARRY HEWLETT-DAVIES, AUTHOR, BRIGHTON

Naybuz or is it *Neighbours*? Australian, predictable, about as exciting as a dead fart . . .

COLIN JOHNSTON, AGED 16, LEEDS

Cable layers under observation. 'You never know what you might find under here'

UNWANTED LEAKS
The simple act of switching on and watching is not always without problems when vandals, or enthusiastic drillers, are around.

We were just settling down (about 5.30 p.m.) to our usual evening in front of the telly, when there was a knock at the door. Apparently some senseless youths had damaged a gas pipe on an outside wall of our block of flats, causing a dangerous gas leak. With the arrival of the Fire Brigade, police and gas men, we were all ordered to evacuate the premises. Television off, fire off, lights off and out we go into the dark, cold night . . .

GILLIAN McGEE, UNEMPLOYED, WIRRAL, MERSEYSIDE

Received a call from Diamond Drillers that they have cut through mains cables at a tower block in Windsor. Visit the site and instruct them to stop digging and drilling. Visit the Windsor and Maidenhead housing officer and inform him of our problems. We agree to wait until we receive complaints from tenants, with fingers crossed . . . The housing department report at 5 p.m. that a 78-year-old lady has had her electricity cut off, and has no lights or heating. They agree to look after this lady for tonight . . . I later found she had slept on a friend's sofa. Unfortunately she had a weak bladder and pee'd on the sofa . . .

TONY SMALL, AREA ENGINEER, WINDSOR (CABLE) TELEVISION

> BUILDING BRIDGES
> *Some uncherished but dedicated broadcasters work on programmes designed to give on-air access to the television audience. Among this number is Andrew Curry, producer of Channel 4's talk-back show for viewers,* Right to Reply. *This morning he has had meetings about the possibility of a mobile video box, for viewers to record complaints, and about the threatened move of his Charlotte Street unit.*

The idea is that we should be moved from No. 60, the building in which the graphics, studio and tape library are housed, to No. 76. The rationale is that they want our office for the new Early Morning Television Team, on the grounds that their crises are likely to be a good deal more serious than our crises. Probably right: I wouldn't want to supervise the day-to-day of the early morning programme. But there is considerable anger that it should be an either/or decision, when there are other departments in the building that have less urgent need of access to the facilities in No. 60.

I know that the decision has been taken, and that there's no point in fighting it; Channel 4 is quite capable of simply moving our stuff to the new offices one weekend if we don't sort it out ourselves . . . But the fact remains, as always, that no one who actually works on *Right to Reply* has been consulted about the move. 'Mad, but typical', says presenter Linda Agran, well used to the madness of other television companies.

During the afternoon Simon Meyers, who's directing an insert from Manchester, rings to say that they're having a nightmare. The people who were fluent and talkative the previous day, with researcher Seetha Kumar, have clammed up completely at the sight of the cameras . . . Our

Linda Agran does her best to ensure a public *Right to Reply* on Channel 4

trainee researcher, Marion Sumerfield, has been talking to some viewers from the Architectural Association, who sound as if they have an interesting line on the Prince Charles *Omnibus* programme; more than just attacking him for traditionalism, but talking as well about the way television treats architecture . . .

As the discussion is looking like a runner I ring the *Omnibus* producer, Christopher Martin. He makes the reasonable point that as our potential participants are raising the matter of overall balance, it's not really one for him as the producer of one programme, but should be addressed to someone further up the line . . . I get the impression that he's not keen on breaking into his sabbatical in Oxford to trek back to London for a discussion. I don't think that I would be, in his position . . .

Rod Stoneman (assistant commissioning editor, independent film and video) tells me that *Mother Ireland*, a film made by Derry Film and Video, which C4 had been in endless negotiation about, asking for cuts and changes, but which had been finally scuppered by the Government ban, is to be shown simultaneously in Derry and London tomorrow evening. The programme is about the way that the image of Mother Ireland became embroiled with republican and nationalist politics over a period of 200 years.

Two of those interviewed, who are apparently judged to fall foul of the Government restrictions, are women who were involved in Cumn na Ban, a feminist organization associated with the IRA in the 1920s. There's also a piece of 1920s archive footage showing a woman speaker at a public meeting saying: 'The IRA have struggled, and the IRA have won', which looks to me like it's on the wrong side of the order.

There's also an interview with Mairead Farrell, who the Workshop believed no longer to be active in the IRA, but who was shot in Gibraltar by the SAS, at about the same time that the programme was delivered to Channel 4. C4 had asked the Workshop to replace her with another republican woman (this before the ban made such things academic) on the grounds that her presence would be offensive to public feeling in Britain, a phrasing that is uncomfortably close to Douglas Hurd's justification for his restriction . . .

ANDREW CURRY, PRODUCER

> *The BBC Community Programme Unit was born as a response to the
> 1960s demand, largely made at media conferences, for public access to
> the television screen. Over the years it has given a voice to many
> outsiders who would not otherwise have achieved air-time and, maybe
> for that very reason, has never been one of the BBC's most favoured
> offspring. It is now to be found, with difficulty, on an industrial estate
> and a one-way system in the Acton area of West London. Access is
> difficult. So, as producer Giles Oakley records, are other things.*

We're making a film under the editorial control of the Brighton Unemployed Centre, where we had our first meeting last week. The group includes two paid, part-time workers and several unemployed people. It's not clear exactly who or how many will work on the programme; it's up to them to decide, and I don't want to push them too early into a decision on how they should work. That does, however, create problems, as shown by a draft programme outline I've received in the post this morning. I'm somewhat downhearted that it isn't more developed and coherent . . .

Today there have been numerous distractions. There's much speculation over whether our 'boss', Tony Laryea (Editor CPU), will get the job as Head of Topical Features, a new department into which we are being amalgamated. Along with eight others he was boarded yesterday. Afterwards Tony gave himself an 80 per cent chance; now apparently he reckons he has no chance . . . After lunch we have to assemble in front of our office for a team photo. There's a feeling that it perhaps marks the end of an era; shortly before it we heard that Tony had not got the Topical Features job. It's gone to Peter Weil, with John Morrell as his deputy.

Tony seems subdued. We all know our independence and autonomy is at risk. We fear it will mean that Tony no longer has direct access to the channel controllers. At best he will be number three in the new hierarchy. It's ironical that, at a time when the BBC is being forced to take 25 per cent of production from independents, in the name of diversity, we are seeing strengthened centralization, with lengthened formal chains of command. What we want is devolved decision-making and more competing powers of commission. Instead we're getting greater

Diminishing access at Acton: Tony Laryea (man in spectacular jersey and dark glasses) leads his Community Programme Unit in a team photograph that 'perhaps marks the end of an era'

concentrations of power at the heart of a system based on increased casualization. Not so much independents as dependants.

We don't know much about Weil (there's doubt about how to spell it: Viall? Vyell? Vile? . . .), editor of *Wogan*, ex-editor of *Open Air*. He's said to be more 'liberal' and likeable than some. 'Could have been worse', we say to ourselves hopefully. There's a fear that he'll be too malleable, no more likely to stand up to pressure than most of the people currently running the Beeb. Above all we resent being arbitrarily banged in together with programmes most of us don't much like, or even respect. Especially as no one even bothered to discuss it with us. Morale is low.

Most of us are strongly committed to the ideals of Public Service: broadcasting in the public interest, not for profit, and not for the State. Most of us feel deep suspicion of the much-vaunted deregulation of broadcasting, which we fear will undermine such ideals. We don't see much sign that the BBC is prepared to make much of a fight of it. Appeasement is seemingly the main external strategy, while 'tidying up' dissent inside. Meanwhile the ratings pressure builds remorselessly. As I leave the office just after 6 p.m. someone calls out: 'When do you think we'll have the first *Open Space* featuring a talking dog?'. . .

At home I caught the end of *Channel 4 News*. I always like this, much more than the BBC News or even ITN on ITV. It treats the viewer as an adult, giving intelligent and reasonably fair analysis. I later saw the *Nine O'Clock News* (BBC1), the first time I'd seen its 'new look'. It still seems to have that faint aura of bullshit; not so much lies as a subtle undertow, dragging news values into line with those acceptable to the Establishment, and especially the Government. On Nigel Lawson's spending announcement the Labour spokesman's views were included but marginalized. As usual City analysts predominate. Working with the unemployed people from Brighton for *Open Space*, makes me realize how different their perceptions of the economy are from those of City people in smart suits . . .

GILES OAKLEY, PRODUCER

DOCUMENTARY WRAPPINGS
As 6 p.m. approaches broadcasters fortunate enough to be working something like office hours begin to drift home or wherever, and to ruminate about their working day. For Thames, producer Nina Burr is making three programmes on the reasons for, and possible ways out of, depression.

And there's a lot of it about, especially at Thames . . . By 2.30 p.m. I was in the car and driving to Newham in East London to talk to people who run groups to help the depressed. I decided against doing any filming there because this group mainly concentrates on depression through bereavement and I feel that the conditions that cause a slow, living death are probably more relevant to my programmes.

However, they do run groups to help Asian women to cope with the shock of Tower Hamlets. I might film that, if I can get them to agree, that is. People don't like talking to the tele about their problems. It's my job to persuade them, but I often suspect the motives of those who do agree . . . As we drove back towards the City, a round red sun was sinking over the rich wastes of Docklands. Here, Jean-Michel had his concert. Here, the City Airport, there, the Docklands Light Railway. I felt depressed enough to include myself in my programme . . .

NINA BURR, PRODUCER-DIRECTOR

> *For greying Bob Saunders this has been BBC Kensington House dubbing day on his* Wide World *documentary, turning up the real man behind the Australian myth of Crocodile Dundee. Recording problems are complicated by the fact that narrator Kos Evans, who plays the photographer assigned to find Crocodile, is inexperienced and dyslexic. By 5 p.m. all seems to be well.*

Recording is finished and we all compliment Kos, a photographer, not an actress, by profession, on her determined performance. I began work on this film on 12 March. It seems an eternity for a one-hour film, but it is not unusual. Kos departs, to drive home to Winchester. I take advantage of the final hour in the theatre to listen to music tracks. I composed and played the music for the film in my home studio on a multi-synthesizer set-up and have been anxious to check the quality on BBC monitors. Brian Watkins, our mixer, judges all but one track to be up to standard. I'm delighted and relieved . . .

BOB SAUNDERS, PRODUCER

> *Today producer Jonathan Gili is at the editing stage of his film* The Day I Met the Queen, *the jewel in the crown of the current BBC2* 40 Minutes *documentary season. He cuts at John Jarvis Associates, off Goldhawk Road, 'a little too near my office in Kensington House for my liking'.*

The idea arose in the usual haphazard way, a year ago. My wife and I were Don Everly's guests at the Everly Brothers' Albert Hall concert. After the show we were invited back to Don's hotel, together with Lucy Lambton and Peter and Chrissie Blake. The subject of Peter's CBE (OBE?) came up and he described, most entertainingly, his visit to the Palace to collect it. This prompted me to tell the story of how I met the Queen at a wedding, and what she had said to me. The next day, in the office, I was describing the evening to Catrine Clay (researcher-interviewer), who said: 'Wouldn't that make a great film, *The Day I Met the Queen*? . . .'

At 3.55 p.m. I finally managed to get hold of Eddie Mirzoeff (series editor), whose telephone has been engaged all afternoon – hardly surprising since he is someone who adores the foul instrument. I wanted to arrange for him to come and see the to all intents and purposes final version of the film on Thursday . . . One of his great strengths as an executive producer is his ability to pinpoint the strengths and weaknesses of a film. His advice is usually both perceptive and intelligent; we don't always follow it, but often it sets us thinking in directions that improve the film no end . . .

At 4.20 p.m. we returned to reel one and made a whole lot of little changes, improving the pacing, removing a phrase here and there. This took us up to 5.30 p.m., when we stopped. I am grateful to Graham Shipham (film editor) for not wanting to work overtime, it's a great help for the budget. The day went pleasantly and quickly; it was quite ordinary really. I didn't watch television in the evening as we have no television set . . .

JONATHAN GILI, PRODUCER

> *For production assistant Jane Bywaters this has been a recce day for a BBC2 Arena film on Graham Greene. The biopic started two years ago in Panama; today she was on the 8.10 a.m. from St Pancras to Nottingham with producer-director Nigel Finch. They have seen the cathedral where Greene was converted to the Catholic faith, the lodgings from where he took his first job as a journalist, and the Nottingham Journal offices where he worked, before driving on to see the Monseigneur in Derby.*

The BBC Library map is completely out of date and we arrive a little late. The Monseigneur is very courteous, however; he reads out the early conversion ceremony and explains how it differs now and where it would have taken place. He himself was converted on the battlefield of the Somme and since then, he said, he has not had one moment of doubt. The Convent smells of cabbage, but tea is politely brought in and Mgr Wilson (aged 90) suggests somebody who might take part in our filming in December. We leave to catch the 5.30 p.m. train back, a useful and enjoyable day . . .

**JANE BYWATERS,
PRODUCTION ASSISTANT**

> *Catharine Seddon, an assistant producer who is making her own film, has spent the day on her BBC1 Everyman documentary exploring the concept of forgiveness through the experiences of four victims of severe crime. She has met Bernard Proctor, who has spent eight years in pursuit of the drunk driver who killed his son; and the parents of a 19-year-old girl sexually assaulted and murdered while they were asleep in the next-door room.*

It's been one of the rare days which reflect both the best and worst sides of being a television producer: the best being the variety of subject, the contact with people and the privilege to have those people entrust to you not just their opinions, but their emotions too; the worst, the moments, allbethey fleeting, of self-doubt, when you wonder whether these individuals will really benefit themselves and others by talking on camera, or whether they'll just be seen as 'good telly' and afterwards come to regret what they said. If they trust me, I owe them a lot.

**CATHARINE SEDDON,
ASSISTANT PRODUCER**

V

LOCAL TIMES

6 p.m. – 7 p.m.

15 VARIATIONS ON A
REGIONAL THEME

My television debut! Yorkshire's *Calendar* magazine has just broadcast our film shot this morning. We were seen demonstrating our media studies equipment, watching the *Lucky Ladders* quiz and giving it the thumbs down. It was a harrowing experience . . . My edited speech was a source of much sarcasm the following day. I still think the main point of the film was nervousness and embarrassment . . .

**TIM NUNNEY, AGED 15,
RALPH THORESBY HIGH SCHOOL, LEEDS**

The hour from 6 p.m. is the hour in which all the regional television stations, both ITV and BBC, transmit their local news magazines. For the most part these are not scheduled to compete directly with each other; regional news gluttons can see the local ITV show at 6 p.m., followed around 6.30 by the BBC effort. Viewers who happen to live near a newsroom producing a regional magazine, anywhere from Aberdeen to Plymouth, know they will be particularly, and unfairly, well served.

The regions are far from uniform, in either size or character, their boundaries mainly drawn by the engineers who made the transmitter map. The editors of Channel Television may wonder, as they while away the afternoon in their studios on Jersey and Guernsey, if there is going to be any news for Channel Report of any kind. In faraway Belfast, as Ulster Television prepares its Six Tonight and its BBC rival assembles Inside Ulster, the problem is just the opposite. Irish hostilities ensure that Belfast has the only BBC newsroom, outside London, that is manned 24 hours a day.

NORMAL FOR SOME

Just now the all-important BBC chair of Controller, Northern Ireland, is occupied by an open-minded but hard-headed Lancashire man, Dr Colin Morris. Unlike most broadcasting mandarins his experience of life has extended far beyond the camera and the microphone. As a young man, and devoted Methodist, he went to what was then Northern Rhodesia to do missionary work. He stayed to become a close friend and adviser of Kenneth Kaunda, first President of Zambia, whose portrait dominates one wall of his Belfast office. He had already seen troubles enough for most when he became the BBC's Head of Religious Broadcasting in 1979.

His translation to Ireland was unexpected and worrying. No sooner had he moved with his wife, into the beautifully sited Co. Down village of Crawfordsburn, than the house of his civil servant neighbour was bombed. This morning, as on all mornings, he was the only BBC controller who checked under his car for explosive devices before driving to work. He is fast approaching his 60th birthday but, we may be sure, he is regarded as much too useful to be touched by BBC retirement rules.

1 November was a normal day by Northern Ireland standards, which means that it was abnormal by the standards of broadcasting anywhere else in the United Kingdom. It was a day dominated by news coverage of a dramatic nature: the usual attack on security forces, the usual arms find, the usual clutch of rumours about the Government's intention of banning Sinn Fein, bringing in a broadcasting ban, setting aside the Anglo-Irish agreement etc., etc. Meanwhile, as news and current affairs offer the images and sounds of conflict, the rest of the output struggles to find the images of normality.

COLIN MORRIS, CONTROLLER, BBC NORTHERN IRELAND

Similar vigilance is required across the way at Ulster Television, something which becomes clear with the laconic diary entries of security boss Ian Leathem.

Inside Ulster: presenter Sean Rafferty (left), floor manager Kevin McCrudden and Lynda Bryans get their wires crossed

8.25 a.m., stopped at paper shop for *Daily Telegraph.* 8.30 a.m., police

road block. 10.30 a.m., party of fire officers shown round building to acquaint them with the layout. 2.55 p.m., constant deliveries of tapes and packages, all to be checked out by security officers before they go to departments. 3.35 p.m., strange cars round building to be checked out and owners identified. 4.20 p.m., informed that switchboard has received a bomb warning. Top management told and all departments asked to check their areas. I had little doubt that this was a hoax and did not vacate the building. 5.30 p.m., police road block outside the building, extra awareness required. 5.45 p.m., security officer asked to check car parks for anything odd . . .

IAN LEATHEM, HEAD OF SECURITY

> SCOTTISH STORIES
>
> *In Scotland there is much less certainty about what might be the story of the day. Reporter Jane Franchi, soon to be promoted to Glasgow as BBC Scotland Correspondent, today reports on the North-East from her Aberdeen base.*

Phone Bob Allen, Scottish Fishermen's Federation, about the implications of a ban on seal culling announced the day before. Both of us agree the implications are zero, as there hasn't been a cull since the early 1980s . . . Phone David Burnside, Piper Alpha Legal Group, to find out if the meeting tonight would mean an end to the compensation wrangle. It won't. 'A nuts and bolts meeting', he said. Michael Park, Occidental's lawyer, was on the phone within minutes. 'Was David Burnside making any statement today?' he asks. Also, would we remember to get a response from him, if David does go into print. It occurs to me that we, the media, are being used, by both sides . . . Conference hook-up with Glasgow. Asked to check out Piper Alpha, seals, teachers' demo and industrial tribunals involving seamen sacked during the P&O dispute. Probably sound smug that I've already done so . . .

Definitely the telephone call of the week, if not the year. From Geoffrey Joseph, whose two-year-old daughter Sharona was murdered by a 12-year-old boy. The story hit the headlines last week and I had included it in my *Sunday Mail* column. We talked for a long time, on the understanding that I would not repeat what he said to me . . . The fact that he wanted to talk to a complete stranger about the worst tragedy in his life, on the basis that my column had touched him so much, was the most moving and extraordinary proof of the power of words. I hope I never abuse that power . . .

Grampian Police say they've found two more bodies in the Piper Alpha module at Flotta, and have identified another seven. No words will ever describe the horror and grief of Piper Alpha . . . Bob Allen arrives to be interviewed about dismantling oil platforms. *Reporting Scotland* producer, Gordon McMillan, phones to say his programme is full and he doesn't want the interview. Will it hold for tomorrow? No. Apologize profusely to Bob, make him a cup of coffee and listen in on the interview he does for

Radio Scotland. Just in case. It's useful info to have. Tell crew, who've spent 45 minutes setting up an interview corner in the club, to stand down.

Phone call to Grampian Regional Council re the number of schools closed by teachers' strike action: three secondaries, 31 primaries, 48 per cent on strike. Phone Glasgow with that. Check out protest planned by divinity students for tomorrow. Sounds a riot, will probably cover it . . .

JANE FRANCHI, REPORTER

WELSH WORRIES
The pressures are more apparent at BBC Cardiff, where Ioan Kidd, a sub-editor acting as producer, is preparing the 6 p.m. Welsh-language news. At lunch he had a long wait in the canteen queue, found there were no vegetarian lunches left and 'felt like complaining'. Back in the office . . .

It all started again. The phone did not stop ringing, everybody wanted to speak to me, I felt harassed and wanted to run away . . . I went to the afternoon meeting instead of my fellow producer and I felt impatient to leave and get on with my programme. I wish he had been available to attend . . . During the next hour I went through a mountain of copy that had piled up, and one or two changes were made in the running order.

I felt other members of staff were beginning to grumble at some of the changes. We are always short of staff and some colleagues only see their own tasks in isolation. I began to feel alone again and sensed some hostility. I thought there was a silent criticism, by some, of the way things were going and I felt such criticism was totally unfair and unwarranted. I felt like turning on them and challenging them to produce a programme with few staff and few facilities. They know the problems, but under pressure people often lash out.

It was 5 p.m. and I was over-running by about two minutes, and had to cut back. Decisions, decisions. I was given misleading information regarding how much time we had to fill (or lose) and this was grossly complicated when nearly all the reports came on with durations longer than requested. Panic took hold of some colleagues and it began to rub off on me. I felt oppressed and cheesed off and everyone was looking to me to solve their problems. My own problems were more numerous and more pressing.

After weeding out and cutting back we were on course, but one of the reporters had not yet returned to base. It was 5.45 p.m. and we were on air at 6. Terror and panic! Where was he? He finally arrived and the deputy editor helped out. I rushed to the gallery and all was well. The programme output was no reflection of the panic earlier . . .

I went for a drink in the canteen and began to reflect on the afternoon. I decided to go to the boss to clarify matters and to have a moan at the way items turned out too long in duration. I was really glad I went to see him.

He was pleased with the programme. He put my mind at rest and restored my confidence . . .
**IOAN KIDD, SUB-EDITOR,
ACTING PRODUCER**

> BORDER LINES
> *It will be a relatively calm day for Shirley Hewitt, consumer reporter for the Tyne Tees magazine* Northern Life. *As she leaves her Tynemouth home, and points the car towards Newcastle, she has one regret.*

I muse that it is such a pity that the consumer spot has just been moved to Monday evenings. We might have been logged for posterity . . . My day is to be spent checking round the student population of the region. I have appointments with the president of Newcastle University Students' Union, Rob Williams, and later Sigrid Fisher, president of Newcastle Polytechnic Students' Union. I want to know if the students are having a tough time finding accommodation . . .

Also I make contact with wheelchair-bound Sue Clements who is to co-operate on an item about the lack of disabled access in shops, and a new guide for the handicapped to the Tyneside Metro system . . . We are keeping an eye on dangerous fireworks, with the Guy Fawkes anniversary in four days' time . . . I am reminded that Christmas is not far off. It brings its own difficulties, people are too busy to make news, so items must be planned ahead . . .
**SHIRLEY HEWITT,
CONSUMER JOURNALIST**

> *Across in Cumbria, reporter-presenter Jane Askew also has a mixed day preparing items for Border's* Lookaround.

We set off in the van for our first job, at a tiny place called Town O'Rule near Bonchester Bridge in the Borders. The job was a military and civilian exercise to find a simulated leak in one of British Petroleum's ethylene pipelines. It involved about 50 troops . . . Unfortunately, when we arrived at our designated time of 11 a.m. we found nearly everyone had left 15 minutes earlier. I managed two quick interviews with a BP boss and an army colonel. It was extremely cold and I was glad to hurry off to a café in Hawick to liaise with a Beta cameraman who had filmed some of the operation for us. I wrote voice-overs and cutting notes in the café, recorded the piece in the van, and a driver sent from Carlisle took the item back to be edited.

After lunch the newsdesk told us to go to the Market Square in Selkirk to meet the entertainer Jesse Rae. We arrived early so we had coffee and I bought a Selkirk Bannock, I had always wanted to try a real one . . . Our interviewee arrived in his green Land-Rover, bedecked in kilt, sporran, leather tabard, iron mask and carrying a claymore (large sword formerly used by Scottish Highlanders). Apparently he's never seen in public without all his gear on. I did a walking interview with Jesse up one of the main streets. At 2.50 p.m., with a flurry of his claymore, he was off, slowly followed by a rather more sedate and sombre crew.

Dozed in the van on the way back to Carlisle. In the city we alerted the newsdesk about three fire engines screaming through the town centre, but it turned out to be nothing. Got back just in time to go into rehearsals at 4.45 p.m. I was reading the news. The lead item in the show was the teachers' strike in Scotland . . .

JANE ASKEW, REPORTER-PRESENTER

> YORKSHIRE CULLS
>
> *At BBC Leeds, as the Tuesday evening* Look North *is put together, there are one or two envious thoughts about the superior resources of the Yorkshire Television rival,* Calendar. *Copytaker Sheila Clarke has other things on her mind.*

Our main local news story today is a murder remand. A 16-year-old girl has been strangled and her body dumped at the side of the M1 motorway near Wakefield. It will be our lead story in *Look North* tonight. During a typical day the bulk of the news stories we take down and send on to local radio stations and other BBC television centres will be made up of murders, robberies, child abuse, assault and battery, muggings and fatal road accidents. Sometimes it's hard to remain detached, and often a particularly nasty story involving young children will affect us deeply.

Fortunately, we have Horace the Hamster to keep us sane today. He disappeared in a chemist's shop in Malton two weeks ago and was reported missing by his distraught owner. Luckily, a passing policeman spotted the hamster in the shop at the dead of night and effected a rescue. Horace didn't appear to be too grateful . . . he bit the policeman's finger and is now in custody at the local police station . . .

SHEILA CLARKE, COPYTAKER

At 9.30 a.m. our programme prospects are mapped out and our four camera crews assigned to all parts of the region. It's the only time I feel envious of our counterparts in Yorkshire Television. They have 12 crews at their disposal. It's a very thin day, no real lead story. But this is typical for regional television. Some days we have too much news to digest . . . and then there's today.

As presenter of the programme I usually get out on stories myself two or three times a week. A lot of my work is doing public relations for the BBC. This morning I have to open a dangerous drugs campaign in Sheffield, and then give a lunch talk to a group of local businessmen . . .

At 5 p.m. the producer asks me to look at one or two scripts, can I rewrite them in my style? This is something we've been encouraging; too often 'intros' into items are badly written . . . Into the studio to record the headlines. Standard practice now, in the old days we always went live, not any more. A good start is always important . . . A special feature on a children's hospice has proved to be very powerful and a moving piece. It might upset a few people. The producer decides, quite rightly, in my opinion, to run it uncut . . . Not as bad a programme as we thought, for a thin day. I'm told the opposition programme was full of technical problems. No gloating about that, though, it could easily happen to us tomorrow . . .

HARRY GRATION, PRESENTER

> *The supposed technical problems did not apparently much exercise*
> Calendar *presenter Richard Whiteley. He has spent his day in YTV's*
> *Studio Four recording several editions of the Channel 4 parlour game*
> Countdown. *Number one was the first programme on the first day of*
> *Channel 4 and it is now into its 17th series.*

The normal target is to record six programmes per day, in a four-day block. On this particular day we recorded seven. . . The morning audience consists of 50 ladies from the Bridlington Voluntary Women's Association and a party from Bransholme, a large estate near Hull . . . The seventh game ends at 5.20 p.m. The studio is booked until 6.30, but as we have run out of contestants, we call it a day. We could have done more . . . At 5.30 I go to Studio Two to prepare for the live transmission of *Calendar* at 6 p.m. Cup of tea, script and autocue check. Talk with producer about items. Main presenter . . .

RICHARD WHITELEY, PRESENTER

Yorkshire's Richard Whiteley, heavily employed on 1 November presiding over both *Calendar* and several recorded editions of *Countdown*

> *There were no worries about technical problems for a teacher and 33*
> *children, at St Andrew's primary school in Sheffield, who were filmed*
> *for the programme.*

A group of my pupils had worked on the song called 'The Final Cull', about the plight of dying seals, featured in recent news programmes. I sent a cassette to *Calendar* and here we were now singing in front of the cameras. My normally bubbly, talkative 10- and 11-year-olds were filled with a sense of great achievement as they realized they had fulfilled their aim, in alerting the public to their plea, and some were even stunned to silence when questioned by the friendly reporter . . .

Rushed home after school, hurriedly phoned my family and friends, fed the dog, sat down and tried to watch *Neighbours*. Little did Mrs Mangel know what trauma and apprehension I was experiencing. Maybe I could claim compensation for an attack of nerves, at the thought of seeing my class and myself on television for the first time? At 6 p.m. *Calendar* began, and yes, our story was mentioned in the headlines. When we were featured in the final news item I hugged the dog with joy. He showed little interest . . .

**ANGELA HOGG, TEACHER,
SHEFFIELD**

When it was advertised in *Calendar* my Mum was on the phone to my Nan and everybody. Then the moment came. There I was, standing there

and singing: 'The seal is our friend who did us no harm. He swam round
the sea when the world was calm. He was healthy and strong in the clear
green sea' . . . where we went wrong at the back. And there was Carrie
being interviewed . . .

**KATIE FIELDS, AGED 10,
SHEFFIELD**

Then it was time for *Calendar* on the other channel and my song sung by
my J4 class at St Andrew's School. It was very exciting to see myself on
television. It was even more thrilling when the four television people
came to our class that morning to film us all. I had butterflies in my
tummy but it was really exciting when we sang the song for them. I am
really glad this has happened on this special day, on 1 November 1988 . . .

**CARRIE SHIRTCLIFFE, AGED 10,
SHEFFIELD**

GRAINS OF GRANADALAND

*On the western side of the Pennines news editor Barry Flynn is handing
over much of his Granada Reports space to a report on the supposed
economic regeneration of the English North-West, marking the launch
of a 'Fast Forward' conference in Manchester. His out-of-town
reporters nevertheless keep going. Here is Paul Crone, based at the
Lancaster office.*

I decide to do a follow-up story on the Preston bank robbery, which took
place seven weeks ago. The gang haven't been captured yet and neither
has the £500,000 they took . . . The producer at our Liverpool
headquarters readily swallows our Preston idea. Yesterday, four stories
fell down and he wasn't a happy man. Today we are back in favour again
. . . We arrive at Preston and are greeted by Detective Superintendent
Barrie Walmsley. When I spoke to him earlier he'd said most of the
enquiry team had caught colds, rather than any bank robbers. In
sympathy I took him a jar of Vick to rub on his chest. Fortunately, he
laughed.

We then filmed the ops room and interviewed Walmsley on how the
enquiry was going. It's a cracking yarn and he's a good talker, so it's not
difficult to make it an interesting story. After filming we chatted for 20
minutes on the robbery and theories about the whereabouts of the gang. I
felt a lot of sympathy for Barrie Walmsley. He's a good copper and has
the unenviable task of solving what's been described as the perfect crime
. . . Back at the office to record my voice-overs I find out that my story is
being held over for a day. I'm not too disappointed because I have been
given more time, two minutes 30 seconds . . .

PAUL CRONE, REPORTER

*Back at base, regional editor Mike Short has some more generalized
thoughts.*

With all the problems we face because the Government is planning to move the goal posts, change the size of the pitch with the proposed White Paper, I sometimes wish I wasn't a lapsed Catholic . . . Quite a number of things are being turned over in the mind. For one the news that Anna Ford is to present the BBC1 *Six O'Clock News* against us and how would that influence the ratings. We are climbing back from a downturn in the summer. My hatred of the BBC is confirmed. Michael Grade's last clever move at the BBC had been to give adolescents their own soap, *Neighbours*, which put more pressure on regional news. Ms Ford's good looks, though she would wish it weren't the case, will have an effect. I suppose one answer will be more Barbie dolls presenting in the regions . . .

ITN will have to retaliate. Their *News at 5.45* team is being squeezed. Still, it makes me sick how they slimed into Mrs Thatcher to get her personally to intervene to protect them. So much for the market force philosophy. I think their national news presentation has a Southern bias. There's a standing joke that when it snows in London their desk starts ringing round for snow pictures. The Grampian reporters have usually been wearing Eskimo outfits and snowshoes for about three months when the call floats in. During the great storm, I have it on good account, the BBC national news announced with great pomp that everything was going to be all right because 'the hurricane is moving north'. . .

MICHAEL SHORT, EDITOR

EAST ANGLIAN CLOUDS
Specialist contributors have a constant battle to win space on local news magazines. Sports reporter Stuart Jarrold, working for About Anglia, *is no exception to the rule.*

I had high hopes of this day being reasonably fulfilling. My idea was to report on the only known woman rugby correspondent, from Australia, covering the present Wallabies tour of England. As they were in our patch today, playing the Combined English Students at Cambridge, it seemed a worthwhile profile piece, including comments from the Australian players. I had spoken to the woman at her hotel the night before, to research the story and check on her movements, so we knew where to meet her. I had also made provisional arrangements with a camera crew to be available . . .

Then came frustration number one. Too many other news stories were deemed more important than my sports feature. These included visits by the Princess Royal, and a politician, Norman Tebbitt, plugging his autobiography. As we are supposed to reflect regional happenings I argued against allocating four minutes in a 24-minute programme to a book-plugging item. This could have little interest to local viewers compared with my story, I said. It didn't cut any ice and, in the end, compromise was the order of the day.

Go to Cambridge and report briefly on the match itself, I was told, forget any mention of the woman rugby reporter. Logistically this meant organizing a motorcycle despatch rider to collect the video tapes from the crew at the ground, and playing back the action from the nearest district office, 40 minutes away, to our headquarters in Norwich. The round trip to the rugby ground, of 120 miles or so, produced about 30 seconds of material on air the same evening.

There were other frustrations. Several other sports stories I had spent time researching, telephoning people about and writing, were all dropped. Another waste of effort. I would say the frustrations were typical, although it was not a typical day. No day is the same. In a sense that is one of the pleasures, I suppose, of working as a television reporter . . .

**STUART JARROLD,
SPORTS REPORTER-PRESENTER**

After his canteen lunch, weather forecaster Jim Bacon walks about Norwich with his eyes tilted towards the sky. He notes that the wind has picked up and it is quite cold, despite the sunshine. He detects a small amount of low-level cumulus cloud.

By 3.15 p.m. I have identified the main theme of the forecast for *About Anglia* tonight. It is now clouding over in Norwich and this confirms my feelings about the lack of frost overnight . . . At 4.15 p.m. I am asked if I can cope with 15 seconds less time for my evening forecast. I am not over-keen to do this, but the weather is not so complicated today that it cannot be done in less time. I reluctantly agree . . . By 4.45 p.m. I am 'graphically' committed to no air frost (perhaps a ground frost in the south) and no fog. If the cloud breaks become larger during the next few hours the first part of the forecast will be in trouble . . .

By 5.15 p.m. I have a complete set of charts stored on the computer. I can run through the forecast and check that it is possible to cover all the important detail in the shorter time available. I can also test for awkward phrases . . . At 5.30 I have a telephone conference with the Norwich Weather Centre to exchange ideas and latest observations . . . At 5.45 it is time to visit Make-up. I take my usual short cut across the car park to get a look at the sky . . . At about 6.11 I start the forecast; it lasts for about two minutes and finishes when the floor manager gives a count-out signal. I think it worked out reasonably well . . .

JIM BACON, METEOROLOGIST

MIDLAND SCHEDULES
Sound recordist Don Young, employed on the Birmingham version of
Central News, *begins his working day outside the Coventry press conference where the council announces its pioneering ban on outdoor drinking.*

Discover that my recorder has been left in a cold car overnight (minus four degrees Centigrade), I having been on leave the previous day. Condensation has formed on the head drum during the trip to Coventry.

The tape is stuck to the head and the machine is not working. Quiet panic. Pull case apart to get to the problem. The back of a car makes a poor workshop, I am feeling nervous and pressed. Twenty minutes later the recorder is working, I am relieved and a bit chuffed at my ability. We go into the press conference, but it is almost over.

Morning interviews with police and council, filming around the city centre. We try to hurry the reporter along, as we have a job in Birmingham at 12.30 p.m., but he doesn't care, only interested in his story. Silently annoyed, I'm used to this typical attitude. Arrive 25 minutes late for story about planned changes to Birmingham roads. Reporter very understanding, has kept things waiting for us. The reporter's attitude pleasant and a refreshing change . . .

At 5.35 p.m. we are back at base, exhausted. The day is over but . . . Panic. NUPE announcement about a nurses' strike. Race off to the Children's Hospital. Despatch rider takes the tape. Back at base ten minutes after the programme's 6 p.m. start. Will the nurses' piece make it? Watch item go out, most impressed with the team. At 6.30 p.m. about to go home, but the news editor wants a crew to stand by for possible reactions to the Clinton McCurbin case in Wolverhampton. Agree to go out later at night, silently thinking it to be a waste of time. Rest of crew willing to co-operate but share my view. Still, the mortgage interest rate is up again, the overtime will be handy.

Cameraman and I go for an evening meal at a local bistro. Relax and chat about the company, the job, the future. A little apprehensive but we enjoy each other's conversation, specially off the job. At 8.20 p.m. we return to base to meet the sixth reporter of the day for our vigil in Wolverhampton. We arrive at 9.10 and begin to cruise around the town centre, visiting all the known likely places for trouble to brew. It would be good in television terms if there was some sign of unrest, with us on the spot for a change. We all agree that this is unlikely.

The reporter repeatedly calls to police and new agencies on the car radiophone, but everywhere is as quiet as the grave and very cold. At 11.15 p.m. there is not even a hint of trouble from any sector, black or white, not even at pub throwing-out time. Arrive at base very tired, cold and fed up. Put batteries on charge for tomorrow. Lock recorder and camera in a warm storeroom for the night. Reach home at 12.45 a.m., too tired for a cup of tea. Fall into bed next to my sleeping wife . . .

DONALD YOUNG, SOUND RECORDIST

BRISTOL ROVING

The rivalry at Bristol is between the BBC's Points West *and the English version of* HTV News. *Taking an overview as the HTV magazine is assembled is news and current affairs chief Stephen Matthews. Starting the day at his Chew Magna home, he is another ITV regional executive concerned about the BBC's latest, expensive signing.*

Get papers from village shop. Disappointed to see Anna Ford is to make a comeback on the Beeb's *Six O'Clock News*, wonder how many viewers she'll steal . . . Editorial conference at 9.30 a.m., yes to backbench revolt on teeth, yes to future of countryside conference, no to save the hedgehog campaign . . . Phone call from managing director (Patrick Dromgoole). He's an ex-journalist, wants to know what's happening, has plenty of ideas himself . . . View two unedited features as there's a question mark over them. Yes to the one about the musicians who play ironing boards, and maybe to the middle-aged minuet dancers drawing crowds in Bath. Shades of *Nationwide* at its most eccentric; carefully placed they'll raise an eyebrow . . .

At 11.30 a.m. THE DAY CEASES TO BE BORING. Industry reporter receives leaked document from contact at British Aerospace. It says that factory which made Concorde and now Airbus, and employs 8000, might close. Great story, exclusive. Go through possibilities with editor and reporter Steve Scott. Is it genuine? Can we substantiate it? How shall we play it? Can't call Aerospace yet, they might put out a statement, take out an injunction even. Decide to construct it from library pictures and talk, off the record, to many contacts. Tell editor not to run Aerospace story at lunch-time, better to surprise and annoy the BBC at 6 p.m. . . .

At 12.15 p.m. DAY GETS BETTER. Story in that radioactive waste found in Portishead. Crew and reporter despatched, lead story on any other day, now two to choose from. Love it, no such thing as a boring day in news . . . Lunch of ham, egg and chips. Realize too late this will look bad in diary, should have had beansprout salad. Never mind, still not fat . . .

Managing Director calls. Discuss problems over BBC rugby contract. Funny how we defend freedom of the press, and then pay money to stop the opposition enjoying that freedom . . . At 5 p.m. watch rehearsal on monitor. Aerospace have confirmed report now, denied the closure move. Still excellent exclusive . . .

Man from IBA calls in for occasional chat about life in general. Mentions White Paper and wonders how both our lives will change. It's *déjà vu*. There's been a pistol at the head of broadcasting since I can remember, just a different hand on the trigger this time . . . Watch *HTV News*, pleased generally. Watch *Points West*, relief, nothing we missed . . .

**STEPHEN MATTHEWS, HEAD OF NEWS
AND CURRENT AFFAIRS, HTV BRISTOL**

> *Across at the BBC producer-presenter Michael Dornan had a more nerve-racked day. As producer he was preoccupied with the final edit of a documentary to be transmitted the following Friday. He was also required to deputize for Chris Vacher as presenter of* Points West. *His problems started soon after noon.*

The pictures break up badly when we try transferring the final section of the documentary to VT. No success in trying to trace fault, after 45

minutes. Have now missed slot for dubbing sound track. Persuade
Andrew, the dubbing mixer, to give up his (and my) lunch to do it . . .
DISASTER! Picture editor has left out two vital shots; commentary,
interviews and pictures won't fit. He hasn't checked it. I can't believe it.
Begin scouring the building for him, but he's gone out to lunch . . .

Two editors and three engineers have come up with possible emergency
method of rectifying picture fault. It doesn't work. The section will have
to be re-edited, but the only machinery available is the suspect suite
where it was cut this morning . . . Look into the newsroom to see how
evening magazine is shaping, I have studio interviews to record at 4 p.m.
and 4.30 . . . To faulty edit suite where engineers have machinery in bits.
Somebody has a 'bright idea, which might just work'. . .

Before the interview go to the gents' washroom, put on make-up, put in
my one contact lens. (The lens is for close reading of scripts; the eye
without the lens reads the autocue, which is at a distance; the brain
simply selects whichever image is sharp) . . . Look into VT: an extra
machine and wires everywhere; the 'bright idea' is probably breaking all
regulations, but appears to be working . . .

At 4.05 p.m. interview a toxicologist (who's in a Leeds studio) down the
line. He's flummoxed by one question, so two takes needed. We lose line
during final question, sizable editing needed . . . Second interviewee
arrives, for Hinkley Point power station story I suggested myself this
morning. It's not the person I expected, but a lady who's done no
television before and is paralysed by nerves: three takes, getting
progressively worse, much editing needed. Suggest second interviewee
dropped altogether. News editor and producer unwilling as we are already
short of material and programme is three minutes longer than usual
tonight . . . Asked to take over editing both interviews . . .

The *Points West* director (Jan Blyth) calls on phone, frustrated by the
shortage of equipment. She needs to get on and record other items, how
long will we be? We have one remaining edit to do, two minutes . . . We
have tried, perhaps 20 times, to edit on a line saying, 'There we must
leave it, thank you very much', but it's still not right. I cannot believe this,
it should be so simple. The director orders us to stop, so she can get on
. . . Look at programme scripts, for the first time, at 5.50 p.m. . . . Begin
recording headlines at 6.05 p.m. We have recently changed the format.
Co-presenter Viv (Vivienne Creegor) is used to the new one but this is only
my second time . . .

The pace of the programme is frantic. During each item the director is
issuing instructions for the next one. It isn't usually like this. Suddenly an
argument flares up between the producer, director and news transmission
assistant, about whether we are over-running, under-running or on time.
Viv, at the adjoining desk, carries on reading a sequence of news stories
(with the argument belting along in her earpiece) without any outward
sign that anything is wrong. What a pro!

Ian Cameron, the producer, overrules everybody and instructs us, via
the earpieces, to read a sequence of spare news stories, at the end of the

present sequence which Viv is reading. I will do most of them to give her time to reorganize her scripts. I bless the fact that I took time to put in my contact lens, the first story is not on autocue . . . Ian was right, we were under-running, but we're back on time. Viv hands over to the newsroom for the final summary, which is read by a reporter up there. She and I begin to relax and have a moment's giggle. At the end of the summary I will close the programme . . .

The news summary under-runs by seven or eight seconds and I'm caught on the hop, a wretched lapse in concentration. I say 'Goodnight', especially to viewers keeping a diary of today, and hope that their day is proving as eventful as some of ours have been. I am preparing to take off my microphone, as a further animated discussion begins in the gallery, when somebody tells me I am wanted in VT. I had temporarily forgotten the other programme for which I am responsible . . .

In VT I find, to my astonishment, that they have re-made the last five minutes of the programme, by a method I didn't think possible, and rectified the break-up of the picture. The programme is almost complete. MAGIC! . . . At 8.30 p.m. I put on my coat. When I came in here, 13 hours ago, there were only two people in the room – the early morning journalist and a copy typist. Now there are only the late evening journalist and another copy typist. In 13 hours I have not had five minutes' respite, but I did have a ham sandwich. I think it is probably time to go home.

**MICHAEL DORNAN,
PRODUCER-PRESENTER**

CAPITAL PRESENTER
*Regional news magazines for London and the English South East face
two particular problems. One is the richness of news choice generated
by a population larger than that of many nation states. The other is that,
because national television journalists congregate in London, the
national news often mops up stories which might more properly be
treated as local. The resulting duplication is one of the matters
exercising Penny Smith, as she moves towards the end of her stint as
co-presenter of* Thames News.

My assignment for the morning is sniffer dogs in Surrey. Let's just hope they keep the sniffing at ground level. Apparently there aren't enough wet noses to go round, particularly with the extra call on them for security reasons. Wonder if I can write the entire story without resorting to puns and talk of dogs' breakfasts . . . Stop en route to Guildford to get prawn mayonnaise sandwich and custard doughnut for breakfast. Is it any wonder my hair looks startlingly peculiar these days? . . .

Very friendly lot at police headquarters. They take us to where the doggies are trying their hands (paws) at sticks of gelignite. I thought gelignite was one of those unstable substances. Like my sister, or something. Stand well back. Organize where we're going to do the shoot, a lovely sunny spot with a stupendous view over the Surrey countryside.

What a job this is. But then I also think that, only in a different tone of thought, when it's cold, wet, windy and I'm doing a story of interest to nobody but a one-legged armadillo with ringworm . . .

Half an hour late and still no sign of the crew. *Quelle surprise.* Phone back to the office, who say they're in Guildford and trying to find their way out of the one-way system. Yup, and I also believe in fairies. Apologize yet again, to the dog trainers *et al.*, who've been waiting patiently for everyone to turn up . . . Crew arrives 40 minutes late, obviously did a detour via Dumfries. Cameraman usual supercilious self. God protect me from prima donnas. Enough problems with one of me. At least the soundman's a lovely guy, and the rigger driver.

The doggies set off at a straining trot round the quadrangle. One golden labrador has decided his owner's arms need stretching. Cameraman gets very short with the sergeant who's helping show us what happens. Cringe inside and wish he was a car riveter. Part of this job is public relations, not helped by recalcitrant technicians. Eventually get the shots and do the interviews. By this time I have taken off my scarf and coat and have rolled up my jacket sleeves. Could an Indian summer be round the corner?

Story in the can, discuss my imminent departure to Sky Television. Is it the right move? Who knows. Why am I going? Why not. Will satellite survive? How the hell do I know. But there's always turkey plucking . . .

Thames's Penny Smith
about to take off to Sky

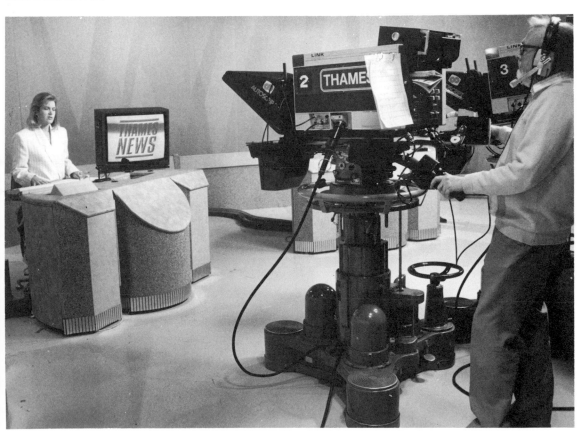

Arrive back at Thames, suddenly to remember that I'd missed the
mandatory NUJ meeting about the Government's new ruling on interviews
with some terrorist groups and their supporters. Terrorists or freedom
fighters? It's all a matter of perspective. It is considered permissible to
deal with the PLO, the Contras etc. What are they if they're not terrorists
in the countries where they operate? . . .

Quick rehearsal of afternoon bulletin, of which I make a complete hash.
Must have added about ten seconds stumbling over everything. A real
case of getting mords in a wuddle. Maybe I really should look at
bricklaying for a living . . . The two-and-a-half-minute bulletin flies by,
no mistakes . . . Swiftly up to the newsroom, and join the queue for the
trolley. Have a bacon roll and a disgustingly awful cake, stupendously
ravenous by now . . . Sniffer story not needed tonight, so write it up at a
leisurely pace, not normally the case . . .

Into studio where I read through links and discuss the current state of
co-presenter Andrew Gardner's wols – our nickname for the barn owls
that he's been raising. Lead story is about Vauxhall cars being recalled,
those between December last year and September this year, because of
brakes failure. Three of our stories have already been done on ITN.
Typical! . . .

I'm supposed to be reading a boxing story, about a world title fight
which has run into difficulties because one of the guys is South African.
But it misses its slot. One of the reporters who's at the House of
Commons, doing a live link, comes out of his piece 30 seconds early.
That's not so bad, but then I have to keep a straight face after a piece
about London Zoo, where, behind the interviewee, a Lord somebody or
other who I probably should know, there is a chimpanzee violently
shaking a tree and making strange noises. Cut to me and the story about
the boxing, which has finally made it into the programme . . .

PENNY SMITH, PRESENTER-REPORTER

SOUTHERN HEIGHTS

*At Southampton the co-presenters of TVS's Coast to Coast come to
agree with each other. A reporter, wounded after being apparently
caught out in a rude gesture, is less quick to hide his ego behind
communal harmony.*

They are running a story called Worthington Trial, about parents who are
accused of murdering their three-year-old daughter. Apparently the
pathologist couldn't tell at first whether the child was black or white, due
to her injuries. Ghastly and shocking. I asked whether we had to report
that fact but the boys like that stuff. I don't think it's necessary . . .

A short show tonight . . . Sadly one of the reporters did not allow
enough editing time and the piece that went on air had him accidentally
giving two fingers to the camera. He actually was indicating a take two.
Quite amusing for viewers, devastating for him and the producer. Poor
chap got grilled and booted after the show. All other reporters were

relieved it wasn't them. Afterwards he came to talk to me and I reassured him, saying it happens to everybody at least once, and perhaps he'd now allow more editing time. He agreed, saying he was renowned for doing things at the 60th minute, that it had always worked until now . . .

FERN BRITTON, PRESENTER

There is discussion, and argument, about how we should deal with a murder case at Winchester, in which two young people are accused of the brutal murder of their child. Fern feels this will be upsetting to our viewers, and should be used only as an item in the News. She loses the argument but later I feel that she was right – the report was gory and upsetting. But we have some nice 'light' items as well, including a film on a parrot for sale at £60,000. (The buyer will also get a house.) . . . Apart from one technical error the show goes well . . .

FRED DINENAGE, PRESENTER

> *An altogether more perilous day was experienced by Peter Pardo, a sound mixer seconded to the Southampton newsroom from TVS Maidstone. He and his cameraman are first despatched to Portsmouth to meet the expensive parrot. Then on to Salisbury, where the Dean is to cement the final stone of the restored cathedral spire.*

Standing in the autumn light, where John Constable perhaps stood for one of his greatest paintings, we discuss the possible shots and angles and their potential artistic merit. There is what appears to be a ladder on the outside of the spire. It's a long way to the top . . . Suddenly, behind us, the Dean has arrived in a flurry of scarf and cycle clips, giving a wonderfully lifelike impression of Derek Nimmo playing a Dean. He informs us that he really must catch the 3 p.m. train to London as he has a meeting, this very evening . . . 'with HRH' (Prince Charles) . . .

We walk to the lift that propels us skywards for the first 50 feet. Pete, a freelance electrician bounding with enthusiasm, aids us by carrying the tripod; a hefty bit of equipment that digs into your shoulder over a distance. Paul has the camera and I have a lightweight mixer unit on my shoulder, plus the infernal radio receiver round my neck. I don't fancy the climb to the top but we've discovered from the hard-hatted gentlemen (we didn't trust the Dean) that the steps to the top are inside . . .

Paul and I agreed, before the Dean arrived, that the coffee we had around 9.10 a.m. now needed to get out. The need of a beer and sandwich had not been the only reason for our desired visit to a hostelry. I ask if there is a loo available. Silly question, not a lot of people go up in the spire . . . Our gear is now in a canvas bag, being lifted by a rope worked with an electric motor. It sails slowly up through a latticework of ancient woodwormed beams into the mysterious heights above, as we begin to climb the stairs . . .

We continue upward into a section of spiral stone staircase. This I find claustrophobic as my awareness of the stairs above and below tells me I am rotating within a stone tube, gradually closing in around us . . . Finally there is daylight from a tiny door above . . . Pete, our electrician, is behind me as I burst out through the door. The sunlight hits my eyes and I need a moment or two to readjust. I step out on to the planking at around 430 feet up and there is wild space visible through the cracks. Pete discovers, for the first time, that he has no head for heights and reacts with: 'Oh, Jesus Christ'. The Dean, following on his heels, responds with: 'Er, perhaps I can help you with that.' Absolutions and blessings are too late for Pete but, being a well-brought-up lad, his manners outweigh his panic and he waits for the Dean to clear the door before diving back towards the safety of ground level. Graham Simmonds, our reporter, is also none too happy at this altitude and hangs on to anything that appears firm and reassuring.

The press boys, with their stills cameras, have preceded us to the top and are busily snapping away on the other side of the spire as the Dean applies cement and mortar to the final stone, leaving a dry bit for us when they've finished. The Dean is wonderful, he's obviously done all this sort of thing before. He knows exactly what's required even to the placing of a penny under the mortar for posterity to laugh at . . . Back to ground level, the Dean heads off for the station, Graham takes the tape back to the studio and we, at last, can go and find a loo and lunch . . .
PETER PARDO, SOUND RECORDIST

DARTMOOR BOGS
In Plymouth the staff of TSW's Today South West *are not seen to be without blemish by security man Adrian Baker.*

Alarm call at 5.30 a.m., corn flakes and a cup of tea. I jump on my pushbike and pedal the three-quarters of a mile to work, evading the mobbing seagulls who are fighting each other for last night's remains . . . Gents' toilets over by graphics badly blocked, could I sort it? So over I go, armed with my trusty plunger, which has seen quite a lot of action. Both cubicles blocked and overflowing. Holding my breath and, hopefully, my corn flakes I try the plunger . . . Sod this, it is a job for Dyno-Rod. Besides, I'm supposed to be a security officer, not a toilet attendant . . .

Dyno-Rod arrives and I show him the battle scene. He tells me we will have to deal with it from the manhole cover position. While we're peering down at the sludge, with its powerful stench, guess who comes stepping over the abyss. It is the head of education. He has a slight look of horror written on his face and I muse that we must have given him a bit of education . . .

When the battle of the bogs is over I check the car park and find, surprise, surprise, a couple of cars illegally parked. 'Oh, but Adrian, I will only be there five minutes.' One of the first things you learn here is that TSW staff have got a very strange idea of how long five minutes is. Like a traffic warden, I have heard all the excuses before. With looks that could kill they drive off in their nice new cars. If they can afford such cars surely a measly quid in the meter isn't going to cripple them. It would me, hence the pushbike. We aren't allowed to use the car park, even though I'm here saying 'Good morning' when they arrive, and still here saying 'Goodbye' when they go home . . . At last the chairman arrives and I direct him into the parking spot we've been guarding with our lives. His big, powerful Mercedes fits, I guessed right again . . .

ADRIAN BAKER, SECURITY OFFICER

> *There are different grumbles across the city in Seymour Road, Mannamead, where the BBC's* Spotlight *is being assembled. Newsreader Donald Heighway has been around for a long time.*

BBC Plymouth's Donald
Heighway: 'I must be a bit
of an anachronism'

Yesterday's news that even more of the work of the department to which I belong, Presentation, has been redistributed among journalists and programme presenters, means that today I'm faced with the unenviable task of constructing a new rota. This means that the part-time people will lose a considerable amount of work, though I, as a full-time staff member, will continue in regular employment.

In fact I must be a bit of an anachronism in today's BBC. When I joined, 20-odd years ago, 'career' announcers and newsreaders were still a fairly common feature of the Corporation. Today the BBC's attitude seems to have changed; its former reverence for the spoken word has evaporated and broadcasters are valued primarily for their ability to catch the short-term interest of the public. In the present financial climate presenters are engaged mostly on short-term contracts, so that they can quickly be disposed of when the personality no longer fits the current vogue. And, of course, the BBC is not embarrassed by having to pay out pensions and compensation.

Uncertainty among broadcasters is bound to increase with the publication of the Government White Paper next week. Many, including myself, fear that deregulation will lead to a financial free-for-all and a depreciation in programme standards. How can it be otherwise when advertisers call the tune?

Nevertheless, I shall hope that there are still intelligent and artistic television programmes on screen to entertain me in retirement, which is not now so far off. Meanwhile I shall press on with my announcing craft, a bit pedantically perhaps for modern tastes. Which leads me to the news: I must check that the typists have made no punctuation errors and the scriptwriters no syntactical gaffes. As you can see, I'm a bit of a dinosaur . . .

DONALD HEIGHWAY, ANNOUNCER

> NO NEWS IS BAD NEWS
> *The immediate concern at Channel Television is the shortage of news. At the Television Centre in St Peter Port, Guernsey, the staff of seven is not greatly stretched. Roger Bowns, doubling as manager and chief reporter, is willing to admit by the end of the morning that 'the plain*

fact is there's little or no news about'.

*For want of anything better to do he has despatched his
camerawoman, Rosemary Anne Henry, to the harbour. Here she shoots
film of 'vehicle chaos due to the ridiculous position of the new customs
shed' and then sends the results down the microwave link to the main
studio in Jersey. Meanwhile reporter Mary Maher has embarked on a
round of checks on running stories.*

Progress on opening of Guernsey's first building society . . . Fire Brigade
to show a firework safety video starring *Fireman Sam* at a local primary
school on Thursday . . . Local civil servants held a meeting last night to
discuss remarks by a committee president blaming his staff for the need of
extra work costing £1 million on the North Beach Marina project, which
has already cost £16 million. It's a bit like a UK minister blaming his staff
and refusing to resign over a major blunder, but, true to form, civil
servants will do anything to avoid a row and their statement is very
wishy-washy . . .

A press release from Crédit Suisse arrives, telling us about their new
local services. I put it in the bin. In my opinion it's little more than a plug,
or rather it is a plug. But the duty editor in Jersey wants it as a line for
business news, so I fish it out of the bin again . . . Check on progress in
finding an alternative route to a quarry earmarked for use as a tip for
builders' rubble . . . Check with local politician on whether he's made any
move to get an 'eyesore law' drawn up . . . Check on when and where
inquest into man's death in States prison resumes . . .

Back to the studio, after an afternoon previewing an auction of Channel
Islands memorabilia. I start looking at the news scripts for tonight.
They're still in the computer and if I feel something is not clear I can
challenge it and possibly get it changed . . . Time to tackle my hair and
make-up. The problem is not make-up, though I have to make sure I don't
look too much like a panda because I have really deep-set eyes. But my
hair! It's very fine and sometimes it won't go where I want it to go. At
5.30 p.m. I'm still trying to get my hair right . . .

The computer bleeps to alert me that messages about changes are
coming through. I have to run between my desk and the mirror to keep up
to date while wrestling with my hair. In the studio at 5.55 p.m., five
minutes before *Channel Report* is on the air. A straightforward read for
me. Mary Green in Jersey will hand to me for the news block. I enjoy
presenting and I'm pleased Guernsey is able to broadcast live . . .

MARY MAHER, REPORTER

*On Jersey senior announcer Tony Scott Warren has met the Channel
Report director's request to relieve him of 45 seconds, 'as he is short of
material'.*

As I leave I reflect that I've done quite well today, considering it is my
first day back after two weeks' leave. A major problem as always is that

we're on the end of TVS's dirty feed, our presentation is dependent on them getting it right, and all too often they don't. We have to fill our promotion gaps on the spot while they have a promotions scheduler; we have to work with fewer resources and often have to slot a trailer to fit a gap, rather than promote effectively; and we are dependent on their time-keeping. They are very often late meeting breaks and almost always over-run into the front of programmes. It's very frustrating to finish an introduction to a programme at the correct time and then wait five seconds before we are able to join the programme, because TVS haven't joined it on time. The audience think that we've made the mistake . . .

I do tend to watch other companies' trailers as much as possible because promotions work depends on fresh ideas and something one company does often sets off a train of thought as to how ours could improve. At the moment I'm using one format which is based on something I saw on French television, which I quite often watch at home.

We actually get better reception of three of the French channels than we do of our own, and get an extra view of the world, because their news programmes have far more international news than ours. They also do better light entertainment programmes . . . Our scheduling is predictable to the extent of being boring, perhaps the 1992 watershed will shake in some new life to it. Situation comedy has run out of situations, current affairs is insular, sports coverage is too narrow . . . I think it's a myth that Britain has the best television in the world . . .

**TONY SCOTT WARREN,
SENIOR ANNOUNCER**

VIEWERS' RESPONSES

Thousands of viewer diarists from all parts of Britain mentioned at least one of the magazines serving their area, either BBC or ITV. Many detailed the contents of the programme they saw. The responses were so uniform that they can safely be summarized in a few lines. The main message is that local programmes are appreciated and that they would be still more appreciated if they were more local. There is some feeling that regional programmes lack the finish of shows made for a national audience. This idea will sound as music in the ears of broadcasters who work in regional television, specially at the BBC, and complain of being denied the resources to do the job properly.

Viewer diaries suggest that the choice between an ITV or BBC show depends on three main factors. One is ingrained habit. Another is the attraction, or otherwise, of the surrounding programmes on a particular channel. Maybe more important are the screen personalities of the presenters. This judgement probably applies to both sexes, though female viewers are more forthcoming about the visible attractions of male presenters than the other way round.

Technical upsets, causing such agonies among broadcasters, are hardly noticed at all. On 1 November, for instance, there was something that looked like a complete technical collapse at the end of Look North, from BBC Newcastle. What mattered to viewers was that genial presenter Mike Neville was present to laugh his way through. A Carlisle viewer complains that she now receives North West Tonight from BBC Manchester instead of the Newcastle Look North. She is not interested in the news of Merseyside and Manchester and, more crucially, much prefers Mike Neville to Manchester's Stuart Hall. In this case the efforts of Border's Lookaround, providing a local service on ITV, do not seem to matter.

The regional magazines are most appreciated by the middle-aged and elderly, people cemented into identification with their area. The young who reckon to be bored by news programmes, especially if their parents habitually watch, are liable to be doubly scornful of parish pump television. Yet all the specific complaints from viewers are about the neglect of their town or area. At one extremity Guernsey people consider that Channel Report has too much Jersey news. At the opposite end Gaelic speakers, and others of the Highlands and Islands, feel Grampian's North Tonight to be a bit remote. Only in London and the English South-East is there a tacit acceptance that a truly local story, in Thames News or London Plus, would be akin to a lightning strike.

Giggling through. Popular BBC Newcastle presenter Mike Neville (centre) laughs over the imperfections with Tom Kilgour and Wendy Gibson

> *In addition to the regional magazines there were other programmes in*
> *the 6 to 7 p.m. slot. Many professionals consider that the Six O'Clock*
> *News, read this evening by Nicholas Witchell and Laurie Mayer, is the*
> *best BBC1 news programme of the day. Viewers do not necessarily*
> *agree.*

What annoys me about the News is the way that it is put together. First
they tell you about what they will be telling you about, then they tell you
about some of it, then they tell you about what they have still to tell you
about, then they tell you about that, and finally they tell you about what
they've just told you about . . .
JANE BENTLEY, AGED 15,
MAIDENHEAD, BERKSHIRE

The *Six O'Clock News* has too much politics in, which I think is very
boring . . .
LOUISE HINCHCLIFFE, AGED 10,
POTTERS BAR, HERTFORDSHIRE

We watched *The Cosby Show*. That was after an argument between my
brother, my Dad and my brother's girlfriend, against me. I was for the *Six*
O'Clock News . . .
SIMON TYERS, AGED 9,
LEICESTER

Leave the office. Good grief, the traffic in Norwich is appalling, it takes
twice as long to cover half the distance I travelled to and from work in
Durban . . . Stop complaining, Margaret, remember all the reasons you
left South Africa for, and all the pleasure you've derived from the past
two years in Norwich . . . Home at last . . . Switch straight across to BBC1
for the early news there. After years in a society where press freedom is
an absolute myth, I never fail to be amazed at how well informed I feel
here in England . . .
MARGARET FIELDEN, MEDICAL
RECRUITMENT MANAGER, NORWICH

I sit down at 6 p.m. to watch the BBC evening news. I get very cross, in
fact I get furious, when they mention the IRA in some sort of revered
tone. I wish they would show a sort of distaste. I'm really pleased that the
Government is banning interviews with them. Never mind the terrorists,
let's give more viewing space to their victims.
    I feel sadly that television is becoming riddled with producers etc. who

want to put over their views, with total disregard of impartiality. And why, I often think, do we have to have the Middle East war every night? What's it got to do with us? Sometimes I think television whips up hysteria to make viewing more compulsive. It's not very hysterical tonight, my husband has dropped off to sleep . . .

PEGGY HENSON, RECEPTIONIST, AMBERGATE, DERBYSHIRE

During the day I listen to radio news bulletins because I find them more informative . . . I have developed the habit of watching the *Six O'Clock News* because the sight of news makers adds a gloss to their actions. Tonight, for instance, there were pictures of sleek, well-fed Cabinet ministers outside No. 10, after cutting support for the sick and poor, whose interests seemed better represented by Gordon Brown. He succeeds in making statistics live. We heard the Prime Minister say that 'many people could be quite put out' if they were not permitted to pay for eye and dental checks. Can this educated woman really be so stupid as she often manages to sound? . . .

JOAN MacKINNON, RETIRED GRADUATE HOUSEWIFE, EDINBURGH

The *Six O'Clock News* today . . . Nicholas Witchell's in blue, he's even managed to match his eyes to the set . . . The usual types of news. Mrs T. reckons that many members of the public 'want to pay' for eye and dental checks. I'm so angry I'm going to write to her now . . .

STEPHANIE ANTOINE, MUSIC STUDENT, BIRMINGHAM

We never miss the *Six O'Clock News*, Nicholas Witchell is my favourite newsreader. Apart from being gorgeous, he also reads the news very well indeed, with compassion and kindness where needed, and on the lighter stories, with a great sense of humour and an impish smile. I have a personal interest in him, because I write to him quite a lot, and he writes back. The news was a bit dull tonight, though. There was no sign of the usual amusing story at the end. Nick was on his best behaviour and made no mistakes. We love it when things go wrong . . .

MARY HART, PART-TIME WORKER, ST HELIER, JERSEY

I like the way the news headlines are given half-way through the bulletin. I am often distracted during the *Six O'Clock News*, so this is useful if I miss an item. I also saw *London Plus*. Quite a good mix but why are all these newsreaders wearing the Flanders poppy? It is now 1 November and the official Armistice Day is 11 November. Why not wait until that date? . . .

JOAN REED, TEACHERS' ASSISTANT, BROMLEY, KENT

Westminster outsiders: 'that piece of grass' does duty as political platform while the television cameras are still excluded from the mother of parliaments

We watch the *Six O'Clock News*. At the sight of MPs being interviewed in

the open area, with Big Ben in the background, there are subdued groans. 'Not that piece of grass again.' That piece of grass is round the corner from our flat by the Embankment. The children have built snowmen on that piece of grass; and there is a feeling at home that constant interviews on this open space look amateurish, make interviewers, MPs and camera crews cold, and are boring. A proper studio would be so much better, we all feel . . .

**ANN CARLTON, RESEARCHER,
LONDON SW1**

DIABOLICAL GUNS

The BBC2 alternative from 6 p.m. to 7.20 was Guns of Diablo, *a 1963 cinema movie adapted as a vehicle for Charles Bronson from the television series* The Travels of Jaimie McPheeters, *and shown as* The Tuesday Western.

I watched a film called *Guns of Diablo*, or something like that. It was the fakest film I have ever seen. For instance, this man was shot in the chest and he walked on with not even a sign of pain on his face. A man was shot in the arm and not a drop of blood could be seen. Anyway, I thought it was a boring film all the same . . .

**ROSHI ROWSHANAEI, AGED 11,
NEWCASTLE UPON TYNE**

My Dad has put on BBC2 to watch some stupid cowboy film called *Guns of Diablo*. I think it is a load of rubbish, so I am going upstairs to draw a picture . . .

**ANGELA LAFFERTY, AGED 10,
LIVERPOOL**

We turned over to BBC2 and watched *Guns of Diablo*. This was a good film with just enough action for me. It even had a girl for one of the main parts (for a change). It had a lovely ending, just how I like it . . .

**LOUISE McDONNELL, AGED 13,
READING, BERKSHIRE**

My brother turned over at 6 p.m. (he thinks he rules the television) and we all had to sit through a film called *Guns of Diablo*. I was half watching it and half doing homework. Kurt Russell was in it, when he was just a wee tot. I thought the film was very boring, although maybe if I'd been watching it, that would have helped . . .

**CLAIRE ANDREWS, AGED 15,
WORTHING, SUSSEX**

My viewing started with the film *Guns of Diablo*. I began watching with an antipathetic attitude, due partly to the possibility that I had seen it at least once already, and partly due to the cult of ugliness that has overwhelmed film-makers since the advent of the Bronson and Matthau-style faces. Odd bits of the film were familiar enough to suggest yet another repeat. With its absurdly wicked 'baddies' and casual acceptance of murderous violence, the whole thing was unreal and distasteful. A good story should leave one feeling better for the experience, most films make me feel worse . . .

**MR G. W. BURRANS, RETIRED,
NORTH WALLINGTON, HAMPSHIRE**

RASPBERRIES FOR CHRIS

The ITV network was split for the whole of this hour. At 6.30 p.m., while the Scottish regions went their own way with the local Take the High Road *soap and the Thames* Strike It Lucky *quiz show, the rest of Britain was offered* Prove It, *the fifth show in the first series of this TVS entertainment. Chris Tarrant presides over a gathering of 'extraordinary people with eccentric talents', or, as they might once have been called, a bill of novelty acts.*

Now it's time to *Prove It* with Chris Tarrant. It is a show that seems to spend all its time proving that Chris is a wally. It comes quite close on occasions to being good, only to be ruined by the presenter. I don't know why I watch . . .

**MRS C. BETTIS, HOUSEWIFE,
HIGHLEY, SHROPSHIRE**

Avoiding the low road: the cast of Scottish Television's *Take the High Road* congregate beside the Luss pier

I think the opening titles to a show are an important feature . . . with imaginative titles and good music, people's recognition should be gained . . . *Prove It* proves it. Tonight it started by showing a group of five people riding on a motorcycle going backwards, with the leader playing the

mouth organ, and the rest singing 'Oh, Susannah'. This was followed by a glossy title sequence accompanied by glossy music. All this helped to get you into the right mood for the show, and keep your concentration. The mood being one of lunacy.

The items included John Styles of Sidcup, making enough items out of balloons to fill a zoo; audience volunteers involved in a memory exercise with an elephant; an inventor showing off his personalized dance master; and a man who did 40 impressions in under 90 seconds. It is a wacky show and I think TVS provides a good example of an entertainment programme not too taxing on the brain after a hard day's work . . .
MARK CHALKLEY, AGED 16, CAMBERLEY, SURREY

Prove It was really good, with an impressionist who made me laugh so much I had to pop out to the bathroom for a minute. (I hope I didn't miss a good advert.) Chris Tarrant is a very funny, fast and witty personality . . .
JAMES HOFF, AGED 12, HOUNSLOW, MIDDLESEX

COSBY AND AFTERMATH
During the hour the ITV audience steadied around 9 million, the BBC1 figure hovered between 8.1 and 8.3 million, the BBC2 movie attracted 4.6 million (the highest figure of the day for this channel), and the selective C4 audience was the one that showed considerable variation. At 6 p.m. Michael Grade maintained his all-American schedule with The Cosby Show, and was rewarded with an audience that grew from 2.5 to 2.8 million. At 6.30 p.m. he switched to the worthy home-made Design Matters, and saw the figure drop from 800,000 to 500,000.

The only programme I watched during the day was *The Cosby Show*. It is a sitcom about a black American family. They are not poor, they are sort of middle class, their home is nice and big and they never have to worry about money or anything. The whole family are very well fed and clothed and the parents are very sympathetic. Really the programme is a shining example of what a real family should be like. Sometimes it's too perfect . . . When daughter Denise has little problems I feel I know how she feels, because it's happened to me . . . The relationship between the husband and wife is very good but sometimes I think it is a bit biased because they show the husband at work and never the wife at work . . .
JOANNE JULIUS, AGED 14, LEAMINGTON SPA, WARWICKSHIRE

I think this show is hilarious. It has real life dramas but the parents never get annoyed. They sit down with the child and talk it out. I wish my parents were the same . . .
LORRAINE STEVENS, AGED 13, HARLOW, ESSEX

We watch *The Cosby Show* while we eat . . . I can't understand it being tucked away, it is a top rated show in the USA. Do the planners think that we couldn't accept a successful black family in England? . . .

**DEBORAH DE VALL, TEACHER (RESTING)-
MOTHER (NON-STOP), RAINHAM, KENT**

It's humorous, believable and, perhaps most importantly, it is the only good programme about a black family. It may not be a very typical black family, but the high middle-class attitudes are on the increase, slowly but surely. It does not give a stereotype of a black family in the usual situation . . . There is a desperate need for a similar programme to be made and shown in Britain, with British actors. There is also a need for many more multicultural programmes. A person watching could really believe that there was only one, white, race . . .

**MS S. GORDON, STUDENT
NURSERY OFFICER, LONDON SE18**

Cliff and Clair at home:
The Cosby Show maintains
an American-biased
schedule on Channel 4

Why aren't there more black people on television? Especially in the UK, where we have a public broadcasting system paid for by everyone, which

is supposed to represent everyone fairly? And why is America's most watched show put on a minority interest channel in this country? It is so nice to see positive images of black people, who aren't criminals or drug addicts (the usual stereotype) on television. When will programme-makers in this country realize that the black community is as diverse as the white community? And show it.

In fact the phrase 'the white community' is wrong because it doesn't take in all the variety of English life, variations of class, education, gender, age, etc. 'The black community' is an accepted phrase, we're perceived as a homogenized mass, often a problem. That is, if we're shown at all. I guess this is because television is mostly made by white people who think all black people look alike, and don't think about it any further from there . . . I could go on, but it would stop me watching television . . .

HILARY BUCHANAN, MEDIA SKILLS TRAINER FOR THE UNEMPLOYED, MANCHESTER

The Cosby Show is beloved of the trendies. It is claimed to be a 'breakthrough' comedy, portraying blacks in a positive light. In fact it is old-fashioned beyond belief. The themes tonight – 'lovable' daughter refusing to eat her greens, elder daughter planning to stay out all night at a concert – were not even funny when Dickie Henderson and June Lavorick were performing the like 30 years ago. Just substituting Bill Cosby's black face for Dickie Henderson's white one hardly constitutes a revolutionary comedy. If showing Bill Cosby as a doctor, and his wife as a lawyer, is 'positive', what a pity the scripts are so unfunny and dated . . .

JOHN SAUNDERS, LIBRARIAN, MITCHAM, SURREY

I find *The Cosby Show* quite witty, and my nine-year-old daughter Rosie likes it, but today I disliked the stereotypical situation of black people wanting to dance. This seemed very outdated, surely we've moved on. I realize that we get the series later than the USA, but I don't think this will do for one of the few series in which black people challenge stereotypes . . .

I watched Channel 4's *Design Matters* because it was about Newcastle, where my family is from. But where are the Geordies? All the voice-overs, and the management and architects interviewed, had BBC accents. Only the ordinary man in the street, the council house tenant, sounded like a Geordie. Again, a total failure in breaking down stereotypes. The final insult came at the end of the programme when a BBC voice said: 'The Geordie mentality today, don't worry about tomorrow.' How patronizing . . .

LIZ MURRAY, LONDON N5

I thought *Design Matters* was very interesting because it was about Newcastle architecture and I come from very near there. I enjoyed the local scenes but I think if I came from anywhere else I may have found it a bit boring . . .

**VICTORIA BALDWIN, AGED 15,
GATESHEAD, TYNE AND WEAR**

Under the sub-title of *Cities with a Future* this repeat purported to deal with my home town, Newcastle upon Tyne. It never got to grips with the initiatives which are making the place fit to live in. And why is a programme about design so dull to look at? It's sketchy and undramatic and self limiting. Andrew Robinson, from the Northern Development Company, speaks to us from his company office, but what is the Northern Development Company actually doing on the ground? Talking about enterprise is all very well, but where are the building sites, where the bricks and mortar? I cannot recall a single programme, fictional or documentary, that has given a living, breathing portrait of this city. We've seen enough complacent talking heads at ease with themselves, it's time for something more vivid, more heartfelt . . .

**MARK RICHMOND, UNEMPLOYED,
WINLATON, TYNE AND WEAR**

THESPIAN THOUGHTS

There is not too much clock watching among television thespians absorbed in their work. Not all have started the homeward trek by 6 p.m., though maybe they should have done. Not actor Rupert Baker, for one, who has been in his fireman's uniform, at work in a London

Fireman Rupert Baker
canning another episode of
London's Burning for LWT

Weekend studio on a new series of London's Burning, *since soon after 7 a.m.*

It is 5.40 p.m. Have just returned to the green room with fellow thespians, having spent the afternoon completing the shooting of Scene 24. A lot of dialogue across the table about Blue Watch's one-day non-smoking drive. Concentration wanes after a while and the scene can attain a quality of unreality. It can be an odd experience, specially when you are saying the same things over and over again.

At the later stage of the day it is interesting to observe how the cast changes. Filming is always a long haul, people become ruminative, pensive, and performance goes flat. One has to make a big effort to gee oneself up to deliver. Much of television and cinema work is about pacing oneself. In a short while we are hoping to begin Scene 64, also set in the mess. The wrap comes at 6.55 p.m. . . . . we shall return to it, refreshed, tomorrow morning . . .

RUPERT BAKER, ACTOR

Drinking singles: Susie Blake (right) and Judy Loe take something stronger than tomato juice in Yorkshire's *Singles*

Actress Susie Blake, working on a second series of Yorkshire's Singles, *has had an easier day. She started at the Oval rehearsal rooms in London at 10.45 a.m., where there was much discussion over the proper*

*pronunciation of the key word in the week's episode, 'chiropodist'. It
was back to family life in the afternoon, followed by learning.*

Soon after 6.15 p.m. settle down with tomato juice and next week's
episode of *Singles* to start learning. I am on a very strict diet, I don't mind
being overweight but it doesn't 'arf show up on camera. Only half a stone
to lose . . .

SUSIE BLAKE, ACTRESS

ONE DAY IN THE DEATH . . .
*Peter Gourd, head of presentation at the satellite Superchannel, did go
to the office, though it was not likely to be the happiest of working
days. A new era of television may be imminent but just now it does not
look too promising.*

My days at the moment are far from typical, due to the desperate period
of uncertainty which we are all going through. For over a fortnight now
we have been waiting to find out who, if anyone, is prepared to buy the
channel and take on the considerable liabilities incumbent on the
shareholders. Ever since Superchannel was launched in a blaze of
publicity, back in January 1987, we have suffered one funding crisis after
another. One by one the shareholders have lost their nerve in the face of
huge losses and too slow a growth in advertising revenue . . .

Yesterday was one of the worst days for me. The total number of
resignations in my department mounted to five, out of eight. To see this
wastage of skilled and talented people is a tragedy, particularly as the
actual presentation of Superchannel is a model of lean and efficient use
of a highly sophisticated system . . . Last night we learned that the Italian
company Betatelevision had bought out the ITV shareholders' 55 per cent
holding, leaving Virgin with 45 per cent. As yet we have no idea what this
will mean in terms of programme strategy or staffing levels . . .

At 3.25 p.m. Mike Roles, head of programming, is summoned to a
meeting with the Italians in the boardroom. From 4.45 p.m. an hour of
grim activity, with the four directors, Mike and the personnel manager,
flitting in and out of each other's offices with stern faces. I get the feeling
that some form of reckoning is going on. This interminable uncertainty is
agonizing. One feels that even bad news would be better than no news.
Finally, all I am told is that there will be a meeting tomorrow to tell us
what is going on . . .

Watched the BBC1 *Six O'Clock News* in the office. Very brief mention
of the takeover. Amazingly the story seems to have been perceived as a
takeover by Richard Branson. In fact, Virgin have just lost control of the
company to Betatelevision. It is extraordinary how Branson always
manages to steal the PR for any project he becomes involved in . . . Offer
to help with a flurry of activity in the Acquisitions Office. Mike is
preparing sheaves of papers for the Italians, listing programmes available
or not available to them.

My help is not required. I feel unable to contribute any more to what is going on and go home, around 7 p.m. Another exhausting day of tension and nothing achieved. This has felt more like One Day in the Death of Television . . . Next day at 10 a.m. I was summoned to see Mike and the personnel manager. I am to be made redundant, along with virtually the entire presentation and programming department. Apparently the new scheme can be run without us, though they want me to stay until the end of the month to help keep things going . . .

PETER GOURD, DEPUTY HEAD OF PROGRAMMING, SUPERCHANNEL

Also wondering about the future is John Suchet, presenter for Superchannel of ITN's World News.

Will it ever be like this again? A daily worry about who's going to buy Superchannel, and hence what will happen to our *World News*. We've lived pretty much on the brink since our launch in February 1987, but this crisis out-crisises all the others . . . For the last two weeks, almost every day has been a deadline. Today's board meeting will decide . . . they're in secret talks . . . Branson wants an all-news channel . . . there's an Italian company involved.

I've found that, much as I try to put it to the back of my mind, it pushes forward. Even varnishing the kitchen floor this morning, I was wondering, 'What if today's our last day?' Not for nothing has the ITN Editor, David Nicholas, described the *World News* team as the 'shock troops of television'. Satellite television will come, I believe it deeply. But there will be casualties. Will ours be the first?

Today, a decision. The Italians have bought Superchannel and Branson has kept a large share. Both want more news. We've survived! Haven't we? . . .

JOHN SUCHET, NEWSCASTER

SHE WHO MUST BE OBEYED
Market forces have no place in Whitehall, or at the doomed Independent Broadcasting Authority. At the Home Office, nominally in command of broadcasting, at least one civil servant feels embarrassed at the delay in the Government's White Paper. Everybody knows that when it is published it will spell out the death sentence on the IBA.

Scrutinized various documents relating to the handling of the broadcasting White Paper, due out on 7 November, involving speaking engagements, press statements, Cabinet briefing etc. We share the frustration of the broadcasting industry at the long delay in publication, due mainly to the difficulties of arriving at ministerial consensus in a field which directly concerns the Home Office, the Department of Trade and Industry, the Treasury and the Prime Minister.

It will be a relief to be able to state Government policy clearly rather than tiptoe round it. But the delay has meant every conceivable body with an interest has been able to put forward its own ideas, and there will be a further year for debate about the detailed content of the White Paper, before it passes into a draft Broadcasting Bill . . . In the afternoon prepared briefing on Granada Television for the Chief Secretary of the Treasury, who is lunching with the top brass of Granada on 8 November . . . Arrived home at Ipswich by 7 p.m. and watched *EastEnders*, *Fawlty Towers* and *Brass Tacks* . . .

MR A. G. HOWLETT, HIGHER EXECUTIVE OFFICER, HOME OFFICE

(Crown Copyright. Reproduced with the permission of the Controller of Her Majesty's Stationery Office.)

> *David Glencross is the television programme boss at the IBA. Attentive as ever, he switched on to TV-am at 7.30 a.m.*

It still has some way to go but I wish those who are so ready to criticize it would actually watch it occasionally, instead of dredging up Roland Rat, who disappeared from TV-am three years ago . . . First thing in the office was to ring Andrew Quinn, managing director of Granada. Wanted to tell him that the IBA ban on a Sinn Fein councillor, taking part in last Sunday's *Media Show* (C4), was not, as Ray Fitzwalter alleged in today's *Independent*, because of timid advice from the IBA lawyers, Allen and Overy. They simply supported the conclusion I and others in Television Division had already reached. Doesn't alter my view that Government ban is misguided . . .

The usual Tuesday management meeting chaired by John Whitney (Director-General) started with congratulations and regrets at the impending departure of Colette Bowe (Controller of Public Affairs) to the Securities and Investment Board. I'm not surprised that Colette is going after only two years at the IBA. Quite apart from uncertainty about the IBA's future I always thought she was more interested in politics and economics than in broadcasting . . .

After lunch with Greg Dyke of London Weekend, Robert Hargreaves (Chief Assistant, Television, specializing in political coverage) and I went to BBC Broadcasting House to meet John Birt (Deputy Director-General) and John Wilson (Controller, Editorial Policy). We were to discuss Northern Ireland coverage, particularly in relation to the Home Secretary's direction that we should not broadcast interviews or direct statements by the proscribed organizations. We met in John's third-floor office, triangular shaped, wood-panelled, no staining or varnish.

General agreement that IBA was right to stop the *Media Show* interview with the Derry Sinn Fein councillor on the previous Sunday, since he was clearly speaking as a Sinn Fein representative. All of us felt the ban was unnecessary and still uncertain at crucial points, particularly in relation to Sinn Fein elected councillors. We felt it was significant that in announcing new measures against IRA terrorism the Government had chosen to start with broadcasting. Both of us felt the Home Office suggestion that cases of doubt in individual programmes should be referred to them was an ominous development which should not be acted upon. John Birt was in cheerful mood, though he said that he and John Wilson had had a rough time with their news and current affairs people when discussing the Government's ban that morning . . .

Returned to Brompton Road in time to take the 4.30 p.m. meeting of senior Television Division people . . . Discussed the visit to the Broadcasting Standards Council the previous day. We felt that in the end Lord Rees-Mogg and his colleagues were too civilized and intelligent to be able to deliver to the strident constituency which had brought them into being . . . I've spent virtually no time in the office today, so much paper will have piled up . . .

**DAVID GLENCROSS,
DIRECTOR OF TELEVISION, IBA**

VI
PRIME TIMES

7 p.m. – 9 p.m.

17 'I COULD HAVE KISSED HIM'

I watch *Telly Addicts* because I quite like answering the questions. After having done so I wonder if the effort was worth it. I also watch it to see what the television omnivore looks like. Do they spend most of their non-working hours glued to the box, and are they the products of what they see? Most of them look as though they come from places like Basildon or Bexleyheath . . . Suburban homogeneous lotus-eaters? . . .

MR A. BARNES, UNEMPLOYED, TWICKENHAM

ON TOP OF THE POPS
Though the majority of the staff have left work by 7 p.m., this does not mean that studios are empty. Now is the time for recording audience shows. At the BBC's rather Gothic television theatre on Shepherd's Bush Green they are recording a Wogan *special marking Cliff Richard's 30 years in show business. Producer Peter Estall has the first word.*

Two traumatic events today. First the rumour, later confirmed, that *Wogan*'s editor (Peter Weil) had been offered the post as head of the topical unit. Second that my assistant producer had been offered a job and was tempted to go to Thames . . . Wrote a series of letters. One to Buckingham Palace with a request for Princess Anne, and two to MPs assuring them that they will be treated fairly when they appear together on *Wogan* . . .

At 7 p.m. the Cliff Richard programme begins sensationally, but there are some disastrous technical faults. Luckily it is a recording for once and all is rectified. Cliff warms up and I am pleased with the latter half of the interview. No panics, apart from over-recording. After the programme met a lot of important people who materialized in our hospitality suite on some pretext or other, all to see Cliff Richard. Against my better judgement I grew to like all three of his songs . . . Afterwards a drink at the Kensington Hilton with a man from Thames, the poacher . . .

PETER ESTALL, PRODUCER

Soon it is 7 p.m. and once the VT machines have run-up we're off . . . Tumultuous applause for Terry. After a special introduction I cut to camera one, lighting changes, the Cliff sign is illuminated and raised and we are into 'Wired for Sound'. The lighting on the sign is not brilliant. At the end of the song Cliff walks over to Terry. I cut to Cliff's close-up on camera five, then for some reason the camera pans off. Gasps in the gallery. 'Oh dear, what happened?' says director Tom Corcoran. 'Don't worry, Terry is being carried', I say. The producer panics and there is a

furore. I just continue cutting and calm soon returns . . . The audience
applaud heartily. Cliff is very bubbly. Terry comments on how Cliff is
only two years his junior yet looks much younger. 'What are your
secrets?' he asks. Cliff's only regret is that he has never 'made it' in the
USA . . .

HILARY BRIEGEL, VISION MIXER

Recording in front of an audience of screaming women. I had no idea that
Cliff Richard still had such a following. But it is easy to see why. He is a
superb performer with a charismatic personality. On the whole it is an
exciting, exhilarating show to work on. (I only regret that the Shadows
aren't here.) It still amazes me that I get paid for enjoying myself this
much. More amazing is the fact that cameramen, who enjoy their work so
much, are currently suffering such bad morale. Could it be something to
do with our bureaucracy? . . .

ROGER BUNCE, SENIOR CAMERAMAN

Terry Wogan and Cliff
Richard prepare. Age shall
not wither them, provided
the make-up staff are
sufficiently attentive

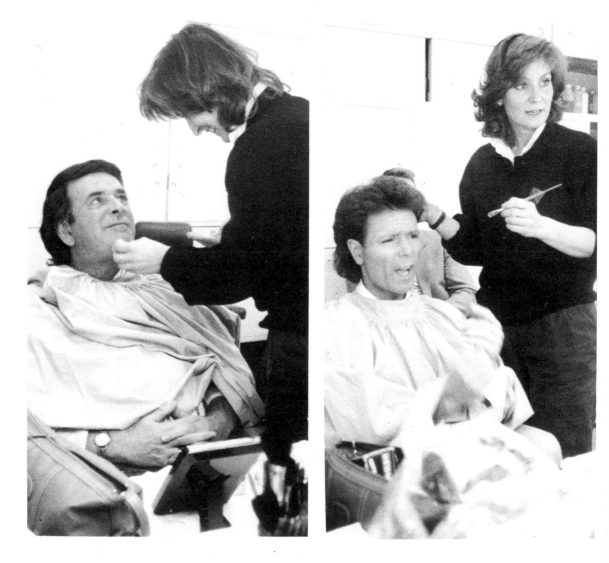

Gill Armstrong, a 25-year-old student who lives at Shepherd's Bush, was in the audience.

I hadn't actually got a ticket for the show, but hung around for over two hours in the hope of getting one or catching a glimpse of Terry or, dare I say, preferably Cliff. When everyone had gone in and the show had started there was just me left on the step, and feeling pretty miserable. Then the person in charge came to the door and let me in, I could have kissed him. I dashed up to grab my seat . . . I was fascinated by the equipment around me and, of course, Terry and Cliff. It was an excellent show which I enjoyed again, when it was transmitted on 16 November. It was marvellous to think that I had been there when it happened, well most of it anyway . . .

GILL ARMSTRONG, STUDENT, LONDON W12

Up the road at the BBC Television Centre the shows being recorded this evening included the durable Top of the Pops, *this week including such performers as Yazz, Tanita Tikaram, Gloria Estefan and the Miami Sound Machine. Production assistant Lynn Schnier spent the morning at the Water Rats public house in Kings Cross, working on one of the* Turns *series, in which writer Jimmy Perry recalls old variety and music hall acts. In the afternoon she did some work for* Jim'll Fix It. *Now she is on duty for TOTP.*

Thumping music: the 'young trendy audience' return to their gyrations for the BBC's *Top of the Pops*

I had to work out my timing chart before the first complete run through at 4.15 p.m. I headed to Studio 3 to sort out the final running times and juggle around with them, as the live numbers were running longer than planned. The first run went smoothly apart from problems with temperamental smoke guns . . . We broke for an hour at 6 p.m. I went back to the office to see what had been going on. Nothing had, but I stayed there to avoid all the young trendy audience piling in through the doors to watch that night's show.

It was back to the studio at 7 p.m., where the cameramen were waiting for any orders from producer Brian Whitehouse. There weren't any so they headed down to the floor, ready for the recording. It's always exciting at this time to hear the warm-up music thumping through the studio, and to see the audience getting into the swing of things, on the preview monitors. At around 7.15 p.m. the red lights are on and the show starts. It all goes very well, the audience are lively and the bands perform brilliantly. At the end of the recording we get the successful 'all clear' and the audience piles out . . . Another show is in the can . . .

LYNN SCHNIER, PRODUCTION ASSISTANT

> *In nearby TC8 the* Paul Daniels Magic Show *is taking rather longer to record. Senior sound man John Hays has an early brush with his supervisor.*

Everything is rigged and working but my good spirits are jolted by the sound supervisor, aggressively demanding that a member of the crew be permanently on headphones during the rigging period to ensure that a two-way check with presentation works smoothly. This is required as we are doing a live insert into *Open Air*. I would be only too happy to oblige if I had been told about the requirement. My protests to the supervisor that this is not the best way to deal with the staff, who have worked hard to get everything working early, eventually smoothes over the situation. I feel that I have achieved what I'm paid for, to ensure a satisfactory interface between the floor crew and the sound supervisor . . .

The afternoon is spent slowly rehearsing the various illusions, mainly for the artists' benefit. Crews are so experienced that they frequently need very little rehearsal. The old convention that shows came into the studio fully rehearsed has long since been abandoned. The consequence is that this rehearsal over-runs by 25 minutes into the evening meal-break . . . The evening recording, in front of an audience, starts late, partly because a radio mike completely fails to work once it is concealed in a lady's dress. We proceed slowly, taking all the allotted time until 10 p.m. . . . .

JOHN HAYS, SENIOR OPERATOR, SOUND

> **THE SOLITARY PRODUCER**
> *Jane French, a BBC South producer, has been at the Television Centre all day, attempting to fill out the natural sounds of birds and animals, and dubbing commentary, for her* Zoo Vet *film.*

We emerge just in time for the evening rush hour out of London. Oh God, if only regions could afford all their own facilities. I hate Shepherd's Bush. Travelling with editor Stan is like bringing the rest of BBC South with you. He excels at imitations (except birds and llamas). The first of his characters is Chris 'I hate television' Jones, the disillusioned director who, while everyone else is being difficult, still manages to 'crack it' and bring his programme in on budget. Then the union man, 'It's getting bloody ridiculous'; the fellow editor, 'My dears, I think I may be getting a headache tomorrow'; the man with the voice who makes everyone reach for a leave chit; 'and finally tonight the top story'; they all come alive on the journey home.

At 7 p.m. I leave Stan, still talking, on a deserted farm track near a village I may never again be able to find. He's muttering something about 'Ain't that lovely, ain't that better than being in a dubbing theatre, freedom, that's what it is . . .' As we leave I hear, or imagine I hear, the notes of a Romany song, and realize his mind has already turned to quotes from the next film about gypsies. I deliver assistant editor Dave back to his wife and children. With an hour's driving to Lymington (Hampshire) I find a measure of comfort in calculating my expenses, but there is still a small voice echoing in my mind which seems to say, 'Now who wants to be the solitary television producer?'. . .

JANE FRENCH, PRODUCER

TEASERS FOR ADDICTS
Tonight at 7 p.m. on BBC1 the Blakemore family from Bolton narrowly defeat the Moores of Sutton in a quarter-final tie of Telly Addicts, *the quiz game where dedicated viewers remember esoteric details from dramas and entertainments of long ago.*

To me, what is most surprising about *Telly Addicts* is that people remember what they saw on television years and decades ago; they remember the names of characters and actors in programmes broadcast back in the 1960s, not to mention the 1980s. They also remember signature tunes, catch-phrases and the like. I can't say what the significance of this might be. I doubt if viewers deliberately try and remember television programmes. Perhaps they remember so much because they see the same characters in television series week after week. Does this mean that educational programmes could bring mass benefit, as Reith dreamed? Does it mean that people who remember television are also influenced by programmes? It is something to think about . . .

**MIRANDA MORTON, LIBRARIAN,
CARDIFF**

Telly Addicts is one of my favourite programmes and led me to become an armchair expert on television. During the half-hour I shout at the contestants, if they get a question wrong, and exclaim about how easy it is. I may enter it some day, if my Mum will let me . . .

**COLIN WOTHERSPOON, AGED 16,
BANGOR, CO. DOWN**

Noel Edmonds makes an extremely good host and it is good to see that he has bounced back after the terrible death of Michael Lush (killed attempting a televised stunt) two years ago. That was tragic . . . The Blakemores won and it isn't for me to say that it wasn't fair, because their questions were easier . . .

**KERRY FAIRBAIRN, STUDENT,
LONDON E17**

GLOOMY AND GAY

Between 7 p.m. and 7.30 the audience for Telly Addicts *climbed from 7.7 to 10.2 million, while the ITV figure for* Strike It Lucky *(plus* Take the High Road *in the Scottish Television area) grew from 10 to 11.2 million. Now, at 7.30 p.m., the ratings lead changes hands. The split ITV network draws only 8.5 million while BBC1 manages the highest figure of the day on any channel, 13.8 million, with* EastEnders. *Although 'gloomy' and 'depressing' were the words most often attached by diarists to this twice-weekly soap, a large proportion of these supposedly disaffected viewers admitted that they still watched regardless.*

Before viewers have their say, here are two of those who help to put the show together at BBC Elstree. First, actor Michael Cashman, soon to end his stint as the graphic artist Colin Russell in the serial. Colin was shy and sincere, a born worrier who had multiple sclerosis to worry about, and was maybe the most virtuous character regularly seen around Albert Square. He is also, like the actor who played him, unaffectedly gay.

Dress in a suit, I have three personal appearances today. The growing number of charities, filling the vacuum left by this Government, is a depressing indictment of our society. It's impossible to say yes to all of them . . . First to Brixton to help launch a telephone help-line for drug addicts (who may have HIV or be antibody positive), their families and friends.

Time was tight and of course we started late. I knew I had to leave by 1.05 p.m. to get to rehearsals for 2.45. But it was a good launch . . . I focused on 'scapegoating' by sections of the media, in particular tabloids like the *Sun,* the *Star* and the *News of the World.* I stated very strongly that such 'scapegoating' was wrong and highly irresponsible. 'We are all affected by AIDS and to reinforce the myth that only gay men, drug addicts and prostitutes get AIDS is to actively encourage young heterosexual teenagers to be promiscuous in the mistaken belief that AIDS has nothing to do with them . . .'

Caught the tube to St Pancras and the British Rail train to Elstree. The usual looks of disbelief from the people on the trains. I think they expect soap stars to be above public transport. Playing Colin, the gay character, I'm pleased to say I've had hardly any negative encounters, so far . . . Gossiped in the sixth-floor green room while awaiting rehearsals. We concluded that the undue tabloid interest in our private lives replaced spontaneity with mistrust. How sad.

Rehearsals are generally interesting on Tuesdays because the producer (Mike Gibbon) and his team, along with the writers, give notes to the director in the light of the runthrough of the two episodes that we do on a Monday afternoon. Today there were no notes but we managed to find some subtleties in the scenes between Colin and Guido (Nicholas Donovan) . . . I spoke to my agent about some offers that were coming in for next year. Then June Brown (Dot Cotton) and I adjourned to the tea bar.

I do like June, very much indeed. We sped away to her 'bolt-hole', where she got changed, very glamorous. Then off we went to the launch of Hilary Kingsley's new book about soaps. On the way we picked up Wendy Richard (Pauline Fowler), she's another favourite of mine, her fiancé Paul and my Paul. The place was alive with photographers and journalists and we only stayed about 45 minutes . . .

Soon I was at the Lesbian and Gay Centre in the City, drawing the raffle with Simon Fanshawe. The raffle was to raise funds for the Lesbian and Gay Switchboard. Each winner was called by Simon or me on the telephone. It was hilarious. One man accused me of making 'dirty phone calls', and another asked his boyfriend to explain how he knew me. Only one person in the audience won a prize. The prize was a haircut and he was virtually bald . . .

MICHAEL CASHMAN, ACTOR

Properties buyer Monica Boggust left home in Hertfordshire that morning with the flashback to the 1940s Albert Square at the front of her mind.

Blowing bubbles?
EastEnders rehearsing for
a sing-song round the
little-used piano at the
Queen Vic

Back to the house, forgot the angostura bitters needed as a prop. Drive through the village and stop at the greengrocers. Need some white free-range eggs, because the producer (Julia Smith) says you didn't get brown eggs during the war, and you don't argue with her . . . Drive to Cambridge, where there's a good secondhand furniture shop. Need some armchairs for Dr Legg. They must be a certain colour because the set is already wallpapered, they must be a certain size because the set is so small, and they must have an 'aged elegance'. If I can't find them I'll have to suggest to the script department that the chairs got lost in the move . . .

At the office. The senior designer comes in to borrow my chicken coop. It turns out to be too big to transport and too big for the Fowlers' backyard. I'll ring round some friends and try to find one that fits . . . Props supervisor comes in to say that a cat has got into the studio and left its mark. Bribe someone to clear up the mess and arrange for a cleaning contractor to come in and deodorize the carpets and furniture . . .

Script editor wants to know how the Queen Vic bank their money, goes away happy . . . Friday's team come in to discuss car stunt, how to do a head-on collision without damaging cars? . . . Local garage rings in to ask for tyre tread gauge back . . . Write letters to garage and police, who loaned us a breathalyser last week . . . A drinks rep has arrived, can I spare a few minutes? Better meet him, must keep up with new packaging while being discreet about advertising. We do try to spread it around, but everyone seems to be owned by the same main company. Can't show him the studio or the lot as we're recording a secret programme for Christmas . . .

Ring John in the boilerhouse. Could he look at the tea urn in the café set, the tap leaks and the actors may get scalded . . . Production team in again. Could I get them three mattresses to rig the back of the car, then there'll be no damage to either car. They're sure they'll get the camera angle right and no one will notice. Don't believe them but I can't override them. Ring Oxfam . . . no, not the beds, just tacky mattresses they can't sell, and yes of course I'll make a donation . . . This week's recordings will be transmitted in January, better make sure we've 1989 calendars on the walls. The designer has mocked up last year's Guinness calendar for the pub, but have just checked and Guinness are not producing one for 1989 . . . Designer rings in, thinks the chairs sound OK . . .

MONICA BOGGUST, PROPERTIES BUYER

| *And what of the viewers?*

I enjoyed watching *EastEnders* best, because I like Ethel and her little dog Willie. He makes me laugh a lot with his little tail wagging, and when Ethel says 'my little Willie' she makes me laugh too . . . My favourite characters are Ethel and Willie, but best of all is Dirty Den. I like it when he says: 'I don't want to talk about it, all right?' . . .

**ROBERT YOUNG, AGED 6,
WAKEFIELD, YORKSHIRE**

EastEnders is all right but is a bit too violent. It is about the second favourite programme in my class, first is *Neighbours*. Den is the character we talk about. We seem to talk about television when we are changing for games or PE. The accent in *EastEnders* is horrible. People leave their t's out and definitely talk like people from London. I can't keep track when Dot and Ethel are talking. They just blab on and on and on . . . I get scared when Den starts to argue with other men in jail, because of the evil look on his face. I quite like Cath except that she is always unstable and nervous. She could at least try to pull herself together . . .

**SARAH MILLER, AGED 11,
SCARBOROUGH, YORKSHIRE**

I like *EastEnders* but I think it's a bit offensive to Londoners because it makes out that all Londoners are drug addicts and get into trouble with the police. Also there is a bit too much shouting going on. I don't watch it with any of my family because they don't like it, because of the violence and language . . .

**JACKIE HILL, AGED 13,
DONCASTER**

In our house watching *EastEnders* is like going to church. We all sit down for half an hour and there is peace. I like this because it deals with everyday life. I live in a widowed family, so we can relate to the programme. Well done, Beeb . . .

**REBECCA SWINFIELD, AGED 15,
LEICESTER**

I try to watch every episode, without slitting my wrists or just going into a manic depression. Why can't something nice happen? Everyone goes around moaning and swearing at each other and the story hasn't changed for weeks . . .

**ELIZABETH SMALLMAN, AGED 16,
CARDIFF**

We have, and for the first time ever, banned our children (a girl of nine and a boy of seven) from one programme, *EastEnders*. I have no wish to watch it myself but the children sometimes feel the need to see it. I am sure it is enjoyed by thousands but perhaps it should be moved to a later slot in the evening, due to the vast amounts of swearing, crime, sexual issues that arise. I agree that children need access to information but, as much as possible, I feel a need to protect my children's innocence. That is something that doesn't seem to be considered by the planners of early evening viewing . . .

**JANE DUPREE, TEACHER,
GLEMSFORD, SUFFOLK**

Being East Enders ourselves we do watch at 7.30 p.m. tonight. But this programme is as far removed from our type of East End environment as a Martian entering our orbit. It is dull, depressing, full of whingeing and whining characters. They have none of the true East End grit and character which my mother possesses, which she inherited from my lovely grandmother, Agnes Dance, who was a true East Ender. I could write a book about her, what an amazing, lovely lady . . .

**PATRICIA AINSWORTH,
LONDON E16**

I used to watch *EastEnders* at this time on a Tuesday night, but it is now SO AWFUL. The characters are so aggressive, making their faces ugly. I always thought the East End meant warmth, real living but a cheerful optimism. Too romantic a view? Well, if you ever turn off the sound and watch the faces you will see what I mean. The awful social worker, are they really like her? The Den saga is hysterical, pathetic. Ethel is the only person you can enjoy and smile about. I used to tape *EastEnders* and watch it later. Then I could fast forward the bits I didn't like. When I was fast forwarding most of the programme I knew it was time to give up . . .

**MS J. P. OLSEN,
BRISTOL**

Being one of the many single Mums does not fill me with pride. (Single is what I am dubious about, Mum's great.) Being one of the millions of *EastEnders* viewers is something I could loyally and righteously defend against any opposition. The company of the familiar characters is a welcome pleasure. The script and storylines are beyond reproach. Not dazzling Oscar Wildean, but admirable acting and direction, good entertainment. Sometimes *EastEnders* contains excellent drama. Today's episode was more touching than dramatic, but I enjoyed it as always . . .

**E. J. HAMILTON, HOUSEKEEPER,
BRIGHTON**

For me as an American, raised without a television, British television continues to be a treat . . . I love *EastEnders*, it's the *Hill Street Blues* of soaps . . . They are dragging out Den in prison a bit too much, and prison is far worse than they can show at 7.30 p.m., but I respect the way the show weaves in the issues quite naturally . . .

**PAMELA COTHEY, WRITER AND
HOLIDAY FLAT CLEANER,
ST IVES, CORNWALL**

Like so many I watched *EastEnders* in its early days. I couldn't wait for 7.30 p.m. on Tuesdays and Thursdays. Who was the father of Michelle's baby? Would Mark be found? Would Michelle marry Lofty? 'I'm not going out tonight, it's *EastEnders*' (I had no video). 'Don't ring me between 7.30 and 8 p.m. because I won't answer.' The next day it was discussion time, on buses, in shops, at school and college. To avoid hearing about the lastest instalment before the Sunday omnibus was impossible unless you avoided human contact completely. Storylines and acting alike were brilliant, specially the story of Arthur's mental illness.

The episode today was, I am afraid to say, boring. Arguments and gossip in the pub, nothing much better than deadly dull *Coronation Street*, except the characters are more realistic. I feel that Colin, the gay character, is being pushed to the sidelines these days . . . Maybe I'm wrong but I wonder if the BBC is inhibited now that Clause 28 (banning the promotion of homosexuality by local authorities) is law . . . A case of too much political pressure on broadcasting? . . .

**KAY CLARKE, TEACHER,
OLD HARLOW, ESSEX**

EastEnders is as interesting as ever. It points up the problems faced by blacks, lesbians, gays and women in a very positive way and puts them in context, so that you feel you can understand and identify with the problems and pressures yourself. At work we discussed the question of the programme's treatment of AIDS. We agreed that it was good that Colin, the gay man, had not automatically been singled out to be HIV positive, and that the other risk groups had been highlighted. The programme is excellent at confounding stereotypes . . .

**RICHARD JOHNSON, LOCAL
GOVERNMENT OFFICER, BRIGHTON**

EastEnders is compelling to watch but I wish some of the characters would cheer up a bit. My main criticism is that homosexual behaviour seems to be portrayed as a normal thing for decent, young, hard-working men . . .

**JOHN FOWLER, RETIRED FARMER
AND AIRPORT SECURITY MAN,
BROAD OAK, SUSSEX**

I don't own a television set because I don't have time to watch one. I prefer to spend my time experiencing life at first hand and if I need entertainment then I can find plenty of it through personal interactions with friends, or simply by studying the everyday lives of the people of Northampton. Who needs soap operas when real life is happening all around them?

I know this is going to contradict what I've just said but I did happen to be at a friend's house today, so I did see some television. I watched the last ten minutes of *EastEnders*, the only soap I do sometimes see, since the demise of the likes of Ena Sharples and Hilda Ogden in *Coronation Street*. I like to see how Colin is getting on. Although he isn't exactly a 'positive image' he is one of the very few homosexuals allowed on mainstream television (I don't count the likes of John Inman and Larry Grayson) and us gays do want our role models. Apart from occasional appearances by sportsmen and women, actors and musicians (who may be closet but we all know about really), the silent Shane in *The Archers*, or anything that Channel 4 or BBC2 puts on late at night, Colin is the best we have got.

I am still waiting for the first lesbian soap star. We haven't even had a stereotype old spinster, or butch lorry-driver yet. But of course we're invisible, aren't we, except when some of us do naughty things like abseil in the House of Lords or invade television studios. I suppose I don't watch more television because I find it still too dominated by heterosexual male images . . .

CHRISTINE ARCISZEWSKA, BIOLOGIST, NORTHAMPTON

YO-YO AND YES, YES . . .

After the wrongs were righted to conclude Guns of Diablo *on BBC2, the channel turned at 7.20 p.m. to* Personal Notes, *a series in which composer-conductor-pianist André Previn relishes the mutual admiration society he forms with other musicians. This time his guest was cellist Yo-Yo Ma, and their conversation was punctuated with quotes from Bach and Elgar.*

For me *Personal Notes* was the pick of all today's viewing. It should be used as a training film for the hot-eyed talking heads, who would have us mesmerized by their pronouncements and edicts. André Previn and Yo-Yo Ma had a conversation. It was as simple as that. There was no sense of camera, no preaching, just two men of charm and humour, each interested in what the other had to say, allowing the viewer a fascinating insight into the mystery and mechanics of music . . .

BRENDA WHINCUP, FREELANCE SCRIBBLER, RUYTON-XI-TOWNS, SHROPSHIRE

Bach again. Mutual admiration from conductor André Previn (left) and cellist Yo-Yo Ma for the BBC's *Personal Notes*

Here was a relaxed conversation between two eminent musicians, much talking, little action. There was insufficient playing by Yo-Yo Ma. The radio could have carried this programme more successfully than television, I thought, as I more or less watched it . . .

MURIEL SOUTAR, RETIRED TEACHER, KEIGHLEY, YORKSHIRE

We have our supper at 7 p.m. and we are still eating when the programme I really want to see comes on. We can turn the television round so that it faces us at the table. Husband makes the coffee and clears the table to give me a chance to watch the whole programme. I enjoyed it enormously but at times I wondered who was interviewing whom. Yo-Yo Ma comes over as a thoroughly likeable chap, adding a new dimension to his playing for me. I shall look forward to André Previn's programme next week . . .

SYLVIA BOWSHER, CELLO TEACHER, DEAL, KENT

I am stuck with André Previn and Yo-Yo Ma praising each other in *Personal Notes*. Reservations over these types of programmes very early confirmed when Mr Ma said to Mr P.: 'You are one of the nicest conductors . . .'

MR H. W. RICHARDSON, RETIRED, DERBY

André Previn talking to Yo-Yo Ma. There are too few music programmes on television. This I enjoyed but am ashamed to say I fell asleep before the end. Like many older people I know I tend to doze even when watching a programme I am enjoying. In my case this is particularly true during talks or music . . .

MARGARET HUDSON, RETIRED, ARUNDEL, SUSSEX

I wish there could be more popular classical music, including Gilbert and Sullivan, on television. I am a kidney dialysis patient and today I had to set up the machine as soon as I got home. From 6 p.m. to 10.30 I was attached to the machine, getting my blood changed and finding little of interest to watch . . .

ANNETTE PARKINSON, CAFÉ MANAGERESS, CHORLEY, LANCASHIRE

RISING PRIZES
Although ITV remained a split network between 7 and 8 p.m., only Scottish Television opted out of Strike It Lucky during the first half-hour, and it had transmitted this well-tried Thames game show at 6.30 p.m. As ever the three competing couples, yearning for a jackpot prize of £3000, and even user-friendly presenter Michael Barrymore, are dominated by a set of garish hi-tech. The questions are simple, the nervous excitement as feverish as possible.

Michael Barrymore of *Strike It Lucky*. 'Oh Michael, I admit to my diary that I love you'

I sat there in my armchair and thought I would know all the answers, but I am no longer well informed in the pop scene, so I fumed and fretted with the competitors one moment, and smiled smugly the next. I thought, just look at that Michael Barrymore, leaping up and down the stairs like a gazelle and grinning. I'm 63 and I'm as slim and supple as can be, but I don't grin for a solid half-hour. Perhaps it's to do with his salary. Oh Michael, I admit to my diary that I love you, love your zany humour and your cheek that never offends . . .

**DEHRA ADAMS, WIFE,
LISBURN, CO. ANTRIM**

As usual I wish Michael Barrymore was my son, he's an absolute darling. But I wish he wouldn't let the audience make so much noise. One lady says she is 80. My goodness, she looks 10 years younger than me and I'm only 73. Wish we had two-way television so that I could ask her how she does it. Would love her to win, but never mind, the winners seem a very pleasant young couple . . .

**MURIEL HALLIGAN, RETIRED HEADMISTRESS,
BEXHILL-ON-SEA, SUSSEX**

I turned to ITV to watch *Strike It Lucky*. My dog Booboo was watching it with me. I don't like Michael Barrymore, he acts so flash. My dog doesn't like him either. When he sees him he starts barking . . .

**YUNCHE CHUNG, AGED 12,
LONDON E2**

I find Michael Barrymore amusing and entertaining, but there's too much chat and larking about with the contestants at the start. I want them to get on with the game. There was an 80-year-old woman who looked 60 to 65. I was surprised and impressed. Hope I'll be like her at her age. I got involved with the show, enjoyed participating from my living-room with my partner. We wonder if we'd have the courage to go on the show. I would like to win even one prize. I would bank every prize I won, but the studio contestants sometimes gamble, and lose . . . The ad for South African Airways annoyed me, I'm anti-apartheid and didn't want it shown . . .

**CATHERINE CRAIG, CLERK-TYPIST,
NOTTINGHAM**

Another programme which I find amusing only because these contestants are the weakest and their answers so often ludicrous. The presenter is another hopeless performer who thinks, like the *Fawlty Towers* chap, that the more he flings himself around the stage, the funnier he is. How wrong he is, his efforts cause no amusement . . .

**HERBERT MARSLAND, INDUSTRIAL CONSULTANT,
MACCLESFIELD, CHESHIRE**

*At 7.30 p.m. the Scottish, Central and Television South West areas
scheduled their own programmes. The rest of the ITV network was
treated to* Pink Carnations, *a repeat from the 1970s Yorkshire sitcom*

series Rising Damp. *As usual the late Leonard Rossiter played the accident-prone Rigsby, and Frances de la Tour his rueful friend Ruth Jones.*

After a while I left my Nan's house (where I'd been since coming home from school) and went home. At home I saw *Rising Damp* and *The Bill*. That Rigsby is a horrible old man and Miss Jones is a silly old maid. I'd seen this episode before but my Dad insists on watching it again and again. Boring . . .

CHARLOTTE EVANS, AGED 15, CARMEL, CLWYD

A hilarious comedy from the 1970s which I was too young to see first time round. I like this idea of repeating shows from several years ago. To me they are not repeats but new shows . . .

ANDREW SMALLER, AGED 16, WARRINGTON, LANCASHIRE

A comedy classic. It seems anything more than five years old is called 'a classic'. Leonard Rossiter's great talent is the best thing about this series. The other actors, although fine in their own right, appear to be there simply to provide the right situation for Rossiter to display his brilliance . . .

CHRISTINE CUMMINGS, STUDENT, BELFAST

Damp Rigsby. Frances de la Tour passes on a home truth to Leonard Rossiter, Richard Beckinsale and Don Warrington in Yorkshire's *Rising Damp*

My husband set the video to record three programmes. We decided to watch *Rising Damp* first. As usual the opening credits were missing. There's nothing worse than videoing a programme only to find the last few minutes missing, so my husband always sets the timer to change channels at 7.32 p.m. We settled down with a cup of tea each and I had a large piece of lemon meringue pie, home-made that afternoon. Although we've seen this episode before the repeats are still enjoyable. We always fast-forward through the adverts, which saves a lot of time.

During the second half of the programme we turned the volume up a bit as I was busy on the exercise bike, a usual practice of mine when there's a programme on television which does not require much concentration. I cycled one kilometre before changing over to rowing. Rowing is a lot easier (and has certainly trimmed up my stomach muscles since my last baby was born), so I continued with this until the programme had ended. Leonard Rossiter has always been a favourite of ours . . .

**MRS U. R. C. BINGHAM,
HOUSEWIFE AND MOTHER,
SITTINGBOURNE, KENT**

Rising Damp is on HTV, but not on Central. A flick of the tuning knob, and Eureka! . . . a faltering vertical hold, a snowstorm in black and white, and unmissable classic comedy. With a name like mine I had to learn to love Rigsby, despite the jibes. I treasured this: Miss Jones: 'Some people have got it, and some haven't. You've got it, Mr Rigsby.' Rigsby: 'But I never seem to get to use it, Miss Jones.'. . .

**CHRISTOPHER RIGBY,
COMPUTER ANALYST AND PROGRAMMER,
WORCESTER**

ALEXANDRA PALACE TO WELLS STREET
On the youngest of the four networks all but a few minutes of the hour from 7 p.m. was occupied with Channel 4 News, *probably the news programme most respected by other broadcasters. Among those admiring this 1988 product from the ITN studios in Wells Street was an 80-year-old Brighton woman who joined the television industry in its prehistoric period.*

My interest in television began in 1937. I then joined the BBC at Alexandra Palace as a make-up assistant. Coming from film make-up I had none of the training expected today. That didn't matter. I was a learner among learners. All the enthusiastic staff, from Gerald Cock, Head of Television, to the youngest property boy, were searching for the techniques demanded by temperamental television tubes . . .

Unfortunately I did not find the 1 November programmes very appealing, on any station . . . I kept my regular date with *Channel 4 News*, whose presentation I admire most, although their choice of news items may not be always what I want to see. An adult naturalness and confidence (which admits mistakes easily) from the presenters holds my attention more than the gentlemanly approach of most of the BBC team.

These are apt to look over-rehearsed or working to a pattern. On all channels the backgrounds of news programmes are a bit forced; in an effort to strike originality? . . .

ISABEL WINTHROPE, RETIRED, BRIGHTON

Tonight *Channel 4 News* was the only one that tried to explain why the Chancellor took the financial measures he did today and how it can affect us (to 1992) with some very interesting projected figures. The programme uses statistics visually so that we can take them in and think about them. It uses graphs in the same way . . . Television news should be visual, with film of actual events and good graphics . . .

BOB HALL, RETIRED LIBRARIAN, WARMINSTER, WILTSHIRE

As the rule in our household is never to watch television until the sun has sunk below the yard-arm, and for much the same reason, we start the evening with *Channel 4 News*. It is the best of the news programmes, lacking the pompous blandness of the BBC's *Nine O'Clock News* and the breathlessness of ITV's *News at Ten*. Above all its presenters, including Nicholas Owen and Trevor MacDonald, manage to combine the knowledge of first-class journalists with an interviewer's determination to get to the root. And they succeed in doing so without Robin Dayish bravado. It's nice to see in Trevor MacDonald a black man who is clearly on terms of easy equality with politicians around the world.

Tonight the major home news is the Chancellor's Autumn Statement. Gordon Brown, Labour's rising star, argues the issues with the Treasury No. 2, John Major. It seems the studio arrangements have been improvised, as the protagonists are awkwardly perched on not very easy chairs and oddly one sees them from the knees up. The television grooming shows in the way they each keep their hands clasped to avoid distracting involuntary gestures. Both seem confident professionals with some liking and respect for each other. Partial and unreliable though such vignettes may be, I really do think they give the voters an insight into the characters and capacities of their rulers which was never vouchsafed in the pre-television age . . .

The *Comment* item following the News, one of the admirable innovations of Channel 4, is contributed by a student, the charming and sincere Jane Rogerson, talking cogently about student grants. A country (Scotland), and an education system, that can produce such people cannot be worthless . . .

MR R. TAIT, RETIRED CIVIL SERVANT, NOW PARISH CLERK, BETCHWORTH, SURREY

Jane Hutcheson is Sandie
Merrick, the nearest thing
Yorkshire's *Emmerdale
Farm* has to a 'sensual
woman'

*By mid-evening, when their largest audiences are settled in front of
domestic screens, many broadcasters are standing together with drinks
in hand and ever louder voices, or swapping memories, gossip,
confidences, ideas across dinner tables. In the West End of London, at
the Hippodrome off Leicester Square, soap stars, publicists and
journalists have assembled for the launch of* Soap Box, *an informative
guide to past and present soap operas, by the informed* Daily Mirror
reviewer Hilary Kingsley.

*Among her guests, along with EastEnders Colin Russell, Dot Cotton
and Pauline Fowler, is Sandie Merrick of Yorkshire's* Emmerdale Farm,
*described in the book as 'the moody dark-haired daughter of the late Pat
Sugden, and the nearest thing the serial has to a sensual woman'. She is
played by the diminutive Jane Hutcheson, a Stockport actress who
began her soap career with a small part in* Coronation Street. *That
morning, far from the bright lights, she had been getting 'frozen' in the
Yorkshire countryside, recording three scenes for her serial. She was
released before lunch to return home to Esher in Surrey.*

Make cup of tea and iron the red strapless dress I have decided to wear to
the book launch . . . Eat Marks & Spencer chicken tikka sandwich my
partner has thoughtfully provided. Insist on opening a half-bottle of
champagne while getting ready, bubbly puts me in excited anticipation for
events ahead. He drinks it in bath; me in front of mirror while stiffening
hair and applying face. Look good, I think, I am pleased with the
results . . .

At the Hippodrome meet Freddie Pyne (Matt Skilbeck of *Emmerdale
Farm*) and our press officer Katy Turner. Also Hilary Kingsley. I like her.
A rival soap opera book author isn't as convincing as her, dressed in
stunning white pearl-covered blouse and black pencil skirt. She is tall; no
wonder she harps on about my height (four feet ten inches) in the book. I
have already read my bits in *Soap Box* and found them very amusing,
apart from a slightly inaccurate account of Sandie's first pregnancy,
which I discuss with Hilary.

A pleasant couple of hours is spent. We meet a few friends from
EastEnders and other press persons and directors. We leave after a couple
of glasses of Bucks Fizz (white wine when that ran out), excusing
ourselves from the publishers' invitation to 'champagne supper' at the
Hippodrome, clutching our signed copy of the book. We make for home,
calling in at our local to boast of our splendid evening and appearance in

a book . . . not to mention what will probably be ludicrous snaps in the Sunday papers . . .

JANE HUTCHESON, ACTRESS

> Granada press officer Graham King, with his special interest in
> Coronation Street, was another guest at this launch.

Feeling ill (virus?) and distinctly unsociable for the evening ahead. Slept for two hours at the White House Hotel, Regents Park, to recharge vital functions before telephoning wife to complain in dismay that this had not been achieved. Decided against calling the hotel doctor and prepared to dress for the evening . . .

Time for kissing ladies' cheeks, shaking gentlemen's hands and sipping, largely, iced fruit juices in deference to my fragility. Conversations ranged from polite or amusing (Hilary Kingsley, her diarist colleague Garth Gibbs and Wordstar agency journalists Stafford Hildred, Tim Ewbank and Geoff Baker); and meaningful exchanges on the ethics of populist tabloids (with Charles Catchpole and Ivan Waterman, *News of the World*); to the mildly ribald (with Nina Myscow and freelance glamour photographer John Paul) . . . Russell Cox and Paul Bennett from the *Sunday Mirror* picture desk asked about the potential to feature some *Coronation Street* cast at home, or with their favoured post-Christmas diets . . .

At 10 p.m., feeling ill and stretched, I resisted persuasion by John Paul and Nina Myscow to adjourn to another club. I returned to the White House at 10.30 p.m., completed my day's record of expenses, finished this week's two *Coronation Street* press releases and picture captions for faxing to Manchester in the morning, and retired to bed at 11.30 p.m. . . .

GRAHAM KING, PRESS OFFICER

> HAMPTON GÖTTERDÄMMERUNG
> The grandest social occasion of the London evening, attracting most of
> the top-ranking television mandarins around, was an event dedicated to
> cinema nostalgia. At Hampton Court Palace the Council of BAFTA
> (British Academy of Film and Television Arts) was entertaining friends
> from AMPAS (American Academy of Motion Picture Arts and Sciences)
> at a dinner marking the 60th anniversary of the Oscars. Many British
> Oscar-winners were present, dressed overall and endlessly
> photographed.
>
> Among the television grandees present was London Weekend
> chairman and managing director Brian Tesler. For him as for his peers it
> was the end of another busy day.

Get out of lift at seventh floor as usual to run up to the thirteenth, my daily concession to exercise. Andrea greets me with mail, coffee and telephone calls. She has already personally received a rude one: writer of hopelessly inadequate play scripts has been offended by my attempts at

constructive advice; informs her he's written 250 plays, doesn't need my advice, and she can tell me to stick it up my . . .

Mail is light. Most bizarre is duplicated missive from British Satellite Broadcasting, accompanying expensive promotion pack and video cassette for their impending service. 'Like us,' it says, 'we hope you are looking forward to BSB's arrival. Thank you for your support.' Seeing that BSB is ITV's dedicated enemy, and that LWT was instrumental in depriving them of the exclusive contract which was to be the jewel in their prospective crown, this little parcel is either an elaborate attempt at irony or a bad mailing list buy . . .

Must finish draft of annual report to staff . . . It's been a traumatic year for the company: every local and national union agreement revised or scrapped, every working practice radically restructured, a programme of redundancies and retirements which will see a total of 300 job losses (20 per cent of staff) by the end of the current financial year. All without disruption, though at great cost . . .

Interrupt draft for conference call to Paul Bonner, whom I am succeeding as chairman of the network's Film Purchase Group. Acquisition of feature films and film series is now a major strategic issue for ITV, with the advent of satellite film channels. Do we continue, with Murdoch or Maxwell or even BSB, to outbid the others for all the rights to this or that package, like the BBC's recent MGM deal with BSB? Or do we go it alone – buy all the rights and sell on the satellite rights when we think it appropriate? Or concentrate on terrestrial rights and be prepared to pay more for what we really want? . . .

Scan duty officer's report on telephone calls during the weekend's transmission. See that one viewer thinks 'David Hockney's work is a load of rubbish, the guy that built the swimming pool has got more talent.' Also that on *Live from the Palladium* 'the word testicles was said just after 8 p.m.' On a live variety show we were lucky it was testicles . . . Meeting of British Screen Advisory Council sub-committee to consider the impact on the British audio-visual industry of the 1992 single European market. Chaired by Dickie Attenborough, isn't everything? . . . I return to office very aware that 1992 will be a year of other problems: it will be start-up year for new holders of ITV franchises, wind-down year for those who did not manage to hold on to them. Beside such problems in 1992, Europe's will hardly be noticed . . .

Leave Kent House untypically early to change into evening dress, pick up Audrey and continue on to Hampton Court Palace. Makes a change: black tie affairs are usually in town and changing done in office . . . During reception talk to Paul Fox (Managing Director, BBC Television) about the White Paper; Michael Checkland (Director-General, BBC) about Superchannel (latest news is its likely decline into a European rock music channel which, having been in on its proud beginnings as a Best of British channel, we both mourn); and Liz Forgan (Director of Programmes, Channel 4) about the ITV and Channel 4 link (latest news is that if Channel 4 can't be linked to ITV it would like to be linked to Channel 5)

The importance of winning Oscar. Television and cinema grandees assemble at Hampton Court Palace for a celebration of British winners of Hollywood Oscars

. . . It's a good dinner, and a magnificent setting. I have one British Oscar winner on my right, sound man Gordon Daniel, and another opposite, David Puttnam. Audrey has John Osborne on her left, angry about everything . . .

**BRIAN TESLER, CHAIRMAN
AND MANAGING DIRECTOR, LWT**

> *Other diarists attending the dinner included Liz Forgan, the highest placed woman in British television; and Michael Checkland who, as BBC Director-General, might be described as the top man in all British broadcasting.*

Routine day at Channel 4 with four screens permanently on in the office – UK channels one to four with an occasional flip into CNN for a breath of US news. I can't say I really watch any of them and the sound is mute, unless I pull out something in particular. Probably the nearest I get to watching television like a normal viewer.

Between a succession of lengthy budget meetings to decide commissioning editors' funds for next year, lunch with Alf Dubs of the new Broadcasting Standards Council . . . I fear he and others may find their roles are rather marginal. We press on him arguments against double standards for free and pay television, against a laundry list approach to sex or violence, against taking on politics as well as taste and judgement. But we are pitting rational argument against some deep rage for puritanism sweeping over our times, and it is ineffective. How can people not see the absurdity of committees adjudicating on the freedom of adults to hear particular phonetic conjunctions (familiar to any bus queue) or to

Channel 4 bosses Michael Grade and Liz Forgan: 'Can't you see we're in a meeting?'

see the work of recognized artists whose vision is of the ugliness and violence that is in every human individual and society? . . .

Day ends with hugely lavish dinner to celebrate 60 years of the Hollywood Oscars. It would all be a great lot of expensive nonsense if it were not being held at Hampton Court in the Great Hall. Swishing through Henry VIII's palace, empty of tourists and floodlit just for us, is an incredible treat. It may be *Götterdämmerung* (Twilight of the Gods) as far as the television industry is concerned, but if so it's a great way to go . . .

LIZ FORGAN, DIRECTOR OF PROGRAMMES, CHANNEL 4

Routine meetings with Board of Management, Directors of Corporate Affairs, the Secretary and the Policy and Planning Unit . . . After which it was a pleasure to contribute a message on videotape being prepared for Frank Gillard's 80th birthday. He was the first Managing Director of BBC

Cutting the formalities: Michael Checkland, BBC Director-General, likes to command in shirtsleeves

Radio and it was his enthusiasm which launched BBC local radio in 1967 . . . Rest of the day spent preparing business for the next Board of Governors meeting, considering the forthcoming White Paper and co-ordinating a future computer strategy for the BBC . . . In the evening it was the turn of the feature films, when my wife and I attended a splendid occasion at Hampton Court Palace, with BAFTA hosting a dinner in honour of the American Academy. 1 November was as wide-ranging, enjoyable and interesting a day as any other . . .

MICHAEL CHECKLAND, DIRECTOR-GENERAL, BBC

A chairman bends the knee: Granada chairman David Plowright defers to the Princess Royal at the Hampton Court dinner. Between them Lord Young of Privatization beams and Sir Richard Attenborough averts his eye

Catch a taxi at 5.15 p.m. and ask to be taken to Hampton Court Palace. At first the driver can't believe what I've said, then he asks for the best way. 'I'll leave it to you', I say . . . We get there at 6.50 p.m., more than half an hour later than I intended . . . For the next hour or so I work hard, photographing our Granada crew filming celebrities . . . A lot of photographers are around, I know a few of them. By hook or by crook I must get our Chairman (David Plowright) shaking hands with Princess Anne . . . Check flash on, check camera speed, right, ready, hope it's all right, please let them have their eyes open . . . More pics in Great Hall, that's a nice one of Anne, good. 'Thank you', I say to Olivia de Havilland as she poses for me, then they all go in to dinner . . .

The film crews and I go to a room that's been allocated to us. My God,

I'm hungry, having had no lunch. 'Where's the food, boys?' I discover no food has been laid on. I try to bribe a waitress with money, just for a snack, 'kidding, of course'. I go to the Minstrels' Gallery, where we have been told we can photograph from. There's no light and it's all too far away, but Peter Ustinov comes in to do an interview . . . Go back to the Great Hall to wait for the end of dinner. Two glasses of champagne and then I ask a waitress for a strawberry. My God, that was good . . . Job over at 11.30 p.m. Dave from Associated Press offers me a lift back to town. We reminisce about the old days, the good times we had at Blackpool conferences. At 12.20 a.m. back at the hotel, starving . . .

**STEWART DARBY, SENIOR PRINCIPAL
PHOTOGRAPHER, GRANADA TELEVISION**

In my humble white Golf I join the line of chauffeur-driven limousines, depositing the television and cinema moguls at the outer courtyard entrance. I attend in my role as chairman of Welsh BAFTA . . . Two-and-a-half hours later dinner is served. The evening is over-subscribed and 100 of us are denied the glorious Henry VIII Banqueting Hall, and seated in a lesser hall. We are given monitors to view the proceedings . . .

Feel less miffed when I discover that many VIPs are off-loaded here, including, on my left, a former Chairman of BAFTA. Splendid evening with witty and short speeches from the Princess Royal, Sir Richard Attenborough, Lord Young, Peter Ustinov and Richard Kahn (President of the American Academy), who presented an Oscar to Princess Anne . . .

**STELLA MAIR THOMAS,
ASSISTANT HEAD OF PUBLIC RELATIONS,
HTV WALES**

Car home at 4.45 p.m., to change into dinner-jacket for BAFTA evening at Hampton Court Palace. Spoke to John Whitney (Director-General, IBA) on the car phone, who confirmed the White Paper would definitely be released on Monday . . . Arrived at Hampton Court. Pre-dinner drinks lasted for ever as 80 Oscar winners were photographed. I discussed video discs with Peter Morley and had a long talk with George Thomson (Lord Thomson, Chairman, IBA) about my guidelines for ITV's response to the White Paper, his forthcoming valedictory speech, and the difficulty of chairing ITV . . .

Lew Grade (Lord Grade, formerly boss of ATV) joined us to say how ridiculous it was to auction ITV contracts. I asked about his Barbara Cartland films. He said he had sold them to the BBC 'because ITV said they had to put it to a committee'. . .

Dinner started at 8.45 p.m. I sat opposite Julie Harris, who won an Oscar for costume design on *Darling*, and my wife Jigga sat next to John Osborne, who was half-cut and still angry. He hated the whole thing. At the next table Betty Box fell sound asleep after the first course and could not be woken, despite much vigorous shaking. It was nevertheless an enjoyable evening, rounded off with an excellent speech by Peter Ustinov. Afterwards, at 11.30 p.m., the cars were all held up by the police, for no good reason. We had to stand for almost half an hour in the cold night air, chatting with Lord and Lady Young (Lord Young, Secretary of State for Trade and Industry), and the Trethowans (Sir Ian Trethowan, Chairman, Thames), who were all in the same predicament.

RICHARD DUNN, MANAGING DIRECTOR, THAMES TELEVISION

> MORE DINNER DATES
>
> *Others, denied BAFTA glitter, were subjected to catering vagaries. The fashionable view is that beauty contests are outmoded. Yorkshire Television publicist Sallie Ryle is obliged to make the most of them.*

Change for dinner at the Post House Hotel in Leeds where I am hosting for two of the three judges to take part in the Miss Yorkshire Television being recorded tomorrow. Arrive at the hotel for 7.30 p.m. Service for dinner is very slow and we complain to the management . . . Home at 11.45 p.m.

SALLIE RYLE, HEAD OF PUBLICITY AND PUBLIC RELATIONS, YORKSHIRE TELEVISION

> *Patrick Chalmers, Controller of BBC Scotland, has today entertained and advised Bill Greaves (Head of Broadcasting, BBC North East England); could not dissuade Keith Alexander, his head of music and arts, from taking an executive producer job in London; and held a programme review with his department heads. In the late afternoon he goes on the prowl.*

I go walkabout around the building; sometimes a little aimlessly but it's amazing where you fetch up and what you find out, and it's a great opportunity for me to meet the troops and vice versa and allows me to have informal chats . . .

Afterwards I go to the Dinner Club in the Western Club. The Dinner Club is a monthly group of the great and the good of business and commerce in the City of Glasgow. We're invited to become members of the Club and it's restricted to about 30 people. It's a very valuable information exchange and an opportunity to meet bankers, stockbrokers and captains of industry.

Bill Brown (Managing Director and Deputy Chairman) was there from Scottish Television and we chatted about the impending White Paper. Jimmy Gordon was also there. He is Managing Director of Radio Clyde and yesterday they confirmed that they had just bought North Sound, the Aberdeen radio station, for £1.2 million, more than just a straw in the wind for television . . .

PATRICK CHALMERS, CONTROLLER, BBC SCOTLAND

> *An Anglia crew is in Strasbourg and has today been shooting bistro scenes for* A Quiet Conspiracy, *an adaptation of an Eric Ambler novel.*

PRIME
TIMES

Alan Cordner takes a sober view of the crew's 'corridor party' on the hotel floor they have taken over.

Conspicuous conspiracy: Joss Ackland (sixth from left) in Strasbourg takes direction, before the shooting of another sequence in Anglia's *A Quiet Conspiracy*

An uneventful afternoon passed with apparent success. The director (John Gorrie) had heard that various of us were diarists for the day, so he decided to be extraordinarily relaxed, hardly anything above a polite whisper . . . And so to a little partying. Heard the one about my five colleagues who went for a quick drink at the local brasserie; quick it was, but how do you drink £140 in half an hour and, even more intriguing, how do you stay upright? My lesser consumption was much slower, so I managed to note the amused/bewildered concierge who peeped out of the lift, and I also managed to entertain the British legal expert who somehow found his way up to the seventh floor. Sometime I went to bed . . .

ALAN CORDNER, OUTSIDE BROADCAST
ENGINEERING SUPERVISOR

Anna Home, BBC head of children's programmes, is taking part in a European Broadcasting Union working party being held at Rethymnon in Crete. During the afternoon there was a presentation of possible co-production projects, a few of which were granted a 'maybe'.

All these programmes were discussed at length before we adjourned for the evening trip up a mountain, to sample some typical Cretan food, drink and entertainment. This proved to be exhausting in terms of the active amount of dancing required but, as always on these occasions, it is fascinating to see such a mixture of people from different countries genuinely enjoying themselves together and participating . . .

ANNA HOME, HEAD OF CHILDREN'S PROGRAMMES, BBC

The BBC's Joan Bakewell, the thinking man's fancy in the heart of Israel

With producer David Willcock, of BBC religious programmes, presenter Joan Bakewell is in Israel. They are making a film for Heart of the Matter, *about a movement of young soldiers refusing to serve on the West Bank. On the kind of low budget which goes with BBC religion they are trying to save money by staying at 'a dump of a hotel' in Jerusalem. This has been the only day they have to look for filming locations.*

All day we have noticed the polling booths being busy. In the Orthodox quarter there are no women in the streets, but crowds of men in large hats and side-curls. They are clearly excited and campaigning hard. A hint that the result might go their way. The colony buzzes with such talk.

We dine in the restaurant there. At other tables there are journalists of all nationalities, shirt-sleeved and eager, tucking into the food and drink . . . and the gossip and shreds of news. This must be one of the best informed corners of Israel right now. Michael Vestey of BBC Radio comes in: I wonder what the count of BBC people in Israel covering the election is? . . . At midnight some of us drift down to await the results. The hotel has coffee, snacks and a blackboard all set up. On each of two television sets Israeli politicians are already discussing the options . . . Seven weeks later they still hadn't formed a government. So I didn't miss much by going to bed at 1 a.m. . . .

JOAN BAKEWELL, PRESENTER

Producer Alan Bookbinder and crew of six are in Managua, Nicaragua, working through the last days of a five-week shoot for a BBC documentary series about missionaries. Before that they had four weeks in Chile so they are now 'tired, irritable and looking forward to going home'. Today they have been filming and interviewing Father Dan Driscoll, an American Catholic priest and a supporter of the Socialist revolution, working in a remote mountain area.

Back again from the local clinic for mothers and babies, and we all set about finding the put-u-up beds and mattresses. The crew settle for the large room on the ground floor, the producer and presenter settle for the basement, and the researcher and I are in the attic . . .

At 6 p.m. we go in search of a local hostelry. The producer goes to Mass to recce the service for the next day's filming. The local rum proves to be OK but there's a lack of Coca-Cola and we have to settle for some local, red fizzy stuff.

Back to Father Dan's for supper. By this time the cameraman is in talkative mood and challenges Dan on his belief in God. The Father gets out a bottle of Jack Daniel's and happily discusses Christianity while we devour the hard-boiled and well-travelled eggs and ham sandwiches we have brought from the Intercontinental in Managua . . . It's lights out at 10 p.m. and in no time at all the whole house is echoing to the sound of snoring . . .

**VIVIEN GRIFFITHS,
PRODUCTION ASSISTANT**

Feeding the hungry of Nicaragua: American priest Father Dan Driscoll celebrates mass, and the masses, in the BBC documentary series about missionaries

> *Documentary film maker Paul Hamann is in Washington. He has been persuading the United States drugs intelligence agency to let the BBC make an observational documentary series with them. He spent the morning 'mainly nodding to up-market waffle' but agreement is reached and, in the afternoon, practicalities were discussed.*

Get back to the apartment of my journalist friend David Blundy and tell

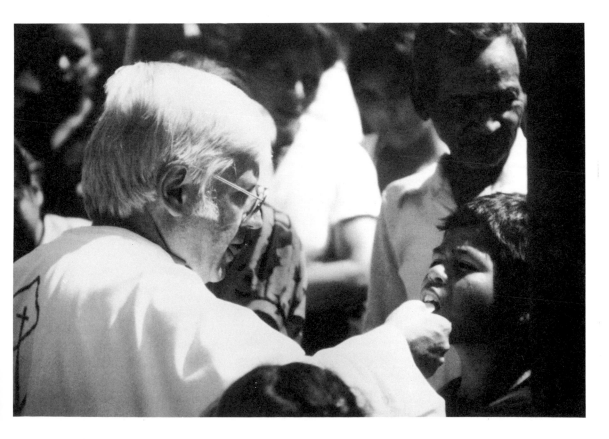

him of my unusually good television day, pulling off a major series. At 8 p.m. arrive at Gulelios' Italian place in Georgetown. Buy Blundy and colleague Roger Courtieura celebration dinner. Conversation is about the lamentable state of the British newspaper business and the forthcoming debate on the White Paper, which we all feel will see the end of the least worst broadcasting system in the world. Despite a very good day we all leave the restaurant feeling depressed.

Back at Blundy's we drink malt whisky and talk of our women, children and changing career in mid-life. Go to bed feeling high and looking forward to getting my annual injection of energy tomorrow, visiting New York . . .

**PAUL HAMANN, EDITOR,
BBC1 DOCUMENTARIES**

> *The 1 November programme which received most unreserved praise, from viewers and broadcasters alike, was an episode of* Fawlty Towers. *Diarists of all ages were not slow to use this comedy with which to beat those of the inferior 1988 vintage. Only two series, each containing six episodes, were ever made. That is one reason for the superiority of this BBC sitcom, set in the most undesirable of small Torquay hotels and written by John Cleese (Basil Fawlty) and his then wife Connie Booth (Polly). The episode repeated on BBC1 tonight was the third of series one, first shown in October 1975. Despite being 13 years old it still drew an audience of 12.2 million between 8 p.m. and 8.30, compared with 11.1 million for ITV's The Bill.*

Fawlty Towers really brightened up my day, being the best comedy around. John Cleese is terribly funny, always panicking and doing the wrong things. There was one bit I didn't like, where Basil was listening at the door and hearing things. My Dad commented on this and switched it over. When we complained he switched it back again . . .
ANDREA ROBINSON, AGED 11, IPSWICH, SUFFOLK

In *Fawlty Towers* it was Manuel's birthday, so he had a day to celebrate his age and thank the others for their help. Sybil was on to her unusual laughing attitudes again, and Basil was back to his moaning and groaning of other people. It was so funny when he kept making silly remarks about customers that I had a breakdown. I accidentally smashed the crystal ball. I was laughing and laughing and I placed my hand on the desk and banged it hard. I had to clean the mess up afterwards. This was the first accident I'd had in the one-and-a-half years I have been living in Eckington . . .
MABEL WONG, AGED 14, ECKINGTON, DERBYSHIRE

Many things in life are never forgotten, old friends, favourite tunes and *Fawlty Towers*. I relish every moment of crazy embarrassment. I watch as Basil goose-steps across the room, insulting anyone or anything that dares to move, and I ask 'Is he human?' As Sybil nonchalantly ignores him I think 'Does it matter?' No, it doesn't matter. As long as there is a universe *Fawlty Towers* will remain for ever tattooed across the backside of history . . .
CAROLINE SMITH, AGED 14, DUCKLINGTON, OXFORDSHIRE

Next day at school we were impersonating Sybil Fawlty's laugh during lessons, to annoy teachers . . .

**SALLY CLARKE, AGED 15,
SOUTHAMPTON**

In the light of our evening watching I was led to reflect, snobbishly, on contexts where 'it' is 'on' unless it is 'off', as opposed to those where 'it' is 'off' unless it is 'on'. My partner and I, both born before mass television, are of the latter camp. But my son, on his regular 'access visits', proves to be of the former camp – a minor source of tension . . .

Fawlty Towers remains endlessly funny. John Cleese's timing, performance, holding of developing tension, nothing short of brilliant. This time a 'bedroom farce' episode of pseudo-sexual misunderstandings, set in pre-AIDS anxiety innocence, another age . . . It is also pre-Thatcher and reminds me of a time when Basil's uglier values were not so openly and successfully celebrated in the dominant discourse. It makes me laugh, and that's enough, for little does . . .

**PETE LATARCHE, LECTURER,
CULLINGWORTH, YORKSHIRE**

Of the four sitcoms I saw on 1 November, *Fawlty Towers* was far the best, despite being 13 years old and repeated for the umpteenth time. I am constantly astonished at the extent of all the Pythons' creativity, but I think Cleese stands out from the others because he is both the most naturally funny and the best actor. He is a master of the nuances of perception: the viewer always knows at exactly what moment his character has become aware of the Fact.

He has been quoted as saying he relies on first-rate material, and I think that is the key to *Fawlty Towers'* success. It has two elements lacking from most sitcoms: a very strong plot, with carefully interwoven sub-plots which feed the final climax, and three inherently funny characters. The humour does not depend on 'witty' one-liners, but on the raw elements of farce: embarrassment, fear of embarrassment, ghastly people, misapprehension, wild dissemblance, panic and surprise (most sitcoms are so predictable). And of course, the quality commented on about Cleese's film *A Fish Called Wanda*, cruelty.

It's also enormously British (which explains rather than detracts from its success abroad): Basil makes a fool of himself time and time again, because he's a snob and a prude and can't express his feelings. He has a strict code of conduct which is without any real rationale, but which he never questions. His sexual morality is untarnished. He is, for example, clearly attracted to the French lady in this episode, but will not consider going to bed with her, despite his wife's supposed absence. His dogmatic application of his own morals to others is the direct cause of the humiliation he fears so terribly.

I am convinced that people will recognize *Fawlty Towers* as classic farce for many years to come . . .

**ANDREW BURNET, ACTOR,
GLASGOW**

Basil Fawlty is an indulgence in nostalgia. He reminds me of that other bigot Alf Garnett, the same xenophobic attitudes. Bigots liked Alf, he legitimized them, he spoke for them. That's one of the paradoxes of favourite television. I love the obnoxious Basil . . .

**JOHN BEVERLEY,
HUDDERSFIELD, YORKSHIRE**

I did not like *Fawlty Towers* first time round, but my personal life is not so tense now so I have probably mellowed towards it. But I could still smack Basil . . .

**MRS D. E. FLOWER,
RETIRED SUB-POSTMISTRESS,
OTTERY ST MARY, DEVON**

I arrive home at about 8 p.m. with a splitting headache. Switch on to *Fawlty Towers*, aware that I must be the only person in the world not to find it uproariously funny. I try to like it but fail again, it's too loud and the humour too obvious for my taste. The day ends with a couple of aspirin and an early night . . .

**JANET WATSON, INFORMATION OFFICER,
INDEPENDENT PROGRAMME PRODUCERS'
ASSOCIATION (IPPA)**

FAULTY MEMORIES

Although the formula for A Question of Sport, *produced by Mike Adley at BBC Manchester, is now 18 series old, it is still enjoyed by people who like televised sport. This was the second of the 1988–9 series. Loyal viewers were still getting used to the idea of resting cricketer Ian Botham as a resident captain in place of retired footballer Emlyn Hughes, who has defected to ITV. Tonight the Botham team, including boxer Lloyd Honeyghan and Rugby Union player Nick Farr-Jones, loses 22–38 to the Bill Beaumont team, in which that former England Rugby Union captain is assisted by footballer John Aldridge and racing driver Martin Brundle. Between them they hold a BBC1 audience of 11.4 million between 8.30 and 9 p.m., while that for* The Return of Shelley, *the ITV sitcom, drops to 8.9 million.*

It is not long since Ian Botham, of Somerset and England, was the hero of Taunton, but times change . . .

I didn't really take much notice of *A Question of Sport*. As usual there wasn't a single woman on either team. The programme is sexist. Why not have one male captain (preferably not the arrogant, chauvinistic Ian Botham) and one female captain? . . .

**DAVID SHUTTLEWORTH, AGED 16,
TAUNTON, SOMERSET**

Goodbye, Emlyn. Goodbye, viewing . . .

**MIKE VALENTINE, SELF-EMPLOYED,
SPILSBY, LINCOLNSHIRE**

A Question of Sport is hugely disimproved since the loss of Emlyn Hughes. Botham seems churlish and humourless by comparison. When faced with a question about racing he says, 'Jesus!' Husband, I think rightly, takes offence. Not the time/place/situation for such language. Botham too boorish for Emlyn's shoes. Where's Emlyn gone, and how much will the BBC be paying him for the next show? . . .

HILARY MORIARTY, TEACHER, MONMOUTH, GWENT

I was very glad to see that awful Emlyn Hughes had been replaced on the sport quiz by somebody decent, Ian Botham. It is a good programme and I like the 'what happened next?' round. I thing there should be more women on, and even a female captain . . .

DANIEL CRIGHTON, AGED 12, CLEVELAND

The next thing I watched was *A Question of Sport*, which is really entertaining. I was a bit disappointed with the pullover of question master David Coleman, plain black. Ian Botham is a good replacement for Emlyn Hughes, who has defected to the abysmal *Sporting Triangles* . . .

JULIAN CRUTE, MUSEUM ASSISTANT, WREXHAM, CLWYD

Ian Botham has taken to the captain's role like a duck to water. He is in some ways better than Emlyn Hughes, well he doesn't have a squeaky voice anyway . . .

BARBARA RODGERS, CLEANER, UP HOLLAND, LANCASHIRE

ANOTHER SLURP OPERA
A man of the English South-West, foodie teaser Keith Floyd was discovered by BBC Plymouth producer David Pritchard presiding with extrovert energy at a bistro-cum-wine bar. After being tried out, talking enthusiastically about fish, in a 1984 local series, he became a networked performer the following year. Tonight on BBC2 at 8 p.m. he is concluding his food series Floyd on Britain and Ireland *in the Orkney Islands. His audience is 2.6 million.*

I wanted to watch Floyd talking about fish because it was filmed on Orkney. I was glad to see he chose native Orcadians to talk to, they were interesting people and Floyd brought them out well. So often when cameras come up to Shetland research is poor and you end up with the same half-dozen people each time. My husband actually works as cook on a fishing boat. I wouldn't hold out much hope for Keith in the real world of cooking at sea but his dishes look delicious . . .

ANNE HUNTLEY, MOTHER, WHALSAY, SCOTLAND

The best news is that Floyd, the offbeat travelling cook, is on again. He is

superb, the locations are interesting, the people he meets are great. And what lovely humour he throws at you, with the rapport between himself and Richard (Elliott) the cameraman. The dishes he whips up look delicious, like you could put a spoon into the cathode ray tube and bring it out again overflowing with delicious sauces. He has invented a novel way to show cooking at its best. I feel an overwhelming urge to say, 'I'd like to meet that man'. . .
**GRAHAM PAGE,
LOCAL GOVERNMENT OFFICER,
WORCESTER PARK, SURREY**

Sadly this is the last of the series, but how enjoyable. My parents actually watched it all the way through, after me going on and on about it, and also enjoyed it. Today's programme was full of good humour. And I'm glad they put that beautiful lobster back where it belonged, in the sea. Keith Floyd is brilliant, a great cook, a great presenter with a great sense of humour, who always seems to come across as being an extremely likeable chap . . . (Any chance of a meeting?) . . . I hope another series comes along in the not too distant future . . .
**EMMA DAVIDSON, AGED 16,
WARWICK**

That king prawn Keith Floyd really is no match for *Fawlty Towers*. I like my cookery programmes to teach me something, not to see food messed about with. Keith can go and boil his head for all I care, if a big enough cauldron can be found . . .
**SUZANNE WHITEWOOD, SCHOOL CARETAKER,
NEWPORT, ISLE OF WIGHT**

As a single male who has sat down to burned boiled egg, I watch this man simply for the strength of his personality. I'd hate to work for him, but

Smiles and slurps: Keith Floyd makes a case for island cooking in the BBC's *Floyd on Britain and Ireland*

love him when it goes wrong. He is far less predictable than the too often repeated *Fawlty Towers* . . .

BOB ELLIS, ELECTRONICS ENGINEER, DERBY

A hen-pecked husband is not looking forward to 8 p.m. I'd quite like to enjoy John Cleese knock the stuffing out of everyone at *Fawlty Towers* but I am afraid I may be forced to watch Keith Floyd slurping his way around kitchens in the Orkneys. I always felt rather sorry for Mr Craddock, having to do the dishes for Fanny, but my wife seems to expect me to produce cordon bleu after 30 minutes of flaming Floyd . . .

'And now the management wishes to announce that he is being allowed to watch *Fawlty Towers*. This is to prevent him moaning. I just hope the service around here never reaches the depths portrayed in Torquay' . . . The fair sex strikes unfairly again, there's always an ulterior motive . . .

ARTHUR WATSON, UNEMPLOYED ECOLOGIST, PLYMOUTH

> FRESHLY POACHED SALMON
> The Brass Tacks *way of reporting, and then discussing, social issues has become established since it was launched by BBC Manchester in 1977. The subject at 8.30 p.m. this evening is the poaching of game. It is a tribute to the efficiency of this BBC2 series that its editor, Colin Cameron, is about to move to London as Deputy Head of Documentary Features. In the event, and before he reached his new chair at Kensington House, a further rung of the hierarchical ladder was vacated and he arrived as nothing less than Head of Documentary Features.*

A morning meeting in Cricklewood with Tessa Sanderson. She arrives on crutches, having just come out of hospital after an operation on the leg that defeated her Olympic bid. She agrees to join the judges . . . Then a race to the airport to catch the 12.45 p.m. shuttle back to Manchester . . .

Phone calls on the way to graphics and others to try and get adequate resources for *It's My City*, to be launched by the Prince of Wales in a fortnight's time. Desperate competition for resources in a very overstretched North-West. Particularly with the start tomorrow of Janet Street-Porter's new show *Reportage*, which is hosted and part-staffed by us. It is eating up everything in sight, including goodwill, so I hope it's worth it. Get an agreement from Head of Graphics that, somehow, *City* would not suffer. HRH is a great name to drop, although I'm not sure it outranks JSP.

Catch the shuttle and the taxi at Manchester is in place for once . . . Alan Dobson, producer of *The Travel Show*, comes in to say that, as I'm leaving, he doesn't think much of my management of his area. I suggest it might have been more useful telling me that before I was leaving. Impasse, but it does leave me angry . . .

Finally I view the roughcut of *Jobs Survey*, which is the *Brass Tacks* for next week. An excellent original idea from Roisin Macaulay, to survey all the jobs available in one week in one average town, Chesterfield. The survey side is fine, with some interesting conclusions, but the film needs to be much bolder about proclaiming the originality of the work and its findings, and less reliant on individual case histories. I discuss the necessary changes with Roisin, who's the reporter, and producer Brian Barr, and will view again tomorrow.

Get home at 7 p.m., just as the kids are going to bed . . . Tonight's *Brass Tacks*, on poaching, is a counterpoint to the last of Floyd's wonderful cookery series. I am well pleased with this, a decent piece of journalism and a stylish piece of film-making from Mike Burke, a very new producer who joined us from *First Tuesday* . . . Watch some of the revamped *Nine O'Clock News*, it looks dreadful. Ring Mike Burke to thank him for his film . . . Back to BBC1 for a muddy discussion on television sport on *Network*. No mention of my pioneering sports journalism series in the summer, *On the Line* . . .

COLIN CAMERON, EDITOR,
FEATURES AND DOCUMENTARIES,
BBC NORTH-WEST

| *And did the viewers think as well of this* Brass Tacks *as the editor?*

I watched *Brass Tacks*, which I found very interesting. I watched with my mother and father, and they started cursing these men who came on trying to justify poaching. I thought that it ended well, with a deer looking straight at you. Seeing him gave me a feeling of peace, until suddenly you heard a shot and saw the deer twist and fall to the ground. Then the credits came up, leaving me with a feeling of pain and sadness for the deer, and hatred towards the poachers . . .

FRANCESCA SAYER, AGED 14,
HOVE, SUSSEX

Brass Tacks started and it was about men killing animals. It was disgusting the way they shoot animals, and then people have the nerve to eat them. I think the men who kill the animals should get back just what they do to them. I had an argument with my big brother about it. He said, 'If they never killed them we wouldn't have a decent thing to eat.' He thinks he knows best . . .

ANGELA BARNES, AGED 14,
GLENROTHES, FIFE

It was about poachers and poaching, salmon and deer. I left it on because I am interested in game fishing and wanted to know about the salmon poachers. Everybody started to watch it, even Mam, who was cutting my brother's hair and made a mess of it in the end. It was saying things about these poachers that I could hardly believe. The poachers can make thousands of money in one night.

The deer poachers were even worse. Before the titles came up at the end of the programme, they showed a scene which I'll never forget, of a deer being shot dead. It was standing there and you could see the bullet hit the deer, and it fell to the floor dead. Terrible! My brother nearly fainted. He was a bit young to be watching it . . .

**MARK RICHARDS, AGED 14,
SKETTY, GLAMORGAN**

Brass Tacks showed the new face of poaching. It is no longer the poor agricultural labourer, taking a bird because the family is short of food, but gangs with sophisticated weaponry, where millions of pounds are involved. It was mainly about salmon and deer poaching. I eat quite a lot of salmon, I wonder if any of it is poached. I've had venison a few times. I roasted it and must have overdone it as it seemed dry and a bit tasteless. It's now, according to the programme, the 'in' meat . . .

**GWENDOLEN PECK, RETIRED TEACHER,
LEWES, SUSSEX**

My husband is a farmer, so when *Brass Tacks* started I called him and Giles in to watch. We all thought it an eye-opener, thought-provoking. Michael said we must keep our eyes open for any poachers on the farm. Dad did not know venison was not covered by the meat inspection regulations . . .

**ELISABETH COOK, RESEARCHER,
CASSINGTON, OXFORDSHIRE**

Brass Tacks was particularly interesting. I live beside the beach at Spittal, across from Berwick-upon-Tweed. It is particularly beautiful as we can see the Tweed estuary, Holy Island and the Farnes. My husband and I own part of the beach. Sometimes at night we see poachers running around the beach. There are scuffling, whispered voices, and then the beam from the bailiff's car alights very quickly upon them.

This film was very true to life. The age-old image of the poacher as a lovable country rogue, pitting his wits against the gamekeeper, was shattered. The public were shown that poaching is now a ruthless, multi-million-pound industry, not afraid to use violence . . . I am glad there isn't any violence around here. Poachers don't enjoy meeting up with the bailiffs but seem to respect them. They are all local people . . .

**MRS M. M. RAPER,
SPITTAL, NORTHUMBERLAND**

BILL STICKERS PERMITTED

The writers and production team, assembled by Peter Cregeen for Thames's The Bill, *are endeavouring to keep their promises. That means that almost all the twice-weekly episodes are self-contained, no continuing stories; and that every frame is seen through the eyes of the Sun Hill police on duty, their domestic upheavals being kept decently out of sight.*

Private weaknesses are not out of bounds and tonight, in Geoff McQueen's Spooky Stuff, the ruffled Detective Sergeant Ted Roach has debt problems and is then doubly wounded when his boss, Detective

*Inspector Frank Burnside, fails to acknowledge the debt he owes to Ted
for a crime 'result'.*

I sincerely hope our police forces are more competent than depicted here.
A senior officer gets his face slapped, and his foot trodden on, by a
suspected shoplifter who keeps demanding that her husband should be
present . . . It is grand to be informed of women police usefulness, and it
is nice to understand how sulky and schoolboyish the senior police get
when reprimanded. But I suggest they get professional advice for this
series . . .

**MR E. F. CHESTER, RETIRED, AGED 82,
GREENFORD, ESSEX**

This is the second best programme on television, behind *Hill Street Blues*.
It is realistic but I live in a country where the police are totally
different . . .

**ALAN McNEICE, UNEMPLOYED,
NEWTOWNABBEY, CO. ANTRIM**

The next programme I watched was *The Bill*, which I think the people in
it swears too much . . .

**SHARON GRIGG, AGED 11,
BIRMINGHAM**

I am very disappointed with this show, it has a very negative effect. I am
fed up with having to watch black convicts come in time after time. They
portray a sort of macho image among the police force, where they have to
act tough and show how disgusting they can be. The language they use is
ridiculous, as for example 'up yours' and, at the market place, 'Where's
that black sod?' . . .

**MICHELLE EDWARDS, AGED 14,
LONDON E17**

Time for a visit to Sun Hill police station. It's good how they leave the
mind to find the conclusion at the end of each episode, unlike other
serials. It wouldn't be half as good if they did continue each storyline . . .

**JACQUELINE MOORE, AGED 15,
BIRMINGHAM**

I never miss *The Bill*, which is supposed to be the most realistic police
series on television. It's good entertainment and it has its funny moments,
as well as providing drama and realism as television should. But maybe
the episode tonight, involving a CIA agent, was a bit unbelievable, a
departure from the usual gritty realism which I like . . .

**ROBERT MUNKS, AGED 16,
HARROGATE**

Ten out of ten, fantastic. It is so realistic and each episode is well thought
out. Nice to see more women police officers being introduced. I was a bit
disappointed today though, due to PC Ramsey (Nick Reding) not

appearing. DS Roach (Tony Scannell) had a difficult part to play, emotional parts are the hardest, but his performance was brilliant. Well done . . .

**PARMINDER HEER, STUDENT,
LEAMINGTON SPA, WARWICKSHIRE**

DID YOU ONCE SEE SHELLEY PLAIN?

The attempt by Thames to round off its Shelley sitcom after six series has failed. With Hywel Bennett still playing the eponymous sloth of a hero, producer-director Anthony Parker has been persuaded to embark on The Return of Shelley, *now at its fourth episode. After a spell abroad the deserted James is tonight faced, in* One of Those Nights *by Guy Jenkin, with a lonely 42nd birthday. But, wearing his humanity on his sleeve, he befriends a man in a wheelchair, and other fellow outsiders, and heartens a number of deserving diarists.*

I found Shelley back on peak form. (Not all of the series' writers seem able to grasp the subtleties of the character's humour.) I find it particularly significant that there are a lot of real values in this programme, the value of friendship for one. As he did with the heroic vicar, Shelley seems here to form a valid friendship with the man in the wheelchair, the alcoholic lady and the Turkish café owner. There is also good comment on disablement, the man is certainly no less a man, etc. . . . It is always good to see valid points being made within the sitcom format . . .

**GEOFF GILBERTSON, SONGWRITER,
STREET, SOMERSET**

A yuppie birthday to you . . . Hywel Bennett (left) as Thames's *Shelley* has a birthday confrontation with his landlords Caroline Langrishe and Andrew Castell

The Return of Shelley is a favourite of mine. Hywel Bennett is excellent
and all the rest of the cast are good. It is a favourite because it is about
what is happening in this country today and, just as important, the way
people are behaving, and what they are thinking. Anyone in the future
who wishes to know what was going on in the UK in 1988 and what some
people, such as myself, thought of it should watch this . . .
**MR K. K. GILLINGS, RETIRED,
BROMLEY, KENT**

I remember hearing Tony Hancock described as 'mildewy' and thinking
that this adjective also aptly applied to myself. I think Shelley is in a
similar vein and see him as the modern successor to Hancock. I find it
easy to identify with Shelley and seem to become more like him with
age . . .
**KEVIN MEGGS, UNEMPLOYED,
LONDON SE15**

Hywel Bennett is very good-looking but I find him one of the most boring
personalities on television. I have watched him many times, but it's like
being in church, with the priest giving a boring sermon. My husband must
have found him just as dull because he started to flick from channel to
channel . . .
**MRS J. M. ROCHE, HOUSEWIFE,
NEWPORT, GWENT**

To my mind *The Return of Shelley* is easily the best of the current crop of
sitcoms. Tonight Shelley, a middle-aged layabout with a university
education, befriends wheelchair-bound David after the latter is asked to
leave a wine bar for (allegedly) constituting a fire risk. Being in a
wheelchair myself, I found this scene, and the ones which followed it, not
only most amusing but also very encouraging.

Having encountered the fire risk excuse/explanation myself in the past,
it was pleasing to see it being dealt with in such a manner, and on such a
wide stage. The appearance of any disabled character on television is an
all too rare sight; to see one featured so prominently, and on such a
popular mainstream programme, was very welcome. David's character
was that of a man who happened to be in a wheelchair and, as such, was
both positive and true to life . . .
**DARREN CHANTER, UNEMPLOYED,
BRADFORD**

DIVIDED SCHEDULES
*While BBC2 maintained audiences of around 2.5 million between 8 and
9 p.m., the Channel 4 schedulers emphasized the network's credentials
as a servant of minority tastes. A mere 700,000 watched* The Divided
Kingdom *during the first half-hour, many of them doubtless wondering
why a concept that needed space should be cut into 27-minute capsules.
This is a series of ten from HTV Wales in which opinionated presenters
give a personal view of a British (or Irish) region which is not their own.*

PRIME
TIMES

Tonight North of England journalist Beatrix Campbell considers Scotland.

The most telling part of this programme was Margo Macdonald's introduction. The 'imposed tartanry' was a bit overdone. No attention was paid to the fact that the tartan was proscribed for a long time after the '45, and some Scots actually like wearing it. My husband always wears a kilt, summer and winter, and he is an island-born Gael who spoke no English until he was six. Beatrix Campbell (English woman? – surely just English born) missed the fact that William Wallace was different from other past heroes. He was a true patriot of the people, not a noble looking for power. The Scots were almost always ill-served by their nobles . . .

MARGARET MACDONALD, RETIRED TEACHER, INSCH, GRAMPIAN

Floating pundits. The opinionated presenters of Channel 4's *The Divided Kingdom* are (from left) Kim Howells, Margo Macdonald, Julian Critchley, Beatrix Campbell and Professor A. T. Q. Stewart

As fully expected the Scots agonized about their identity, a sure sign that they've lost it, or never had it in the first place. Some of my friends tried to imagine such a programme being made in the stockbroker belt in Surrey: brigadiers and denizens of Boodles or Whites, reeling about and declaring they're 'from Surrey and proud of it', worrying if folk up in Glasgow have got the right impression of them. In addition, of course, they'd pass the buck and assert that everything that has ever gone wrong

in their lives was because of the Scots. They would drown their inferiority complex in drink and celebrate the Battle of Flodden. And they, like the blacks, would never seem to know when they are being patronized. Poor devils.

Why can't television documentaries dealing with minorities ever be honest? They let these people air their complexes but never contradict them. A programme about race, for instance, consists almost entirely of blacks complaining about authority. Why is a black who hates all whites not a racist? Why is a feminist who hates all men not a sexist? These are some of the points raised in discussion, and all started by a programme about Scotland. The discussion was between ordinary people, not members of the National Front, or any species of vampire . . . I suppose if television took courage and apportioned blame all round it might be accused of racism, sexism, Fascism, etc. Then presumably the world would end . . .

**DAVID MOSEY, SELF-EMPLOYED,
HULL**

The premise of this programme was correct but it was too short and too superficial. The real Scotland is truly nothing like the tourist brochures . . . The real Scottish history is one of brutality, oppression and poverty. Poverty still stalks the land today, women are still ignored. The people are embittered and inhibited. They still operate in clans and fear incomers. They are still the prey of superstitious fears. The only time they come alive is if someone goes before one in a queue . . .

I was born in one of the Islands. I have travelled all over the world, and returned to live on the outskirts of Glasgow 12 years ago. Since then I have never had a conversation, never been invited anywhere and I know nobody . . . Fortunately I have intellectual resources, so I can live without human friendship, but Glasgow is the most unfriendly of cities to live in and many people living alone are driven to suicide . . . All that the media publishes about this city is rubbish . . .

This programme started to tell the truth but will it be followed up? Margo Macdonald is a prosperous, over-exposed bore. I am sick of seeing her unattractive face. She knows nothing about the real Scotland. She has never been poor as a large number of Scottish people are. When will people like me be consulted by the media? . . .

**MRS A. H. A. HUGHSON,
RETIRED WELFARE RIGHTS OFFICER,
GLASGOW**

WORTH A MILLION?
*At 8.30 p.m., when Channel 4 turned to its consumer investigation
programme 4 What It's Worth, the audience suddenly grew from its
previous 700,000 to 1.9 million. Presenter Penny Junor, and her Thames
team, have a following built up over six years.*

A series obviously made with commitment, it sometimes tends to lay down the law. On the other hand it does appear to get things done. I like the mix of consumer and social problems. It is also a nice idea to provide a free fact sheet . . .

ANNE GRIFFITHS, LIBRARY ASSISTANT, BOLTON

Always worth watching, however frustrating it may be to see decent, ordinary folk being 'done', with so little to protect them, or get redress. It sadly reminds me of Carlyle's dictum: when asked what was the population of the British Isles, he replied, '40 million, mostly fools'. And yet, why should rascals be left free to batten on their decent honesty? . . .

DONALD MORRISON, RETIRED SCHOOLMASTER, AGED 87, KINGUSSIE, HIGHLANDS

The programme took a stand against bent new kitchen salesmen. They have a moustachioed chap presenting, who thinks he's a comedian. He should shave it off and leave moustachioed humour to Ben Turpin and his silent films . . .

DERRICK WATERS, RETIRED FIREMAN, MALTBY, YORKSHIRE

I wonder if Penny Junor has sold many copies of her biography of Prince Charles? How can people be so rich and so silly as to pay anything from £1000 to £3000 for kitchen suites, before they are installed? How can you save people like that from themselves? . . . The presenter of the report on videos is straight out of Boys' Own Bumper Larks. Trying not to make the remote control gadgets so boring, only makes them more so. Who needs the picture enhanced? Who needs split vision? Easier remote controls look even more difficult . . .

LILIAN TRUEMAN, RETIRED PHOTO PRINT TECHNICIAN, FISHBOURNE, ISLE OF WIGHT

VII
NIGHT TIMES

9 p.m. – Midnight

20 'THEN, ALL OF A SUDDEN, IT STARTS TO FLOW'

Changed over to BBC2 to catch the remainder of *Newsnight*. This is my chance to have my say on the political front, and I can tell you I give them what for, even if I do look like the wild woman. My comments may not change the situation, but it certainly gets the day's tensions out of my system. Goodnight . . .

MARY HENERY, EARLY RETIRED, GLASGOW

> *It is now 9 p.m. in the 1 November story. If you write for television it hardly matters what time it is. Some who sit at home creating scripts for soaps and sitcoms, dramas and documentaries, do attempt to work something like office hours. Some succeed in this for some of the time. Some find the creative channel blocked until 9 p.m. and beyond. As a deadline approaches all ideas about clocking off have to be abandoned.*
>
> *A few television writers at the top of the tree will always have as much work as they can handle, or more. A few have semi-permanent jobs as part of soap writing teams. For the majority it is a struggle to win commissions, to be decently paid and to ensure that the work is respected. There is only one Dennis Potter. When material is made for television, rather than merely reported by television, the writer, or the writer's inspiration and perspiration, makes the difference between success and failure. Yet, in an increasingly film-orientated medium, producers and directors are less shy about regarding themselves as authors employing wordsmith servants.*
>
> *Sitcom writers frequently work in pairs, able to enjoy the reassurance of instant response. Other wordies take the precaution of sharing their lives with a fellow writer. For most it is a solitary occupation, maybe attached to a production team but rarely a full member. They choose to do what they do and, when things seem to be working well, life can feel good. But it is not surprising if the diaries, even of relatively successful writers, include intimations of paranoia.*

Like most freelance writers working at home, I find that my efforts at structuring my working day are torpedoed more often than not. Interruptions range from answering the phone and letting the dog out to taking the car to be serviced or my husband to have a tooth extracted. 1 November was another day of minor interruptions, and rather mundane work . . . a Granada sitcom needing adjustments before going into production, a radio sitcom half finished, paperwork for the Writers' Guild . . .

We have become very worried by the relatively small amount of work available for our members. I have taken on the job of going through the *Radio Times* and *TV Times* every week and noting the amount of time taken up with new, creatively written British material . . . There are approximately 1000 scriptwriters in the Writers' Guild and the disgraceful figures I record each week prove how little work there is in this country. Don't ask me what I feel about *Neighbours*, I'm likely to use bad language . . .

ARLINE WHITTAKER, WRITER

I've spent all day typing out the first drafts of episodes 1331 and 1332 of *Emmerdale Farm*. My shoulders are knackered – all those hours hunched over my Amstrad wordprocessor. It has taken since last Wednesday to write the two episodes. I always write them in longhand first. The deadline for their receipt is tomorrow, but they will arrive a day late . . .

There are so very few openings at the moment. I used to laugh at my Mum and Dad watching *Emmerdale Farm* when I was a kid. Now I know how lucky I was to get into the writing team. But progressing on from here is proving very difficult; a foot in the door isn't enough, it's just a start. I reckon you've got to be strong enough to kick the bloody door down. Certainly persistent enough. My motto is 'Don't Give Up'. And I think it needs to be . . .

JACKIE NEWEY, WRITER

A call from Di Baldwin, production assistant on a BBC film I've written, *63 Highmere Park*, which is in pre-production. Can I come in at 2 p.m. and see two actresses for a key role in the film? I say yes . . . Also important is keeping up the flow on the screenplay, where I'm at a critical point in the setting-up of the story . . . I get to my office by 10.30 a.m. It's a hole in the ground, a basement below an estate agent, a godsend. I can't look at anything but a blank wall. The phones ring above but, deliciously, they're not for me . . .

Calls on answerphone, another godsend, from my agent, Norman North. He tells me there has been little progress on the assignation of *63 Highmere Park* by Zenith, who initiated the project and are now selling it to the BBC. Zenith has been efficient but the BBC business side has moved at a snail's pace. I've been paid for the first draft but not for the second, long delivered . . .

Cycle to Television Centre from home in Shepherd's Bush. The film is based on a real story and, although the characters are all fictional, there are endless legal points. Some bits have already had to go and we're fighting for others . . . Eight years ago I did a *Play for Today*, *Minor Complications*, based on a medical negligence case which had similar legal problems, but it now seems much more difficult to get anything strong or controversial through, a constant battle . . .

With producer André Molyneux and director Jenny Wilkes, I see the two actresses. One reads very competently, but it's rather like an audition piece. The other asks lots of questions and is all over the place, but that's because she's subconsciously trying out different aspects, different possibilities of the character. That's actually very thrilling. I'm sure she thought she gave a lousy audition, but I actually like her very much . . .

Cycle back to my hole in the ground . . . Some good stuff goes down the plughole, but I can set the story up in 45 to 50 pages, which may be a bit long, but I feel free to get at the heart of the story . . . Jenny phones at 10 p.m. We speak every evening. We talk about casting and about Scene 177, which is the climactic scene, which she still feels isn't quite there yet . . .

PETER RANSLEY, WRITER

The morning eaten up by angst-ful events. The person who's been living with me doesn't like it when I start writing a television script. (Why ever not?) He therefore suddenly decides to go away. He goes. I am upset. By around noon I'm at my desk and struggling to begin work, when the flautist living overhead begins to practise. I kick the sofa and other soft objects . . .

The project is a London Weekend drama serial, *Wish Me Luck*. I've written the eight storylines for the third series and yesterday had a planning meeting with producer Michael Chaplin. I should be relaxed about it. I'm not, I'm terrified. My mind feels numb and full of question marks. A few of these are noted down for our researcher. I feel as if I'll never write again.

Between 2 and 4 p.m. I drink a pot of coffee and do, limpingly, produce two pages. Quite certain they'll have to be cut from the script. The magic, where is the magic? To write drama is to create a world and its people, and to propel those people, by their own natures and motivations, through a mill of experiences that will catch and hold the imagination of the viewer. Today I don't eat, don't answer the phone and don't go out. Trying to enter France in 1944 . . . It was not a typical day, tomorrow will be better . . .

FRANCES GALLEYMORE, WRITER

Writing until 3 a.m. the night before. Seems to be going well at the moment. Woke up at 9.30 a.m., back to the wordprocessor . . . I am researching for an impending programme about Tarzan, so went into town to see an Indian variation of the genre, *Tarzan Comes to Delhi* . . . On the tube thought about my plans to throw my television set from the top of Centre Point and film myself doing so. Can't afford it. Might hurt someone. A lot of film-makers do have a schizophrenic relationship to their television . . .

Back to the wordprocessor and then call it a wrap at 7.30 p.m. Cooked supper and watched the end half of *The Divided Kingdom*, or whatever it's called. One of the most ill-conceived programmes Channel 4 has put out, I feel . . . Nothing else worth thinking about watching, Tuesday is the worst television night of the week. Though I did watch most of *Brass*

Tacks, about poaching of salmon and deer.

This brought me an idea for my next programme, called *The Lion, the Witch and the Wardrobe*. It will feature Rees-Mogg as the lion, ready to eat us if we make foul-mouthed, over-sexed documentary reconstructions of the latest pile-up on the M25. The witch I leave to the viewers' imagination. Because both the witch and the lion have locked themselves away in a wardrobe, where no one can see them, as they ponder the latest porn movie beamed by satellite television and wonder where they went wrong . . . I was planning to turn my television on again at 10.30 p.m. but there was a power cut, the whole street was out . . .

ADAM KOSSOFF, WRITER-PRODUCER

This was no ordinary day. In a writer's life there is no such thing . . . My official working day is 11 a.m. to 7 p.m., with regular overtime at the back

Craftsman and body of work. Alan Plater's high profile makes him the natural leader of the fraternity of television dramatists

end. Started today completing notes on revisions of a treatment for a feature film screenplay, required for meeting with producer tomorrow . . . The afternoon is occupied with the writing of five letters. I once read that Anton Chekov wrote five letters per day. The theory is that if you receive less than five letters per day on average, in time your in-tray will be empty. After 15 years the system still hasn't worked, mainly because after applying it for two or three days I get fractionally ahead of the game, become complacent and write no letters for a week . . .

Around 4 p.m. we start ablutions. I did say this was no ordinary day. By 5.15 p.m. or thereabouts, I am in tuxedo, my wife in a lovely black number and we set off to Hampton Court and BAFTA's dinner to celebrate 60 years of the American Academy. This isn't because I'm an Oscar winner (but who knows? . . . the notes about the movie and tomorrow's meeting etc., etc. . . . like snooker, movie-making is a funny old game), but because I'm on the BAFTA Council. This is a fairly recent situation, brought about by a feeling at the Writers' Guild that our trade is under-represented at BAFTA. I'm the only writer on the Council, now or in living memory. It could be a giant step for writer-kind, but on 1 November it's a night out at Hampton Court. Among the socializing and the niceties, we have a few television-related discussions with people like David Rose (Channel 4, Head of Drama), Alan Yentob (BBC2 Controller) and Graham Benson (TVS, Controller, Drama). There are five speeches and even a battle-scarred old republican like me considers Princess Anne's the best. It's brief, pointed and she can handle a one-liner . . .

ALAN PLATER, WRITER

Today I was supposed to be flying to Germany to see some people about a film for the New Year, but the money looks shaky, so this is to be a more typical day. It got off to a typical start with the arrival of a batch of research material for a drama-documentary film I'm currently working on. This typically threw me into a panic as, though it was all fascinating stuff, it contradicted the previous material I'd been working from and made several good scenes thoroughly unusable . . .

Rang my accountant to talk about VAT, that put at least two years on my life . . . Realized it was already the afternoon, so I had a haircut. The barber talked non-stop about television programmes I'd never seen and asked me why all the good comedy shows had been produced by the BBC. I muttered something about the commercial break destroying the half-hour structure, but I had my head in a basin of water at the time . . .

Watch *Blockbusters*, of which I am very fond, while preparing tea. Manage to answer a few questions which elude the teenage participants. After the news come upstairs determined to write something, to get over this research-imposed block. Tell myself that even if it's factually inaccurate it's better to get something down and change it later. Pick up the pen and start to write, this diary.

The phone rings: my BBC producer suggesting a meeting on Friday in Claridges. I am very impressed by this and tell him I've never been there.

He tells me he hasn't either . . . Then all of a sudden it starts to flow, not too fast, not too brilliant, but something, a line that makes me laugh, a cut that just might work . . . Goodnight diary, I've got to earn a living . . .

MICHAEL EATON, WRITER

Deal with mail. Am destroyed to learn that an EEC film series, which I wrote with £12 million behind it, involving 12 countries each contributing its own excellent actors, is being shot with each actor speaking a translation of my dialogue into his mother tongue. How will anyone know what anyone else is saying? How will they pick up their cues, judge their reactions? At the end of the day the whole print will be dubbed into the translations of the translations in 12 different languages for the participating countries. The English version is going to sound like Mickey Mouse. Make a note to be out of the country for six weeks when it's shown on Channel 4. Make further note to plan elaborate murders of all the executives involved. Make third note that this is not a bad idea for a play. Daydream for ten minutes about doing it first, then writing the play . . .

Meeting with producer Robert Bradford and director Tony Wharmby to discuss second draft of four-hour mini-series of Barbara Taylor Bradford's latest blockbuster, *To Be the Best*, for US network. Great to meet Tony again, who now lives in the States. We dreamed up *The Gentle Touch* when he was LWT drama chief. Warming to find he hasn't changed in flesh or psyche by so much as a molecule. Delighted to hear Lindsay Wagner is to star. Sandwiches like tower blocks. Claret sumptuous . . .

Take Liz out to dinner with friends. Knowing I'm to write this diary, try to trigger them on the subject of television. Confirm what I have found on other occasions, a stunning lack of interest in any moral or ethical dimensions of the medium. If we want to change it, or even merely to preserve and protect it, we have it all to ourselves . . .

TERENCE FEELY, WRITER

> TEUTONIC THUNDERBOLTS
> *The Nine O'Clock News, considered to be the 'flagship' programme of the BBC Television News day, has had yet another refit. The new format is meant to be simpler and less pretentious than the old, more direct in its telling of the news, but the post-mortems, after the unveiling the previous evening, give little credit to this good intention. It is noted that movements in the newsroom, visible behind the newsreader's head, are distracting; the opening graphics point towards 1930s nostalgia; and there is now one reader, where before there were two. The one tonight is Michael Buerk.*

It's the reporting that matters, but since improvements in reporting are evolutionary, it's the overnight changes in the presentation that everybody will concentrate on. Pity. I don't think last night went too badly. The Wagnerian thunderbolts will take some getting used to. Mercifully, they're brief. Must tell Martyn (Martyn Lewis was the Monday evening reader) he looks suitably Teutonic. Must also tell the editor (Mark Thompson) it looked rather as if Martyn had been left to hold the fort while the rest of the newsroom hopped off to the pub. Tricky. Perhaps they had . . .

Drive in to Shepherd's Bush to find the newsroom humming with a hundred inquests on last night. Triumph – or disaster? The truth, as ever, is somewhere in between, but that's not a good story, still less good gossip. In the hubbub the *Nine* team is trying to sort out today's programme. That's not easy.

The BBC's desire to deploy greater 'expertise' in its news coverage, its energetic recruitment of specialists, can lead to territorial problems. The Chancellor's going to deliver an analysis of the economy, on a political occasion, which will have major implications for the Health Service. A political story? An economic story? Or a social affairs story? The editors of these three new or reconstructed departments naturally think it's basically their story. So who should cover it? The answer, it seems, is that they all will. I loudly express the hope that it really is a big story, not much else is happening, and we don't bore the viewers to death . . .

At lunch we chew through the bean salad and the news diary. On the way back to the newsroom I argue about *Neighbours*. I say it's the worst written, worst acted, programme ever shown. Nobody disagrees, but some admit to being regular viewers. My theory is that the Aussie accents make it the first middle-class soap opera acceptable to a wider audience in this class-ridden society . . .

By 7.45 p.m. the top of the programme is written into the computer. The new format makes taut, impactful writing not just desirable, but essential. The programme starts cold on the newscaster, two crisp sentences, the titles sequence and then a tight summary of the main story and into what really matters, the report, as quickly as possible . . . Back in the newsroom the tension and excitement rises, as it does for all live programmes as the clock ticks round to transmission. I start altering and rewriting the scripts. Some of our producers write them beautifully, others, frankly, don't. Some I alter only because I find it easier to say the same thing in a different way . . .

Time to 'sit in' on the new set, not the long run to the old studio, but just across the newsroom. Earpiece in ear, jackplug in hole, clip on the microphone, switch on the computer monitor, shuffle through the scripts (still only half of them there). Sit on the back of the jacket to make it look right, as they did in *Broadcast News*, and realize once again all it does for me is paralyse my neck and head. Keep up a steady banter with the floor manager, give the level of my voice to the sound gallery far away, and listen to the chanting of the production secretary in my ear, countin away the minutes to Nine. Time for just one rehearsal of the headli

The clock flicks up on the monitor. BBC continuity is saying in ⟨ that the time is coming up to Nine. In the other ear the news galle counts down from ten, the director barks 'cue' and we're on the ⟨

trick is to divide your mind in two. You have to concentrate on understanding and clearly reading the scripts and the autocue, yet still keep up with the flood of information, the to-ings and fro-ings, and impending crises, coming from the director's gallery into the left ear . . .

The principal problem is uncertainty over whether the live satellite link with Keith Graves in Tel Aviv will come off. There's worry that he might not be able to secure the outside broadcast camera set-up at the Labour Party's headquarters. I know Keith, and know they needn't worry. He's not exactly a shy man and even the Israelis would think twice about taking away his camera and microphone. The consequences of trying would be a story in themselves.

The programme moves faster for me than I suspect it does for the people watching it. The coverage of the main story is competent, technically clean; it's an interesting analysis of two important interlocking issues. It won't have the viewers on the edge of their seats with excitement, it's not that kind of day . . . The rest of the programme is a better mix than the night before, better balance and pace . . . Afterwards there's a general feeling that it hasn't gone badly, that it's been a technical improvement on the night before. The adrenalin takes time to settle down . . .

MICHAEL BUERK, CORRESPONDENT-PRESENTER

> *Meanwhile the Monday newscaster, Martyn Lewis, was enjoying a busman's holiday, feeling optimistic and viewing the* Nine O'Clock News *with professional care.*

The BBC's Martyn Lewis, 'The vastly improved quality of the journalism is beginning to come through'

Behind all the early traumas of sets, lighting and graphics on the *Nine*, the vastly-improved quality of the journalism is beginning to come through. John Birt (Deputy Director-General) once said to me his sole purpose was to get BBC journalism right. I'm convinced he's well on the way. There is a tightness of writing intros and editing VT packages which has been endemic in much of ITN for many years. The BBC's 'added-on' value on the *Nine* is combining that newly-acquired discipline with a reservoir of expertise unparalleled in my 21 years of experience in television journalism. It's a combination which is common in Fleet Street and will, I believe, prove to be unbeatable in British television news . . .

I won't go into the White Paper. But despite certain caveats, I am greatly excited by the new opportunities promised. I predict an exhilarating time for anyone who is in television journalism because they enjoy that unique challenge of combining words with pictures across a broadening spectrum of the output . . .

Background to newscaster in the *Nine O'Clock News*, day two . . . People's faces and movements too clear and therefore distracting. Can everyone be asked to try to avoid walking or running across the background during newcaster link. It is a major diversion from taking in what the newscaster is saying. It wasn't helped by Mike being shot most of the time even wider than was normal on the old *Nine O'Clock News*,

right down to the button-fastening on his jacket. This shot also revealed a
huge chunk of the grey desk-front behind him. The shot's message to me
is, 'We can't make up our minds whether we're in a newsroom or a studio,
so we'll stay wide and cover ourselves.' Amorphous mid-shots rule, OK.
Whatever happened to those bold, positive shots we piloted . . .

Clearly Mike opted for the low monitor, he ended up looking down too
far at the end of intros. I cheated the look to just left/below camera on
Monday night, but why should either of us have to do that? . . . We could
still do with one or two more short items to help achieve a better rhythm
and pace . . . Should not the cut and thrust of a big Parliamentary debate
be reflected in the style of the package? For example, snatches of
Parliamentary sound laced with well-crafted linking thoughts, as Michael
Brunson did on *News at Ten* . . . The John Cole voice-over was marred by
a series of overlong night shots of Parliament that distracted the viewer
from his argument. The moving shots of Parliament are a good idea, but
only if used thoughtfully and sparingly . . .

MARTYN LEWIS, JOURNALIST-PRESENTER

*For reporter Michael Smartt the opportunity to perform as an extra
behind Michael Buerk's head provides a rare moment of glory.*

I reluctantly volunteer to sit in one of the desks that forms the backdrop
to the new *Nine O'Clock News* set and, unlike last night, there's standing
room only. Sadly, viewers' reaction is that tonight the background is
distracting. Half-way through the bulletin I forget we're on air and stride
forth to collect a newspaper. More people comment on this brief
appearance than during the entire six months I have just completed,
helping to present the *Six* and *Nine O'Clock* newses . . .

MICHAEL SMARTT, REPORTER

Producer Steve Rose is able to add some distance to the view.

Every news writer has the same dream . . . to be alone in the office when
the 'big one' lands right in your lap. A major exclusive, and it's all yours.
On 1 November, this didn't happen yet again. As Snoopy said: 'One day
my ship will come in and I'll be at the airport.'

Working in News is a strangely mechanistic process. There's a vast,
well-oiled cliché machine. There will always be enough material to fill.
The day is long, 8.30 in the morning until 10.30 at night. Yet, compared to
other areas of television, the pressure is relatively easy to bear. You can
always be sure that the programme will appear, with you or without you.
In other areas of television, you dare not take a day off, dare not leave the
office until late into the night. Nothing gets done without you. The
pressure is organizational, technical, creative. Not so in News, here the
pressure is merely one of speed.

And so 1 November was spent largely in well-mannered preparation
and discussion from 8.30 a.m. until 7.30 p.m. The main story of the day –

the Chancellor's Autumn Statement – was monitored throughout the afternoon. Then a plan was made to report this and all the other news in a sensible running order. At 7.30 p.m. people started to run. By 8 p.m., they were dashing. By 8.30 p.m. they were flying all over the place. At 9 p.m. the News went out – cool, calm, professional. As if no one had stirred.

At the end of the day, people need to wind down. But contrary to expectations, there's very little alcoholism in this branch of television. The News team had really moved in the 90 minutes before the bulletin. The adrenalin had flowed. They sweated. They worried. So, after the News they went to the bar. But just one drink, then home. Back tomorrow. Do it all again.

People who work for the BBC have usually believed in public service broadcasting. They imagine that they are doing more than merely earning a living. They hope to be contributing to society. It's a vague notion, but not lacking in nobility. In a few years, it will be dead. The lure of the market place cannot be resisted. The public servants will be swept away. Most will find other jobs in broadcasting. Undoubtedly richer in pocket. But sadly poorer in spirit.

STEVE ROSE, SENIOR PRODUCER

| *Meanwhile his viewers have more immediate concerns.*

Witnessed the new *Nine O'Clock News*. It is like the bridge of the USS *Enterprise*; with only the smooth, placatory tones and reassuringly familiar face of Michael Buerk to prove otherwise. Having brought the plight of the Ethiopian famine victims to our notice, does he feel anger or shame that so much money will have been spent to create this sterile set? . . .

**PATSY QUINN, STUDENT,
HALIFAX**

I'm loyal to the BBC *Nine O'Clock News* to the extent of taping it every time I go out, and watching it when I get home. That said, its standards have sadly fallen over the last couple of years.

As to the new format, the opening titles are a weird mixture of traditional symbol and hi-tech, and look a bit odd. I don't see that anything is added by the newsroom format, and the increasing influence of John 'sit still while I explain this to you' Birt is very damaging. Saddest of all, the BBC seems to have been browbeaten into submission over the past couple of years by the Government. Why do we have to have ridiculously staged and supposedly flattering clips of Ministers walking along the road or pretending to peruse their boxes? Why is there a distinct lack of 'the Government says . . .' prefacing so many of the tendentious statements which are presented as if they were facts? Why did British interviewers not hang their heads in shame when they saw Mrs Thatcher's recent grilling by an Australian journalist? . . . Weather man Ian McCaskill, a true and lovable eccentric . . .

**CHRISTOPHER BAILEY, LOCAL GOVERNMENT
OFFICER, BRIGHTON**

So far I don't like the new theme tune, but having heard it five or six times on the video I'm getting used to it, and the set is quite good, showing the people in the background working . . .

**STUART SCOTT, AGED 16,
WEST WICKHAM, KENT**

The new format will take a little getting used to, though the opening titles are great after the flying fish fingers we used to have. Solo newsreader Michael Buerk seems a bit lonely, isolated from the aquarium-like newsroom behind. This really did not look busy enough to be convincing. Had they all gone home? . . . I'm always interested in the graphics and captions, because they're computer-generated, but these were hard to read and altogether too arty. They were redeemed by the new format for weather. Ian McCaskill is always good value, but it was obviously a struggle for this larger-than-life character to compress himself into 60 seconds. More time needed . . .

**ED POOLE, TRAINING MANAGER,
SWINDON**

I dare say I shall get used to the new format. The initial graphic is a bit stark, shades of the old Ally Pally mast with reference to the BBC crest, all very logical. The actual bulletin is good and the weather forecast is different . . .

**MRS J. E. M. SAVAGE,
RYDE, ISLE OF WIGHT**

Ian McCaskill, the nation's
favourite weather
forecaster

Not very impressed with the new opening of the *Nine O'Clock News*. It reminds me of the flashing aerial on the old RKO movies, and I preferred the old dramatic music. The format of the News allows me to dip into it while I am preparing for the following day. Definitely don't like the new-style weather, why keep tinkering with it? The maps are too small to take in the detail in the short time they are displayed . . .

**WENDY CARLYLE, PLAYGROUP LEADER
AND HOUSEWIFE, BINGLEY, YORKSHIRE**

I don't like the start of the *Nine O'Clock News*, now. I liked it how it was. And I expect it cost a lot of money to change it. I think they could have spent it all on the old and homeless or the NHS . . .

**NICOLA PEGLER, AGED 13,
DURSLEY, GLOUCESTERSHIRE**

DEPTFORD DEPTHS

Occupying BBC1 from 9.30 to 10.25 p.m. was the second episode of an eight-part drama by Susan Wilkins, South of the Border. *In the geographical sense the 'border' is the Thames, the drama being largely set in the seedy depths of south-of-the-river Deptford. Black, beautiful and honest Pearl Parker (Buki Armstrong) and white, gutsy and thieving Finn Gallagher (Rosie Rowell) are learner private detectives, often as bewildered as the other have-nots they intermittently serve.*

South of the Border is BBC1's private enterprise answer to *Cagney and Lacey*. I was interested both as a feminist-minded English teacher and as a resident of Deptford. The pace and quality was slammed home by the high-octane opening sequence, in which three yobs with beagles coursed a city fox through the night streets, intercut with the knife murder of a smart young Afro-Caribbean man in his own kitchen. This looks classy, I thought excitedly . . .

The private eyes, Pearl and Finn, track down the fox hunters and find evidence to defend Carol Jackson, the dead man's wife, whom the police have routinely assumed murdered him in a 'domestic incident'. The true culprit is found to be a rich, white, upper-class woman with a cocaine addiction, whose 'toy boy' the dead Jason had been . . . I thought this was a good example of quality British broadcasting. I liked the way the climax

Private eyes Pearl and Fin. South London's answer to the splendid *Cagney and Lacey* is discovered in the BBC's *South of the Border*

echoed the opening sequence. The three main women characters (including the solicitor, Mrs Mulligan) were interesting, complex individuals who contrasted excellently . . .

The episode ended with the two women meeting back at their flat. Both have had a beating in different ways, but feel they have 'struck a blow' . . . All you can do? . . . Definitely the highlight of the evening.

MS F. C. MORGAN, TEACHER, LONDON SE8

All the ingredients that are so fashionable with the brainwashed public today. Ugly dialogue, black thugs who are heroes, situations which are fictitious, but presented as if they really do happen, and sympathy for horrible people. I notice that most of the credits are women, obviously libbers setting out to prove political points.

It proves to me that the medium is under the control of the dangerous, loony left, in spite of the proof that Britain is doing better. Television must take the responsibility for the flaunting of all authority, causing the crime rate, vandalism and lack of manners in today's society. Violence, as such, in fictional programmes does not, in my opinion, beget violence. The Saint hit people. It is the brainwashing of viewers to become rebels . . .

ALAN SELWYN, RETIRED FILM PRODUCER AND WRITER, LONDON SW15

What a revolting start to any programme. Switch off . . . horrible. It certainly made me angry and will put ideas into the heads of louts and hooligans. There has been enough violence in the News today without all this blood and gore within the first five minutes of *South of the Border* . . .

BETTY MORTON, RETIRED, WHITLEY BAY, TYNE AND WEAR

I watched out of curiosity, having heard mixed reports. I was not impressed. I found it disjointed and unbelievable. I got the impression that they had commissioned someone to take six familiar ingredients of modern drama – independent girls, violence, racism, feminism, sex and the police – and try to concoct a series round them. I shall not be watching it again . . .

DOREEN HAMMOND, LIBRARIAN AND HOUSEWIFE, IPSWICH

I haven't watched this before but I thought it was great. At last two women are allowed to do something on their own, without a father figure patting them on the back, as in *C.A.T.S. Eyes*. The story was nicely rounded off in the hour. I liked the solicitor, but am not too sure how realistic her defence 'research' was. Altogether it was a good-looking programme, showing the mess of South London I see every day . . .

HENRIETTA HOPE, TEMPING PUBLIC RELATIONS ASSISTANT, LONDON SE15

South of the Border is great. I really like programmes with strong parts for women, especially now that *Cagney and Lacey* has finished . . . My husband watched with me and this means I have to concentrate twice as hard. You see he is blind, and as a lot of things happen when there is no dialogue I have to tell him what is going on . . .

IRENE ARMSTRONG, SHELTERED HOUSING WARDEN, LONDON SW19

I taped *South of the Border* to watch tomorrow. I believe it contains some violence. Mrs Whitehouse is no doubt pounding away at her Olivetti. Daft old bat . . .

MS GLEN MOY, FREELANCE WRITER, SANDHURST, BERKSHIRE

RAILING COLIN

During his working hours Colin, otherwise comic actor Mel Smith, is a 'passenger relations' clerk on British Rail's Eastern Region. To prevent the relationship becoming any worse he is kept grumbling in an office, well out of the way of any aggrieved passengers. Also on the wrong track at home, with his up-market partner and her equally confident friends, he rues and rails with still more fervour. In short he is another variation on the little-man-at-odds-with-the-world, or Tony Hancock, theme. At 9 p.m. today BBC2 scheduled the third of his first six-part sitcom series, Colin's Sandwich, by Paul Smith and Terry Kyan.

I am presently into my eighth week as a hospital patient, undergoing treatment for anorexia nervosa. I received a diary form from a fellow patient, and thought it might be an incentive to actually absorb some of the programmes I watch . . . Mel Smith is brilliant. Most sit-coms are fairly predictable but the mixture, of witty one-liners and Mel's thinking aloud, means you don't always know what is coming. This is one of the rare sitcoms that makes me laugh, rather than just smile . . .

LYNNE FITZGERALD, ENROLLED NURSE, FLEETWOOD, LANCASHIRE

Colin's Sandwich was very funny, but nothing to do with sandwiches. Mel Smith fits the bill perfectly. He's fat and looks like a perfect British Rail complaints clerk . . .

MASTER A. HEATHCOTE, AGED 11, CHELMSFORD, ESSEX

The funniest programme on a Tuesday has to be *Colin's Sandwich*. I think Mel Smith plays this type of role better than anybody else and the way he soliloquizes is perfect. I must congratulate you on such a fine series . . .

GRAHAM BUTLER, AGED 13, WEST WICKHAM, KENT

I went up to my room to watch my favourite programme of the day, probably of the week. The moment Mel Smith starts to speak I just laugh.

I can't help it. He doesn't even have to speak, just the look on his face has me in fits. I specially like it when he's sitting there and somebody's talking to him and you hear his thoughts . . . And then Colin speaks to the other person nicely, as if he hadn't been thinking those horrible things. I have never seen this technique used before in a comedy and hope the idea catches on . . .

The next day at school I chatted to my pals and asked them if they had watched it. Only one had. I talked to her for about 15 minutes about how funny it had been . . . I think it's a shame that it's on BBC2 and a lot of people miss it. They don't think of brilliant comedies being put there . . .
**KAREN PAYTON, AGED 13,
LIVINGSTON, WEST LOTHIAN**

Colin's Sandwich is disappointing, and it's very sad to see Lindsay Duncan wasted in a poor part. I saw her in *Les Liaisons Dangereuses* some years ago, and she was terrific . . .
**NICK RATCLIFFE, CIVIL SERVANT,
ILFORD, ESSEX**

Hmm, *Fawlty Towers* makes *Colin's Sandwich* rather paltry fare to follow. It had its moments, certainly, but not enough of them. The ideas are more interesting than those in most 'Oops, Vicar, where's the pouffe?' sitcoms around at the moment. But I was troubled by the luxury in which the beleaguered Colin (a British Rail employee) was living. I am sure the nice men at Chingford Station don't have leather suites and snooty girl friends. Neither, as far as I know, do they have sufficient leisure time to be writers, even writers as bad as Colin . . .
**ELIZABETH LACEY, LECTURER,
CHINGFORD, LONDON E4**

We had decided to watch this series from the beginning, because we admire Mel Smith. My husband bears an amazing resemblance to the character of Colin and this can be amusing, and also extremely depressing . . .
**FIONA BOISMAISON, EXECUTIVE OFFICER,
DEPARTMENT OF EMPLOYMENT,
ST NEOTS, CAMBRIDGESHIRE**

SEEING COLIN
Following in the tradition of earlier 13-part series attempting to cover huge areas of art, science and the ascent of man, Professor Colin Blakemore is now half-way through his on-screen performance telling what can be told from that little explored region, the human brain. Annina Rive, production assistant on The Mind Machine, *reports from the team's grey cell within the cortex of BBC Kensington House.*

We have spent two-and-a-half years on the series now, co-produced with WNET/Thirteen in New York. It has been a real trans-Atlantic collaboration. Much of the material was also used in WNET's *The Brain*.

Cerebral explorer
Professor Colin Blakemore
half-way through his on-
screen perambulation
around BBC2's *The Mind
Machine*

This has been brought up to date and combined with nine BBC films, making up the 13-part series. The BBC end also contributed material from its film library and BBC film crews were made available for WNET producers who wished to film in Britain . . .

Today I open up the office to find no messages on the answerphone. A year before the tape would be full, packed with urgent requests from WNET producers wanting me to sort out this and that by 2 p.m., when American colleagues arrive at their office. It is now quite a relief not to be living ahead of everyone. Though I do miss the adrenalin of deadlines, and the daily 'Have a nice day' from 3000 miles away.

This is transmission day for programme seven, *Sight Unseen* . . . Search the papers for previews, nothing. I don't expect any reviews either. No one bothered to turn up for our BAFTA (British Academy of Film and Television Arts, Run Run Shaw viewing theatre in Piccadilly) showing the previous Friday. Religiously each week I turn up there with the 'U'-Matic version, as this is of better quality, to show the television reviewers, even though they never come. Some may have seen cassettes at home, but it's the tradition to have these bookings anyway. So 'the show must go on', with or without the critics.

Carry out routine paperwork, and there is plenty created from such a marathon series. Today I have to concentrate on the budget, as costs of *Sight Unseen* have to be submitted to Accounts. Out of the 13 programmes this one has cost the least to produce, primarily because it was filmed in Oxford rather than some more exotic location.

Check and re-check credits and name supers for one of the last programmes due to be edited over the weekend. The Graphics Department are screaming for them. As most of the contributors are American, several phone calls have to be made at the relevant time zones to eminent doctors and professors to find out what their 'job description' is. Are they psychiatrists, psycholgists, psychoneuroimmunologists, neurologists, neurophysiologists, neurosurgeons, neuroanatomists, neuro-endocrinologists, or just plain neuroscientists? Will anyone know the difference?

During one call to Salt Lake City, the doctor decides that 'psychiatrist' will do. Then he calls back three hours later wanting to change it to 'Professor of Psychiatry'. Apparently there are thousands of psychiatrists in Salt Lake City but only a handful of Professors of Psychiatry. I change it again only to be told there is not enough space on the screen to accommodate this long title. So he ends up as psychiatrist after all. I only hope that the eminent Professor is not in Britain when the UK version airs.

Finally go home to watch *Sight Unseen* for the umpteenth time. There is something different about seeing it 'live', almost like viewing it for the first time . . . Only another six programmes to go . . .

ANNINA RIVE, PRODUCTION ASSISTANT

Some viewers were gripped, others less so.

What a superb programme, dealing with the terra not as incognita as it used to be when Descartes thought he had discovered the secret of vision in an ox eye. Sensory cortex, motor cortex, hand/eye co-ordination, recognition, knowing where we are, compensating – all the things we take for granted but can't be reproduced by a computer. We got the jugglers a little too often perhaps, and the Sheldonian Theatre was distracting, but I loved the concave and convex Byron, illustrating that one's internal information rejects evidence that does not fit . . . I hope to watch the rest of the series, very exciting . . .

MEGAN ROBERTSON, RETIRED HEAD TEACHER, BRIERLEY HILL, WEST MIDLANDS

What is it about Colin Blakemore that isn't quite right? Slightly self-conscious? A bit too aware of his own importance? That may be it. I mean, is it really necessary to say, 'When I went to Cambridge as a medical student in 1962 . . .'? Is this relevant? Come to think of it he was pretty awful in the first episode when he dragged his daughter in as well. One of my daughters was watching with us that time and we were all cringing with embarrassment . . .

MRS M. E. BARKER, LIBRARY ASSISTANT, NORTHAMPTON

The Mind Machine is a fabulous series. A member of my family has brain damage and I find the series helps me in dealing with the problem, for the present . . .

DOMINIC FEEHILY, PAINTER AND DECORATOR, CORK CITY

Generally I am able to sit down and fully concentrate on what the young Professor is telling me. But today was a horrible day. What with waiting for the plumbers to arrive (which incidentally reminds me of the brain and its pipes and tunnels), and at the same time waiting for the electricians to see about my mother's storage heaters in the same block, it was difficult to settle down.

I have no video, too difficult for me, and I made no notes for fear of missing my connections on this wonderful journey. I do, however, remember being stunned by what the brain allows us to do . . . Actually, although at the time I seemed to be grasping everything and missing out nothing, it must have been impossible for me to absorb it. As our headmistress used to say at school: 'You have to read everything three times to absorb it once.' How true. Now I am waiting for the BBC to publish a book on the series. I'll read it three times . . .

ELEANOR HUTCHINSON, RETIRED CIVIL SERVANT, SANDGATE, KENT

The Mind Machine has been a very engrossing series, if a bit difficult to follow at times. Tonight was about the brain's effect on vision. My husband came in and asked me to help calve a cow. It didn't turn out to be

too difficult, so I was back before the end of the programme. I may watch
it again on Sunday . . .

**GILLIAN SMALLEY, FARMER'S WIFE,
MOLLINGTON, OXFORDSHIRE**

I find *The Mind Machine* very interesting because it puts faces to many of
the names I came across during my psychology 'A' level course. But it
does make me realize that the animal experiments I wrote about were
actually done on live animals, a point which failed to hit me from just
reading books. Seeing distortion and deprivation experiments on kittens,
which I wrote about frequently, I realize I am being a hypocrite enjoying
this subject as much as I do, because I am against the exploitation of
animals. None the less a very well presented programme . . .

**ALEX HUTCHINGS, UNEMPLOYED,
STEEP, HAMPSHIRE**

A BOON FOR ITV

*At 9 p.m. the unified ITV network regains the ratings lead it lost to
BBC1 at 7.30 p.m. The opening episode in a new series of* Boon, *created
for Central by Jim Hill and Bill Stair, attracted an audience of 12.7
million, easily the biggest of the day on this channel. On BBC1 the* Nine
O'Clock News *holds 7.5 million but this number is reduced, partly due
to the BBC Wales opt-out, to 5.7 million by* South of the Border. *The
respectable BBC2 figures during this hour are 3.2 million for* Colin's
Sandwich *and 2.3 million for* The Mind Machine. *Only 600,000 see* The
Other Europe *on Channel 4.*

Esta Charkham, the Boon *producer, woke up at her London home*

A *Boon* scrum. Enjoying
this disagreement are (from
left) Hywel Bennett, Neil
Morrisey, Amanda Burton,
David Daker and Michael
Elphick

with 'an odd feeling of anticipation', took a train to Birmingham and was delighted to find herself placed in the Princess of Wales Suite of the Holiday Inn.

On the way to the cutting rooms I picked up today's press cuttings from Wendy Dickenson, our press lady. We had nice pieces in the *Daily Star* and the *Daily Mirror* about our smashing new leading lady, Amanda Burton, and a fairly snide piece in the *Sun* (wouldn't you know?) about her pregnancy.

Got to the cutting room of Roland Brason, who is film editor on episode 12. I viewed a rough cut last week and it was almost right except for the last section of the last reel, and some smaller alterations in the earlier two reels. Obviously I give the director the opportunity to discuss the changes I wanted him to make, and in some instances I saw the validity of his claims and gave in. However, there were some points I was adamant about and had to exercise my producer's rights in as charming a way as possible.

Firstly the overlays of dialogue are a little complicated and I feel would be difficult to follow for our audience, and anyway they are not in the style of our show. I feel the same way about fades to black. We've never used them before and can't start using them on the 38th episode. The last reel was the real problem – it was untidy, messy, with overlays of dialogue over shots that didn't relate and the entire climax given away too soon . . .

A nice *Boon* promo at 8.30 p.m. and then on to *Shelley*. I don't know whether it's good or bad that Hywel Bennett is our guest star in the first episode of *Boon*. It means viewers will have an hour and a half of him tonight and next Tuesday night. Oh well, that's the way the cookie crumbles.

It's 9 p.m. and here we go. A recap of the last series – I'll never know whether that worked or not – but it's pacey – then the new opening credits – then to the opening sequence – a dream sequence – I hope the viewers know it's a dream. We've had the print graded pink and have lots of slo-mo and optical mixes in it – It's funny when you watch something that you've toiled so long and hard over. You notice so many tiny little holes in it for the first time and then you think, 'Oh God, I'd never noticed that before.' Still I only think they're apparent to me. You have to make so many mental notes, so that you can remember not to do that (whatever it was) again. Oh well, I suppose the day you think you've produced a perfect television show is the day to give up.

I'm always interested to see who buys advertising time during one of my shows. An odd selection, pet foods, Harpic, Comfort, Skol, Maxwell House, central heating; and I was delighted to see that my two best pals got repeat fees during *Boon*; Pat Hodge for her Tia Maria voice and Tricia George for her Paxo Mum . . .

Well it's over. I watch the credits roll and there is a nice little moment just for me when my name goes up. Not bad after getting two 'O' levels and one CSE. Then the phone starts to ring. It's lovely to get phone calls of congratulations, but I want to watch the last *St Elsewhere* . . . Ring down to reception and order every newspaper for tomorrow morning, to see if we have good reviews. Take off the make-up, clean the teeth, and get into the very large bed – once slept in by Bruce Springsteen . . .

ESTA CHARKHAM, PRODUCER

| *And how many of those 'tiny little holes' were spotted by viewers?*

At last it's my favourite programme, *Boon*. I think he's lovely, even if he's too old for me. I think he's more my Mum's age, but she's already married. I am not allowed to watch any more today as I have school tomorrow.

**LESLEY-ANNE SMITH, AGED 11,
BALLINGRY, FIFE**

Didn't seem to gel tonight. Boon looked ancient or permanently drunk, Amanda lovely as ever, Hywel Bennett non-actor, Matthew Kelly, well, talentless in my eyes. The usual toilet scene, oh why, oh why, oh why? Should this series have been brought back? . . .

**PATRICK WEST, RETIRED,
ENFIELD, MIDDLESEX**

Boon had a stupid start. First no colour at all, then everything pink and yellow. It made me think the television must be on the blink. Also I do object to having to watch men piss, seems the lowest form of entertainment to me. It appears to be Hywel Bennett benefit night . . .

**MRS D. BARRINGTON,
HOUSEWIFE, WORCESTER**

Because *Boon* is set in Birmingham it is that much more interesting. It is good when you are able to spot places you know . . .

**STEPHEN SPENCER, POSTMAN,
BIRMINGHAM**

Boon is an easy programme to watch as the plot and dialogue do not require a great deal of concentration. It is downhill all the way. We like Michael Elphick but find that he is sometimes let down by a weak storyline. But it makes a welcome change from *The Equalizer* and *Game, Set and Match* which, although very enjoyable, do require a lot of concentration most of the time . . .

**FREDERICK PAGE, RETIRED,
ENFIELD, MIDDLESEX**

Turn over to Ken Boon. This we always find innocent and amusing. The plots would be more appealing to a fanciful adolescent, but at least viewing is effortless and mildly entertaining. It is a pleasant relief from violence, child abuse, perverted sex and the nauseating Esther Rantzen. My husband, being an expert motorcyclist, wonders how Boon stays alive,

riding his BSA whilst taking very lengthy nostalgic stares at his former
Fire Brigade colleagues . . .

**ANNE DORAN, LOCAL GOVERNMENT OFFICER,
WINSFORD, CHESHIRE**

COLD WAR, HOT PRESENTER
*For the whole hour from 9 p.m., minus commercial breaks, Channel 4
was occupied with programme three of the six-part Tom Roberts and
Panoptic production* The Other Europe. *This was a lavishly filmed
personal view of Eastern Europe, the Communist bloc, by presenter
Jacques Rupnik. At a time when public opinion was eagerly accepting
signals of friendship and peace from Moscow this series was widely
regarded, amongst its minority audience, as a bit old hat in its apparent
'Cold War' view. On the other hand, Rupnik was admired as a talented
and persuasive front man. And he knew that in his native country,
Czechoslovakia, unreconstructed Stalinism still ruled.*

Eastern Europe pokes out of a globe like frozen plasticine and I wonder
if this film of Rupnik's *The Other Europe* will be as Cold War as
the others. It's not, it's a penetrating analysis of the delicate dialectic
between absence and presence being created by the Party in Poland,
Hungary and East Germany. Expat hard-liners like Kolakowski see little
change, but contemporary East European citizens are both sceptical and
hopeful . . . The inane advertising breaks – Oil of Ulay, McDonald's,
Kenco Coffee, don't really constitute an alternative world. Eastern Europe
is different . . .

MR A. J. DUNN, LECTURER, LONDON SE21

The programme's counterpoint of idealistic 1950s party propaganda and
contemporary film of an East German rally broken up by rain was very
powerful. After describing how the Communist states' faith in a 'scientific
world outlook' underwrote all human affairs during the Cold War years,
this tremendously ironic sequence strongly and poetically questioned such
a position . . . The dichotomy of the stylized and the spontaneous was
graphically illustrated by Young Pioneers marching through the streets,
contrasted with the deeply critical analysts of today . . .

I greatly enjoy this series. It fits in with my academic interests in
politics, history and the cinema. I have recommended *The Other Europe*
on several occasions to people at work, my father, an ex-college lecturer
and various friends. It represents the view of one man and, for me,
Rupnik is too partisan. He does not allow for any of the good which
Socialism must have brought to the Eastern bloc. However, he is a most
articulate and likeable presenter and I wish him well. The series may
confirm the worst suspicion of conservatives in the West. It may also
allow them a window into that huge part of our continent which has been
barred to us by Winston Churchill's 'Iron Curtain' . . .

**RICHARD ARMSTRONG, CIVIL SERVANT,
LONDON N4**

Most television celebrities are off the air most of the time. What are they doing? Here are some 1 November glimpses from the off-screen lives of a few who have been chosen by the mirror in the corner. First to open his diary is entertainer Gary Wilmot, today celebrating his eighth wedding anniversary.

Entertainer Gary Wilmot, 'an inveterate channel hopper'

After Carol and I exchanged gifts this morning I switched on the television and watched TV-am, listened to the tone on BBC2, watched *Breakfast Time* and the Channel 4 test card. The reason? I'm an inveterate channel hopper. I sit in my armchair with my remote control unit at my side and, like others who I'm sure share the same mania, watch all four channels.

My viewing habits have also been changed by the video. I now no longer worry about which programmes the television companies have decided I should watch. If . . . one don't fancy anything on the box tonight, one can just pop down to one's video hire shop . . . and tonight . . . one has done just that . . . hire a film that is. It is a British film, I'm pleased to say, called *Hope and Glory* – and I loved every enchanting second of it.

GARY WILMOT, ENTERTAINER

For Magnus Magnusson this has been the first day of the 17th season of BBC1's Mastermind. He has had to travel from his home in Glasgow to the first 1988–9 location, the University College of Swansea. A muddle over tickets, and a consequently circuitous journey, has caused him to miss his intended lunch at the Dragon Hotel, Swansea, with Mary Craig (chief researcher), David Mitchell (newly promoted from director to producer) and Andrea Conway (new director).

Interesting-looking set of contenders for programme one (to be rehearsed and recorded with number two tomorrow): a classical composer, a police inspector, a steelworks crane driver, and a veterinary surgeon confined to a wheelchair. For the first time in 17 seasons, a contender won't be in the Black Chair itself. It will need a bit of extra stage management and give Andrea an interesting baptism . . .

Andrea arrives to report on the set-up in the Taliesin Arts Centre at the University College: she's enthusiastic and all fired up. We go over the wording of my introduction and links, to fit the camera shots she has been deciding on. We'll make the final adjustments during the camera rehearsal tomorrow afternoon. It's nearly 8 p.m. by the time we finish. I decide to have a meal up in my room, so that I can go over the questions again on my own, and pencil in the emphases. It's nearly 10 p.m. before it's done . . .

MAGNUS MAGNUSSON, PRESENTER

Producer-presenter
Desmond Wilcox, 'I love
you, Daddy'

> *Desmond Wilcox has had a day defending his documentary seam* The
> Visit, *which has so far been made out of Glasgow. James Hunter (Head
> of Television, BBC Scotland) had 'shocked us all' by announcing that
> the series was to be killed because, 'I believe in killing things like this
> when they are strong and at their best, before they go off, or get weak.'
> A morning meeting with Jonathan Powell (Controller, BBC1) has proved
> reassuring. He would keep* The Visit *and the only question was whether
> he took it 'from another output department, or makes me an offer as an
> independent'. Wilcox favours the independent option.*

What an odd squabbling of sparrows on the back lawn. All this bickering about details, and not a word about programmes, from management level in Scotland. It was, I believe, Wellington who said: 'I don't know about the enemy but, by God, my own troops frighten me' . . .

A showing of our two-part documentary on autism for Dr Martha Welch from the USA and 15 other autistic therapists and specialist VIPs . . . In the BBC viewing room both projectors have broken. I apologize to the VIPs. The British ones seem somehow to be comforted by the thought that the licence-funded BBC is trying to keep obsolete equipment on the go. We manage to book an alternative viewing theatre, at the bottom of a condom-filled alley in Soho . . .

At the end of the showing there's nothing but applause and support, very gratifying. We take BBC-paid-for taxis, with bolshy drivers, to the pizza restaurant in Shepherd's Bush, originally organized because it was near to the BBC. Everybody is very jolly . . . I leave them buying Mexican beer for each other at 10.30 p.m. and return home. The family are asleep. Down to my basement office and the wordprocessor. I start on 2000 words for *Woman's Own*. To bed at midnight. I check on the children, Rebecca and Joshua. Both murmur, while still firmly asleep, 'I love you Daddy.' It has been a good day . . .'

DESMOND WILCOX, PRODUCER-REPORTER

> *Barry Norman began his day at home in Hertfordshire, taking his
> customary three-mile jog accompanied by black labrador. By 10.30 a.m.
> he was in the West End to see the first of the day's three films. In all he
> will see six in preparation for his weekly* Film 88, *shown by BBC1 on
> Monday nights.*

The third film at 6 p.m., *High Hopes*, a British picture by Mike Leigh. In foyer of Coronet private cinema in Wardour Street I am accosted by American director Harley Cockliss. He upbraids me, gently but quite properly, for having made a joke on my programme about his name. I apologize gladly: it was a very cheap joke and I'm sorry I made it . . .

Home by about 9.30 p.m. Watch recording of last night's *Film 88*. I rarely see the programme on transmission because the BBC insists on putting it out at the back end of the night; and, after a day of script revision, rehearsal, recording and seeing yet another film, I can't stay awake long enough to watch myself. Television presenting is hardly an arduous job but the increased pulse rate and adrenalin flow that go with it leave you exhausted. I dislike watching myself on television but I do it anyway, to search out any irritating mannerisms that might have crept in. The question you have to ask yourself all the time is: 'What could I do to make it better?' . . .

Then to the night's viewing. First, *Wildlife on One*, an enchanting study of meerkats. This is the kind of thing television does superlatively well. It is also the kind of thing which, I fear, could easily vanish from our screens when, in this brave new Thatcher era of every man for himself, the satellites come zooming in and all the television companies (the BBC included) are scratching desperately about for ratings and any old rubbish that will appeal to the lowest common denominator . . . *Network* next, a discussion chaired by Anna Ford on television coverage of sport. I watch because I recently presented Channel 4's late night Olympic Games programme and wonder, egotistically, whether I will be mentioned favourably or otherwise. In the event I am not mentioned at all. The discussion is almost entirely about the television presentation of soccer and, like most discussions, is totally inconclusive. The critics make their points, the pundits answer them, everyone is satisfied and nobody learns anything . . .

And so to bed. A typical Tuesday: in the course of it I have done nothing on television, met nobody from television, not even talked about television, and yet the whole day has been devoted to television . . .
BARRY NORMAN, PRESENTER

> *For Stephen Fry this was the morning after the night before. This is David Lander, a six-part comedy series about a visible and versatile investigative journalist, had begun on Channel 4 the previous evening. Now Fry, who plays the name part as he did in the Radio 4 original, is not feeling too well.*

Well, it was always predictable that 1 November should see me succumb to the most virulent and unpleasant form of influenza that modern medical science has yet devised. It is no part of my mission with this journal to embarrass the reader with wild talk of vomiting, but we must be fearless and candid. Puking there was, and shivering and moaning. For many, of course, this is a usual response to the *Kilroy!* programme, in my case it was unforced and unbidden. I threw up joyfully and totally without the aid of morning television.

I therefore missed Michael Grade defending *This is David Lander* to Bob Wellings on *Open Air*, an event reported to me by producer Paul Mayhew-Archer. It seems Bob Wellings, whom I'd always imagined to be a person of superior understanding, said 'I saw *David Lander* and wasn't very sure about it.' To which M. Grade tartly replied: 'Yes, that's why you've got your job and I'm doing mine.' Well.

Spent what few conscious, non-vomitous hours I had checking up on reviews of last night's *Lander*. I'm beginning to think we decided on transmission order wrongly. Last night's episode was very Roger Cook-ish and might have given a false impression of the series as a parody of door-stepping confrontational journalism. W. S. Gilbert, and some other nameless poltroon in the *Independent*, made fatuous comments which implied such misapprehensions.

Christ, I loathe those television critics. If only they could say 'hated it'. It's when they try and explain their dislike that ignorance and wild stupidity shine through. 'It fails because . . .' is their style, implying, 'If only the producers could have shown me the script early on, I could have put them right.' W. S. Gilbert couldn't recognize the reason for the success

Stephen Fry, bewigged as dogged Channel 4 investigative journalist David Lander

or failure of a piece of television if he got home and found it peeing on his furniture. Bitter? Not me . . . Fell fast asleep until mid-evening and awoke to be greatly revived by *The Mind Machine*. A hasty channel change and what Britain now calls 'those Meerkats' were on screen again. They stopped the vomiting dead in its tracks.

Any night that has an episode of *Fawlty Towers* on television is a good night. It's just the idea of what an unrestrained arsewit like W. Stephen Gilbert would say when he first saw *Fawlty Towers* – 'frantic and overstretched silly walk comedy from ex-Python', 'fixed formula sitcom', that kind of thing. Thank Christ critics have the power and influence of a prawn cocktail . . . Well, a good day's television on the whole, given the vomiting and the rest of it. I must do this again some time.

STEPHEN FRY, WRITER-COMEDIAN

THE INFLUENCE OF A PRAWN COCKTAIL?
In different, and often excessive, ways the national television networks and the national press use and feed off each other. Most programme-makers will readily agree with Stephen Fry that, with one or two exceptions that do not quickly spring to mind, newspaper critics are obtuse, ignorant, lazy, self-regarding and worse. These same broadcasters will also relish and carefully preserve newspaper cuttings which commend, or even just mention, their work.

At this stage of the night first editions are emerging from the presses with their reflections of 1 November. The broadsheet City pages tell about the Italian takeover of Super Channel, and the tabloids are salivating over the Channel 4 Signals, barely exploring television sex. The Daily Express and the Star are awarding Larry Hagman, otherwise JR of Dallas, a new £2.8 million contract. The Times has lots of letters from architects, bouncing off Prince Charles's television lecture on the subject.

The up-market papers still sustain 'morning after' television reviews, usually on their arts pages. Following in the wake of the Guardian's Hugh Hebert, both Philip Purser of the Daily Mail and Mark Lawson of the Independent write prettily round the One Day in the Life of Television project. Purser also has the wit and perception to look past the presentation of the new Nine O'Clock News to its improved reporting.

Among reviewers Purser is now the respected doyen. After 26 years writing a weekly column for the Sunday Telegraph he was, inexplicably, allowed to leave. He is now installed, for reasons best known to the editor, not as number one but as second string at the Daily Mail.

Because a morning paper reviewer must these days deliver his words by afternoon I have already seen the programmes I am going to write about . . . In the far-off, front-line days when I first reviewed for the *Mail*, and then the *News Chronicle*, almost all television went out live. You frequently had only minutes between the end of the programme and the deadline for telephoning in a measured appraisal. I used to quote a revue sketch I'd seen, in which Dora Bryan and Joan Heal (I think) were secretaries discussing the men in the office.

'I do like so-and-so,' said Heal. 'He dresses so nicely.' 'Mmm, and so quickly,' said Dora. Quickness was all-important as a pioneer television critic, too.

Anyway, this morning I am handicapped by having left my notebook on the train from Milton Keynes the day before. I make copious notes of the content of every programme I see at previews, from a craven fear that when I sit down to write I will have completely forgotten what it was about. In practice I rarely even glance at these notes, but without them I am immediately reduced to panic . . .

Luckily I can begin with the television Domesday project itself, before leading into *Boon* and *The Return of Shelley*, which I couple together on the device of Hywel Bennett being involved in both . . . Since last May I've been using a Tandy, a little portable wordprocessor which you can plug into the telephone and thereby transmit copy directly into your newspaper's system. It's marvellously convenient, though I think it changes your style slightly. It's so easy to correct as you go along that you can lose the rough edges and last-minute amendments which give good journalism its zing.

Ann, my wife, back in the country, rings to tell me there is a message on the answerphone with the welcome news that my notebook was retrieved by another passenger. He turns out to be the librarian of the Arts Council in Piccadilly. The Arts Council is the finest organization in the land. Its officers should be heaped with honours . . .

After a snack lunch I trudge out to the BBC Television Centre. It is every reviewer's least favourite destination. It seems to be 102 stops on the Central Line from wherever you start, the viewing rooms are basement dens that even the KGB would hesitate to use as dungeons, and you have to get past the security staff on the gate. 'I've been coming here, off and on, for thirty-three-and-a-half years,' I've tried shouting, 'which is Our Lord's entire span on earth. And still you don't know me.' It makes no difference. You still have to wait while they make telephone calls . . .

I finish around 5.30 p.m. and take the underground back to Channel 4 in Charlotte Street to see next evening's *Signals*, on the subject of sex on television. Both viewing rooms here are occupied, so I have to watch on a set in the corner of the general press office, using the headphones so that the sound won't distract people. The girl at the nearest desk says the programme has been in demand all day, and she has now seen the naughty examples four times. They are not very naughty . . .

PHILIP PURSER, CRITIC

Fellow veteran Richard Last is the last survivor of the team that used to review for the Daily Telegraph, *and is now that organ's number one.*

This is one of those blessed mornings when I didn't have to attend formal viewings in London. I wrote my review for the day at home in Woking, sitting at my desk on the second floor of my house, looking at the trees, still in my dressing-gown. I wrote about *First Tuesday*, which was reporting on a way-out Evangelical church in Bradford, and offered some scope for what passes as humour in my column. There was also a ten-minute novelty called *Building Sights*, a weekly examination of the quirks of modern architecture . . .

After that I bathed and got up properly and set off for my unfavourite chore in the viewing business: a visit to the subterranean viewing cells at BBC Television Centre. This is, for me, an absolute last resort, when I have missed the appropriate screening at BAFTA and failed to persuade either producer or public relations person to send me a cassette . . . As it happened, I watched the first episode of a particularly good series which has since become a favourite, *Rockcliffe's Folly*, much better than its progenitor, *Rockcliffe's Babies*, perhaps because the action has been transferred to Dorset. Then a terribly worthy but fairly boring documentary about Dr Barnardo's . . . I would have rounded off the day with a spot of private viewing when I got home but it was a pretty wretched evening . . .

How did I start television reviewing? I was a feature writer on the IPC *Sun* (the respectable pre-Murdoch version), with a longish background in the field of music and theatre criticism for the defunct *Daily Herald* and in the provinces, when they wanted someone to take over from Nancy Banks-Smith at weekends. I started my television career as Nancy Banks-Smith's deputy. You can't get better than that . . .

RICHARD LAST, CRITIC

Having seen the television Domesday project on the horizon, Nancy has gone on holiday. Her present deputy at the Guardian *is Hugh Hebert.*

Radio 4 checked for the 7.30 a.m. news summary, my usual practice. If there is some important news item, that could change my plans of what to write about that day . . . My first serious job is to watch the remainder of *Perlov's Diary* (Channel 4), recorded overnight from 12.30 to 1.30 a.m. Then watched tape sent to me by producer of *The Other Europe*. I had not intended to write much about this but news broke only yesterday that the Gdansk shipyard is to be closed down. That makes this programme, dealing especially with the Communist regime in Poland, a much stronger runner for tonight's column . . .

Arrive at the office about 1.30 p.m. and decide to lead on the Polish stuff . . . *First Tuesday* as usual presents the problem that it falls into two contrasting halves. Neither fits very happily after the Poland piece. Decide to opt for the piece about the Restoration Church, a fundamentalist lot I hadn't heard about, rather than the awful but familiar problem of dyslexia. That leaves room for a short piece about *South of the Border*, which, while not a great series so far, is watchable, takes on some

The glamour of television. 'Hi, Mike, it definitely says caviar and champagne in the script' good issues and has stirred some . . .

For most of my time on newspapers I have been a feature writer with a special interest in the arts, and in books. I was not an avid television watcher. Events in the early 1980s – the arrival of Channel 4, the expansion of cable (a false promise as it turned out), two long features I was assigned to write – decided me that it was going to be a much more interesting field to write about than it had been . . . When the vacancy for a television reviewer, three nights a week, came up I asked to take over the job with very little hesitation. It has turned out to be much more demanding than I realized . . .

**HUGH HEBERT, FEATURE WRITER
AND TELEVISION REVIEWER**

> *W. Stephen Gilbert, the man who bumped Stephen Fry's funny bone, is better qualified than most television critics. He has been uncomfortable and successful as both a writer and producer of television drama. He is at present squeezed into the preview boxes of the* Independent's *listing page.*

Today I go to see Mark Shivas, recently installed as the BBC's Head of Drama. I've known Mark (not well) since I first fell into television in 1969. He had the great good fortune to be recruited as replacement to the producer Ronald Travers, who departed rather abruptly and left behind him a little series called *The Six Wives of Henry VIII*. Mark guided the series through transmission and has ever after been known as the producer of the show which, strictly, he wasn't. So he's no mug . . .

My image of him has always been as an exponent of literary, safe but classy drama for a middle-brow, middle-class (or aspiringly so) audience. But in Maggie Brown's interview in the *Independent* the other day he sounded hearteningly bullish and encouraging . . . The thing is I want to get back to producing. This previewing is not a job I can do for long: it's sprinting . . . So I put my pitch to Mark, all about how the BBC has to fight the grim future of television from its traditional strengths and that means domestic plays for the home market; that means the studio, for which I am just about the only advocate alive; that means restoring the continuity of work among writers and directors, and producers come to that. He makes encouraging noises and says he will tell George Faber, executive producer on *ScreenPlay*, to see me. I suppose it's the best I can expect. Will it lead to anything though? . . .

Lunch in the BBC canteen with Roy Battersby, who directed the last production I managed to get on to the air, Farrukh Dhondy's four-part *King of the Ghetto*. He's become a wise and stimulating friend . . . We talk about what it's like going to the brink of ruin, with the work refusing to come, both of us being in debt and precariously placed for some years past. Roy has this superb fall-back position, wherein he rounds up a hit-squad of like-minded technicians and goes out into the street to create work on a wing and a prayer, so that come what may he's still working.

I'm knocked out and envious, the latter because I have no skills that
provide a bedrock for the lean times, save putting words together in
quintessentially futile contexts like previewing for the *Independent* . . .
W. STEPHEN GILBERT, PREVIEWER

> *Elizabeth Cowley may be described as the mother of television
> previewing. She delivered her first listings spread to the long defunct
> weekly* Reveille *in 1955, before graduating to become a producer for the
> BBC's pioneering* Tonight. *Now she is back in print, mostly for the*
> Daily Mail, *and is recognized as one of the three or four truly
> conscientious members of the previewing fraternity.*

I start at Thames around 9.45 a.m., seeing three *Witness* programmes on
the role of social workers . . . Then a brisk walk through icy sun and wind
(picking up sandwiches en route) to Channel 4, where I normally come to
roost of a Tuesday. I tend not to go to organized viewings in theatres or at
BAFTA etc. It's so much quicker to do it yourself, and covertly fast
forward when needs must. The C4 viewing rooms badly need baffles.
There is a lot of gentle, middle-class complaining. 'Could you turn your
set down just a jot? . . . I hate to interrupt' . . .

Home by late afternoon to write Pick of the Day (approximately 300
words a day, five days a week) and phone it over to the copytakers at the
Mail by 7 p.m. . . . I tend to view alone because I live alone and work from
home. The day has been smooth enough. I have to chuckle at how much
easier it is to preview these days, what with press offices falling over
themselves to be helpful and cassettes and despatch riders at the ready.
This was not the case in 1955 . . .
ELIZABETH COWLEY, FREELANCE JOURNALIST

> *Margaret Forwood, a columnist for the* People, *reckons to have been
> hooked by television around 1950. She has never wanted to write about
> anything else and made her reputation, as one who cares about popular
> television, with the* Sun *in the 1970s.*

Today I was on holiday, at a health farm, trying to relax and not watch
television for once. Needless to say I did watch some, but nowhere near
as much as I would normally do. There was *Telly Addicts*, because I am
one; *EastEnders*, I don't think I've missed an episode since it began;
Shelley, because I like Hywel Bennett, because the series was originally
created by a friend of mine, and because it is sharper than the average
sitcom; *Fawlty Towers*, unmissable; *Boon*, because it was the first of a
new series . . . After watching *News at Ten* I fell asleep. It's very
exhausting, relaxing.
MARGARET FORWOOD, COLUMNIST

> *Maggie Brown shares her job but on working days may be said to do the
> work of four women. During working days she is media editor for the*

*Independent, constantly doubling as her own reporter and feature
writer. At home she has a family to care for. This morning she has been
considering the final composition of the Wednesday media page.*

I decide to leave out an opinion piece by me, on the changed *Nine
O'Clock News*. I dislike the new look but I 'pull' the piece because I think
that the essentials, the quality of BBC News journalism, is on the rise, and
that, rather than looks, is what matters . . . I decide to include a late item,
about Sky Television negotiating for a five-days-a-week *The Price is Right*
programme deal. I use this to illustrate how satellite channels may spell
more of everything, including trivia . . .

I have several discussions with a general news reporter who, at my
suggestion, has been to Channel 4's *Signals* preview. She found this
history of television sex pretty tame. John Archer, producer of the
programme, phones to talk about it. I say I wish *Signals* well, but it has
got off to a disappointing start . . . I am phoned by the producer of the
Thames counselling programme, *A Problem Aired*. I fix a media page
feature with her. I think the idea of television counselling needs
discussion, especially after LWT's ghastly *Family Affairs* experiment this
summer. I leave at 6 p.m., arrive home and put the children to bed. And so
to television watching . . .

MAGGIE BROWN, MEDIA EDITOR

*Elizabeth Guider writes about British broadcasting for the American
newspaper* Variety, *and begins the day watching episodes of Granada's*
Game, Set and Match.

It is interesting to us because it has American money and may well be the
last of a breed of relatively costly, slow-paced but well-acted and lavishly
produced warhorses, whose ratings broadcasters in future may feel do not
justify the expenditure . . . Reading the papers on the bus to work, I
resolved to get started on an overall piece on the implications of the
impending White Paper . . . I wanted to address the question: How
American in structure and style is the British broadcast environment of
the 1990s likely to be?

Called by *Daily Variety* and asked to follow up a story about British
Satellite Broadcasting negotiating for a hefty package of US films from
MGM-UA, together with the BBC. Apparently BSB committed to £50
million for the pay television rights to the package, and then sold on the
off-air rights to the BBC's chief buyer, Alan Howden, for about £20
million . . . In the evening I accompanied BBC drama producer Kenith
Trodd to Hampton Court for the BAFTA evening commemorating the
British film industry's links with Hollywood . . .

ELIZABETH GUIDER, CORRESPONDENT

From 10 p.m. the size of the television audience declines as the nation prepares for sleep. Maintaining its ratings lead, ITV has 8.5 million viewers for the start of News at Ten. *This is reduced to 3.3 million at the beginning of* First Tuesday *soon after 10.30 p.m. Still without its Welsh viewers, BBC1 has 6 million for* Wildlife on One *at 10.25 p.m., and drops to 1.9 million when 'those meerkats' are replaced by talk of sport in* Network *at 10.55 p.m. During this two-hour period the BBC2 audience drops from 2.1 million to 1.1 million. Channel 4 does much better with 3 million for* St Elsewhere *and 2.8 million for* The New Statesman *repeat lasting for half an hour from 11 p.m.*

With some thought for One Day in the Life of Television, *BBC1 Controller Jonathan Powell scheduled a third showing of the much-loved* Meerkats United, *first seen in* Wildlife on One *in January 1987.*

My favourite part was when the meerkats took shelter under a termite hill because the sun was too hot for them. I thought it was fascinating the way the camera zoomed in so close that it looked as if the meerkats were playing in my own living-room. I think the meerkats are sweet, the way they make funny little peeping noises and stand on their hind legs looking for predators, there should be more films about them . . .

**VALERIE MELLON, AGED 10,
SOUTHEND-ON-SEA, ESSEX**

Meerkats United. 'Right lads, remember the camera is on us, so we have to get a result'

I would like to have watched the meerkats but my dog finds all animals a challenge to his territory and to save his barking I find it easier to change channels and catch the end of *News at Ten* . . .

MRS A. J. POPE, COMPANY DIRECTOR, STROUD, GLOUCESTERSHIRE

I intended to switch off, but our cat was enthralled by *Meerkats United*. So I ended the day watching our cat watching the meerkats, her reactions were priceless . . .

HILARY HAMMOND, HOUSEWIFE, NORTH BADDESLEY, HAMPSHIRE

This documentary was wonderful in its capture of the hyperactive meerkats. I was left fully awake and exhausted, simply through watching their superb teamwork. Even the cat gazed in amazement at these lovely little creatures in their warm and sunlit land . . .

JANET STEVENSON, UNIVERSITY TEACHER, THRINGSTONE, LEICESTERSHIRE

I had to see the meerkats again. Unfortunately my own cat chose that moment to be sick and by the time I'd cleared that up I'd missed most of the film . . .

URSULA LIGHT, RETIRED BIOLOGIST, ASHFORD, KENT

This was a joy from start to finish. David Attenborough alone is worth the cost of a licence. The skilful way in which commentary ceased, to allow the action of the meerkats full play, and the very sparing use of music, made a delightful end to the day. I liked the slogan 'One for All, All for One', I wish humans could learn from this . . .

HILDA LEEK, AGED 75, BEACONSFIELD, BUCKINGHAMSHIRE

A repeat programme I had not seen the first time round, but friends said it was good. As it was presented by David Attenborough I feared the worst. I have stopped watching his wildlife programmes because he has such a fixation about sex. I am not against sex but I do object to the sight of copulation in my sitting-room, whether it be bird, beast, fowl or human. However, all was well and I enjoyed the antics of these wonderful creatures . . .

JOAN MARKHAM, RETIRED, SEAFORD, SUSSEX

Meerkats United is quite outstanding for two reasons. First the animals are incredibly talented in front of camera; and second, it's not presented by Anna Ford . . .

STEPHEN CHALONER, SCRIPTWRITER, BRIDLINGTON, HUMBERSIDE

ANNA FORD BENEFIT NIGHT

As well as appearing, involuntarily, on page three of Britain's two most sleazy tabloids, Anna Ford now became unavoidable on BBC1. She presented all the remaining programmes on the channel, apart from the 12.35 a.m. closedown weather forecast. First there was Network, *looking at televised sport; and then* The Search for Realism, *an Open University production demonstrating computer graphics.*

Nice to see Anna Ford presenting, she will be a great bonus when she joins the *Six O'Clock News.* Rather self-indulgent of the BBC on One Day to dedicate so much time to reviewing television, *Open Air* all morning and then *Network* . . .

**PERSIS ASTRIDGE, OBSERVING FROM
A HOSPITAL BED, PROGRAMME
DIRECTOR, ITN AND TVS**

The main *Network* topic was the quality, or rather the lack of quality, of football coverage. An angry young man made a short film complaining about the bland analysis of football. One had to agree with him. When ITV won the Football League contract we lost the BBC's *Football Focus.* It was no work of art but the lesser of two evils when compared to the odious *Saint and Greavsie.* Why do producers of soccer programmes insist on treating us like morons . . .

CIARAN KEARNEY, STUDENT, DERRY

This one was a great disappointment. The programme seems to have lost confidence in itself and to have become petty, unambitious, soft-centred and dismissed into an even later slot. The discussions used to be crisp, sharp and relevant, and it was sad to see this rambling and inconsequential talk. The best part of the programme was the introductory film from the viewer. But this new *Network* is giving a nervous and tucked-away impression . . .

**ANN WOLFF, PART-TIME LECTURER
IN TELEVISION STUDIES, LONDON NW3**

Anna Ford not looking the slightest bit interested. Fellow comes on before her wearing a disreputable leather blouse, speaking in some sort of accent, and with a very peculiar manner. So aghast at this appearance that I didn't take in a word of what he was saying. Huge studio, with a lot of men and three token women ranged in some sort of horseshoe fashion. Why they were all there I don't know, three-quarters of them never spoke. Usual 90 per cent blather about football . . . I don't mind what sport is put on as long as I am given some tennis . . .

JEAN BARNES, RETIRED, CHESTERFIELD

Football is one of the joys of life and the appalling television coverage, as with *Saint and Greavsie* on ITV, lets it down. Simon Inglis (our next door neighbour's brother) gives a fan's view on the current state of football broadcasting. Why are the BBC and ITV heads of sport so friendly when they're in direct competition? . . .

**PHILIP CALCUTT, MARKETING
MANAGER, BIRMINGHAM**

At 11.30 p.m. there was sport on three channels and commercials, preceding a sports programme, on ITV Anglia. On BBC1 *Network* was discussing sport, BBC2 was showing championship bowls, Anglia was about to show a programme about boxing and Channel 4 was just starting an hour of American Football. Whatever happened to choice? . . .

**SHEILA BROOME, RETIRED
LIBRARIAN, GREAT BADDOW, ESSEX**

If there is anything more boring than football it can only be a lot of people talking about it. But I am glad I stayed up for *The Search for Realism*. I know nothing about computers, what a thing to confess in the 1980s, and I sit there open-mouthed at what the programmers can do. Goodness knows how big the computers must be, surely not desk-top things. *Son of Luxo* is computer animated and one of the funniest things I have seen, anthropomorphic or not. I laughed out loud, not for the first time tonight, but unusual in an Open University programme . . .

**RUSSELL BRYDEN, MUSICIAN,
KIRKCUDBRIGHT, DUMFRIES AND GALLOWAY**

This was one of the best programmes I have seen for a long time. Although I found the *Radio Times* write-up misleading as I thought I was going to see the latest *Star Trek* film in the making . . .

**MRS J. V. HUGHES, UNEMPLOYED,
WIRRAL, MERSEYSIDE**

The look-out crew, waiting for *Campion* action

PUMPING HYPERBOLE

The fixed 10.30 p.m. start for Newsnight, *introduced this week after
some angst, means that BBC2 is now in the market for ten-minute
fillers. Hence* Building Sights, *a series of personal reflections on 20th-
century British architecture, which opens tonight with Piers Gough
being lyrical about the new pumping station on London's Isle of Dogs.*

I took a quick glance at the jolly façade of the Isle of Dogs pumping
station, like something in a Diaghilev ballet, but only because the Prince
of Wales's entertainingly provocative film the previous week had stirred
things up.
**MS D. M. BENSON, WRITER,
LONDON NW8**

There was this dear little toy pumping station on the Isle of Dogs. I only
caught two minutes of it but wanted it to play with. I like the idea of
highlighting good modern architecture but am apparently doomed only to
see two minutes of it a week, or miss the end of *South of the Border*,
which is unthinkable . . .
**MS H. C. ALLOTT, LIBRARIAN,
HAINAULT, ESSEX**

A ten-minute documentary which only the BBC could come up with. The
programme consisted of an architect waxing lyrical over the new Isle of
Dogs pumping station. The presenter was adrift on a sea of hyperbole and
came up with the quote of the day: 'concrete as yummy as nougat'.
Question, If he's on television why aren't I? . . .
**TERRY REASON, CIVIL SERVANT,
ST LEONARDS-ON-SEA, SUSSEX**

BIRTIST TREASURES

Other programme areas may not regard the cementing of BBC2's
Newsnight, *between 10.30 and 11.15 p.m., as a great blessing. Editor
John Morrison is inclined to think it one of John Birt's monumental
achievements as BBC news and current affairs supremo.*

Leave *Newsnight* at 12.30 a.m. on 1 November. It is the end of a mildly
historic day in the programme's history, the day we achieved a fixed start
time. This has been the holy grail for successive editors down all the years
we have floated about the schedules. Its iconic significance has been
confirmed by regular shedding of corporate blood. Its achievement has a
slightly unreal air. During the modest party afterwards I found myself
asking: is it really true? Has it really happened? When John Birt's legacy
is counted, the fixed start time for *Newsnight* should be one of its
treasures.

Though for most people on *Newsnight* the significance of yesterday was
not the fixed start time, but the coincidental re-design of the programme.
Titles, set and graphics are all new. We kept the original title music (and,
bizarrely, had a phone call complaining about the 'new music'). The effect

is stunning. When I took over as editor a year ago, almost to the day, I found a programme which looked dark, male, gloomy, heavy. Now that's all gone. Everything is lighter, more elegant, more expressive. The show went flawlessly. But what of today? In my experience day two is the real test . . .

Ring today's output editor, Eileen Fitt, from home at 9.15 a.m. A heavy day is in prospect. We have a team in Israel for the closing stages of the general election. And there is also the Autumn Statement from the Chancellor, not to mention the threatened backbench revolt from Conservatives unhappy with planned charges for health checkups. This is before any 'real' (unexpected) news happens . . .

Discussion at the office with political correspondent Nick Clarke about his planned replacement for the producer who normally works with him but who is moving to higher things. These discussions have been going on for several weeks. It is a very important job for *Newsnight*, as politics is the meat and drink of the programme. We settle on a bright young producer, Jim Gray. Tell Jim who is agreeably pleased. If only all personnel matters were this pleasant . . .

Discussions with Home Assignment Editor, Nigel Chapman, and his designated successor Steve Anderson, about our coverage of the forthcoming White Paper. This is a tricky one, a 'house' story and therefore one that attracts particularly close attention from our masters . . .

JOHN MORRISON, EDITOR

At which point it is the turn of presenter Donald MacCormick to continue the story of the day.

In the early afternoon I chat with the programme director about one shortcoming in the 'first night' of the new set. The editor, like most of us, felt we didn't have a sufficient punctuation mark between the news summary and the introduction of the closing item of the show. We agree that a longer pause, coupled with a verbal signpost of the 'Now to . . .' type, would probably do the trick . . .

As usual, the rest of the day flies past, with the script being written and checked, and the odd bit of voice-over being recorded, in an atmosphere of increasing haste. It's also obligatory to keep an eye on how *Channel 4 News*, the *Nine O'Clock News* and *News at Ten* are dealing with the economic story . . .

Then suddenly I'm on air, opening the programme by outlining what the Chancellor has done, and saying who our guests will be. Then Peter (Snow) pops up from Tel Aviv with his 'menu' from the Israeli election. From the start it has the feel of a busy, lively 'live' programme, and afterwards everyone seems satisfied that's how it has turned out.

There are no guests to share a post-programme glass of wine with, but I still fall with pleasure on the Muscadet Sur Lie. Much better than some of the stuff we get, slightly salty, but full and fruity with it. Soon it'll be 'Sur Lit' . . .

DONALD MacCORMICK, PRESENTER

| *Are the customers similarly satisfied?*

Basically a long commercial for the Conservative Government. John Major says 'an investment boom in the private sector' . . . 'expansion in manufacturing'. He doesn't say much about industry being wrecked by them six to eight years ago, or that imports are up 12 per cent while exports are only up 1.5 per cent this year. Any increases in manufacturing are from a very low starting point, even compared to 1979. The US election brings more awful publicity 'hype'.

In fact the media, specially television, have replaced the electorate in deciding who will be the candidates, let alone the President. In other words, they'll go through the motions but Bush has already won. Here we are four years after 1984 and we haven't yet realized that the Orwellian dream really did happen.

CHRISTOPHER HANCOX, GRAPHIC DESIGNER, STOURBRIDGE, WEST MIDLANDS

So, what's new? Looks more bland than before and in two nights' viewing I've seen only one woman interviewed, let alone any woman (or black) presenter. Yawn, yawn, when will they get it right? Roll on white, middle-class maleness. They do include non-South-East accents. Should we applaud? Dismay . . .

PIPPA CURTIS, MANAGEMENT CONSULTANT, LONDON N16

I love *Newsnight*, have watched it for years and catch it whenever I can. John 'new broom' Birt has nailed it to a regular 10.30 p.m. slot now, and that's a shame, as the old irregular kick-off time added a sort of spice. There is also some grisly new presentation. We used to have a pre-title VTR sequence with portentous headline commentary, before banging into the theme tune and title sequence. Whatever the lead story the effect was always dramatic . . . Now, following a scramble of ill-assorted and barely apprehended images that signify nothing much, Donald MacCormick sits sad and cramped in front of what looks like a pile of St Paul's Cathedrals, but could be skulls . . .

GEOFF BULLEN, THEATRE DIRECTOR, LONDON N10

| WATCHING THE WATCHERS WATCHING THE WATCHED
| *At Independent Television News, assistant press officer Judith Lustigman had an early start. From 6.30 a.m. her job at the Wells Street studios has been to mind the Yorkshire Television team who are filming a day in the life of* News at Ten.

We're in the main newsroom, and it's virtually empty. Apart from the YTV crew and me, there's Mervyn Hall, the home news editor; the foreign news editor; and the cleaner. The poor man is being filmed from every angle as he hoovers the same spot. I can imagine the commentary, 'And the only thing to be heard is the low hum . . .'

My first important job is going out to buy the coffees. I buy Merv a big one. Bless him, everything he eats or drinks is big and consequently so is he. Oops, he's just spilt his coffee all over his desk. I nudge the director and he tells the crew to film the action, Merv wiping his sodden newspapers . . . First meeting of the day, in the office of deputy editor Stewart Purvis. With him are the three news editors, senior home news editors and five or six from *News at One*. Presenter Julia Somerville arrives. Hell, she obviously didn't see my memo about the filming. No make-up. She may kill me. I stay outside . . .

Everyone falls on the papers for opinions of the *Nine O'Clock News* revamp last night. Being as objective as possible we all thought it was dreadful. No sour grapes or anything, but it was a mess. I thought they'd gone on air before the set was finished. My old colleague Martyn Lewis looked lost behind the enormous desk. And that odd over-the-shoulder window, floating in mid-air. Why bother? . . . Hmm, Anna Ford. Why did the BBC announce her for the *Six O'Clock News* job, on the same day as the revamp. It stole the *Nine O'Clock News* thunder . . .

News at Ten programme director is in. She's a legend, Di Edward-Jones. Probably the best television news director in the world, a founder member of ITN, I believe, which means she's been here 33 years. She's best known for her unbelievably vivid language. When I told her she would be filmed she said, 'Fuck that, I'd better not say fuck then, fucking nuisance' . . . At lunch Di visits Persis, another director, in hospital . . . Everyone is sure she's ill because she works so hard – days, nights and weekends – for ITN and other companies . . .

At 8 p.m. the YTV crew decide to go off for supper. At 9 p.m. they're back and we're running. We follow newscaster Alastair Stewart into Make-up. He's been on since this morning, presented the *News at 5.45* and is now being re-done for *News at Ten*. I think viewers think this is where the newscaster's day starts . . .

Go into studio for rehearsal, Sandy Gall and Alastair at desk. Amazing scene with autocue lady. She's been at ITN for years and years. She's being replaced by new machinery in ten days, and tells everyone and anyone what she thinks about it. Suddenly she sees 'that machine' next to her friendly old teleprompt and gets hysterical. 'Cover it up! I'm not working with that next to me! Cover it up! Cover it up!' Scene shifters run off in all directions and come back with loads of sheets, and shroud the evil piece of machinery, and pacify her. Christ knows what she will do on her last night . . .

On air Brent Sadler is expected. In the minute his VTR story is running we see him waiting on the monitor, white-suited in a hall in Tel Aviv. Fine. We can hear him, great. But he can't hear us. He's lined up for a live two-way interview with Sandy, in 30 seconds. 'We'll have to drop it if he can't hear us.' Disembodied voice: 'Master control here, we can cue him from here.' 'No, we'll do it later.' Five seconds to go. 'No, we'll do him live now.' He's cued in but there's a momentary delay. For three seconds

we, and nine million viewers, see Brent waving frantically to an unseen body to get out of the way . . . Then the voice, phew. My nails have gone. Brilliant producing, brilliant directing, what a team. At the end of an amazingly fraught programme Nick Pollard (senior programme editor) smiles, wipes away the sweat and murmurs, 'Nice day at the office, dear?'
JUDITH LUSTIGMAN, ASSISTANT PRESS OFFICER

| *Fraught? Newcaster Alastair Stewart apparently did not notice.*

The new *Nine O'Clock News* is on its second night. The general newsroom judgement is that it is an uninspiring birth. I don't like the idea of starting with the newscaster in vision. I hate the new logo and sound sting. The new graphics are dull. The stories are dull and their analytical content doesn't justify their extended duration. In short, not impressive . . .

It is 9.30 p.m. and I put my contact lenses in (no vanity here) and have my make-up put on. Last cigarette and into the studio about ten minutes before transmission. The usual rigmarole of checking tie, collar and cuffs. I'm told I fiddle incessantly with my watch . . . It's a good programme. The Autumn Statement is made interesting and we do get the vote on eye test charges, just after the commercial break. We take the Speaker, live, reading out the vote. A Government majority of just 16. That's a good late story. Just before the finish we get news that Charles Hawtrey, of *Carry On* fame, has died and we squeeze the news into the last 40 seconds of the programme. I wash, have a drink and go home by car . . .
ALASTAIR STEWART, NEWSCASTER

| *A good programme?*

Most evenings I try to see *News at Ten*, it's always differently slanted in comparison with the Beeb's bulletin. But I had one main motive in watching tonight. Cardiff City, my favourite football team, were playing at home to Bury. I had to wait, full of suspense, until the very end of the bulletin, for the score. Joy of joys. My team, which I have felt an affinity with for 45 unbroken years, won 3–0. My heart leapt for joy and I immediately turned the television off . . .
REVD C. F. WARREN, CLERGYMAN, NEWPORT, GWENT

We watched *News at Ten*. The main issue was the vote on dental and eye checks. Later in the programme we were told that the Government had won the first vote. I will be prepared to pay, even though we have no choice in the matter. I prefer to watch the local news as the readers are sometimes light-hearted. I like this because there are so many sad stories around. It can reflect on to you and change your mood. Towards the end of the News I began to feel tired and so I didn't put my full attention on to what was being said . . .
TRACEY ENGLISH, AGED 17, LINCOLN

We never watch *News at Ten*. It is irritating and trivial and I would rather remain ignorant than use it as a source of information . . .

**BRIDGET WHELAN, ADVISOR,
LONDON N19**

Olivia O'Leary, an Irish intelligence to focus Yorkshire's *First Tuesday*

AND THE WORD WAS DYSLEXIA

Next on ITV followed Yorkshire's First Tuesday, *the current affairs documentary magazine shown in this slot on the first Tuesday of every month. As often happens, presenter Olivia O'Leary had two films to introduce. The first touched on the Restoration Church, a relatively new manifestation of evangelical Christianity. The second, 15 hours after Susan Hampshire contrived to preach about the subject on both TV-am and BBC breakfast programmes, concerned dyslexia.*

Among those watching part two was Peter Griffiths, an educational producer at Thames.

An appalling item on dyslexia. Two case studies gave no insights, and the programme became a plug for those who believe that the one word is sufficient for the diverse and myriad problems with language which were evoked. A lot of emotional twaddle – yes, of course, we all sympathize with people with problems, but we want more about solutions – smokescreens galore. Thankfully, the head of a private school for kids with specific learning difficulties talked of 'small groups . . . individual tuition . . . intensive work on specific difficulties' and never mentioned 'dyslexia'. As somebody once said, 'Even if you agree to dump all these problems together under that heading, how do you treat them except by good specific teaching?' . . .

**PETER GRIFFITHS, SERIES PRODUCER,
'THE ENGLISH PROGRAMME'**

I watched the report on dyslexia. Certainly, one little boy featured got little of my sympathy. I didn't feel the programme got anywhere at all. In fact it produced a largely soporific effect which I was unable to ignore. And so to bed . . .

**MRS A. JOHNSON, HOUSEWIFE,
RUYTON-ELEVEN-TOWNS, SHROPSHIRE**

Not unexpectedly the film about the Restoration Church of Bradford provoked anger in the Restoration Church of Bradford.

Both my husband and I were totally shocked by the allegations in *The Apostle and the Prophet*. The programme was totally one-sided, to the negative. A local couple were interviewed, who spoke ill of the church and the terrible things they had experienced when they hadn't come under total submission of the church elders. Even to the point of the 'lady' having lost her baby. It did sound bad, but they were not telling the truth . . . *First Tuesday* didn't speak to anybody who attends the Bradford Church today. The couple were talking about incidents of nine years ago.

As for the allegations, they are totally false. Nobody at this church has to do anything. The amount of money a person gives is up to the individual. Nobody is oppressed. Nobody *has* to attend and anybody is free to leave whenever they want. The programme was totally unfair and biased. Now, because of the prejudiced view of the *First Tuesday* team, the British nation has the wrong idea of the 'Abundant Life Church' in Bradford. We know the truth because we belong to that fellowship and are proud of it . . .

**LINDY HYMES, SECRETARY,
BRADFORD, YORKSHIRE**

As active Christians of no fixed denomination (that is, followers of Jesus Christ rather than Runcie, Hume, Bryn Jones or anyone else), my husband and I did at one point belong to a church under the large Restoration umbrella. We are also interested in Christian action anywhere, so this programme was of great interest. It seemed to present some indisputable facts but a great deal of it was the misleading result of editorial cutting to make up a fairly biased documentary. The effect must sadly be to further cover Christianity in general with a black blanket and confirm people's worst fears . . .

The truth is that all churches are made up of human beings and therefore no church is perfect. Sometimes an obsession with side issues builds up and leads to stagnation or complete downfall. This seems to be the sad case with part of the Restoration movement. The programme has caused a lot of discussion among our Christian friends, and the editorial of our present church's paper was devoted to the subject, using it as a vehicle to examine the issues in a Biblical light, with suggestions as to how to avoid anything similar . . .

**KEELIN HOWARD, PARENT-HOUSEWIFE,
PRINCES RISBOROUGH, BUCKINGHAMSHIRE**

It dealt with some dangerous distortions of contemporary Christianity. Well done *First Tuesday* for putting people on their guard . . .

**DAVID HOUSTON, CLERGYMAN,
CARRICKFERGUS, CO. ANTRIM**

First Tuesday restored my faith in television and went a further step towards destroying my faith in society. The picture of hot-gospelling fundamentalist sects showed how they take a grip on their converts. All authoritarian groups, whether political or religious, want total control over their members. In a way, those who give themselves over body and soul to some self-appointed leader, are asking for it . . .

**MR R. G. JONES, UNIVERSITY TEACHER,
BORTH, DYFED**

MOVING ELSEWHERE
Returning to American output, Channel 4 gained its largest audience of the evening, climbing between 10 p.m. and 10.30 from 2.4 to 3.3 million. The attraction was the 23rd and last episode of the fifth series of St Elsewhere. The episode concluded with the demolition of the Boston

inner-city teaching hospital which has so far provided the setting for the medical drama.

My absolute favourite programme of all time. I do not apologize for gushing my praise for this as it is justified. In the same vein as *M*A*S*H* and *Hill Street Blues*, it mixes a perfect blend of humour, tragedy and entertainment. Many times I have been in tears due to *St Elsewhere* and this final episode was no exception . . .

TERESA ROGERS, HOUSEWIFE, GRIMSBY

Ausslander, the symbol of the helplessness of the aged and the young in one, was crushed with the hospital building. Despite the vain efforts of the caring staff, this bastion of protection for the poor, the hospital, was destroyed under orders from a company the contractors can't even name. The traditional helplessness of the comic hero, at the mercy of external factors he cannot comprehend, yet without the comic denouement, is horribly involving.

It may not be comforting to ally oneself with these tragi-comic creations yet they articulate a view of mankind which is much more sympathetic and empathetic than television drama in this country. These women and men who smile at life and at death, while getting on with the task of living, confront the helplessness we all feel at some time. They present the disillusionment which is familiar to our own lives. It is

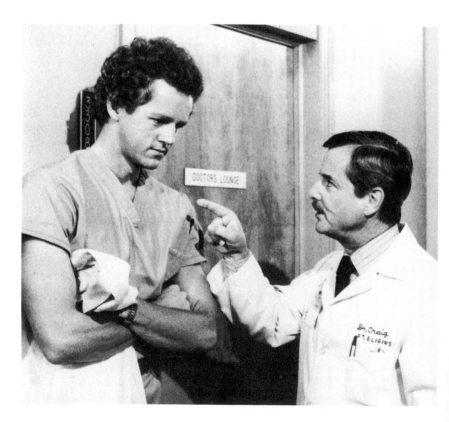

Boston whitecoats: Dr Craig (William Daniels) and Morrison (David Morse) reflect on the demise of Channel 4's *St Elsewhere*

abstracted; perhaps made safer because it takes place 'elsewhere', abstracted but none the less valid . . .

MERIEL LLAND, STUDENT, KINGSLEY, STAFFORDSHIRE

A friend told me to make certain I watch this episode as everything comes to an end. Not that I would consider missing one minute of the mayhem from that batty bunch of crumpled, white-coated, would-be medics who've given me more giggles, gasps and soggy paper tissues than all the weepy 'Who's dying of what disease this week?' television movies put together. No disappointments here . . .

Then it struck again, that sharp sense of *déjà vu*. Surely the last time I felt like this was two *Dallas* series ago, when I blubbered through wads of tissues over Bobby Ewing's untimely demise. Then a disembodied voice-over said: 'Another series of *St Elsewhere* starts in the New Year.' Well, swing my appendix for believing it was last gasp time, and I can't wait to find out how they're going to be brought back . . .

RHONWEN CROFT, RESEARCHER-WRITER-COMPILER, ROCHFORD, ESSEX

THE MEMBER AND THE WHIP
Before embarking on a second showing of its American Football coverage, Channel 4 is repeating the first series of The New Statesman, *originally made by Yorkshire for ITV. This Laurence Marks and*

The Thatcherite hold: Alan
B'stard MP (Rik Mayall)
happily submits himself to
the whips in Yorkshire's
The New Statesman

Maurice Gran episode, Three Line Whipping, *has Tory MP Alan B'Stard
(Rik Mayall) being caught out in a televised election result programme.*

B'Stard makes a fool of himself on TV-am after rushing to get there from
a brothel. He also tries to kill a taxi driver. 'Is this fact or fiction?' I
thought. 'It seems too believably real' . . .
**ALI YASSINE, UNEMPLOYED,
CARDIFF**

The B'Stard character is obsequious, obnoxious, duplicitous and
hypocritical, a characterization that has the appalling ring of truth . . .
**DARRON NORTHALL, UNEMPLOYED,
BRISTOL**

Best laugh of the evening, especially the Thatcher sequence in a taxi . . .
**PRISCILLA MACNAMARA,
LONDON NW6**

The highlight of the evening. I am recording it as well as watching it so I
have the whole series on tape. Rik Mayall is totally brilliant as Alan
B'Stard and the scripts are original, and very funny. I promote it among
friends and we often relive the jokes . . .
**DARYL KAYES, AGED 17,
READING**

I don't normally watch *The New Statesman* because of the lateness of the
hour when it is screened. But as I am staying with my mother at the time
of writing this I was able to watch it. The rules about bedtime are more
lax at my mother's than at my father's . . .
**MICHAEL APOSTOLOV, AGED 15,
LONDON N6**

AS THE SUN RISES IN THE EAST
It is nearly midnight now, and the end of One Day in the Life of
Television. *Let the last word be given to BBC assistant producer Linda
McCarthy. She has had an unprecedented 17 hours, seconded to assist
the Yorkshire Television team covering the BBC Television Centre day.
She alone now knows what it is like to work for both sides at once.*

A rather special day at the fun factory. At 8 a.m., with the rigours of the
Circle Line behind me, I'm greeted by smiling faces at Television Centre.
YTV, eager and raring to go, are unloading their van. Can it really be in
MD Tel's (Paul Fox, Managing Director, BBC Television) parking space?
Will heads roll? I can't wait to see what the day will bring. Peter
Kosminsky, the YTV director, stands on his own, for the moment
redundant. Suddenly his eye lights on Paul Fox and he's off, his crew
padding the regulation four steps behind. They're in business.
    Four crews, one YTV and three BBC, will today film a day in the life of

BBC television. I'm here to make sure all goes smoothly. My thoughts turn to the first BBC crew which, with YTV director Anne Webber, have been on the go since 4 a.m. with *Breakfast Time*. A quick check with the production assistants outside studio two, and all seems to be well at that ranch. Time for the first coffee of the day in a rather dreary, windowless conference room, lost somewhere in the labyrinth of studios and make-up areas on the ground floor of the concrete doughnut. I sit with my feet up on the table, beside a bowl of last night's peanuts spattered with cigarette ash. Is this the glamour I yearned for as a child? The thrill, the excitement of showbiz? . . .

No time to ponder more, it's a dash to meet the third crew, BBC chaps these, loaded with camera and sound boxes and heading for *Top of the Pops*. After a dash to film the weather being transmitted live at 1.30 p.m., just in time . . . Hang on a minute. I've missed out on lunch somewhere! Another check on the YTV crew. All seems quiet on the sixth floor as they follow Jonathan Powell (Controller, BBC1) from one meeting to another. Bright lights under the door, and the sound of softly modulated voices, reassure me. Down to *Top of the Pops* rehearsal, and director Derek Jones is hard at work capturing the flavour of the gallery for posterity. Then the crew is off (after a few final shots in the BBC Club – well, where else do you do better for a final shot?) packing their van, still gracing Mr Fox's space.

The remaining BBC crew dash up to the Duty Office to monitor a few viewers' calls coming in. The crew quite outnumbers those on the phones. It's *Newsnight* next, and once more the equipment is humped down to TC2 to record their offering for the evening. A pause to check out

Northern intruder. A Yorkshire Television van bravely occupies the car parking space of BBC MD Paul Fox while filming the opposition

Network Control and can there really be footsteps on the stairs already? Funny how time goes when . . .

Network control, the heartbeat of the service, are monitoring the transmission of the last programme for the day. It's past midnight now and the screen is still telling us of the joys of computer graphics. The continuity announcer prepares herself for the final announcements in her booth and the cameras turn. At 12.47 and 40 seconds she puts on the National Anthem, not quite standing to attention, and our thoughts turn to home. A few cutaways and it's time to say our goodbyes and thank yous.

We're not alone. A figure glides by the door, the Controller 2 (Alan Yentob, BBC2 Controller, just back from that dinner at Hampton Court Palace) is still on duty. On second thoughts, maybe he's just in early. As the sun prepares to rise in the east, over the bastions of Television Centre, I sneak out of White City and head south. Just another day in the life of television.

LINDA McCARTHY, ASSISTANT PRODUCER

VIII
TWILIGHT OR DAWN

We talk about television, we criticize television, we appear on television, our whole lives are dominated by television, and increasingly our careers can only advance by being good on television. The only thing we don't do is watch television. And that says something.

GEORGE ROBERTSON MP
(LABOUR, HAMILTON)

AROUND THE HOUSE

On 8 February 1989 there was a House of Commons debate on the Government's White Paper, Broadcasting in the '90s: Competition, Choice and Quality. Hardly had Home Secretary Douglas Hurd opened his case, asking the House to 'take note' of the document, than he felt obliged to give way to one of his own backbenchers, Derek Conway (Conservative, Shrewsbury and Atcham).

'Does he accept that some of the comments made about his proposals, notably in television discussions by the media intelligentsia, reject the very reasonable point that he is making, which is that there is not much to be defended, particularly at the BBC, at the moment? Programmes such as That's Life *and* Panorama *would not recognize 'unbiasedness' if it smacked them on the head. There is not a great deal to brag about in the present system, and there is much scope for improvement,' said Conway.*

In a paragraph this MP managed to encapsulate the way most politicians look, or do not look, at television. It is either a medium which reflects their view of the world, or it is indefensible. Yet it is the Derek Conways of this world who have the future of British broadcasting in their hands. They heavily outnumber the handful of MPs who genuinely know and care about television and radio.

On the Conservative side a few will have considered the arguments and may feel faintly troubled as they pass through the 'ayes' lobby. All have had to be persuaded that any new legislation would not lose them too many votes at the next general election, and would not remove the platforms provided by national and regional news and current affairs. Otherwise they will ensure that the Government can order the television future it wants.

All 650 MPs were invited to keep their diaries of One Day in the Life of Television. *Of these 58 replied and seven filled out, or wrote a couple of sentences, on their diary forms. Only Bryan Gould, four years a presenter-reporter with Thames's* TV Eye, *managed to slip out from the debate on health check charges long enough to watch something.*

A typical evening's viewing for me, on the rare occasions when I am able to get to a set. On this evening I was able to get home for a bite to eat, and was able to see the *Nine O'Clock News* before returning to the House for later votes. *Fawlty Towers* was a joy and I try to keep up with *Coronation Street*.

**BRYAN GOULD MP
(LABOUR, DAGENHAM)**

I was unable to watch any television at all, as is the case most days. I see about five minutes a week as a general rule.

**MICHAEL MEACHER MP
(LABOUR, OLDHAM WEST)**

As a busy MP I usually can only have limited television viewing during the Parliamentary week and this particular day happened to be rather more frenetic than usual with my involvement in the campaign to persuade the Government to change its mind on charging for teeth and eye tests . . . Normally I try to pick up an hour's viewing during the evening. *Channel 4 News* is my favourite but if that is not possible I catch the *Nine O'Clock News* or *News at Ten*. For television relaxation I enjoy a good thriller series like *Game, Set and Match* but often have to miss an episode so value the brief synopsis before each programme. Being an opera buff I look for one at the weekend. I do not enjoy panel games or comedy series, except one or two using exceptional comedians. Nature programmes and good films are my choices plus topical current affairs.

**JOHN HANNAM MP
(CONSERVATIVE, EXETER)**

I saw no television on this day, due to work commitments in Parliament . . . But I did video the film *The Childhood of Maxim Gorky* (ITV, 2 to 4 a.m.) which I saw the next day.

**HARRY COHEN MP
(LABOUR, LEYTON)**

I regret that due to the political high drama of the House of Commons today . . . I saw no television at all. If it had been a day in the recess I would have watched News and, possibly with my wife, something in the evening. My children watched children's programmes before tea, and if I'd been at home, I'd have seen what they watched. I'd have hoped to watch the local news, to see if I was mentioned and what issues are going to land on my desk next week. We've often thought of getting a video, but I'd still have no time to catch up on the old tapes.

**DAVID PORTER MP
(CONSERVATIVE, WAVENEY)**

At 10.35 p.m. I saw 30 seconds of an advertisement on ITV, I think about someone's dinner. I saw this in the House of Commons family room while spreading the word on the eye test charges vote.

**MRS LLINOS GOLDING MP
(LABOUR, NEWCASTLE-UNDER-LYME)**

BUILDING THE FUTURE

One feature of the legislation foreshadowed in the White Paper is the winding up of the Independent Broadcasting Authority and the creation of an Independent Television Commission. Armed with whatever powers the Government chooses to give it, this ITC will have the future of all television, apart from the BBC services, in its hands. Soon after publication of the White Paper the Government announced its selection of George Russell as the last Chairman of the IBA and first Chairman of the ITC.

His diary of 1 November is succinct. 'Spent the day in California, visiting plants of Marley plc, of which I am Chief Executive,' he wrote. When at home he was also Chairman of ITN and Deputy Chairman of Channel 4, having previously served on the IBA itself. He was a very rare person, perhaps unique, respected by both the Prime Minister and her ideologues, and the broadcasters with whom he has worked. It seemed essential to ask him to expand on his diary.

Sean Day-Lewis: The White Paper looks to me like a patchwork of ideas, some still half baked, from a variety of sources that do not have a lot of care for broadcasting. Do you find it coherent?

George Russell: It seemed that somebody came along and said that advertising is a monopoly situation and we have got to break that monopoly. First split Channel 3 and 4, then suddenly everybody says a Channel 5 is possible, then there are all these satellites coming along. It is thought that there should be still more access, so let's have a couple of night franchises. Each one of these is a good idea in its own right. All of them together can be overwhelming.

The White Paper comes in with all these ideas and it is technically very hard to argue that they are all wrong. What it seems to do is put the old guard in the position of being very defensive. It's always hard to defend what is. Everybody thinks you are trying to hold on to what you have got. It's hard to bring forward the argument that a change in what is can remove the lot.

Sean Day-Lewis: Who does the Chairman of the IBA or ITC represent? Is it the public or the Government?

George Russell: I will have to represent everybody's interest. You are expected to collect the levies for the Government. You are expected to run the transmitters: effective running of them enables you to be paid. You have to represent the advertisers in some sort of balancing way, to ensure that rate cards aren't used in a monopolistic fashion. You seem to have to represent the public in terms of making sure that the programmes aren't too violent, aren't too sexy, and are balanced.

Sean Day-Lewis: What about programme excellence?

George Russell: That is what the public is supposed to want. The paternalistic view of programme excellence is one that I think we have been very lucky has been accepted for so many years by both those who have been doing the job and those that have been receiving it. The public have been very willing to have the programme shapes that have come through in the last 35 years . . . So there is this representative job where you are supposed to represent everybody, which as you know leads eventually to doom for the person doing it. It's a balancing act all the time.

Sean Day-Lewis: I suppose it is just possible that somebody in Government will take note of the submissions pointing to the flaws in the White Paper. What are the essentials from which the Government will not be budged?

George Russell: Heavens, I don't know these people well enough to be sure which are their real key points, but I do see three major Government thrusts. One is that there should be more competition for advertising, less of a monopoly position. Second, I would think that anything that went back to where we are would not be acceptable. The other one, whether you talk of auctions or tenders, is that the Government wants to find a way of getting a proper sum of money for giving companies a going concern.

The levy on ITV companies should have served, but they all minimize the levy. There is nothing for them to be ashamed of in that, but the corporate tax departments minimize the tax that is paid, and it looks as if the levy hasn't served. Nobody has said this to me but everything points to the fact that there is unhappiness that past levy changes have brought less money in.

Whatever happened it would have been difficult to move from where we are now to 1992. Strangely, the White Paper will probably permit this to happen in an easier fashion. Something was needed to pull the cork out of the bottle where everything had got stuck in these set positions. With all the best will in the world the broadcasters that know it best haven't succeeded in coming up with an effective ITV network system. It's a nightmare, they all know that.

SANS EVERYTHING?

While George Russell prepares to shake the bottle, those inside on 1 November wonder if they will be tipped out, or if the mixture will become so lacking in fizz and body that it can no longer sustain worthwhile life. The first pessimist is Peter Eveson, an Anglia cameraman on location in Strasbourg shooting A Quiet Conspiracy.

As we move towards the end of the day I look around at the assortment of characters who make up the crew (make-up, stage crew, sparks, riggers, wardrobe etc.) and realize how easy it is for outsiders to think that we in television are overstaffed. So many seemingly idle people standing or sitting around, watching one tiny television screen and whispering private chat during the pauses in takes. One day, I thought, it's possible that a show like this will be done with half the numbers, at half the cost, producing half the quality. 'You get what you pay for' is a very true comment. The golden age of ITV is certainly gone forever. I fear a replacement 'dark age' of deregulated, multi-choice cheap crap is soon to relegate British television to moving wallpaper status. In the meantime I'd better check focus again on that zoom in, we're up to take six.

PETER EVESON, SENIOR CAMERAMAN

| *At Television South West an initial shake-up is imminent.*

At 4 p.m. a special meeting of the executive directors, which I had called, to go through and approve the major 'radical change' package which we are planning. This involves job reductions, early retirement, redundancies, cuts in overtime rates, expenses etc. The unions will probably not accept it, but it will be imposed. There is no alternative. At 6.30 p.m. the meeting ends with full support for the package . . .

**IVOR STOLLIDAY, COMPANY
SECRETARY AND DIRECTOR OF
PERSONNEL, TSW**

| *For union man Alan Cridford, at HTV West in Bristol, the blow has
| already fallen.*

A long phone conversation with the personnel officer clarifying the early retirement situation for myself. The company now seems to have a definite policy for reducing the staffing levels which is somewhat selective. I don't like it, but as members of the staff have accepted the situation I am a little powerless to negotiate any improvements, assuming the company would even agree to negotiate.

I talked to my wife this evening about the industry and the current situation. Many of my colleagues are very depressed about the changes that are being forced on us. These are being brought about as a result of the Government wishing to have more control of what is said on television. In plain words, Mrs Thatcher wants all television to become the mouthpiece of the Government. Any Tory Minister wishing to gain 'Brownie Points' attacks television and sets the wolves baying at our heels . . .

Despite what the companies might be saying publicly, most of the ITV managements are actually compliant with all these changes. The main people that are bearing the brunt are, as usual, the members of staff who have little or no ability to change their circumstances. It is not surprising therefore that many staff have decided to leave HTV. The remaining staff are very demoralized. We all love this industry, hate what is happening to it and wonder when will it all end.

ALAN CRIDFORD, SOUND SUPERVISOR

| *As the ITV companies shake out their unwanted ones, perhaps the place
| to be is in independent production. With such enthusiastic backing from
| Government surely these little companies are set to inherit the earth.
| Jane Bigger has been working for Hat Trick Productions on two
| Channel 4 series,* This is David Lander *and* Whose Line is it Anyway?

I think that in this country we still make the best television programmes in the world, and they sell all around the world. We have so much talent and expertise in the industry and, after all, this is where television started. I am very worried that our sets will soon be flooded by more and more cheap, imported, bad programmes, which are just churned out as if from a mass-production line . . . I hope we can continue to make excellent programmes, through the coming changes in the industry, and that expertise will be nurtured, not crushed . . .

JANE BIGGER, RESEARCHER

Is Robert Eagle, of Holmes Associates, any more optimistic?

A day spent pursuing many projects which probably have little chance of becoming television programmes. The work of an independent producer is highly stimulating when you have work, and deeply depressing when you have none. I completed my work on a large drama production three months ago. Since then I have been 'developing projects', the equivalent of an actor 'resting'. It is not a restful activity, however, trying to interest the BBC, Channel 4 and the ITV companies . . .

Though four of my television proposals have brought kind words from potential commissioners, they know and I know that good ideas in this business are abundant. The chances of even a well-thought-out proposal reaching the screen are about 100 to one against. But, like many independents, I prefer to live this way than take a salary from a large employer. Nothing sharpens your wits like the prospect of bankruptcy.

ROBERT EAGLE, PRODUCER

The White Paper will describe the BBC as 'the cornerstone of British broadcasting'. It will also threaten this cornerstone with a change of funding, from licence fee to subscription, which should ensure that the entire edifice collapses. Even now the inmates are not necessarily in high spirits.

The Government's obvious intention to privatize public service broadcasting is the beginning of the end of the two things in which it does serve the public. Farewell freedom of speech and easily available artistic excellence. Here come totalitarianism and profit motive. The new opium of the masses is with us. Sit on your bum, close your mind, square up your eyes and rot. The only hope of escaping the compost heap is that it will be so bad no one will watch any of it. The lute will be taken from the wall, the tongue unglued in the mouth, neighbour shall speak to neighbour and we'll vote for the opposition, if only to get a certain egotist off her throne.

What was it: 'Entertain, inform, and educate'. Here endeth the fun, information, and the lesson. The best broadcasting in the world came from one of the most civilized nations and was vital to its health. It was

Androcles to both Lion and Unicorn. But the beasts have forgotten and are turning and rending Androcles.

**NICK HEATH, MUSIC LIBRARIAN,
BBC WALES**

There are similar worries at BBC Glasgow, where religious researcher Anne Muir feels the cold wind blowing from ITV.

Part of me wants to believe that high-quality programmes will always find a place in the schedules (even post-deregulation). But my natural optimism has been dented by the recent *Highway* affair. The main argument, it seems, for replacing *Highway* with a current affairs programme is not that ratings are poor (a reasonable 7.8 million according to the latest BARB figures), but that the audience (predominantly female and middle-aged to elderly) does not have sufficient buying power to attract advertisers. And if that is so, there will never have been a greater need for religious programmes which will raise questions about the materialistic assumptions of our society. The irony is, of course, that these are the very programmes which the market, by definition, will not provide.

ANNE MUIR, RESEARCHER

Arts producer Keith Alexander has just decided to leave BBC Scotland for London and a music and arts job at BBC Kensington House.

Agree with drama producer Peter Broughan that BBC Scotland, because of its size and relative autonomy, should be uniquely placed to adapt to the New Age. But neither of us is wholly confident that traditional BBC attitudes and modus operandi will alter fast enough. We rhapsodize about our love of film, supposedly a dying medium, but still the most tactile and malleable for crafted programmes . . .

As usual Shakespeare provides the quote of the day, from Jacques' 'All the world's a stage' speech in *As You Like It*. A little pretentious perhaps but, given One Day and this diary, I immediately seize on it as a fitting epitaph for the coming New Age of Television:

> . . . Last scene of all,
> That ends this strange eventful history,
> Is second childishness and mere oblivion,
> Sans teeth, sans eyes, sans taste, sans everything.

**KEITH ALEXANDER, HEAD OF
MUSIC AND ARTS, BBC SCOTLAND**

THE WAY TO THE STARS
As politicians go about saying that the public should receive the kind of television the politicians think fit, and broadcasters similarly hold that the audience should receive the kind of television which the broadcasters think fit, the viewers remain unconsulted. A vote based on

*the returns from One Day diarists produces a large majority in the
'noes' lobby against television change, but there is a minority willing at
this stage to give the satellite entrepreneurs the benefit of the doubt.*

This little black box underneath the set can shut off the nasty gremlins
that seem to send out constant repeats. After all, how many times can you
watch *The Guns of Navarone* or *The Great Escape* without starting to
memorize the script? The video can be a godsend antidote to boredom.
Renting epics from the local outlet is much cheaper than going to the
pictures and far more entertaining. Buying favourite series from previous
showings doesn't cost the earth, unless you lash out on the blockbusters
featuring Joan Collins and her ilk. Videos give you freedom of choice.

   Long live satellite television . . . British offerings are known world-wide
for their quality, especially in the historical sector. Quality and accuracy
are the flagship assets on the box, but because the UK is such a tiny
country, the television channels and choice are limited. North American
television has dozens of channels for different time zones and regions.
You don't get bored and there is plenty of choice . . .
**MS R. A. HIPWOOD, WRITER,
LIVERPOOL**

I think television should have at least 20 channels, and it should not have
commercials. I think it should have a special channel for children, elderly
people, parents, people in hospital and schools. And one with just soap
operas . . .
**LINSEY ROBINSON, AGED 10,
HUYTON, MERSEYSIDE**

As soon as *Rising Damp* ended *Fawlty Towers* started. I wasn't so thrilled
about that because I'd seen it so many times on video I practically knew
the script. It was then I paused to use our satellite dish, our best and most
appreciated facility . . . Constant news from CNN was not to my interest,
constant pop music and heavy metal from MTV did not thrill me either,
everything else seemed to be in German, French or include Des O'Connor.
So I returned to English again . . .
**REBECCA BROWN, AGED 11,
WEM, SHROPSHIRE**

We think that we may have already lived through the golden age of
British television, and fear somewhat for the future. The prospect of
multi-channel viewing in the next decade fills us with misgivings. We fear
that quantity will be at the expense of quality and pray for a strong index
finger to switch off what we don't really want to see. But who knows?
Perhaps, with the satellites, we are heading for the stars?
**CHRISTINE BARNES,
SCHOOL ASSISTANT, LEEDS**

LESS MEANS BETTER
Another constituency believes that there is already too much television.

We're on the cable here and sampled satellite programmes for a few months. We had it taken out, not because we can't afford it, though it is rather expensive at £15 a month, but because cable is just American television and just rubbish. It's all 'lowest common denominator' stuff and I don't want it . . .

ROGER HIGGINS, SCIENTIST,
BRACKNELL, BERKSHIRE

And so to bed. I may have missed good, even excellent things. I hope I did, for it would be nice to know they still existed. But, from what I see, programme-makers lack the courage to raise standards, and they fall back on patronizing the public. Television is spread too thinly over too many hours. It would be better to have two hours a day of prime time television . . .

JAMES SMITH,
LEWES, SUSSEX

My son says I am a television addict. I do enjoy the programmes I watch, but I pick them. I sometimes feel guilty about watching too much, but my viewing usually finishes about 9 p.m. My wish would be that we all have two days a week in which the television stations shut down. This would enable people to go about their lives without worrying about what is on television, and what serial they are missing. Time to talk, relax, go out with the family, play a game, read a book. Sorry, but I think television intrudes into too much space in our lives, and I certainly will not be buying a satellite for more stations . . .

JOAN BRYANT, HOUSEWIFE AND
DOMESTIC CLEANER, SOUTHAMPTON

This miserable Tuesday strongly indicated a television weakness. Is it necessary to radiate 24 hours a day? Would it not be better to radiate two or three hours during daylight and three or four in the evenings, releasing more money to produce good, meaty programmes? We do not expect cinemas, opera houses, sports stadia etc. to function 24 hours a day. Even if it had been a good thing there is not the material or talent or money available to fill the hours . . .

JOHN BULL, RETIRED
HEADMASTER, ROMFORD, ESSEX

NONE IS BEST

For a few the best solution to the increasing number of television hours offered is to have no set at all. At least one non-viewer has contrived to avoid the entire Thatcher era of small-screen news.

I don't have a television. It was a positive decision not to have one. I felt it has more of an effect on the present society and its behaviour than people realize. Values have changed, styles of living altered. These things have occurred rapidly and not much thought goes into its results. I live in a village in mid-Wales. The programmes that are shown here are mainly from America or London, where the money is. There are no role models for people in small rural communities. Points of reference have disappeared. The screen is a fantasy of glamour.

Many grow up believing this is something to be emulated. Today, travelling to work, I venture on to the top deck of the bus in search of a seat, forbidden territory, school pupils only. I hear whispered obscenities at my approach, then the conversation settles into television talk. I overhear the mumble on the latest in *Neighbours* and at Albert Square. Some kids speak of the characters with such familiarity it almost feels like you are eavesdropping on personal gossip, private lives made public . . .

**MR S. EVANS, MUSEUM
TECHNICIAN, LLANDRE, DYFED**

I don't have a television set and today didn't visit anyone who does have one. Why? I can't afford it. Although I am retired I wouldn't have time to watch it; I can't think how anyone has time to sit in front of the box unless they are elderly or sick. I'm not physically capable of sitting in comfort for more than about 20 minutes. I was brought up on radio and listen to it a great deal.

I do not miss having a set in my personal life. I am astonished that television programmes play such a large part in people's conversation. For them television seems to be the real world, and they think I live in an

Mrs Sybil Hopkins of Seaford in Sussex approaches her 101st birthday in a television-equipped rest home called 'Channel View'

unreal one. I take the contrary view . . . Pope remarked, in a letter to Dr Arbuthnot, that we are 'born to write, converse, and live with ease'. I wonder what he would have thought of television?

MISS A. GABELL, RETIRED
UNIVERSITY RESEARCHER, WORCESTER

Tuesday is school, work, bagpipe practice and a prayer meeting. With three young children ours is a busy household . . . We haven't got a telly, in fact we've never had one in nine years of marriage . . . Are our children deprived? Some people think so. We were told authoritatively, by more experienced parents, that a telly would be obligatory when the children started school. Othewise they would be social outcasts and be ignorant of the ways of the world.

The children are full of life and have remarkable imagination, the school comments on it . . . Something large came in a cardboard box and they played for over a year with that box. Last week, for the first time, they converted a shopping cardboard box into a 'television'. They cut out a window and spent several hours colouring in a sheet of paper to act as the screen . . .

At work people discuss last night's programmes . . . Then they all claim it is rubbish and they don't really watch it. Why all the guilt about watching? Why do 'thinking people' not wish to be linked with telly watching, except the nature programmes of course? . . .

DAVID RAFFERTY, PROJECTS MANAGER,
KILSYTH, STRATHCLYDE

I gave up watching television's own product about ten years ago, since which I have watched only bought-in cinema films . . . I don't think I've ever discussed or argued about a television programme with anyone on a bus or anywhere else, though I do often hear people talking about programmes I've never seen. The last time I watched television News, Harold Wilson was Prime Minister. I listen to, but do not necessarily trust, Radio 4 News, otherwise relying on the *Guardian*. Early this year we were burgled: the video was stolen, the television was not. The set was never switched on in the three weeks it took Granada to supply a new recorder . . .

DEREK OWEN, GRAPHIC DESIGNER,
NOTTINGHAM

I now live in the Catalonia region of Spain. I've seen television in the USA, England, France, Germany and Spain. I find it all dreadful. I do not feel that my life has been enriched, in any way, at all, ever, by television. My wife says she can learn things from it. I couldn't. In my childhood I watched television like everyone else. I resent that. I resent that I was living in a world which did not allude to Greek myths, but to *Bonanza* . . .

In my teens I took my homework seriously up in my room while my parents watched television downstairs. They kindly kept the volume down to help my concentration, but it was no use: it makes a ghastly whine that pervades the houses of the possessed. My loathing of television dates from then . . .

I feel that the worthwhile things require effort. Which is exactly contrary to the spirit of television. Come home from work, as likely as not work that induces a 'sub-human condition of intellectual irresponsibility', collapse, press button, watch, pick nose or masturbate . . . My parents used to vote Labour and hold *Coronation Street* in contempt. Now they vote Thatcher and chart the Street's destinies with rapt attention. Is this what getting old is all about? . . .

KEITH ADAMS, CALLIGRAPHER, BARCELONA, SPAIN

I have no television of my own, and see it only at friends' houses. I feel most strongly that the mass communication media, most of all television, is a destructive force whose few valuable contributions are totally overwhelmed by their damaging effects . . . I bitterly oppose the presence of an unnecessary noise producer in a room. I have frequent arguments with people whose constant exposure, to the deadly radiation of garbage rays, renders them immune to their effects, on the surface.

I am appalled by the elevation of television personalities to the status of important or valuable people; as much as I am dismayed by television's belittling of the truly useful . . . I cannot imagine that society would look like it does today without the iron grip of the Spectacle: life lived by someone else, anyone but oneself, and then viewed, consumed, discarded, replaced . . . The ability of television, with its avalanche of images, to sweep away all freedom to think for oneself, is its most insidious and dangerous quality. And I welcome this chance to insert, somewhere in the mountain, a toothpick of dissent.

SIMON GWINNELL, STONE WALLER, PLYMOUTH

I did not watch any television today because I prefer reality. Television absorbs rather than stimulates . . . We cannot hope to change society for the better when more than 90 per cent of the population spend their evenings in their living-rooms around a television set. It will not be long before a more ruthless ruling class takes advantages of this weakness . . .

PAUL RICHARDSON, SHOP WORKER, MANSFIELD, NOTTINGHAMSHIRE

A COFFIN OF COMFORT
The majority welcome television into their homes, but some are more ready to admit to the viewing weakness than others.

People are not themselves under survey conditions, the fact that they are being surveyed will force them to change their habits. A truer test is to survey the men who are at the grass roots of television habits, your local friendly television engineer. In my job, repairing sets in people's homes, I have to listen to endless comment, good and bad, about the programmes of the day.

If there is one thing I have learned in my 28 years in the trade it is that very few people will admit to television addiction. This may be partly to do with the viewer's opinions of what he reluctantly watches; and partly a worry that people who admit to liking television are perceived as inane characters.

Perceptions of different channels often stay fixed. Channel 4 is still regarded by some as being rather avant garde, over the top, even weird; BBC2 is still thought of as highbrow. People who think like this could not name any programme to support their view. Large numbers of the older generation still stick to a single channel, mostly ITV. In my area that means Granada. (I nearly wrote Grandma, as those of that age and gender make up a large part of the Granada audience.)

A favourite complaint of mine is that programme-makers try to push too much into too short a time . . . In these days of high programme costs it should help to leave less on the cutting room floor and put more on the screens . . .

MR A. EASTHAM, TELEVISION ENGINEER, BRIERFIELD, LANCASHIRE

I'm the sort of viewer who bumps up the statistics . . . It's all the lovely documentaries that I really enjoy: *40 Minutes, Out of the Doll's House*, lots of lovely cookery programmes, the wondrous gardening programmes, antique shows, other people's houses, other people's hobbies, other people, architecture, politics (not party), philosophy, the whole wide world in my living-room, from the beginning of time to right now. Also a succession of talking heads, looking right at me – royals, medics, comics, criminals – would that my friends were as diverting . . .

SHELAGH ROBERTSON, TELEVISION WATCHER, WEYBRIDGE, SURREY

Thank you everyone who helps fill my life with events, excitement, laughter, pathos, facts and facts and facts – including amazing demonstrations of how to roll condoms on to fingers. At which my dear mother would have passed clean out with shock or excitement, or something.

FRANCES WEBBER, HOUSEWIFE, CARDIFF

Today is my 70th birthday. I have been a widow for 25 years, stay in most evenings enjoying television. What a marvellous invention: to be able to sit in the comfort of my armchair, press a switch and be transported across the world, seeing the colour and beauty. Never in my wildest dreams as a young girl did I think I would be getting this enjoyment . . .

What pleasure television has given to millions of folk, to some of the elderly it is the only contact with the outside world . . . I am proud to tell friends I'm an addict. A thousand thanks for all my days of television and for being able to record this on All Saints Day . . .

VERA HATCH, PENSIONER, CHELTENHAM, GLOUCESTERSHIRE

**TWILIGHT
OR DAWN**

The black box that sits in the corner of the room looks very innocent, but it has played a great part in changing society and affects us every day . . .
**JOANNA JONES, AGED 14,
RINGWOOD, HAMPSHIRE**

I sit opposite the television set which glows with warmth and excitement. I think of all the programme presenters, quizmasters, entertainers and newsreaders who will appear today . . . Everyone seems to come so alive on the 'box'. I hate that word 'box', to describe a television set, it makes it sound like a coffin. Television is far from a dead end . . .
**GORDON PHILLIPS,
NEWCASTLE UPON TYNE**

At this stage the word 'deregulation' comes into the story. Those in high places, who hope to control 'deregulation', say that it recognizes television's coming of age and frees the industry from bureaucratic control. Sceptics see 'deregulation' as freeing those who hope to make money out of television and, in their own interest, are bound to strangle political dissent. As a fail-safe, 'deregulation' is accompanied by the creation of a Broadcasting Standards Council, invited to further restrict programme-makers on behalf of the puritans.

Granada news manager Barry Flynn thinks that the Government is moving in the right direction.

I'm more worried about Government attempts to censor broadcasters than I am about deregulation itself. As a libertarian (if a leftish one) I don't really see in my heart of hearts why the air waves shouldn't be open to everyone. Historically, British broadcasters have colluded in excluding marginal voices and views from our screens, and it's time their cosy duopoly was exploded. The only thing going for it was that it produced programmes with high production values – probably the best in the world – and of course I don't want to see 'quality' disappear.

But is it really so impossible to allow greater communal access to the means of television production, and to open up the airwaves, without losing all quality programming? I have to say I think it's special pleading: television broadcasting technology just isn't that expensive any more. It used to be, which was the justification for the duopoly, the little man couldn't just start a television station. Now he can and he should be allowed to. If I can produce a magazine in my front room, using a cheap computer and some desk-top publishing software, why shouldn't I compile and broadcast a programme generated on my home VHS set?

If you think these are odd views coming from a Granada employee, perhaps they are. What the Government is proposing doesn't really come close to the utopian situation I describe above, but it's a step in the right direction. Broadcasting shouldn't be any more regulated than editorial expression should be. That British television is good because it's regulated doesn't excuse the fact of regulation. The end, when all's said and done, doesn't justify the means.

BARRY FLYNN, NEWS EDITOR

Viewers who mind about television nevertheless look at the future with foreboding.

In years to come 1 November 1988 may be considered as a day from the

golden era of British television. With the BBC regarded as the best
broadcasting organization in the world, ITV extended to 24-hour output,
and Channel 4 established as a complementary alternative to the other
three channels, British television merits 99 marks out of 100. There is
always room for improvement, but the only neglected tastes are very
specialist. Future developments look likely to result in a decline.
Deregulation will push profit before public service. More channels must
mean the investment in programming is spread more thinly. More
competition is likely to lead to more ratings consciousness and less
diversity. Subscription payment is bound to induce cost consciousness in
the viewer, whereas the licence fee system encourages viewing . . .

**EDDIE HALL,
OXFORD**

To envisage what deregulation could mean for British television, one has
only to look at the appalling standard of British newspapers. Or what
passes for entertainment in the United States . . . There is no shadow of
doubt that the Tory Government move is entirely political. Not only will
they be pleased at the prospect of rich pickings to come, but they will take
considerable comfort from the anticipated removal from our screens of
much political analysis . . . I foresee political dissent being squeezed out
of the mass media into ineffectual ghettos . . .

**KEITH DANCEY, SCIENTIFIC OFFICER,
OXFORD**

The people running television must realize that they have the most
powerful weapon that has ever been invented. They have the most
tremendous responsibility to the general public, and they should fight to
the last breath all forms of censorship and Government interference . . .

**TOM WHITTON, RETIRED,
SHEFFIELD**

I believe that television has a great influence on the way we think. In the
light of this programme-makers should be united and careful in analysing
their stations' relations with certain power groups, most obviously the
Government. If we allow monstrosities such as Clause 28 to become
commonplace, tomorrow's television will be bleak and a mere weapon in
the hands of the haves against the have-nots. As a result our children's
sense of democracy may not relate at all to ours.

**JULIAN McDOUGALL, STUDENT,
SHEFFIELD**

The single truth which seems to me obvious and unchanging is that there
is only one struggle in television: between the principles of public service
broadcasting on the one hand, and the lowest common denominator logic
of television as product, on the other.

You cannot privatize truth or value: you cannot one minute claim our
television to be the best in the world and next subject it to forces which

will reduce it to the level of others; world-wide there is no example where unrestricted market forces produce better television than ours. In fact we sell well because we are different. Cost-effective reasoning would banish most drama, inquisitive documentary-making and, ultimately, minority interest television in any form. Our television should provide service over the whole spectrum of viewer interest, not the sponsor's commercial interest over the whole spectrum of viewerdom.

In other places, other rooms, I would defend television to all comers because I love it. Then on this day of days I open the London *Evening Standard*, page three, and despair. 'SKY TV BRINGING BACK GAME SHOW AT A PRICE'. The prospect of wall-to-wall game shows on British television comes ever closer with the news that Rupert Murdoch's Sky Television plans to resurrect the nearest thing to television bingo, *The Price is Right*. Sky is considering showing the programme, dropped by ITV because it was too down-market, five times a week in a new 30-minute format . . . Sky claims it is third in popularity, behind ITV and BBC1, in those 250,000 or so British homes already receiving cable television . . .

**RAY JENKINS, WRITER,
LONDON W5**

I am perfectly happy with the quality of programmes as they exist at present. What I am most certainly not happy about is the extent of Government interference in the content of some current affairs programmes. Our television and radio was once world renowned for integrity, an export we could be proud about. I am afraid the Government will strangle the carefully nurtured independence of broadcasting, as it has in other areas . . . Why is it that many of those who seem to have a lot of say on how television is run prefer to watch so little?

**DAVID SYMONDS, HELICOPTER
ENGINEER, ALFORD, LINCOLNSHIRE**

Satellite and cable, I firmly believe, will destroy television in this country, in the ways so eloquently put by so many television people. It's strange that the arguments of politicians and money moguls don't sound half as strong, and yet they get their way and we, the poor plebs, suffer. I suppose that's democracy? . . . What I want to know is, who among the British public wants all this satellite garbage? I've heard no groundswell of opinion for it, like you get for hanging, flogging etc. So who is the Government bringing in satellite for? Us, or its friends? . . .

**GARETH HUGHES, SALES EXECUTIVE
AND MEDIA ANALYST, NEWBRIDGE, GWENT**

Knowing the penchant which most governments, throughout the world, have for censorship, how will they manage when international free communication becomes a reality? I must admit to being cynical about these projected new channels. I think they will be the means of importing low-grade rubbish, which will threaten the jobs of those who work to produce our very own, home-grown rubbish. However, it takes all kinds to make a world and if that's what people want, somebody will provide it for them.

**ANTONY BULPIN,
CARDIFF**

We discuss television quite often, lately whether the satellite age will mean a situation such as we have experienced in Canada, 16 channels filled with programmes of an appallingly low standard. The existing UK mix we find very good, apart from the tendency of producers to establish and blindly follow trends . . .

It is not difficult to make a case for control and censorship. A rebuttal has to depend primarily on emotional pleas for freedom of speech and democratic rights. Fortunately, only a rigid dictatorship can exercise effective control. In democracies the rule of law and public opinion is the final arbiter.

Because of its wide appeal and immediate impact television is, to a large extent, self-correcting, provided that broadcasting is not a State monopoly. So far as the majority of viewers are concerned, the function of television is to entertain, divert, inform and amuse its customers. When the producer forgets this and adopts a crusading attitude it has an initial novelty appeal, followed by apathy if not antipathy. And, particularly on commercial channels, no censorship or control is more effective than the viewers' off switch.

**FREDERICK DE FRIAS, RETIRED,
EAST MOLESEY, SURREY**

'Oh well, perhaps we'll get it right next time.' A moment of repose for an Anglia cameraman

Are we to lose public service broadcasting? What a crime it would be if this were to happen. Today's schedules show what a good selection of programmes there are at present, but how long is this to last? Are cheap laughs and cheap thrills good for people? I think that the books a person reads influences that person's character. Surely the same is true of television.

Is the unquestioning acceptance of rubbish good for the British character? No. It will sap initiative, and I am not speaking of Mrs Thatcher's 'everyone can start a grocer's shop' mentality. I mean the initiative towards the improvement of the quality of one's life. It will also further divide the nation into those who are discriminating and those who are undiscriminating, the latter having their brains mashed to pulp by a diet of easily understood, unrealistic storylines, trite dialogue and banal subjects. The British people deserve something better . . .

**MARGARET LITTLEDALE, OFFICE JOB
AT THE MOMENT ALAS, BRIGHTON**

I was a BBC studio cameraman for 28 years until I took early retirement in 1982 . . . There was a period in the early 1960s when the BBC, under the directorship of Hugh Greene, gained a reputation as the finest television service in the world and gave us what many now call 'the golden age of television'. I pride myself as having had some small part in this process, working on programmes like *Hancock's Half Hour* and the original *Z Cars* . . .

As the BBC, and television in general, is now out of favour one cannot expect a return to such a period of excellence. It would be nice, however, if one were to see more good acting and less posturing; and the presenters of programmes talking to the viewer rather than reading from the autocue, a tall order as most of them are completely lost without this aid. Also there ought to be a reduction in the long parade of 'celebrities', many of whom I have rubbed shoulders with over the years and found quite ordinary and very boring . . .

For the future I am afraid I do not have very high expectations. One could be naïve and believe it is all about more choice, one could be cynical and see it as the many friends of the Government about to gain their expected reward – in hard cash . . . It is said, with a good deal of justification, that people get the government and the press they deserve. I am afraid they are now about to get the television they do not deserve.

**MR D. J. THOMSON, RETIRED
CAMERAMAN, WESTBURY, WILTSHIRE**

AN END FOR KISSING

The 'clean-up television' campaign, instituted in the Hugh Greene era by Mary Whitehouse, may be said to have reached its fruition with the establishment of a Broadcasting Standards Council. It is still not clear that the clamorously puritan constituency, for which she spoke, can be sufficiently placated through a Council led by such 'media intellectuals' as Lord Rees-Mogg (chairman) and former BBC and IBA man Colin Shaw (director).

There should be more sport on the television. It's very entertaining and, at least, it doesn't end up with kissing or violence in it. Most things these days are not suitable for young children, even people my age. It's stupid having violence and kissing etc., etc., on the television, as it just encourages youngsters. But I suppose violence and kissing is life these days . . .

**SARAH FINDLAY, AGED 11,
DUMFRIES**

Violence and sex are on the increase in television, so is it any wonder that today's children are as badly behaved as they are. The youth of today will be tomorrow's adults . . . It makes me sad to see this deterioration of standards in television and I hope that, with the expansion in the number of channels, I can still have a choice of good, decent, clean programming to watch.

**MARTYN TAYLOR, VT OPERATOR,
ORPINGTON, KENT**

While I have the opportunity, may I say that I have become concerned

over the last few years about some of the sex scenes and bad language
that has crept into many programmes. Unless someone is a complete idiot
it doesn't seem necessary to show people naked, half-naked or whatever,
simulating sex. I, as an adult, know what happens and don't have to see it
portrayed.

I also feel I shouldn't have to have someone swearing in the corner of
my room, any more than I should have to tolerate someone swearing
while sitting next to me on a bus shall I say. And I don't pay an arm and a
leg for a television licence to switch it off if I feel offended by something,
or turn to another channel to watch something which may be boring or
equally offensive . . .

**JULIE PERRIN, UNEMPLOYED,
GOSPORT, HAMPSHIRE**

We haven't now got a television set and I didn't watch any today . . .
Television (and other media) have made sex into a spectator sport and
screen violence and death a commonplace. For most of us life is not at all
really like that. I used to feel uncomfortable sitting down with my teenage
children (I have five children altogether) and finding, as we watched a
play or film, that together we were witnesses to characters simulating
making love. In life it's generally not a public activity, but something you
experience rather than witness.

As for violence, whatever the researchers say about the connection
between screen violence and violence in society, it seems clear to me that
if we want our children to be non-violent and respectful of others, then
we should not colonize their imagination with the fantasies of violence
that are available to them all the time if they watch much television . . .

**JANET TYRRELL, FREELANCE
PUBLISHERS' EDITOR, RUTHIN, CLWYD**

I went out to dinner this evening. If I had been in I would have watched
Floyd on Britain and Ireland and *Wildlife on One*, provided I was not
preached at by some environmental fanatic. I never watch the News on
television, it is heavily biased against decent behaviour and patriotism.

**MR P. BARNISH,
SEMI-RETIRED CHARTERED ENGINEER,
HALIFAX, YORKSHIRE**

I work at BBC Norwich and this week I am doing location camerawork
. . . I was told we had a job in Colchester this afternoon and, using our
own car phone, reporter Michelle Newman arranged with Mary
Whitehouse our expected time of arrival at her house in Ardleigh . . .

We arrived at Ardleigh about 4 p.m. and, as it was starting to get dark,
we decided to do the interview indoors. The job was rather unusual as we
were doing it for BBC Bristol, but ours not to reason why . . . We were all
crammed close together, the office contents not allowing us much room to
move. After we started the interview a bulb blew, and we had to start
again. Thank heavens for everyone's patience. After the interview we did
a few cutaway shots of papers on Mary's desk and she did a piece to

camera for the Children in Need appeal.

I like Mary Whitehouse. As we packed the gear away in her kitchen we had a discussion about the soaps on television. I asked her for some forms about her National Viewers and Listeners Association . . .

**GERARD KELLY,
SENIOR TECHNICAL OPERATOR**

I resent Mary Whitehouse and all her works. As a 58-year-old, I reckon I know what I want to see. I don't need her, or any of the other puritanical guardians of the nation's morality, to tell me if a particular programme is suitable for me.

**JOHN GOODE, UNEMPLOYED,
WELSHPOOL, POWYS**

I don't think censorship of any description is right. I am not particularly well educated but I can monitor my own and my children's viewing. It seems a shame that a noisy minority, such as Mrs Whitehouse, forces ideas on us, the quiet majority . . .

**MRS P. A. POZZI, HOME CARE ASSISTANT,
CHESTER**

My big grouse is that present television politics treats me like a child. Adult films, even those on late, have sudden cuts (for commercials) at erotic moments. Some are cut before being shown. Too many people are playing God. There is nothing obscene in the human body naked, or in love-making. The obscenities to me are starving children while food mountains grow, homelessness and slums, closing of cancer wards and hospitals, long waiting lists for operations, war (those that start them should fight), killing and corrupt government, hypocritical MPs and those supposed to be leaders . . . I wish these people who set themselves up to dictate what I watch would acquire the Swedish view of sex. The Swedish films of the 1960s were funny and sexy but are never seen now. All humour is going out of the country. I worry where it will all end.

**DEREK NIXON, ARTIST,
LONDON W3**

Madeleine Barnett came round this morning briefly to tell me that William Rees-Mogg had sent a letter to our union (ACTT) asking for our thoughts on sex and violence on television for his Standards Council. We need to draft some kind of response. I don't know whether the whole silly business is worth bothering with but if we don't get our views across then the Mary Whitehouses of this world will hold sway and all television will become suitable for less intelligent 9-year-olds.

It grieves me how childish people are about television generally. The only kind of bad language there is, is if it's ungrammatical and incomprehensible. Saying 'fuck' and the like is no big deal, especially in context, yet people get hysterical about it. I think it's a way of deflecting attention away from the real substance of a play, documentary or whatever.

The same with sex on television. People only get upset because there's such an immature attitude in the country as a whole about sex. So people who wish to stop other people from expressing sometimes uncomfortable, disagreeable or joyous truths about human relations and experience, can highlight this one area and use it to prevent other messages getting through. This isn't to say I think people get things right all the time or that the depiction of sex and violence, especially when they are together, is always right. But it isn't the tremendous problem Rees-Mogg seems to think it is . . .

It makes me angry that television is still put down in the way it is, as not being quite okay, and how it is said that people are enslaved. It is absurd to think that people are incapable of switching off, if they don't want to watch something, or that they cannot choose what to watch in the first place. I suspect there's a certain amount of cultural snobbery at work here . . .

**THERESA FITZGERALD,
WRITER-JOURNALIST, LONDON NW1**

Many people complain about sex, violence and drugs on television. I feel these have to be shown because they are part of life, whether we like it or not. If they are all cut out think what it would mean. At one end of the scale there is *Coronation Street*, cut because of the drinking in the Rovers Return. At the other end there are cartoons like *Tom and Jerry*. These show Tom constantly being beaten up by Spike the dog . . . Will we have to watch the BBC test card all day? . . .

**JENNIFER JORY, AGED 15,
REDRUTH, CORNWALL**

Satellite television will not offer more choice: this is a fallacy. It will only give us more to reject. Nor will it pollute our minds. No, the danger won't come from that direction. The real danger comes from that frightening self-appointed group of censors who use their ignorance and narrow views as a yardstick with which to beat the rest of us. Of course, this sort of campaign is backed up by a hypocritical tabloid press and a culturally deprived Prime Minister.

The bottom line is that what is disliked or not approved is labelled 'filthy' or 'subversive', so that debate is stifled, so that any sense of proportion or perspective in our society is flattened. From this follows intolerance and bigotry. Television, which can embrace many views and opinions, even possibly break down prejudices, may yet be forced into a quasi-state-run, propagandist medium for a government and its unthinking supporters, who cheat by changing the rules under the guise of democracy. It is the responsibility of television to fight this incursion with all its might.

**PETER JAMES, BOOKSHOP MANAGER,
LISKEARD, CORNWALL**

Censorship takes on a new meaning today. The newly formed Broadcasting Standards Council is quite frightening. Television is after all show business, and the acumen needed to control it, and the standards it follows, cannot, I believe, be provided by a small group of people selected from the list of the 'great and the good' by the Government. Let the public decide what is or is not acceptable on television, and the ratings be the final arbiter . . .

MR A. F. WEBSTER,
BROMLEY, KENT

COLOUR BARS
At Lewes Prison in Sussex there are additional restrictions. Weekday television viewing for the 560 inmates is contained in the 'evening association' period between 5.45 and 8 p.m. Stephen Plaice is the present 'writer-in-residence'.

I get into the nick about 9 a.m. While moving along the landings I pass the C wing television screen, standing imperiously on its stilted trolley. It is ten feet tall, and an Orwellian sight during evening association. Then it looks over depressed cons, slouched in their low-slung armchairs, flooding them with bright images of an outside world some have not seen for more than two decades . . .

There are homely criticisms of the permitted programmes. They think Dirty Den's current prison experience in *EastEnders* is very unconvincing. 'The screws would never get away with that sort of wind up' – 'Den should know better, he's done bird himself' . . . A week hardly ever passes without the evening news flashing up gratuitous shots of inmates leaning morosely over the landings of an over-crowded Victorian jail, like heavies. Television can never accurately reflect prison life, however, because that life is actually a separate culture. You have to live or work in the prison to understand it.

Today the cameras want to come in again. Both BBC South and TVS have picked up the news item about our involvement with the One Day project on the local radio. They want to send in camera crews at the drop of a hat, presumably to film inmates watching television or filling in their diaries. 'Television looking up its own arse', as one of the cons comments. The prison management resists these belated requests and one of the journalists gets quite heated about this refusal, starts ranting about the public's right to know . . . Television people do seem to consider they have a divine right to breeze into anyone's backyard when they wish . . .

But I shouldn't complain. TVS have funded my writers' residency here, for the last two years, and they made a very sensitive documentary film about the work I do here. When the crew came to film that, one of the inmates slipped them a blue and white striped shirt so that the TVS newscaster could read the news that night wearing a Lewes prison shirt ...

Working partly in the anti-naturalistic medium of theatre, and in a prison, where you daily get to see the bottom line of society's problems, I am hypercritical of television as a vehicle of entertainment and of reportage. Mostly I see it as a superficial medium geared to a superficial

Porridge watch. Prison
television viewing is
permitted during 'evening
association'

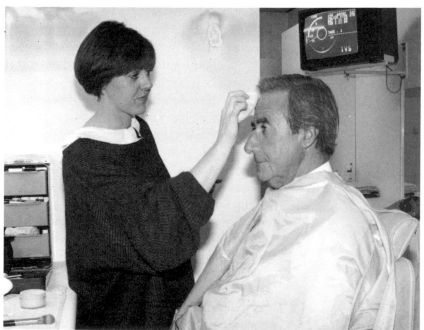

Shaw Taylor of TVS's
Police 5 is fitted up . . .
'rubbing salt into an open
wound'

age. It's a self-contained and self-contented world too, though many
imagine it is the larger world beyond the confines of their insignificant
lives, as prisoners do.

It is self-important, like that great monster standing on its hind legs in C
wing, spouting a mixture of information and implicit attitudes, which you
hear garbled the next day in the pub, read rehashed in the tabloids, or
even hear talked across the landings of C wing. Like the mediaeval
church, like the 19th-century press, it is an instrument of control, first and
foremost, and its major tactics are generalization and trivialization. But
the extent of its institutional power can be measured by the effect it has
had on my life today, which I have recorded here. Yet I have not seen a
single frame of television all day.

**STEPHEN PLAICE, WRITER,
BRIGHTON**

> *Prisoner John Williams is described as the institution's guru and scribe.
> He's been on television and radio talking about, and reading extracts
> from, his prison diary and autobiography. 'It's hard to remember he was
> an armed robber before he took to writing,' records Stephen Plaice.*

The two television sets placed high on wooden stilts begin their evening
stint of distraction for the desperate, when the cell doors are unlocked for
two hours of what is euphemistically referred to as 'association'. A few
prisoners, who prefer the isolation of little contact with their neighbours,
drift towards the hard functional chairs. They are like sullen kids on a
stony beach, who have long since grown weary of the charms of the
Punch and Judy show.

To be seen watching the television at such an early hour is an admission
of failure. Everybody knows that the real entertainment begins when the
children are safely tucked away in bed; that the only possibility of drama
and involvement with what appears on the screen, might occur with the
Six O'Clock News and a report about some gruesome sexual offence
committed by some hapless individual receiving a hefty long prison
sentence. If this occurs it will provide the one opportunity, during the
evening's viewing, for the manufacture of ritual solidarity. Another
deliciously bizarre occasion when incognito sex offenders, murderers and
thieves, all metaphorically join hands and sit as a mob of righteous
citizens, pouring scorn and abuse on the offender shortly to be admitted to
our ranks.

John Ruskin once said: 'In order for people to create beautiful things
they first need to be surrounded by beautiful things.' It takes no great
imagination to perceive the long-term benefits which might occur if this
maxim was applied to the bleak environment which brutalizes even
further the psyches of men in prison. With this thought in mind and with
a few minutes to 'unlock' I peruse the pages of the *TV Times* and *Radio
Times* for a preview of this evening's limited diet.

Who is in charge of scheduling at TVS? Is someone trying to make a point to Her Majesty's guests? Shaw Taylor, *Police 5*, that's like rubbing salt into an open wound. I think I'll give it a glance, might after all see someone I know. The following programme is called *Prove It*. I wonder if Fat Bob, three cells away, will be watching. He has been using the same words for 12 years now. I know *EastEnders* is on. Sometimes I laugh openly at the BBC's sincere effort to portray Dirty Den in a realistic prison setting. Their mistake has been to focus on the extremes of such an environment, and unfortunately from a negative perspective. Still, if it provides a chuckle the evening isn't completely wasted . . .

I've just returned from the evening's entertainment. I don't think I saw anything of great beauty. There was a documentary about British cities, which nobody wanted to watch, so with the prison settling down for the long night ahead, I'll have a glance through the programmes I'm missing and content myself with the hope that by the year 2000 television sets will be optional extras in every prison cell.

**JOHN WILLIAMS/IAN SIMMONS,
WRITER, LEWES PRISON**

I didn't watch any television programmes today. I would have watched *American Football* on Channel 4, but at 11.30 p.m. I'm locked up in a cell and haven't access to the telly. I like the atmosphere that the game creates and the cameras are used to good effect in that not only do you see the action on the pitch, but also the 'drama' off it.

I did watch a Bond film on the video this afternoon, *Diamonds Are Forever*. It'd been taped some while previously off the television. Great film. Connery was at his best and looked the 'mean machine', until he took his shirt off that is. Didn't look like Adonis to me, and that spoilt the idea of Bond a little . . . I enjoyed watching the film and so did the other prisoner who watched it with me. We laughed a lot at the corny bits and at the blasé way with which he went about his duties . . .

**RICHARD DENNICK, PAINTER,
LEWES PRISON**

IN THE PRISON OF OUR DAYS
Television is also a comfort for those imprisoned by disability or bereavement, even to people obliged to take a sideways look.

As usual the television was the most important thing in my day, apart from my husband. Being disabled with chronic back pain I watched from a sitting-room bed lying on my right side. My television stands on its side so that it is the right way up for me lying flat . . . My husband came home in the middle of *Neighbours* as usual, and so he managed to see some of it with me. He lies on the floor to watch . . .

**KATHERINE HUDSON, DISABLED,
MORETON-ON-LUGG, HEREFORDSHIRE**

I am a hospital social worker mainly dealing with elderly patients. Some are housebound and when asked how they cope alone they say that television is their 'company'. I think this is sad, but some of the people are really thankful for it. I visit a young disabled man who spends most of his day in front of the television. Now his hands are getting stiffer and he finds it almost impossible to work the remote control. He mostly uses his set to watch videos, as do a lot of my bed-bound or housebound clients . . .

ANNA MINERS, SOCIAL WORKER, LONDON E15

Television is a window on the world for me and a help in daily life, as I care for a friend with pre-senile dementia. Both off-air programmes and video recordings keep her interested while I am busy . . . We watch *Blockbusters* regularly, my friend can follow a quiz . . . *EastEnders* is too involved for my friend to follow easily and I am not keen on the characters . . . *Fawlty Towers* is interrupted by nurses coming to put my friend to bed. I switch on her set and continue watching in the sitting-room . . .

HESTER LEE, RETIRED TEACHER, EXMOUTH, DEVON

Television is an absolute boon for the lonely. At a flick of the switch one's room can be peopled. When my husband died 10 years ago, the loneliness was dreadful. I never heard my own voice for days as there wasn't anybody to speak to . . . I remember many sleepless nights and the utter relief when the sunrise opening of early morning television meant that there were other people awake in the world besides me. It really was a godsend in the early years . . .

IVY RYALLS, RETIRED, ALVASTON, DERBYSHIRE

COMMERCIAL BREAKINGS
Some are willing even to take note of the commercials as they look out at their 'window on the world'.

I am 75 next birthday and have osteoarthritis, and some heart trouble, so I am in a wheelchair both indoors and out. I see much more television than the normal person. I have a window on a world I can rarely visit or take part in now. There is fun and laughter when life is lonely and frustrating, and items of interest when we feel in more serious mood, and sometimes it gives us the opportunity to sharpen our brains . . .

As for the adverts . . . We who are on pension welcome the fact that we don't have to pay for ITV, and would willingly put up with any amount of advertising for that. It is not easy to live on the old age pension these days, in spite of what certain lady politicians say . . . I find the advertisements in good taste, and well thought out, and have fun discussing them, and the programmes of course, when I go to my club on Thursdays . . . I must admit it does make me wonder where one buys these fabulous things advertised; like the washing machine that turns out clothes that are not only ironed but look as if they have been folded as well. I should like a machine like that . . .

**IVY PARKER, HOUSEWIFE WITH HELP,
WESTON-SUPER-MARE, AVON**

Sound is important to me as I am mostly blind. Do you know that the quality of broadcast sound from the BBC is very high? . . . The sound on IBA channels is not so good. Their sound pressure levels vary tremendously between and sometimes within programmes. One always knows when commercial interludes are imminent. The level takes a dramatic increase and compression is applied to make the sound component uniformly loud, immediate and, I imagine, persuasive. Television commercials are a true exercise in high-pressure selling – at least from the aural point of view . . .

**CHRISTOPHER BRIDGMAN, PIANO
CONSULTANT AND JOURNALIST,
WINDSOR, BERKSHIRE**

I would like to see advertising restricted to factual information, in contrast to the highly ridiculous, facile and expensive montage that is now the vogue on television, with each agency trying to outdo the other in putting across the attributes of a bag of crisps, a bottle of lager . . . or worse still the blandishments of a supposedly responsible bank or insurance company treating what is a serious financial transaction in a completely facetious manner.

**JACK MOFFATT, RETIRED,
LONDON W5**

Our favourite participation viewing is to watch the commercials with the sound off, fitting in our own voice-overs, or trying to guess what the advert is all about, good family fun . . .

**MR F. C. McMAHON, RETIRED,
HILLSBOROUGH, CO. DOWN**

TOO OLD AT 40?

Sexism, meaning female belittlement, is now stamped upon wherever it shows its arrogant or innocent face. Could ageism, meaning wrinkle belittlement, now become a fashionable target?

And yes, there was the first of my programmes, the right channel, the right time, and all managed by mother, all by herself . . . Usually any adult over 40 has a mysterious relationship with the world of video technology. They only have to approach a machine and it ejects tapes left, right and centre, begging to be programmed by their 10-year-old child, who can ensure a recorder will tape every episode of *Neighbours* for a fortnight, while they are on holiday . . .

**STUART MACRAE, STUDENT,
AGED 19, GLASGOW**

I am 82 years of age and as a youngster I had one of the very first crystal sets. I have never ceased to be interested in radio and television . . . A sore point with me is the discrimination by the planners re the young and the old. Why can't we also have the chance to take part in game shows? I've campaigned for this and sent applications, but when one returns the questionnaire stating one's age etc. there is never a reply . . .

**CLAUDE WALKER, RETIRED,
NEWCASTLE-UNDER-LYME, STAFFORDSHIRE**

Bill Oddie, 'Some extra, slightly grumpy, thoughts on television'

Some extra, slightly grumpy, thoughts on television as it involves (or doesn't) me these days. Sure, I'm working quite a bit in a variety of areas. But, considering that I have written/co-written and appeared in many, many hours of, I think, popular television in the past, I think it is permissible to express a soupçon of irritation. I find myself 'scuffling' as if I were a beginner most of the time.

One ingredient that I think has definitely become more insidious in recent years is ageism. This particularly applies among producers and heads of comedy when 'non-straight' sitcom is concerned. I have actually heard it expressed as: 'If you're over 35 it can't be funny.' This is obviously a bit daft, tell it to anyone from the Marx Brothers to Milligan. It's rather as if, after a 'certain age', you have to consign and resign yourself to the cosy backwaters of safe domestic comedy or, worse still, panel games. Personally, no thanks . . .

**BILL ODDIE,
WRITER-COMPOSER-ACTOR, AGED 47**

THE MEDIUM IS THE MESSAGE
For many viewers, perhaps the majority, the fact of television, and its place in our lives, matters much more than any of its messages.

I use television programmes I enjoy as a 'reward' for having done some of my work. As I am a mature PhD student I often have no outside pressure to get the work done (apart from the grant ending in two years' time). Television and radio are part of my internal reward system, not only for academic work but also for routine domestic work . . .

**MONICA DOWLING,
POSTGRADUATE STUDENT, SHEFFIELD**

The television set is the focus of my aggression towards my children in the house. When they were small *Play School*, *Rainbow*, and *Sesame Street* provided moments of peace for us parents and enabled meals to be prepared, fires to be lit safely, quick dashes to the milk box over the field, and telephone calls of some coherence. Now I'm paying the price: children who flick the on switch automatically each time they enter the room, children who have to be driven out to play on sunny Saturday mornings, endless plot summary monologues about inane comedies.

Do you put your television in the warm room of the house to provide a comfortable environment, or could you turn off all the heat to drive viewers away? No use, they wrap themselves in sleeping bags and doze in front of deliriously happy bright young things throwing water and paper at each other. I once removed the fuse, but my husband replaced it to watch football. Is there a miracle time-switch with a monitor, so each child watches just an hour a day? Perhaps the set should be placed in a very small, totally bare room, on a shelf high enough to ensure that all viewers had to stand to watch . . .

My children know far more about the world than I did at their age, but I wonder how far the knowledge is fully absorbed, and whether it is adequate compensation for the passivity engendered by such convenient entertainment. Furthermore, parental control is a myth when your children simply cross the garden to sit in front of a neighbour's television if you turn yours off. Or are these just the complaints of a working mother who has allowed the television to compensate for her abdication of the role of companion?

**MRS O. MULLEN,
NORWICH**

I do watch a lot of television most days as it is very rare that I go out in the evening, and I have recently found myself with nothing to do during the day. I live alone with my mother, so it's the television or nothing.

**TRACY STANGER, UNEMPLOYED, AGED 18,
SHOTTON COLLIERY, CO. DURHAM**

There was a programme about the brain. Now that I am studying anthropology I can justify watching nearly anything on television and this was definitely anthropological. It was very good too, as such programmes almost invariably are. Don't ask me anything about it, though. Why is it always impossible to remember a single thing about what you watch on television?

Once I child-minded two children who were almost overcome with guilt every time I came into the room where they were watching television. I was actually quite pleased that they were not practising the cello or knocking holes into their father's garage, but they did not realize this. My own taboo against uncreativeness was a lot less than theirs, and is diminishing still. So perhaps it is fortunate that I cannot pretend to myself that I am learning anything as I goggle.

**TIM FRANCIS, UNEMPLOYED,
BELFAST**

It's funny, but I had never liked David Coleman until he appeared as quizmaster in *A Question of Sport*. It is good to see his true personality coming out. For me this is unusual as I have always felt that a personality shows through on television as quickly as it does in real life; that you like or dislike people on television just as you take an instant liking or dislike to people you meet. I want to put my fist through the television screen when some people are on, but I usually resist and turn it off instead . . .

**ANN FRETWELL, REPRESENTATIVE,
ELY, CAMBRIDGESHIRE**

I like television. I like it for the same reasons that many other people have for disliking it. They tell me that I am being brainwashed, that my powers of conversation and independent thought will atrophy and that my body will age prematurely as my mind is lulled into a state of passive quiescence. I tell them that I am having my horizons broadened, that learning to listen carefully is essential to good conversation and that a few quiet evenings at home each week may be better for health than seven evenings crammed full of worthy activity.

Six years ago I did not own a television set. Work and 'leisure' kept me away from home an average of ten hours a day, seven days a week. I was also off sick an average of three hours a week. Perhaps a little bit of 'vegetating in front of the box' would have helped my body to recover . . .

**JACQUELINE STEVENS,
SOCIAL WORKER, BRISTOL**

Although I watch very little television, an average of seven or eight hours a week out of the cricket season, I find it attracts my attention like a magnet. At someone's house, or in a bar, where a television is on, I have to watch it, however ghastly the output, in preference to any conversation, however interesting. If anyone arrives at my home, when the television is on, I have to turn it off before they can get any sense out of me. Homes where the wretched thing is left on as a permanent background are anathema to me. How odd that I cannot ignore it.

Someone once said that television was a medium because it is neither well done nor rare. Funny, but unfair. One cannot so lightly dismiss something with the range to encompass, at one end, the incomparable *Brideshead Revisited* (to me television's finest achievement) and, at the other end, the gruesome spectacle of Leslie Crowther conducting hours of cheerful, ritual humiliation of the loud and greedy, to the sickening cry of 'Come on down'.

**PHILIP WARREN, BARRISTER,
BATH**

The nature of my viewing has changed a lot. As a small child, growing up in rural Ireland, I had two different viewing experiences. Our village school class used to pack into the headmistress's parlour to watch any especially important educational programmes. At home we used to have people round on a Saturday night, just to watch such programmes as *Juke Box Jury* or *Six-Five Special* on one of the few sets in the village. Both were communal viewing experiences. Both were experiences which had something almost mystical about them. People stopped everything to watch pictures in black and white, of uncertain quality, using camera techniques that now look amateurish and clumsy.

Now my television viewing is much more erratic, and tends to be done at the same time as something else, whether it be eating (no, not breakfast television, that's too much for my morning state of mind), knitting, sewing, making phone calls or even reading . . . As television has become technologically more remote it has also become more accessible. Everybody has the opportunity to be 'famous for 10 minutes' and we can see friends and family appearing on the box, ordinary people looking quite unlike you used to have to look to take part in the magic world of television . . .

**ELIZABETH PENNY,
DRAMA ORGANIZER, BELFAST**

A look back over the day's viewing. At work, I use the television to present texts and ideas to pupils. It's a medium they feel comfortable with – much more so, in many cases, than with the written word. Shakespeare, even, if he's on television, gets some street cred. I suppose it's silly to feel saddened by this, but I do. I also help to bring it about, I offer the television as a sop, a palliative. 'Look!' I cry, by implication. 'It's OK, you'll like it, it's on this small screen here!' And they can all work the video more efficiently than I can. They are very kindly about it. 'It's OK, it's only the tracking, I'll see to it,' they soothe.

At home, I demand entertainment from the television. I read a great deal, think, work hard at school things in my house, and if I'm going to go up all the stairs to the television, it is not with a sense of duty that I wish to go, but with a sense of pleasure anticipated and even a hope that I will have fun. I know, too, that I treat the television – The Box – like a Puritan would a box of sweets. If I consume too much, I feel glutted and guilty. Sometimes a hard-centred, bitter selection gives sophisticated pleasure. More often, conscious of self-indulgence, I select a limited ration of the most appetizing flavours. Too much cloys. A taste untried is not missed. It is absurd and unhealthy to treat it as the staff of life.

**JANE LINDSAY,
TEACHER, LONDON SE10**

I nearly always discuss the previous night's viewing at work. I have found it a very useful topic when interviewing candidates for a job. People will open up and feel relaxed when talking about what they like to watch, and I will now only employ people who seem to like the same sorts of programmes. If a candidate said they watched sport and soap operas mostly, I'd know they wouldn't fit in with the rest of the team – which is most important. Television is a very binding medium, when people live such different lives . . .

**LYNNE FARRAR, INFORMATION MANAGER,
LONDON W2**

THE BAIRD TON
This is the centenary year of John Logie Baird who, in 1926, gave the first demonstration of a television image. He is not forgotten.

All I say is that so much of our television is useless and not worth watching. We want far more programmes that are worth watching and cheaper emissions the rest of the time. Then we'll all be able to take advantage of the good films and this marvellous invention John Logie Baird bestowed on us . . .

**KARL JEFFERY, AGED 15,
COWBRIDGE, SOUTH GLAMORGAN**

From the 'impossible dream' of John Logie Baird we can now, in the spirit of Shakespeare's Puck, 'Throw a girdle round the earth . . .' in a lot less time than was originally suggested . . .

**PHILIP LEIGHTON,
COMPUTER OPERATOR, SUTTON COLDFIELD**

This is the centenary of my late husband's birth, at The Lodge, Helensburgh, in 1888 . . . I have been busy doing programmes for Scottish Television . . .

**MARGARET BAIRD,
HAMILTON, STRATHCLYDE**

A Mickey Mouse medium? Early television viewing really was a shared experience

25 A MESSAGE FOR
THE MEDIUM

In the House of Commons broadcasting debate, mentioned at the start of this section, the Home Secretary pronounced himself 'glad of the way in which the BBC, in contrast to some of its friends, has reacted to the White Paper'. Douglas Hurd is a politician who speaks in emollient tones and likes others, however threatened, to pitch their public discourse at the same well-bred level. Those in command at the BBC, managers as well as the trusties forming the Government-selected Board of Governors, consider the softly, softly style to be politic.

Thankful for any reprieve, the BBC knows it will survive the next round of broadcasting legislation. This is confirmed by Hurd as he repeats the now familiar phrase about the BBC 'remaining the cornerstone of public sector broadcasting'. He concedes it another five years of licence fee income before it is required to raise its funds by subscription. Like anybody else who gives this plan a moment's thought, he knows that subscription is a device that will destroy the public service cornerstone, existing to make the best available to all, as surely as any direct demolition.

As a first step the proposed legislation is likely to leave the BBC in impoverished isolation. The new Channel 3, to replace ITV, will not have the means, much less the incentive, to offer the BBC any further competition in excellence outside the most popular programme areas. Channel 4, denied its present link with ITV, will have to measure its innovation against its need to survive in the market place.

As 1988 moves into 1989 the nation is apparently in resigned mood, television people and their viewers as much as anybody. The wider disintegration of political opposition has had far-reaching effect. As the ever more zealous cleansing operators, from Thatcherite ideologues plc, career about our painstakingly evolved institutions, there is a feeling that those who speak quietly enough might just escape the dreaded brush for a little while longer. But only for a little while. Television, it seems, has already had its golden ages and such things cannot be permitted again.

The message from the viewing public, as represented by the thousands of diarists who helped to record *One Day in the Life of Television*, is of diffused but nearly unanimous dissent. Contributors do not suggest that existing arrangements are flawless, there are lots of complaints; but through almost every diary runs the implicit acceptance that BBC1 and BBC2, ITV and Channel 4, should and *could* deliver what a discriminating public wants. And, if nothing else, the weight of diaries demonstrates that there is a lot of discrimination about.

Wanting to represent in this book every strand of opinion, I looked carefully for diaries commending deregulated market forces as a means of providing either genuinely different programme strands or improved production values. I could not find one, not even from any of the few Conservative MPs who acknowledged our invitation to participate in One Day.

Looking towards the future from Tuesday 1 November 1988, it is clear that the status quo is not an option. Even a national dictatorship would be hard pressed to prevent the satellite transmissions of determined operators from being seen by all the people all the time. The British Government has to recognize the new age of broadcasting and, at least, propose realistic institutional change to meet whatever is now unavoidable.

It may be rational to argue that, as far as possible, broadcasting outlets should be restricted, because talent and finance are finite and become less effective when more thinly spread. In the long run such restriction could only postpone the inevitable multiplication. Though the majority of diarists look with foreboding at what multi-channel television may bring, a substantial minority relish the possibilities, if only in the hope that sport may be banished to its own ghettos.

If Margaret Thatcher and her Ministers were content to welcome new channels, viewers could have no reasonable quarrel. But it appears that they are using the arrival of the satellite era as a pretext to sweep away, or undermine, existing institutions. At a time when they are paying much green-tinted lip service to the cause of environmental conservation there is a compulsion to attack the broadcasting heritage as though it were an active evil.

The word 'quality' is spattered all over the White Paper, used with so

One Day diary prizewinners meet the *EastEnders*. At the front, adult winner Stephen Pegg and under-12 winner, Sing Yu Jackson. Back row (from left) Sara Smith (teenage winner), Gillian Taylforth, Mike Reid, George Nicolis (Pegg family friend), Pam St Clement, Corinne Hollingworth (associate producer) and Bill Treacher

many meanings that it is soon rendered meaningless. In the subsequent debate the 'quality threshold', towards which the new Channel 3 franchise holders must genuflect, has been raised to a 'quality hurdle'. Either way, it is a phrase sufficiently vague not to commit anybody to anything, and is left for definition by the new Independent Television Commission.

The financial hurdle is decidedly more concrete. 'Competitive tender . . . would secure a proper return for the taxpayer in the use of a scarce resource,' declares Douglas Hurd. Television viewers are taxpayers and, to judge by their diaries, they do not regard the filling of Treasury coffers as the medium's prime function. If it is really still a 'scarce resource', despite all the new channels, then a government's priority should be to insist that the money it generates is put back into diversity and excellence in programming.

Those lines of W. B. Yeats have been used sadly often in the 70 years since they were written, anarchy threatens too often. But without apology here they are again:

> The best lack all conviction, while the worst
> Are full of passionate intensity . . .

The barbarians dismiss as elitist the Reithian idea of making the best, including material of minority appeal, available to all. Many liberal-minded people working in television, feeling vaguely guilty that they have held the ascendancy in the industry for so long, worry that there may be something in what the barbarians say. Few cultural warriors outside the industry are willing to worry for an instant about a medium that is so far from elitism. The result is silence or apology and an impression that the best are lacking conviction.

Take Anthony Smith, a distinguished BBC current affairs producer who went on to direct the British Film Institute and, incidentally, to open the doors that made the One Day project possible. One of the best. For his BFI leaving present he was allowed to conduct public interviews with a group of industry luminaries who believed in the public service broadcasting idea. Afterwards he reflected (*Sight and Sound*, Winter 1988–9) that 'my problem was and is that I support the whole package of attitudes and beliefs, but am scared for their future political liability . . .

'If I had been Mrs Thatcher listening to all four of them, I should have grimaced with the realization that this was exactly how I thought they were. I should have wanted to shake them all until the last licence fee fell from their pockets . . . But I am not Mrs Thatcher. I am a conservative and want the system we have, based on public service, and gradually augmented over the decades as new technologies come along. It's a sweet old-fashioned view, I know, but I can't help it . . .'

Sweet? Old-fashioned? It seems the liberal mentality simply cannot match Mrs Thatcher's conviction that her view is right, even when the shortest pause for rational thought confirms that it is being entirely reasonable. Alas, such gentle irony will do no good on the barricades that now have to be defended. It will certainly not impress the enemy, as it advances with shrill assurance brandishing its iron whims.

Another approach by the best is to hold that nothing about television matters very much. Sure, it can sometimes be fun for a while, especially for the performers, but it is absurd to take it seriously. The arch-exponent of this artificial insouciance is that much-loved institution Ludovic Kennedy. He was so pleased with the critic who saw his style of television presentation as that of a man who has dropped in *On My Way to the Club*, that in early 1989 he used the phrase as the title of his autobiography, both on television and in print.

In his likeable film he advanced a memorable image where television was equated with the passing view seen from a railway carriage window. No sooner out of sight than out of mind. It could have been added that each half-glimpsed stretch of town or landscape matters a lot to the people more at home there than in the Beefsteak or Brook's, the Army and Navy, the MCC or Puffins (Edinburgh). The passing traveller might not mind what ugliness and destruction is inflicted after the train has passed. But everywhere, in every corner of the land, there are people who do care.

That is the message from those who recorded *One Day in the Life of Television*. They are not a co-ordinated opposition, and they are usually silent, but politicians should note that they are a substantial constituency and will not lightly forgive any government that carries out the vandalism now threatened.

GENERAL INDEX

INDEX OF CONTRIBUTORS